DEPRESSION
Behavioral and Directive Intervention Strategies

edited by

John F. Clarkin
Howard I. Glazer

Garland STPM Press
New York & London

Copyright 1981 by Garland Publishing, Inc.

All rights reserved. No part of this work covered by the copyright hereon may be reproduced or used in any form or by any means—graphic, electronic, or mechanical, including photocopying, recording, taping, or information storage and retrieval systems —without permission of the publisher.

Library of Congress Cataloging in Publication Data
Main entry under title:

Depression, behavioral and directive intervention strategies.

   Bibliography: p.
   Includes index.
   1. Depression, Mental—Therapy. 2. Behavior therapy.
I. Clarkin, John F. II. Glazer, Howard. I.
RC537.D42757   616.85′2706   81-6546
ISBN 0-8240-7125-5   AACR2

Published by Garland STPM Press
136 Madison Avenue, New York, New York 10016

Printed in the United States of America
15 14 13 12 11 10 9 8 7 6 5 4 3 2 1

Contents

Contributors   *v*
Preface   *vii*

PART I: **Assessment**   1

1   Assessment of Depression   3
Howard I. Glazer • John F. Clarkin • Howard F. Hunt

PART II: **Major Models of Depression and Related Treatment Strategies**   31

2   Behavioral Treatment of Depression: *A Social Learning Approach*   33
Peter M. Lewinsohn • Michael Arconad
3   A Self-control Therapy Program for Treatment of Depression   68
Lynn P. Rehm
4   Cognitive Therapy for Depression   111
Ronald E. Coleman • Aaron T. Beck
5   Attributional Reformulation of Learned Helplessness and Depression: *Therapeutic Implications*   131
Steven R. H. Beach • Lyn Y. Abramson • Frederic M. Levine

PART III: **Clinical Behavioral Treatment of Depression**   167

6   Multimodal Therapy and the Problems of Depression   169
Allen Fay • Arnold A. Lazarus
7   Remediation of Skills and Performance Deficits in Depression: *Clinical Steps and Research Findings*   179
Peter McLean
8   Clinical Behavior Therapy for Depression   205
Herbert Fensterheim
9   A Social-Behavioral Analysis of Suicide and Parasuicide: *Implications for Clinical Assessment and Treatment*   229
Marsha M. Linehan
10   Somatic Treatment for Depression   295
James Kocsis

PART IV: **Special Population Groups**   309

  ✓**11** Active Treatment of Childhood Depression   311
      Theodore A. Petti
  12 Behavioral Treatment of Elderly Patients with Depression   244
      Joseph P. Cautela

Appendixes   367

- **A** Activity Schedule   369
- **B** Daily Mood Rating Form   373
- **C** Daily Monitoring Form for Relaxation Technique   374
- **D** Samples of Daily Monitoring of Relaxation   375
- **E** Daily Monitoring of Relaxation in Problem Situations   376
- **F** Self-monitoring Log   377
- **G** Mood and Activity Exercise   378
- **H** Immediate Effects versus Delayed Effects   379
- **I** Self-evaluation Worksheet   381
- **J** Attribution of Responsibility   382
- **K** Elderly Reinforcement Survey Schedule   384

Index   393

Contributors

Lyn Y. Abramson, Department of Psychology, State University of New York at Stony Brook
Michael Arconad, Department of Psychology, University of Oregon
Steven R. H. Beach, Department of Psychology, State University of New York at Stony Brook
Aaron T. Beck, Department of Psychiatry, University of Pennsylvania
Joseph P. Cautela, Department of Psychology, Boston College
John F. Clarkin, Department of Psychiatry, Cornell University Medical College
Ronald E. Coleman, Department of Psychiatry, University of Pennsylvania
Allen Fay, New York, New York
Herbert Fensterheim, Department of Psychiatry, Cornell University Medical College
Howard I. Glazer, Department of Psychiatry, Cornell University Medical College
Howard F. Hunt, Department of Psychiatry, Cornell University Medical College
James Kocsis, Department of Psychiatry, Cornell University Medical College
Peter McLean, Department of Psychiatry, University of British Columbia
Arnold A. Lazarus, Department of Psychology, Rutgers University
Peter M. Lewinsohn, Department of Psychology, University of Oregon
Frederic M. Levine, Department of Psychology, State University of New York at Stony Brook
Marsha M. Linehan, Department of Psychology, University of Washington
Theodore A. Petti, Department of Psychiatry, University of Pittsburgh School of Medicine
Lynn P. Rehm, Department of Psychology, University of Houston

Preface

One of the most exciting developments in the field of behavior therapy has been the application of intervention strategies to the behavioral excesses and deficits related to depression. Although the literature on behavioral intervention strategies for depression has been accumulating, at the time this text was prepared there was no single volume that provided comprehensive coverage of the subject. There seemed to be a clear need to present in one volume those advances in both theory and practice that were dispersed throughout the literature. A unifying theme conveyed by our contributors is that depression can be conceptualized and effectively treated using the constructs of the behavioral tradition.

In its initial conception, this book was designed for use by behavior therapy practitioners. However, the contents of these chapters should make it an equally valuable resource for those involved in more traditional practice, clinical research, and graduate and undergraduate instruction.

The book is divided into four parts that cover the salient issues in the field: assessment of depression; major behavioral models of depression and related treatment strategies; clinical treatment of depression, including intervention with suicidal clients and the use of somatic treatments; special population groups, namely, children and the elderly.

The editors, in association with Howard Hunt, have written the initial chapter on the assessment of depression. Topographical and functional analyses are emphasized, and steps in the behavioral assessment are delineated. Self-report instruments, interview rating scales, and recent advances in the assessment of overt verbal and motor behavior are discussed. Overall, there is an attempt to link the assessment concepts and procedures with the intervention methods in the rest of the volume.

Part Two includes chapters on the current major behavioral models of depression. Lewinsohn and Arconad (Chapter 2) focus on the loss of response-contingent social reinforcement due to inadequate social skills as an important antecedent of depression. Treatment techniques include directed activity schedules and behavioral rehearsal techniques designed to enhance social reinforcement skills. Rehm's model of depression (Chapter 3) is based on a tripartite analysis of self-regulatory processes in terms of self-monitoring, self-evaluation, and self-reinforcement. Remedial interventions for dysfunctions in each of these areas are presented. Beck's cognitive model of depression (Coleman and Beck, Chapter 4) emphasizes the importance of unrealistic negative self-referent cognitions as important precursors of depression. Strategies to change these cognitions are presented. Beach, Abramson, and Levine

(Chapter 5) present a reformulation of Seligman's learned-helplessness model of depression, adding a self-referent attributional processing stage to the perception of response-outcome dependence.

Part Three focuses on clinical treatment of depressed clients, often involving combinations of various techniques and strategies. Fay and Lazarus (Chapter 6) describe the use of multimodal assessment and treatment in the area of depression. Case histories are presented within the framework of the BASIC ID acronym emphasizing the importance of assessment and intervention in what they consider to be the seven key modalities. Drawing on his years of research in the treatment of ambulatory patients with depression, McLean (Chapter 7) describes a treatment approach designed to reverse behavioral performance deficits. He has found that when behavioral performance (interpersonal communication, social interaction, behavioral productivity, etc.) improves, this is followed by similar improvement in cognitive, physiological, and motivational functioning. A valuable contribution is McLean's description of the complications that commonly arise in the actual practice of behavior therapy with depressed clients. Fensterheim (Chapter 8) presents opposition to the unitary model of depression based on phenotypic depressive characteristics. He emphasizes the need for a functional behavioral analysis and describes target behaviors, including general tension, automatic emotional reactions, obsessions, unwanted habits, and assertiveness, with many case illustrations. A social behavioral model of suicidal and parasuicidal behavior is developed by Linehan in Chapter 9. She discusses environmental, demographic, and behavioral factors associated with suicide and parasuicide and delineates assessment techniques and treatment strategies, including numerous specific recommendations. The specific indicators of the need for somatic intervention in depression are discussed by Kocsis in Chapter 10. He differentiates depressive subtypes as related to medication use and summarizes symptoms and syndromes of modal responders to tricyclic antidepressants, monoamine oxidase inhibitors, lithium and electroconvulsive therapy. Although this chapter does not tackle the difficult and relatively unresearched question of the interface between psychopharmacology and psychotherapy in the treatment of depression, it will be helpful to behavior therapists unacquainted with the clinical guidelines for the drug interventions that may enhance other treatments.

Part Four is concerned with the application of behavioral interventions for depression appearing in the various age groups. In his chapter on treating childhood depression, Petti (Chapter 11) notes the particular difficulties in dealing with childhood depression, as well as the absence of models and treatments specific to this age group. Petti describes the rationale for an active treatment approach in this area and presents methods of active treatment for symptoms and behaviors associated with depression in children. Cautela's chapter on behavioral treatment of elderly depressed clients, Chapter 12, draws on the theoretical approaches of Beck, Lewinsohn, and Seligman and applies this information in modified form to an elderly population. He focuses on the use of operant and respondent covert conditioning procedures as strategies to decrease aversive stimuli, increase reinforcement, and increase self-control. Several self-report inventories are presented, along with case histories and detailed procedural instructions.

We would like to thank all our contributors for their diligence and care in manuscript preparation and Camelia Castro, Carol Homa, Karen Janiver, Lynn Sillcox, and Lillian Conklin for proofreading and typing of manuscripts.

John F. Clarkin
Howard I. Glazer

Assessment

PART 1

Assessment of Depression

Howard I. Glazer
John F. Clarkin
Howard F. Hunt

Clinical depression is a pervasive phenomenon that affects some 12% of the population at some time during their lives (Beck, 1973). However, its wide prevalence is not accompanied by clarity of definition, either conceptually or behaviorally. The term "depression" is used to describe a range of moods (including sadness and feelings of guilt, worthlessness, and hopelessness) and to describe a syndrome of correlated behaviors (including dysphoria, somatic changes, negative self-referential thoughts and verbalizations, and decreased levels of activity and socialization).

The current trend in psychiatric diagnosis is toward a more descriptive system (e.g., *DSM-III: Diagnostic and Statistical Manual of Mental Disorders*, 1980). This is consonant with the practice of behavioral assessment and treatment of depression, which emphasizes topographical and functional analysis and treatment via cognitive, reinforcement, and social skills methods. Each treatment chapter that follows will describe a prevalent behavioral model of depression with related interventions. The purpose of this chapter is to describe behavioral assessment of depression as it is currently practiced. We shall examine instruments and methodologies that are useful in behavioral assessment of depression and highlight those that are most consonant with the intervention strategies described in this volume.

Symptoms of Depression

A major impediment to the development of a functional classification system (classifying behaviors in terms of what controls them) is the lack of agreement on the symptoms of the behavioral syndrome. There is disagreement not only on which behaviors (reported symptoms, overt verbal and motor behaviors) are typically included in the depression syndrome but also on which combinations of behaviors are most significant for assessment, treatment, and prognosis. In the lists that appear in the literature, the symptoms presented are neither exclusive to depression (Harrow et al., 1966) nor universally ascribed to depression (Levitt & Lubin, 1975). Levitt and Lubin reviewed the literature and listed the symptoms of depression cited in at least 2 of 13 selected sources published between 1961 and 1969 and the symptoms of depression appearing in at least 2 of 16 depression measurement instruments. Beck (1973) provided further data by reviewing the proportions of depressed patients manifesting various symptoms. Table 1.1 selectively summarizes the findings of Levitt and Lubin and Beck.

Using patient reporting as the criterion reference (Beck's data on severely depressed patients), the cardinal symptoms of a depressive syndrome, as defined by their presence in at least 75% of cases, include feelings of inadequacy and helplessness, loss of motivation, psychomotor retardation, indecisiveness, crying spells, loss of interest and enjoyment, fatigability, sleep disturbance, pessimism, dejected mood, and self-devaluation. Such an approach (phenomenological description of cardinal symptoms or behaviors that must be present to define a syndrome) is gaining prominence today. For example, this approach is being used empirically to define schizophrenia (Carpenter & Strauss, 1979) for research and intervention purposes. The new and much debated diagnostic and statistical manual of the American Psychiatric Association (DSM-III) also uses this approach to make syndrome specifications more reliable.

Classification of Depression

In addition to tabulating the percentages of patients who experience the various symptoms, one can further the phenomenology by empirical investigation of symptom clusters. Using ratings from the 16 items of the Brief Psychiatric Rating Scale, Overall and associates (1966) identified three clusters via factor analysis. These were labeled anxious-tense depression, hostile depression, and retarded depression. The typology was found to be related to some differential response to pharmacologic intervention. Paykel (1971) derived a similar typology

TABLE 1.1 Symptoms of Depression and Their Prevalence

Symptom	Percentage of Sources Using Symptom[a]	Percentage of Measurement Instruments Monitoring the Symptom[b]	Percentage of Severely Depressed Patients Showing the Symptom[c]
Self-devaluation	54	100	81
Dejected mood	92	87	88
Suicidal thoughts	100	81	74
Pessimism, feelings of hopelessness	77	81	87
Loss of appetite	77	75	72
Sleep disturbance	77	75	87
Loss of libido	84	44	61
Fatigability	46	81	78
Loss of interest, enjoyment	46	62	92
Guilt feelings	70	62	60
Social withdrawal	38	69	64
Crying spells	38	44	83
Indecisiveness	30	50	76
Constipation	30	44	52
Psychomotor retardation	30	81	87
Loss of motivation	46	62	86
Diurnal mood variation	40	20	37
Feelings of inadequacy, helplessness	30	20	90

[a] The 13 sources reviewed by Levitt and Lubin (1975).
[b] The 16 instruments reviewed by Levitt and Lubin (1975).
[c] The study of Beck (1973).

using data from a semistructured interview to obtain ratings of previous history, life stress, permorbid behavior, and symptoms. A cluster analysis revealed four types. What he called a psychotic cluster was composed of middle-age patients with severe depression, sometimes delusional, and good premorbid history. The anxious group were elderly and severely depressed, with high neuroticism scores on a personality inventory (the Maudsley Personality Inventory), and much anxiety. The third group was younger, less depressed, and hostile. The fourth group was similarly young and less depressed, with marked "personality disorder," as measured by the Maudsley neuroticism scale. Although these data were entirely dependent on self-reports and lacked observational material, this work was well done, and it derives validation from subsequent responses to chemotherapy (Paykel, 1972).

Because of its official status with the American Psychiatric Association, government agencies, and insurance carriers, the DSM-III classification system is, in practical terms, the most important system for clinicians. DSM-III departs substantially from its predecessor, DSM-II, and thus it serves as an indication of changes in psychodiagnostic strategy. The most notable change is a shift away from diagnostic categories based more strongly on theory and toward syndromes based more strongly on description. Whereas in DSM-II an attempt was made to select items that would least bind the judgment of the user, DSM-III is clearly a move toward increasing diagnostic reliability through greater descriptive specificity. The system is multiaxial in its approach, so that each patient is assessed on five different dimensions: axis I, symptoms; axis II, enduring personality traits or behaviors; axis III, contributing medical disorders; axis IV, stress; axis V, most adaptive functioning in the past year. In terms of depression, this means that an assessment is made in terms of the course of the depression (episodic versus chronic) (axis I), the presence or absence of manic behavior in addition to depressive behavior (bipolarity) (axis I), personality pattern (axis II), the presence of life stress (axis IV), and the highest level of adaptive functioning in the past year (axis V).

DSM-III distinguishes three subtypes of purely depressive disorders: episodic affective disorders (major depression, single episode 296.2, recurrent 296.3), chronic affective disorders (dysthymic disorder 300.40), and atypical affective disorders (atypical depression 296.82). Other affective, but not exclusively depressive, disorders include bipolar disorders (mixed 296.6, manic 296.4, depressed 296.5), chronic affective disorders (cyclothymic disorder 301.13), and atypical bipolar disorders (296.70). We shall restrict our discussion to purely depressive disorders.

Major depression is defined by the presence of specific behaviors over a period of at least 1 week. In behavioral terms, the diagnosis depends on the verbal-cognitive symptoms of dysphoric mood and loss of interest and pleasure in all or most usual activities or pastimes, accompanied by at least four of the following verbal-cognitive behaviors and overt motor behaviors: feelings of self-reproach or guilt; slow thinking; indecisiveness; thoughts of suicide; poor appetite or overeating; weight loss or weight gain; sleep difficulty or sleeping too much; loss of energy; psychomotor retardation or agitation; decreased sexual interest and activity.

The dysthymic disorder (or depressive neurosis) is described as a long-standing (at least 2 years in duration) condition of depressed mood or loss of interest and pleasure, accompanied by at least three of the following: insomnia or sleeping too much; low energy level; feelings of inadequacy; decreased productivity at school, work, or home; decreased concentration or attention or ability to think; social withdrawal; loss of interest in and/or enjoyment of sex; restriction of involvement in pleasurable activities; feeling slowed down, less talkative than usual, or pessimistic about the future.

Atypical depression is a residual category for individuals with depressive symptoms who do not meet the criteria for diagnosis of major depression, dysthymic disorder, or adjustment disorder. Examples might include the following: a major depressive episode in a schizophrenic, residual type; a dysthymic disorder, but with intermittent normal mood periods of long duration; a brief depressive episode that does not meet the criteria for major depression and is not reactive and thus cannot be diagnosed as an adjustment reaction.

The reader should note the thrust of the preceding discussion, and of DSM-III, away from normal "classic" categorization toward "prototypic" classification (Cantor et al., 1980). The formal classic approach, with its necessary and sufficient conditions or features for defining membership in a category, has numerous (and increasingly recognized) defects, not only for psychiatric diagnosis but also for classification in general. These include the following: difficulty in identifying features suitable for all members of a category; too many borderline cases; heterogeneity among members of a category with respect to their features; variations among members with respect to their typicality and ease of classification; the problem of atypical subsets of a category lacking some of the supposedly necessary features of the supraordinate category (incomplete nesting).

In prototypic classification, the defining features need only be correlated with category membership, rather than being necessary and/or sufficient. To determine whether or not an instance belongs to a category, the overlap in features between instance and category is crucial. Thus prototype categorization is probabilistic, with typical instances having greater overlap with the prototype, and atypical instances having less overlap; each prototype may have few or many features in common with others and thus be correspondingly more or less distinctive. DSM-III presents diagnostic criteria as prototypes, as sets of correlated features rather than as sets of rigidly defining qualities and the overlap in features across the different diagnostic categories is dealt with in sections on differential diagnosis; see the work of Cantor and associates (1980) for an extended discussion of these issues. The new emphasis on the probabilistic nature, rather than an absolute nature, of diagnostic classification, with diagnostic assortment based on the degree of fit between a patient's cluster of symptoms and the prototypes for the different diagnostic categories, provides a more realistic basis for behavioral approaches to treatment than do diagnostic classifications according to formal categories of presumed "disease" entities.

Behavioral Assessment of Depression

Generally, the behavior therapist is expected to direct attention to an assessment (a behavioral analysis) of the individual case and its total context, which will reveal the circumstances that evoke or are the occasions for occurrences of the target behavior (the cause for complaint, here depressive responses), as well as the consequences of the behavior that reinforce and thus maintain it. The therapist attempts to alter these occasions and consequences, to rearrange the patient's circumstances, and to educate or train the patient to make more appropriate and more effective alternative behaviors possible and more probable. This desirable behavioral repertoire is expected to replace the target behavior, and it is developed, mutually with the patient, through goal setting and the use of rewards, both tangible and intangible. For the reasonably intact depressed patients who will be considered in this volume, cognitive restructuring, which alters the patients' perspective and thus their expectations and their interpretations of events, plays a major role.

Rather than seeking explanations and rationales in terms of underlying causes in the recapitulation of intrapsychic conflicts, behavioral analysis emphasizes primarily a "psychology of the here and now," focusing on overt behavior and its direct and indirect control by environmental events. The remote history of the patient participates only insofar as it is represented in the present. An enormous amount of detailed work and genuine clinical skill are required, of course, to penetrate beyond these easy generalities (Hunt, 1975).

The goals of the initial behavioral assessment of depression include the following: evaluation of the intensity of depression, including suicidal risk; identification of specific problem behaviors, including excesses and deficits; description of antecedent and consequent events and behaviors; formulation of functional hypotheses concerning the factors controlling and maintaining the depression; description of intervention plans that include specific behavioral goals and appropriate procedures for reaching them; development of a formal or informal working contract with the patient. Subsequent assessment, including self-monitoring by the patient, has as its goal the evaluation of the effectiveness of the interventions, both during the course of treatment and during follow-up.

Kanfer and Saslow (1965) discussed at some length the theoretical foundations of behavior analysis and the tasks that a behavioral analysis must accomplish; see also the work of Goldiamond and Dyrud (1968), Kazdin (1974), and Gambrill (1977). The practical steps in analysis, as they apply to depression, are the following.

Defining the Problem

The first step is to describe the problem in terms of salient symptoms, the topography of depressive behaviors, and the mode or modes of depressive expression.

A topographical analysis of depressive behaviors would delineate all the modalities affected (see Chapter 6): affective (depressed mood, feelings of worthlessness, guilt), verbal-cognitive (poor concentration, negative self-referential thoughts, suicidal thoughts), overt motor (agitation, retardation), biologic (sleep difficulties, increased or lowered appetite for food, lowered appetite for sex, constipation), social (avoidance and/or negative or unrewarding interactions with others, assertion difficulties), sensory (blunting of positive sensory experience, increased internal negative sensory experiences), and imagery (visions of failure and personal humiliation). This assessment of the possible affected areas should also include a measure of severity in terms of frequency and intensity, as well as a measure of the interaction of each modality with each other modality.

A topographical analysis defines depressive behavior and identifies indicators that serve to reflect the patient's progress and success in treatment. Most discussions of depression and its treatment are in this descriptive topographical tradition, attempting to define classes or types of patients and classes of target behaviors to be modified, in terms of the external configurations of behavior, and to determine how these configurations covary with one another (as in factor-analytic studies). Thus a topographical analysis emphasizes how things look, permitting objective identification of diagnostic categories and objective monitoring of progress and change, quite in keeping with the pragmatic thrust of the behavioral approach. However, as noted earlier, phenotypical symptoms of depression are distributed throughout the broad range of psychiatric disorders; they are not unique to persons formally classified as being depressed. Further, depressive reactions can be protean in their external manifestations, appearing as restricted-substance abuse or as sexual aberration or in somatized form as headache or other physical disabilities, to mention just a few of the "depression equivalents" (Linn, 1975).

Functional Analysis

In contrast to topographical analysis, functional analysis seeks to classify and comprehend behaviors and their significance in terms of what actually controls them, not in terms of how they look; it seeks to classify stimulus contexts in terms of which behaviors they actually control and how, not in terms of their presumed a priori significance.

In this second step, one assembles data on the people and the circumstances that occasion the patient's symptomatic behaviors and how these people and events reinforce and maintain these behaviors.

This approach grows out of Skinner's emphasis on functional classes of stimuli and responses in operant conditioning. It makes the telling point that the functional identity (the significance) of a stimulus context is given by what it produces, what it does, not by what it appears to be nor by what effects it "should" have (Hunt, 1975; Sidman, 1960; Skinner, 1938, 1953). Thus all behaviors that are positively reinforced by a particular stimulus, such as a food, will belong to one response class, whereas those controlled by a different stimulus, such as a shock, will belong to a different response class, even though the overt behavior involved may be the same, such as a lever response. Similarly, all stimuli or contexts that have the same effect on a particular behavior when they occur in the same temporal relationship with it (e.g., following it) will belong to the same stimulus class. Operationally, such functional relationships identify, empirically, the "meanings" of behaviors and their contexts. And, as in everyday life, behaviors and stimuli can have multiple "meanings" (belong to several classes) simultaneously.

An understanding, a hypothesis, should emerge from the functional analysis regarding what the patient is working for (what the patient is trying to get by way of reinforcers) and how these consequences are being sought (how the patient is trying to get them). With such a provisional hypothesis in hand, the therapist can begin to consider alternative strategies and tactics the patient can employ to achieve the desired ends and to estimate both the effects of these alternatives on the environment and how the environment can be engaged to support them (Goldiamond & Dyrud, 1968; Hunt, 1975).

For example, functional analyses of depressed patients often reveal that symptoms are related functionally to a reduction in the rate of response-contingent reinforcement (Chapter 2), to deficits in self-control (Chapter 3), to cognitive distortions (Chapter 4), to lack of opportunity to work to produce significant improvements in life situations (Chapter 5) and other variants of the learned-helplessness model, and so on. And a patient's depressed behavior may be reinforced by attention, by permission to withdraw and become socially isolated, or by being excused from some frightening obligation, among other things. Because one person's reward may be another person's punishment, and because functional relationships arise out of the particularities in life experiences, functional analysis must be, in principle and in practice, individualized and detailed to accommodate idiosyncrasies among the diversity of patients with their diverse life circumstances.

When taken seriously and used properly, the functional approach can be of enormous analytic benefit as a source of hypotheses concerning what controls the behaviors of interest and, accordingly, where and how to intervene. The clinician always meets the dependent variable in the patient (the "problem behavior") in an experiment of nature in which this problem behavior may be seen as the end result of the operation of numerous independent variables in the patient's life, as "causes." In contrast, in most laboratory work the experimenter manipulates the independent variables of interest to influence already identified and isolated outcome variables, with a lattice of control conditions limiting the intrusion of extrinsic confounding influences. The natural experiments one encounters in dealing with patients are rarely that simple. Clinically important symptomatic behavior ordinarily turns out to be maintained by a complex of contemporary intercurrent reinforcing circumstances, and it often floats largely free of the original initiating conditions. Rarely is this behavior a monument to one or a few Pavlovian conditioning experiences, except in some cases of traumatic disorder, and it usually has grown by accretion to become embedded in the ecology of the patient's life (Hunt, 1975). Functional analysis, as a search algorithm, is a powerful aid to intelligent guessing in the service of disentangling the web to identify points for effective intervention.

The details of functional analysis are complex (Reynolds, 1968), incompletely worked out with respect to the human clinical context and beyond the scope of the present discussion, but important aspects are touched on in numerous ways in the chapters that follow. Running through all of them, in addition to descriptions of the classic pathology in mood, we find several major behavioral themes, including the following: Depressed patients lack positive reinforcement; they expect to have insufficient control over events to gain rewards, and this is a continuing condition largely due to assumed defects in themselves. They undervalue positive things that happen to them and overrate reverses (or, perhaps more important, they are unable to overvalue their virtues and strengths in the way normal people seem to do, to provide for themselves a cushioning flux of positive hedonic experiences). Congruent with these expectations and cognitions, they curtail their behavior output and thus fail to attempt to earn those ordinary day-to-day rewards that sustain most of us in the face of normal difficulties.

The therapeutic strategies address these themes directly by simultaneously attempting to increase the flux of positive reinforcement and alter cognitions and expectations, both of which seem to be required. The global cognitions of helplessness and hopelessness are undercut by redefinitions and by rational confrontations that break them down into less plenary components, each of which is more manageable and more easily falsified in direct life experience. In addition, therapists contract with their patients for increases in specific behavioral performances that imply worthy subsidiary goals that can be achieved and thus are productive of success experiences and experience of their own agency. Discussion aimed toward cognitive restructuring through logical persuasion alone appears insufficient; first-hand contact with a schedule of reinforcement also seems necessary. Similarly, redressing the debit in positive reinforcement simply by giving the patient free (noncontingent) reinforcement is not effective for anything more than a brief term, and in the experience of some clinicians this appears to make depressed patients feel even more hopeless. Apparently, rewards that are earned (deserved) pack the greater therapeutic punch.

Parenthetically, it is interesting to note from the standpoint of functional analysis that the condition of depression, thought to derive at least in part from mother love that is too contingent and conditional (and insufficiently unconditional), responds best to increased flux of positive reinforcement when that reinforcement is made clearly contingent and conditional.

Finally, depression presents a more complex challenge to functional analysis than the more episodic disorders, such as anxiety attacks, phobias, and obsessive-compulsive behaviors. In these disorders, the waxing and waning of target behavior as a function of circumstances and consequences are easier to pin down than they are in depression, with its more tonic, more pervasive changes in mood, for which the analyst must rely on verbal reports of subjective states and highly inferential observer-based estimates. Beliefs and attitudes loom large in the case of depression, and often a hallmark of the state is to be found simply in reductions in overt behavior.

Identification of Specific Behavioral Excesses and Deficits

An examination should be conducted to determine if the depressed patient exhibits behavioral excesses (e.g., crying, self-depreciation, self-punishment) or deficits (e.g., absence of rewarding social interaction). Usually, more attention is paid to behavioral deficits, such as in social interaction, communication, decision making, and problem solving. Rehm (Chaper 3) emphasizes self-control deficits, Lewinsohn and Arconad (Chapter 2) reinforcement deficits, McLean (Chapter 7) skill-area deficits, and Coleman and Beck (Chapter 4) cognitive deficits.

Selecting a Monitoring Procedure and Determining a Baseline

A hallmark of behavioral assessment is its continuous monitoring throughout the treatment, with continuing input into the form the treatment intervention takes. The gathering of baseline data regarding specific problem behaviors, either excesses or deficiencies, provides a standard against which one can later assess the efficacy of the intervention procedures. The baseline should be constructed on behaviors that are considered salient to the problem, and this will vary with the model of depression one uses. Subsequent chapters will detail the behaviors in the areas of depression that are typically monitored: activity (Rehm, Chapter 3), reinforcement (Lewinsohn and Arconad, Chapter 2), mood (Lewinsohn and Arconad, Chapter 2), and thoughts (Coleman and Beck, Chapter 4).

Identifying Personal and Environmental Assets

The assessment should not be focused entirely on problem areas, lest one lose sight of the assets the patient brings to the situation that might conceivably be used in a strategic intervention plan. Social skills, cognitive and intellectual skills, and recreational and vocational skills, for example, may be important in designing a treatment plan for depression.

Specifying Behavioral Goals

It has been pointed out (McLean, 1976) that whatever specific behavioral intervention techniques are selected, an important general strategy in the treatment of depression is to avoid a problem/pathology orientation; instead, the strategy should concentrate on goal-directed performance. This strategy, in and of itself, will probably be conducive to improved mood. The modeling of such an orientation should begin during the assessment phase. Specific measurable goals, both mediating and terminal, often include positive self-referential statements, assertive behavior, and the rehearsal and performance of appropriate social behaviors.

Establishing a Patient-Therapist Contract

This step in treatment, often glossed over with easy informality, is one of the most important and powerful tools in behavioral therapy and its evaluation; for an extended discussion, see the work of Goldiamond and Dyrud (1968) and Schwartz and Goldiamond (1975). The contract may be verbal, but preferably it should be written. It should be explicit and should be developed out of the joint enterprise and discussion by patient and therapist. It addresses the patient's goals and hopes, spells out commitments to action in order to reach them, describes how achievement of the goals will be determined with specific satisfying results, and details the mutual obligations and responsibilities of both parties. In its concreteness and specificity it can break down the seemingly immense and impossible task of recovery into component parts, with subgoals, giving the depressed patient that experience with success, self-control, and agency or autonomy so desperately needed. Because of its development out of the expressed needs and wishes of the patient and its implications of how to fulfill these needs, it not only involves the patient in making affirmative choices among positive outcomes, with the side effect of promoting an experience of choice and freedom (as opposed to aversively controlled coercion) (Hunt, 1977; Skinner, 1971), but also demonstrates that the patient and the patient's interests are placed front and center. In addition, the discovery that someone (the therapist) thinks that something can be done about the patient's hopeless situation, and the discovery of some ideas regarding how to start, can have powerful and beneficial nonspecific effects (Frank, 1961). The discussion during the development of a contract often provides important information for the functional analysis, because the potential benefits the patient can or cannot accept, does or does not value, what the patient will or will not do, and so on, will emerge in concrete form. Finally, as the patient improves, the contract will in most instances have to be rewritten and upgraded, not only as to performance but also as to the level of reward. The kinds of results anticipated and the prosocial level of reward that the patient is working for can exert important influences on self-perception and the organization of the patient's behavior. A patient may start out working for something as mundane and tangible as "points," but as improvement occurs, the patient may graduate to receiving honest appreciation from another adult for the accomplishment of a difficult job well done. These are very different levels of reward. Thus, in specifying consequences and goals, the contract exerts powerful implicit influences on the patient's self-perception and self-respect.

Assessment Tools

We shall review the instruments commonly used in behavioral research and practice and shall categorize them according to source of information: self-report, interview techniques, and observational techniques. Physiological measures and markers of depression are of little clinical use at the time of the assessment, and they will not be included. Assessment of the risk of suicide (not synonymous with assessment of depression, but certainly an essential part) will be discussed by Linehan in Chapter 9. Tests specific to children will be discussed by Petti in Chapter 11. Those instruments most relevant to adolescents and the elderly will be mentioned briefly here. For each instrument, we shall review content, psychometric properties, ease of clinical administration, and potential uses (initial assessment, monitoring, outcome).

Self-report Instruments

As Franks and Wilson (1978) pointed out, there is only a modest correlation between self-report measures and directly observable behavioral measures. For example, the correlation between psychiatric ratings of depression and various self-report instruments (Table 1.2) ranges from .33 to .56 (Rehm, 1976).

Persons who are depressed are likely to assess their own performances differently than would others in their natural environments. Whether because of cognitive distortions (Chapter 4), self-motivating deficits (Chapter 3), or pervasive negative self-attributions, the self-reports of depressed individuals bear examination.

Whereas from a research point of view one may decry the less-than-perfect correlation between self-reports and observer ratings in the treatment of depressed individuals, this very discrepancy is useful for assessment and intervention. A self-report is especially important in the cognitive and affective modes, as it is the only entrée to the individual's internal behaviors that are central to dysphoria and are the reason for seeking help. During treatment, the self-report can be used to show the connection between affect and activity (Chapter 3). Particularly in the areas of interpersonal skills and performance, marital adjustment, and work performance, the self-report should be supplemented by other sources of information, such as therapist observation of the home environment and/or reports from significant others (spouse, parent, employer, etc.).

Of the 24 self-report scales reviewed by Levitt and Lubin (1975), only the following 4 scales remain after elimination of scales for which complete source documents are unavailable, scales aimed primarily at differentiating between depression and other pathologic processes or proneness thereto, and scales composed of items drawn entirely from other depression rating instruments: the Minnesota Multiphasic Per-

Table 1.2 Intercorrelations for Self-rating Measures of Depression

	MMPI Depression Scale	Beck Depression Inventory	Zung Self-rating Depression Scale	Depression Adjective Checklist	Psychiatric Rating
MMPI Depression Scale		.58	.64	.46	.33
Beck Depression Inventory			.83	.50	.54
Zung Self-rating Depression Scale				.52	.56

sonality Inventory (MMPI) depression scale (Hathaway & McKinley, 1951) the Beck Depression Inventory (Beck, 1967), the Zung Self-rating Depression Scale (Zung, 1965), and the Depression Adjective Checklist (Lubin, 1967). These four instruments and two additional self-report measures (the Pleasant-Events Schedule and the Pretreatment Questionnaire) will be described next.

MMPI Depression Scale The MMPI (Hathaway & McKinley, 1951) is the most widely used psychodiagnostic instrument available and the one most widely studied psychometrically. Of the 60 true/false items constituting the depression scale, 11 items were chosen on the basis of discriminating between depressed patients and other psychiatric patients, and the remaining 49 items were chosen on the basis of discriminating between a normal group and a group of manic-depressives, depressed type. The median split half reliability on the depression scale is .73 (Dahlstrom & Welsh, 1960), and the mean concurrent validity is .33. The MMPI has several drawbacks. First, factor analysis (Harris & Lingoes, 1955) has shown that the depression scale is rather heterogeneous, containing factors such as mental dullness and brooding that are not reliably associated with depression. Other factor-analysis studies (Comrey, 1957; O'Connor et al., 1957) have also given clear evidence of the multidimensionality of the scale. Second, because many of the depression-scale items also appear on other clinical scales, the discriminant validity is modest. It has been found that elevations in scores on one or more of the other 10 clinical scales, across a broad range of psychiatric disorders, reflecting the ubiquitous distribution of responses associated with dysphoric affect among maladjusted people. Similarly, patients who have been diagnosed as depressed frequently (even characteristically) show elevations in their scores on other clinical scales, reflecting the broad ranges of symptoms that depressed persons may show. The profile of the score pattern across all of the clinical scales, not the score on any single scale, commonly serves as an empirical basis for clinical diagnosis from the MMPI (Dahlstrom et al., 1972; Gilberstadt & Duker, 1965; Marks et al., 1974).

Mezzich, et al. (1974) developed a regression formula for combining the scores on the MMPI D, Pd, Pa, Sc, and Si scales to improve the differentiation of cases with diagnosed depression from cases with other diagnoses, in the face of the ubiquitous elevation of the D score in psychiatric populations. This approach appears to have some promise for differential diagnosis of depression as the formula has demonstrated its discriminative power in a recent cross validation (Post and Lobitz, 1980), largely by reducing the probability of false positive diagnoses from the test.

From a behavioral perspective it is worth noting that because the MMPI item selection procedure was empirical (i.e., items were not selected for face validity), analysis of the statements used in the depression scale offers little help in identifying specific symptoms or the antecedents and consequences of depressive behaviors. Although attempts have been made to increase the internal consistency (Dempsey, 1964) and discriminative validity (Costello & Comrey, 1967) of the MMPI depression scale (D scale), the resulting measures, being drawn from the same item pool, are still of little use in helping to design an effective behavioral intervention for depression. However, the MMPI D scale remains useful as a behavioral research tool for defining clinical populations, measuring therapeutic outcome, and making comparisons between studies.

An MMPI depression scale for adolescents has been derived by Mezzich and Mezzich (1979). Items judged to have face validity for depression in adolescents were used to test a group of hospitalized adolescents, and the scale was found to be successful in differentiating between those diagnosed as suffering from depression and the others. Although this scale suffers from some of the same drawbacks mentioned earlier for the MMPI depression scale, it does provide a pool of items, some distinct for adolescents, that might serve as a research tool for this population.

Beck Depression Inventory For the behavior therapist, the Beck Depression Inventory (BDI) (Beck et al., 1961) appears to be one of the best self-report instruments available for measurement of depression severity proving itself useful as a pretherapy and posttherapy measure (Fuchs, 1975), as well as a periodic measure to gauge therapeutic progress (Rush et al., 1975). The test scale is administered in an interviewer-assisted manner; that is, a trained interviewer reads the statements to the patient while the patient reads along from another copy, and the interviewer scores the responses. Beck has developed a completely self-administered version that correlates highly with the original BDI (Beck & Beamesderfer, 1974). The 21 items on the inventory were selected to represent depressive symptoms (Beck, 1972), each item consisting of four or five statements listed in order of symptom severity. Item categories include mood, pessimism, crying spells, guilt, self-hate and accusations, irritability, social withdrawal, work inhibition, sleep and appetite disturbance, and loss of libido. Various factor analyses (Cropley & Weckowicz, 1966; Pichot & Lemperiere, 1964; Weckowicz et al., 1967) have been somewhat inconsistent, but they have revealed three similar factors having to do with guilty depression, retardation, and somatic disturbance (Mayer, 1977). Schwab and associates (1966) pointed out that the content of the BDI emphasizes pessimism, sense of failure, punishment, and self-punitive wishes, all consistent with Beck's cognitive view of depression and its causes (Chapter 4). However, the result may be that this scale emphasizes symptoms from the cognitive mode of expression at some expense in assessing symptoms from the other modes. In scoring the inventory, each statement is assigned an empirical weighting factor from 0 to 3. The odd-even reliability has been reported as .86 (Beck et al., 1961), and the test-retest reliability has been reported as .75 after 1 month (Rehm, 1976) and .74 after 3 months (Miller & Seligman, 1973). The concurrent validity studies on the inventory have yielded coefficients ranging from .19 (Seitz, 1970) to .57 (Nussbaum et al., 1963), with the mean for the studies reviewed being .54 (Table 1.2). The construct validity has been supported by a number of investigations in which the BDI has been used as the criterion measure (Beck & Beamesderfer, 1974). Beck (1972) has also demonstrated the high discriminant validity of the instrument, finding a correlation of .72 between the inventory and clinical ratings of depression and a correlation of .14 between the inventory and clinical ratings of anxiety.

Self-rating Depression Scale The Self-rating Depression Scale (SDS) (Zung, 1965) consists of 20 items to which one responds as being true of oneself little or none of the time, some of the time, a good part of the time, or most of the time. Zung used previously reported factor-analysis studies to select symptoms and behaviors most characteristic of depression, regardless of cause. The items selected tapped three areas that characterize depression: affective (2 items), biological (8 items), and psychological (10 items). No reliability scores have been reported for this instrument, but the concurrent validity has been reported as .20 (Seitz, 1979).

The problems with this inventory include the following: (1) Answers are easily faked, especially in the direction of symptom admission. (2) The inventory correlates −.28 with education level, thus suggesting that better-educated individuals are less likely to admit depressive symptoms. (3) Both normal adolescents and normal elderly persons tend to score in the clinical range. On the whole, this instrument is of limited utility because of failure to provide reliability data, inadequate scaling, and overreliance on self-reporting of psychological dysfunction.

Depression Adjective Checklist The Depression Adjective Checklist (DACL) was derived from a list of 171 adjectives using the responses of 95 neuropsychiatric patients rated as markedly or severely depressed and a matched normal group of 279 persons. There are seven different forms of the DACL (A through G). The first four forms consist of 32 self-descriptive adjectives, 22 positive and 10 negative, and the remaining three forms include 34 such adjectives, 22 positive and 12 negative. The subject is asked to check those adjectives descriptive of "how you are feeling now, today."

The first four forms of the DACL were developed using 48 female patients and 179 controls. The last three forms were developed using 47 male patients and 100 controls. Psychometric data have been presented by Lubin (1967). Interlist correlations have ranged from .80 to .93, and concurrent validity rating has ranged from .30 to .71 (Rehm, 1976). Fogel and associates (1966) have reported a correlation of .95 between patients' global self-ratings of depression and the DACL scores. The manual (Lubin, 1967) reported that depressed patients scored higher on the DACL than did those diagnosed as having personality disorder, psychoneurosis, or schizophrenia. The internal consistency has ranged from .79 to .90, depending on the form used and the sex of the subject. The DACL does provide a brief, reliable, valid self-report measure of depression. Because the DACL is restricted to measuring depressed affect and does not tap cognitive, motor, perceptual, or behavioral symptoms, its usefulness is in providing a quick and repeatable measure of mood over time, either for assessing the mood of an individual subject or for research.

Pleasant-Events Schedule An important self-rating instrument developed within the framework of the behavioral theory of depression is the Pleasant-Events Schedule. This instrument is based on the assumptions that depression intensity (Lewinsohn & Libet, 1972) is a reflection of the frequency of positive reinforcement and that depressives engage in fewer positively reinforcing activities than do nondepressives. The schedule consists of 320 events and activities generated from 66 subjects' lists of positive events (MacPhillamy & Lewinsohn, 1972a). The instrument is used either as a retrospective report of events for the preceding 30 days or as a daily log of ongoing behavior. The subject rates each item on a 3-point scale for frequency and on a 3-point scale for how pleasant each event was or potentially would be. The scores derived from the rating are the following: (1) activity level, the sum of the frequency ratings; (2) reinforcement potential, the sum of the pleasant ratings; (3) obtained reinforcement, the sum of the products of frequency and pleasant ratings for each item.

Different forms of the schedule are available for a college population and for the general population. Lewinsohn and Grof (1973) demonstrated a significant relationship between mood ratings and the number of pleasant activities engaged in for normal controls and psychiatric controls, as well as for depressives. MacPhillamy and Lewinsohn (1974) showed that depressives scored lower on the Pleasant-Events Schedule scales that measure pleasure, activity level, and reinforcer potential than did either normals or nondepressed psychiatric controls. The test-retest reliabilities for 37 subjects over a period of 1 to 2 months were reported as .85, .66, and .72 for the three scores, respectively (MacPhillamy & Lewinsohn, 1972a, 1972b), and internal consistency coefficients were reported as .96, .98, and .97 (MacPhillamy & Lewinsohn, 1972b). The Pleasant-Events Schedule is particularly useful as a tool for identifying behavioral deficiencies and developing a graded-activity intervention strategy, and it has also been used to assess intervention outcome (Chapter 3). A note of caution should be made here on the accuracy of the Pleasant-Events Schedule as a reflection of *in vivo* activity levels and enjoyment. Because cognitive distortion is a major component of depression, underestimations of activity frequency and enjoyment are likely. This problem is far more significant when the schedule is used retrospectively than when it is used on an ongoing daily basis.

Pretreatment Questionnaire The McLean Pretreatment Questionnaire (McLean, 1976) asks for a self-report from the subject in three response modes: cognitive/affective, behavioral, and somatic. The severity of the depression is judged by the amounts of functional impairment in the three response modes and by the score on the DACL (Lubin, 1967), which is included as part of the instrument. The amounts of information in the three areas are unequal, with emphasis in decreasing amounts from behavioral functioning, thoughts and feelings, and somatic functioning. This emphasis, the author explained, reflects the treatment orientation of first changing behavior, then changing thoughts and feelings, if necessary, and somatic complaints will improve as a result. In the behavioral response mode the subject is questioned in the area of work performance, eating, social interaction, and physical exercise. The cognitive/affective mode includes data on suicidal ideation, decision making, memory and concentration, laughter and crying, depressive thoughts of worthlessness, hopelessness, and helplessness, and worry. Sleep, aches and pains, agitation, fatigue, appetite, and weight loss are covered in the somatic response modality.

This questionnaire has much to recommend it for the behavior-oriented therapist. As the author emphasized, it is a test of the patient's motivation, and it serves as an indication of commitment to the treatment program. Obtaining the information from the patient before the first therapy session ensures that the therapist can prepare for the first meeting and thus make more efficient use of the first session. The questionnaire covers the symptoms and behaviors of depression in response modes familiar to those who think in behavioral terms. Finally, the questionnaire asks the patient to list specific behavioral goals and specific behavioral changes the patient would like to bring about, thus putting the patient in the frame of reference for a collaborative goal-oriented mode of treatment.

Interviewer Rating Instruments

Hamilton Rating Scale The Hamilton Rating Scale is composed of 17 variables, each of which is rated on either a 3-point scale or 5-point scale. The instrument provides a method for rating the severity of depression in a patient already known to be depressed. The 17 variables measured put heavy emphasis on behavioral and somatic symptoms of depression. The intravariable content is heterogeneous, including cognitive, behavioral, and physiological symptoms of depression. Hamilton (1960) reported an interrater reliability of .90, but the internal consistency of the scale is quite low. No further reliability or validity data have been provided, making this instrument psychometrically weak. Two factor analyses have been performed on the scale (Hamilton, 1960, 1964), both resulting in ambiguous factors. Because of its emphasis on somatic symptoms and its relative neglect of the cognitive/affective mode, it may be more useful for assessment of severely ill patients in a hospital setting than for assessment of outpatients. Although this scale has been helpful in research, problems such as differences in the specificities of anchoring points among items, the heterogeneity of symptoms within a given variable, and the lack of psychometric development suggest that considerable refinement will be required before it can gain wide acceptance in clinical use.

Schedule for Affective Disorders and Schizophrenia The Schedule for Affective Disorders and Schizophrenia (SADS) is a semistructured interview guide that enables the interviewer to quantify symptoms and information on the patient's functioning in terms of the preceding week, during the worst period of the most recent illness episode, and historically throughout the patient's life. As the name implies, the content covers symptoms related to affective disturbances (depression and mania) and thinking disturbances (schizophrenia). The data obtained from this interview (which can last anywhere from 1 to 2 hours, depending on the age and severity of disturbance of the patient) will enable the therapist to make a detailed and quantified phenomenologic assessment in these content areas and also arrive at a Research Diagnostic Criteria (RDC) categorization (Spitzer et al., 1975). The RDC system has gained prominence because of its reliability and usefulness for identifying homogeneous groups for research, and it is almost synonymous with the recent DSM-III. The SADS has been used to diagnose homogeneous groups of depressives for behavioral research (Chapter 2). It is probably too lengthy and too detailed for routine office work, but an inspection of the interview guide is useful for informing a behavioral interviewer on the typology of depression.

Feelings and Concerns Checklist Grinker and associates (1961) presented data on both the Current-Behavior Checklist and the Feeling Checklist. The Current-Behavior Checklist consists of 139 items rated as present or absent during general ward observation and on nursing records. The items are overt observable behaviors and physical symptoms, because this rating scale was intended as a supplement to the Feelings and Concerns Checklist, in which the content of the items is exclusively verbal/cognitive. Although the Current-Behavior Checklist has undergone factor analysis (resulting in 10 factors), reliability data are lacking, and its concurrent validity is very poor.

The Feelings and Concerns Checklist consists of 47 items rated on a 4-point scale from 0 (not present) to 3 (markedly present). Factor analysis using 96 depressed patients produced five factors: (1) dismal, hopeless, bad feelings; (2) projection to external events; (3) feelings of guilt; (4) anxiety; (5) clinging appeals for love. The mean interrater reliability over 23 patients for the full checklist was reported as .43. Interfactor reliability based on single raters ranged from .61 to .90. Neither interrater reliability nor internal consistency figures were given for the total scores.

The attempt by Grinker and associates (1961) to separate the verbal/cognitive symptoms from the behavioral/physical symptoms by factor analysis would seem to represent the same desire for increased descriptive specificity shown in DSM-III. Although both these checklists may be useful in symptom identification and assessment of depression intensity, their main drawback is that they remain psychometrically weak instruments. Lewinsohn and Arconad (Chapter 2) recommend these instruments as a diagnostic tool for initial assessment of patients.

Observational Methods

The most recently opened and least developed area of depression assessment involves the observation and measurement of overt verbal and motor behaviors. The limited research conducted in this area has tended to rely on the case study method using hospitalized patients, leaving open the question of applicability to the less well controlled outpatient situation.

In the area of overt verbal behavior, Lewinsohn and associates have proposed that depression represents a social skills deficit, and they have developed a method of coding verbal communication (Lewinsohn et al., 1970; Libet & Lewinsohn, 1973; Libet et al., 1973). The verbal behavior variables measured include total amount of verbal behavior emitted by the patient, total amount of verbal behavior directed to the patient, use of positive reactions by the patient, use of negative reactions by the patient, interpersonal efficiency ratio (number of verbal behaviors directed toward the patient divided by the number of verbal behaviors emitted), range of interactions with others, and latency to respond to another's reaction.

Lewinsohn and associates have used their verbal communication coding system in both intergroup research designs and case history studies. The interrater reliability measures have ranged from .63 to .99 (Libet & Lewinsohn, 1973). In the group studies, depressives have typically been selected on the basis of MMPI and Feelings and Concerns Checklist criteria. Findings have included depressives manifesting lower total activity levels, slower responses to others' reactions, fewer positive reactions, and a narrower interpersonal range for males, but not females. Libet and associates (1973) reported that in self-study groups, depressed males made fewer comments, responded slower to the reactions of others, asked fewer questions, elicited fewer positive reactions, and were more affected by aversive reactions. Depressed female members of the group showed results in the same direction, but these findings were not statistically significant. In the home environment, depressed males emitted fewer actions, were more silent, were slower to respond to the reactions of others, and elicited less frequent positive reinforcement. Depressed females were less active, elicited less frequent positive reinforcement, and were slower to respond to the reactions of others.

McLean and associates (1973) coded patients' tape recordings of problem discussions with their spouses. Couples receiving behavior oriented treatment showed a significant decrease in negative reactions as compared with control couples, who did not change. Fuchs (1975) counted the numbers of statements made by depressives in a 10-minute time period in a self-study group and found a significant increase in the verbal activity of a treatment group as compared with a placebo therapy group.

Assessment of overt motor behaviors among depressives is another area in which relatively little work has been done. Williams and associates (1972) measured (1) talking, (2) smiling, (3) motor activity, and (4) time out of room every half hour for 10 depressed inpatients. A high concordance coefficient (.70) justified the summing of the four measures into a single behavioral index of depression severity. This index correlated .71 with the Hamilton Rating Scale and .67 with the Beck Depression Inventory. Furthermore, on the basis of follow-up data for 5 patients, improvement on the behavioral index during hospitalization was more predictive of posthospitalization adjustment than either the Beck Depression Inventory or the Hamilton Rating Scale. Hersen and associates (1973), using the same behavioral index to assess change, found that inpatients under a token economy system showed improvement on the index.

Recommendations for Assessment of Depression

Although the method of data collection (e.g., self-report, rating scales, etc.) offers a convenient approach for classifying the instruments used for assessment of depression, this is not the most useful approach in the clinical situation. Rather, when faced with the problem of assessing a patient with depression and formulating a treatment plan, we think it is most important to have data from various sources covering the major areas of behavior that could conceivably be targeted for change and in which there is some developing methodology for effective intervention. The authors of the subsequent chapters in this volume describe the major behavioral methods for the treatment of depression. They emphasize the following areas of depressive symptoms that need assessment, some of which (e.g., environmental reinforcers, recent stress events) do not fit neatly into the five typical modes of expression: emotional response systems, including depressed mood; cognitive response systems, including faulty attributional processing, self-monitoring, self-evaluation, and self-reinforcement; biological response systems, including food intake, sexual activity, and sleep; social response systems, including social skills, rate of response-contingent reinforcement; motor response systems, including motor slowing or agitation and rate of speech.

Conclusion

The goals of behavioral assessment of depression, as presented earlier in this chapter, are the following: (1) identification of specific problem behaviors, both excesses and deficits; (2) evaluation of the intensity of the depressive behaviors; (3) description of antecedent and consequent behaviors; (4) formulation of functional hypotheses; (5) recommendation of specific intervention plans; (6) evaluation and monitoring of treatment progress. At the present time, behavioral assessment is variable in its ability to fulfill these goals. Specific problem areas that are typical in depression have been defined, and the intensities of their disturbances can be measured with self-reports, interview ratings, and observations of verbal and motor behaviors. Depressive symptoms in the cognitive/affective mode are assessed via self-report instruments. Although one must question their accuracy, they are the only way to approach the inner behavior of the patient. Several self-report instruments for affective states have been moderately successful (DACL, BDI), but there must be further development of self-report instruments for the helplessness hypothesis as enunciated in this volume by Coleman and Beck (Chapter 4) and Beach and associates (Chapter 5). Measurement via self-report is, of course, quite convenient and cost-efficient for the clinical practitioner. Such a cost-efficient method is not currently available for measurement of verbal and motor depressive behaviors. Further developments likely will include the use of technology (e.g., audio tapes, telemetry) to reduce the cost of home observation (Weiss & Margolin, 1977). Reports of the patient's depressive behaviors in all modes made by significant others (e.g., spouse, parent) could also be explored in the future. Such an instrument might be like the Katz adjustment scales R form (Katz & Lyerly, 1963), which has the significant other persons rate functioning and occurrences of symptoms. Antecedent and consequent behaviors and events probably are best observed during home visits, for example; but, again, self-reporting is an aid, as in the Pleasant-Events schedule. The formulation of functional hypotheses can grow out of advances in the behavioral models of depression. As models are developed and tested, they will have feedback effects on assessment and will spur the development of assessment techniques.

A major goal of assessment is the formulation of a specific intervention plan. It is a basic assumption of social sciences that different problems require specific treatments and that treatments can be designed to fit the idiosyncratic problem (Mischel, 1968). This assumption is quite appealing. It seems obvious that when a patient presents with a problem, the therapist must carefully, efficiently, and scientifically (with reliability and validity) define the problem area so that a specific treatment can be devised.

Differential treatment planning that flows from a detailed assessment is in its infancy, especially in the area of depression. Hypotheses are beginning to be enunciated, as evidenced in this volume, and they await research corroboration. For example, Beach and associates (Chapter 5) suggest that when cognitive deficits are present, with social skills still available to the client, cognitive treatment of the depression is most relevant. However, when social skills deficits and cognitive deficits are present simultaneously, one should begin intervention with social skills (Chapter 8).

Although the symptoms in the somatic mode (so-called endogenomorphic symptoms) have shown promise of response to chemotherapy (Chapter 10), others have questioned the use of such treatment when the patient is only moderately depressed, and Rush and Beck (1978) have asserted that some of these patients respond best to cognitive interventions. The data of Klerman and associates (1974) suggest that chemotherapy and verbal therapy have significant but different effects.

When several behavioral interventions (or a range of behavioral interventions) are planned for a patient, it is not clear to what degree a given behavioral intervention has a specific effect on a limited area of deficits or problems. For example, McLean and Hakstian (1979) recently reported that cognitive treatment for cognitive deficits is effective, but not more effective than social skills treatment. They argued, as did Zeiss and associates (1979), that the operative elements in the treatment package may be more general elements, such as using a structured intervention that has a clear rationale that is communicated to the patient, or formulation of the problem in a goal-oriented model rather than in a problem-oriented or medical-illness model. Rehm discusses this issue (Chapter 3) and recommends further examination of the subject variables as predictors of differential responses to different areas targeted for change.

In concluding, it seems important to emphasize that depression is not an isolated phenomenon that has a life and existence of its own. To think of it in such a way would be to falsely reify it, analogous to reification of such psychoanalytic constructs as ego and id. On the contrary, depression in the narrow sense is a particular mood, and in the broader sense it is a syndrome of related thoughts, feelings, and behaviors. It rarely occurs alone; rather, it is a thread woven into the context of a person interacting with an environment. This means that the assessment of depression never occurs in isolation but rather is an aspect of a more complete assessment of the person in an environment. By the same token, when the person becomes more effective in one area of life, positive changes often occur in relation to other areas even though they have not been specifically targeted in treatment.

The issue of how the assessment of depression relates to other areas of assessment deserves further exploration. For example, there is abundant evidence that depression often is related to marital distress (Rounsaville et al., 1979). When such a condition is discovered on initial examination, the growing body of knowledge and expertise in behavioral assessment of marital conflict should be employed (Weiss & Margolin, 1977).

Behavior therapists have discarded much of personality theory, and although they have rightly reacted to a reification of personality and personality traits, they have found themselves searching for a set of constructs to guide behavioral assessment lest this enterprise be overly piecemeal, fragmented, and incoherent (Goldfried & Linehan, 1977). The behavioral assessment and treatment of depression are only in their infancy, but it is hoped that the models presented in this volume and the assessment procedures related to them will further the effort.

REFERENCES

Beck, A.T. *Depression: Clinical, experimental, and theoretical aspects.* New York: Hoeber Division, Harper & Row, 1967.

Beck, A.T. *Depression: Causes and treatment.* Philadelphia: University of Pennsylvania Press, 1972.

Beck, A.T. *The diagnosis and management of depression.* Philadelphia: University of Pennsylvania Press, 1973.

Beck, A.T., & Beamesderfer, A. Assessment of depression: The depression inventory. P. Pichot (Ed.), In *Psychological measurements in psychopharmacology. Modern Problems of pharmacopsychiatry* (Vol. 7). Basel: Karger, 1974.

Beck, A.T., Ward, C.H., Mendelson, M., Mock, J., & Erbaugh, J. An inventory for measuring depression. *Archives of General Psychiatry*, 1961, 4, 561-571.

Cantor, N., Smith, E., French, R., & Mezzich, J. Psychiatric diagnosis as prototype categorization. *Journal of Abnormal Psychology*, 1980, 89, 181-193.

Carpenter, W.T., & Strauss, J.S. Diagnostic issues in schizophrenia. In L. Bellack (Ed.), *Disorders of the schizophrenic syndrome*, pp. 291-319. New York: Basic Books, 1979.

Comrey, A.L. A factor analysis of items on the MMPI depression scale. *Educational and Psychological Measurement*, 1957, *17*, 578-585.

Costello, C.G., & Comrey, A.L. Scales for measuring depression and anxiety. *Journal of Psychology*, 1967, *66*, 303-313.

Cropley, A.J., & Weckowicz, T.E. The dimensionality of clinical depression. *Australian Journal of Psychology*, 1966, *18*, 18-25.

Dahlstrom, W.G., & Welsh, G.S. *An MMPI handbook*. Minneapolis: University of Minnesota Press, 1960.

Dahlstrom, W.G., Welsh, G.S., & Dahlstrom, L.E. *An MMPI handbook* (Vol. I) (revised). Minneapolis: University of Minnesota Press, 1972.

Dempsey, P.A. Unidimensional depression scale for the MMPI. *Journal of Consulting Psychology*, 1964, *28*, 364-370.

DSM III: Diagnostic and statistical manual of mental disorders. Washington, D.C.: American Psychiatric Association, 1980.

Fogel, M.L., Curtis, G.C., Kordasy, F., & Smith, W.G. Judges ratings, self-ratings, and checklist reports of affects. *Psychological Reports*, 1966, *19*, 229-307.

Frank, J.D. *Persuasion and healing*. Baltimore: The Johns Hopkins Press, 1961.

Franks, M., & Wilson, G.T. Recent developments in behavioral assessment. In C.M. Franks and G.T. Wilson (Eds.), *Annual review of behavior therapy, theory and practice*, pp. 167-191. New York: Brunner/Mazel, 1978.

Fuchs, C.Z. *The reduction of depression through the modification of self-control behaviors. An instigation group therapy*. Unpublished doctoral dissertation, University of Pittsburgh, 1975.

Gambrill, E.D. *Behavior modification: Handbook of assessment, intervention, and evaluation*. San Francisco: Jossey-Bass, 1977.

Gilberstadt, H., & Duker, J. *A handbook for clinical and actuarial MMPI interpretation*. Philadelphia: Saunders, 1965.

Goldfried, M.R., & Linehan, M.M. Basic issues in behavioral assessment. In A.R. Ciminero, R.S. Calhoun, & H.E. Adams (Eds.), *Handbook of behavioral assessment*, New York: Wiley, 1977.

Goldiamond, I., & Dyrud, J.E. Some applications and implications of behavior analysis for psychotherapy. In J.M. Shlien, H.F. Hunt, J. Matarazzo, & C. Savage (Eds.), *Research in psychotherapy* (Vol. III), Washington, D.C.: American Psychological Association, 1968.

Grinker, R.R., Miller, J., Sabshin, M., Nunn, R., & Nunnally, J. *The phenomena of depressions*. New York: Harper, 1961.

Hamilton, M. A rating scale for depression. *Journal of Neurology, Neurosurgery & Psychiatry*, 1960, *23*, 56-61.

Hamilton, M. A rating scale for depressive disorders. *Psychological Reports*, 1964, *14*, 914.

Harris, R.E., & Lingoes, J.C. *Subscale of the MMPI: An aid to profile interpretations*. Unpublished manuscript, University of California, San Francisco, 1955.

Harrow, M., Colbert, J., Detre, T.P., & Bakeman, R. Symptomatology and subjective experiences in current depressive states. *Archives of General Psychiatry*, 1966, *14*, 203-212.

Hathaway, S.R., & McKinley, J.C. *MMPI manual* (revised). New York: The Psychological Corporation, 1951.

Hersen, M., Eisler, R.M., Alford, G.S., & Argraf, W.S. Effects of token economy on neurotic depression. An experimental of analysis. *Behavior Therapy*, 1973, *4*, 392-397.

Hunt, H.F. Behavior therapy for adults. In D.X. Freedman & J.E. Dyrud (Eds.), *American handbook of psychiatry* (Vol. V) (2nd ed.), New York: Basic Books, 1975.

Hunt, H.F. Behavioral perspectives in the treatment of borderline patients. In P. Hartocollis (Ed.), *Borderline personality disorders: The concept, the syndrome, the patient*, New York: International Universities Press, 1977.

Kanfer, F.H., & Saslow, G. Behavioral analysis: An alternative to diagnostic classification. *Archives of General Psychiatry*, 1965, *12*, 529-538.

Katz, M.M., & Lyerly, S.B. Methods for measuring adjustment and social behavior in the community. I. Rationale, description, discriminate validity, and scale development. *Psychological Reports*, 1963, *13*, 503-535.

Kazdin, A.E. *Behavioral modification in applied settings*. Homewood, Ill. Dorsey Press, 1974.

Klerman, G.L., DiMascio, A., & Weissman, M.M. Treatment of depression by drugs and psychotherapy. *American Journal of Psychiatry*, 1974, *131*, 186-191.

Levitt, E.E., & Lubin, B. *Depression: Concepts controversies and some new facts*. New York: Springer, 1975.

Lewinsohn, P.M., & Grof, M. Pleasant activities and depression. *Journal of Consulting and Clinical Psychology*, 1973, *41*, 261-268.

Lewinsohn, P.M., & Libet, J. Pleasant events, activity schedules and depression. *Journal of Abnormal Psychology*, 1972, *79*, 291-295.

Lewinsohn, P.M., Weinstein, M.S., & Alper, T. A behavioral approach to the group treatment of depressed persons: Methodological contributions. *Journal of Clinical Psychology*, 1970, *26*, 525-532.

Libet, J.M., & Lewinsohn, P.M. Concept of social skill with special reference to the behavior of depressed persons. *Journal of Consulting and Clinical Psychology*, 1973, *40*, 304-312.

Libet, J.M., Lewinsohn, P.M., & Javorek, F. *The construct of social skill: An empirical study of several measures on temporal stability, internal structure, validity and situational generalizability*. Unpublished manuscript, University of Oregon, 1973.

Linn, L. Clinical manifestations of psychiatric disorders. In A.M. Freedman, N.I. Kaplan, & B.J. Sadock (Eds.), *Comprehensive textbook of psychiatry, II*. Baltimore: Williams & Wilkins, 1975.

Lubin, B. *Manual for depression adjective check lists*. San Diego: Educational and Industrial Testing Service, 1967.

MacPhillamy, D.J., & Lewinsohn, P.M. *The structure of reported reinforcement*. Unpublished manuscript, University of Oregon, 1972. (a)

MacPhillamy, D.J., & Lewinsohn, P.M. *The measurement of reinforcing events*. Presented at the 80th annual convention of the Americal Psychological Association, Honolulu, 1972. (b)

MacPhillamy, D.J., & Lewinsohn, P.M. Depression as a function of levels of desired and obtained pleasure. *Journal of Abnormal Psychology*, 1974, *83*, 651-657.

Marks, P.A., Seeman, W., & Haller, P.C. *The actuarial use of the MMPI with adolescents and adults*. Baltimore: Williams & Wilkins, 1974.
Mayer, J.M. Assessment of depression. In P. McReynolds (Ed.), *Advances in psychological assessment* (Vol. 4), San Francisco: Jossey-Bass, 1977.
McLean, P. Therapeutic decision-making in the behavioral treatment of depression. In P.O. Davidson (Ed.), *The behavioral management of anxiety, depression and pain*, New York: Brunner/Mazel, 1976.
McLean, P.D., & Hakstian, A.R. Clinical depression: Comparative efficacy of outpatient treatments. *Journal of Consulting and Clinical Psychology*, 1979, *47*, 818-836.
McLean, P.D., Ogston, K., & Grauer, L.A. A behavioral approach to the treatment of depression. *Journal of Behavior Therapy and Experimental Psychiatry*, 1973, *4*, 323-330.
Mezzich, A.C., & Mezzich, J.E. Symptomatology of depression in adolescence. *Journal of Personality Assessment*, 1979, *43*, 267-275.
Mezzich, J.E., Damarin, F.L., & Erickson, J.R. Comparative validity of strategies and indices for differential diagnosis of depressive states from other psychiatric conditions using the MMPI. *Journal of Consulting and Clinical Psychology*, 1971, *12*, 691-698.
Miller, W.R., & Seligman, M.E.P. Depression and the perception of reinforcement. *Journal of Abnormal Psychology*, 1973, *82*, 62-73.
Mischel, W. *Personality and assessment*. New York: Wiley, 1968.
Nussbaum, K., Wittig, B.A., Hanlon, T.E. & Kurland, A.A. Intravenous nialamide in the treatment of depressed female patients. *Comprehensive Psychiatry*, 1963, *4*, 105-116.
O'Connor, J., Stefic, E., & Gresock, C. Some patterns of depression. *Journal of Clinical Psychology*, 1957, *13*, 122.
Overall, J.E., Hollister, L.E., Johnson, M., & Pennington, V. Nosology of depression and differential response to drugs. *Journal of the American Medical Association*, 1966, *195*, 946-948.
Paykel, E.S. Classification of depressed patients: A cluster analysis derived grouping. *British Journal of Psychiatry*, 1971, *118*, 275-288.
Paykel, E.S. Depressive typologies and response to amytriptyline. *British Journal of Psychiatry*, 1972, *120*, 147-156.
Pichot, P., & Lemperiere, T. Analyse factorielle d'un questionnaire d'autoevaluation des symptoms depressif. *Revue de Psychologie Appliquee*, 1964, *14*, 15-29.
Post, R.D. & Lobitz, W.C. The utility of Mezzich's MMPI regression formula as a diagnostic criterion in depression research. *Journal of Consulting and Clinical Psychology*, 1980, *48*, 673-674.
Rehm, L.P. Assessment of depression. In M. Hersen & A.S. Bellack (Eds.), *Behavioral assessment: a practical handbook*, New York: Pergamon, 1976.
Reynolds, G.A. *A primer of operant conditioning*. Glenview, Ill.: Scott, Foresman, 1968.
Rounsaville, B.J., Weissman, M.M., Prosoff, B.A., & Herceg-Baron, R.L. Marital disputes and treatment outcome in depressed women. *Comprehensive Psychiatry*, 1979, *20*, 483-490.
Rush, A.J., & Beck, A.T. Adults with affective disorders. In M. Hersen & A.S. Bellack (Eds.), *Behavior therapy in the psychiatric setting*, Baltimore: Williams & Wilkins, 1978.

Rush, A.J., Khatami, M., & Beck, A.T. Cognitive and behavior therapy in chronic depression. *Behavior Therapy*, 1975, *6*, 398-404.

Schwab, J.J., Bialow, M.R., Clemmons, R.S., & Holzer, C.E. The affective symptomatology of depression in medical inpatients. *Psychomatics*, 1966, *7*, 214-217.

Schwartz, A., Goldiamond, I., & Wishowe, M.W. *Social casework: a behavioral approach.* New York: Columbia University Press, 1975.

Seitz, R. Five psychological measures of neurotic depression: A correlation study. *Journal of Clinical Psychology*, 1970, *26*, 504-505.

Sidman, M. *Tactics of scientific research.* New York: Basic Books, 1960.

Skinner, B.F. *The behavior of organisms.* New York: Appleton-Century-Crofts, 1938.

Skinner, B.F. *Science and human behavior.* New York: Macmillan, 1953.

Skinner, B.F. *Beyond freedom and dignity.* New York: Knopf, 1971.

Spitzer, R.L., Endicott, J., & Robins, E. *Research diagnostic criteria (RDC)* (2nd ed.). New York: Biometric Research, New York State Department of Mental Hygiene, 1975.

Weckowicz, T.E., Muir, W., & Cropley, S.J. A factor analysis of the Beck inventory of depression. *Journal of Consulting Psychology*, 1967, *31*, 23-28.

Weiss, R.L., & Margolin, G. Assessment of marital conflict and accord. In A.R. Ciminero, K.S. Calhoun, & H.E. Adams (Eds.), *Handbook of behavioral assessment*, New York: Wiley, 1977.

Williams, J.G., Barlow, D.H., & Agras, W.S. Behavioral measurement of severe depression. *Archives of General Psychiatry*, 1972, *27*, 330-333.

Zeiss, A.M., Lewinsohn, P.M., & Munoz, R.F. Nonspecific improvement effects in depression using interpersonal skills training, pleasant activity schedules, or cognitive training. *Journal of Consulting and Clinical Psychology*, 1979, *47*, 427-439.

Zung, W.W.K. A self-rating depression scale. *Archives of General Psychiatry*, 1965, *13*, 508-516.

Major Models of Depression and Related Treatment Strategies

PART II

Behavioral Treatment of Depression
A Social Learning Approach

Peter M. Lewinsohn
Michael Arconad

This chapter will describe a comprehensive treatment approach for unipolar depression developed over the last several years at the University of Oregon Depression Research Unit. The comprehensive treatment approach that we use has a theory, a strategy, and a group of tactics. The treatment strategy translates our basic theoretical conceptualization into a set of specific operations and procedures that can be used to formulate treatment goals for the depressed patient. The tactics are the specific interventions used to accomplish the strategic goals of therapy. In large measure our approach is derived from social learning theory (Bandura, 1977). The techniques that will be discussed extend the social learning conceptualization to the specifics of clinical work with depressed patients.

Treatment Components: Theory, Strategy, and Tactics

Therapists need some kind of theory of depression to guide their treatment efforts. Because depression is a complex phenomenon, therapists without some systematic theoretical conceptualization are likely to have vague and confusing treatment goals and have little success with patients. In general terms, the theory specifies functional relationships between certain antecedent events and the occurrence of depression. These events presumably account for, or "explain," depression. For a given patient, the theory represents a statement about the likely reasons for the patient's depression (i.e., Mrs. T is depressed because of x). Consequently, the theory dictates the intermediate goals for therapy (i.e., in order for Mrs. T to feel less depressed, there must be a change in x). To the extent that the theory is valid, accomplishing the intermediate goals (changing x) should lead to a change in the level of depression.

But a theory is only a set of abstract statements suggesting general treatment goals for depressed patients. A comprehensive treatment approach must also have a strategy. A treatment strategy translates the theory into a set of specific operations and procedures that can be used to formulate treatment goals for the depressed patient. The first step in the strategy is diagnostic assessment of the patient. Diagnostic assessment must first determine whether or not depression is the problem (or at least a problem) for the patient. But assessment of the level of depression is not enough. The assessment must also begin to identify concrete events that may account for the patient's depression. In this way the diagnostic process can guide the formulation of a treatment plan to change the events accounting for the patient's depression. Thus an initial and ongoing evaluation involves not only measurement of the level of depression but also measurement of concomitant changes in the events presumed to be related to the patient's depression. For example, a therapist may believe that a patient's marital difficulties are causally related to the patient's depression and may conclude that marital therapy aimed at changing the quality of marital interaction is the appropriate treatment. The efforts at evaluation should include periodic measurements of the patient's depression level during the course of treatment, as well as regular assessments of the patient's marital adjustment. This two-pronged approach to evaluation allows the therapist to evaluate the effectiveness of the specific treatment (marital therapy) vis-à-vis the patient's depression level, as well as with regard to its impact on the marital interaction.

The third and final component of a comprehensive treatment approach is the group of treatment tactics. Tactics are the specific interventions used to accomplish the strategic goals of therapy. Useful tactics are those that dependably produce clinically desired changes in the events related to the depression. This is probably the aspect of therapy on which clinicians differ the most, in that different therapists often use different tactics in order to reach similar strategic goals. There are probably several reasons for this. Therapists must feel comfortable with a tactic and must be convinced that they can use it effectively. Also, the tactics must be tailored to the patient. The treatment literature describes many potentially useful tactics. Although many of these are presented as all-purpose tactics (e.g., family therapy), often they can be adapted to specific uses. It is the clinician, in collaboration with the patient, who chooses from among several possible tactics.

Social Learning Theory: Basic Conceptualization

Within a social learning theory framework, the cause of depression is assumed to reside in the person-behavior-environment interaction and to be explainable by what are commonly known as "principles of learning," "schedules of reinforcement," and "social learning theory," terms that do not negate the potential importance of mediational and other internal (cognitive) events.

Social learning theory has always involved an attempt to integrate stimulus-response theory and cognitive theory. First introduced by Rotter (1954), it has more recently been extended by Bandura (1977). Social learning theory assumes that psychological functioning can best be understood in terms of continuous reciprocal interactions among personal factors (e.g., cognitive processes, expectancies), behavioral factors, and environmental factors, all operating as interdependent determinants of one another. The relative influences exerted by these interdependent factors differ in various settings and for different behaviors. In the social learning approach, behavior is an interacting determinant, not simply an outcome of external events. From the perspective of social learning theory, people are seen as capable of exercising considerable control over their own behavior, not just as reactors to external influences. They select, organize, and transform the stimuli that impinge on them. This conception of human functioning does not cast people in the role of powerless objects controlled by environmental forces, nor does it cast them as free agents who can become whatever they choose. People and their environments are reciprocal determinants of one another.

We assume that depression and reinforcement are related phenomena. In previous publications (Lewinsohn, Weinstein, & Shaw, 1969; Lewinsohn, Youngren, & Grosscup, 1979) we have advanced hypotheses about the relationship between positive reinforcement and depression, focusing on the effect that a reduction in the rate of response-contingent positive reinforcement is assumed to have on the behavior and on the affect of the individual. Reinforcement is defined in terms of the quality of one's interactions with one's environment. Person-environment interactions with positive outcomes constitute positive reinforcement. Such interactions strengthen the person's behavior. The use of the word "contingent" refers to the temporal relationship between behavior and its consequences. In the social learning approach to the study and treatment of depression, a low rate of response-contingent positive reinforcement is assumed to constitute a critical antecedent for the occurrence of depression. The basic assumption is that the low rate of behavioral output and the associated dysphoric feelings are elicited by a low rate of positive reinforcement and/or a high rate of aversive experience; that is, it is assumed that the behavior of depressed persons does not lead to positive reinforcement to a degree sufficient to maintain their behavior. Hence, depressed persons find it difficult to initiate or to maintain their behavior, and they become increasingly passive. The low rate of positive reinforcement is also assumed to cause the dysphoric feelings that are so central to the phenomenology of depression. Thus the concept of reinforcement is crucial to our approach to depression. The experience of little or no rewarding interaction with the environment causes the person to feel sad or blue. The key notion is that being depressed results from few person-environment interactions with positive outcomes for the person. The corollary hypothesis (Grosscup & Lewinsohn, 1980; Lewinsohn, Youngren, & Grosscup, 1979) is that a high rate of punishing experiences also causes depression. Punishment is defined as person-environment interactions with aversive (distressing, upsetting, unpleasant) outcomes. Punishing interactions with the environment may cause depression directly or indirectly by interfering with the person's engagement in and enjoyment of potentially rewarding activities. Figure 2.1 illustrates the different notions of this working model.

Low rates of positive reinforcement and/or high rates of aversive experience in the person-environment interaction may occur for several reasons: (1) The person's immediate environment may have few available positive reinforcers or may have many punishing aspects (availability). (2) The person may lack the skills to obtain available positive reinforcers and/or cope effectively with aversive events (skill deficits). (3) The positive reinforcement potency of events may be reduced and/or the negative impact of punishing events may be heightened. These notions, and research results consistent with them, have been discussed elsewhere in more detail (Grosscup & Lewinsohn, 1980; Lewinsohn, 1975; Lewinsohn & Amenson, 1978; Lewinsohn, Biglan, & Zeiss, 1976; Lewinsohn & Talkington, 1979; Lewinsohn, Youngren, & Grosscup, 1979; MacPhillamy & Lewinsohn, 1974). In these studies we consistently found that depressed persons experienced lower rates of positive reinforcement and higher rates of punishment than did relevant control groups. As the depression level decreases, the rate of obtained positive reinforcement increases, and the rate of experienced punishment decreases. It has been found that these changes are greatest for depressed persons who improve the most during therapy. Other studies have shown that depressed patients often are deficient in the social skills needed to interact effectively with others (Lewinsohn, Mischel,

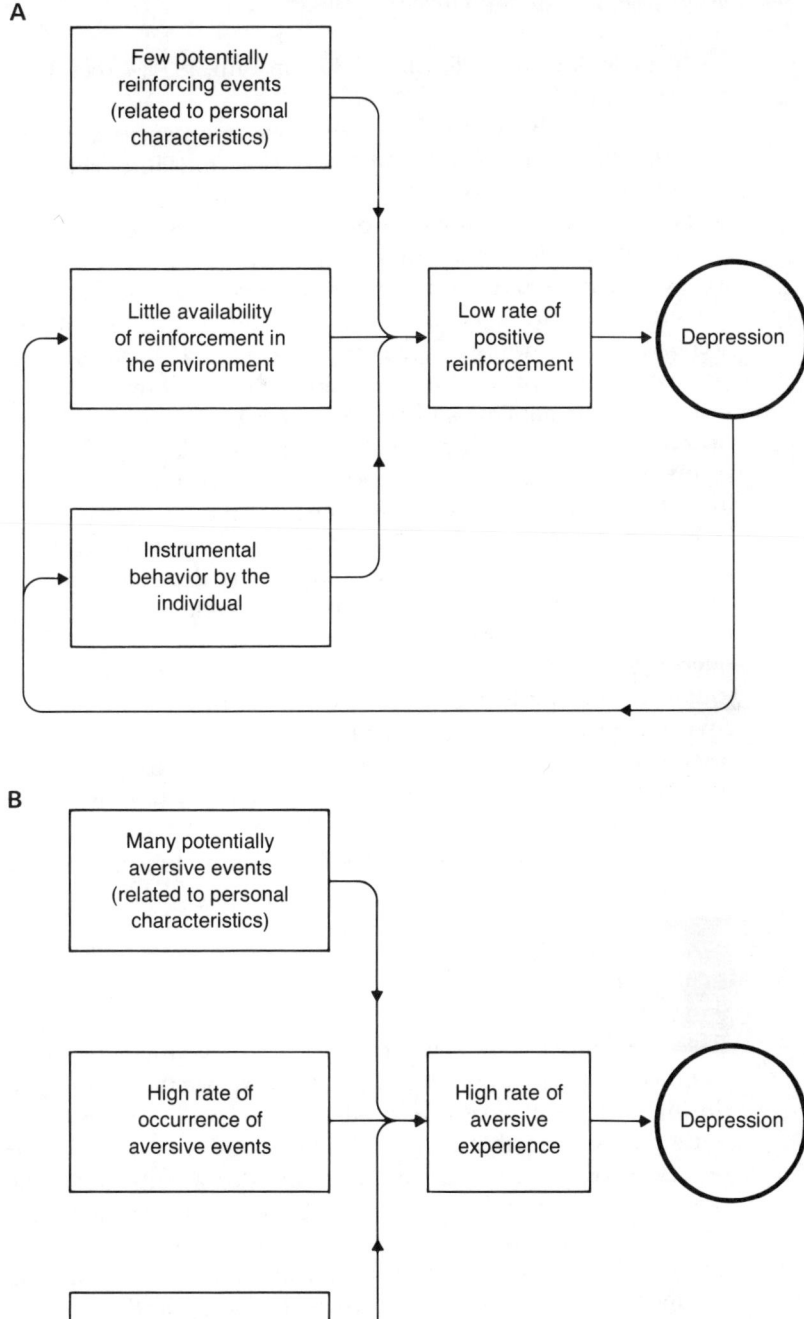

Figure 2.1 Social reinforcement for depression.

Chaplin, & Barton, 1980; Libet & Lewinsohn, 1973; Libet, Lewinsohn, & Javorek, 1973).

The positively reinforcing events whose absences are particularly relevant to the occurrence of depression fall into several clusters (Lewinsohn & Amenson, 1978): positive sexual experiences, rewarding social interactions, enjoyable outdoor activities, solitude, and competence experiences. Examples of these clusters include "being noticed as sexually attractive," "expressing my love to someone," "being with friends," "being relaxed," "doing a job well," "seeing beautiful scenery," and "doing a project my own way." Punishing events particularly important for depression fall into three clusters: marital discord, work hassles, and receiving negative reactions from others. Specific examples of these sorts of events include "arguments with my [spouse, living partner]," "working on something when I am tired," and "having someone evaluate or criticize me."

Within the previously mentioned theoretical framework, it is expected that to the extent that a person is depressed, that person's interactions with the environment have elicited a low rate of positive reinforcements and/or a high rate of aversive experiences. Consequently, treatment is aimed at assisting the person to increase the rate (quantity and quality) of positively reinforcing interactions with the environment and to decrease the rate (quantity and quality) of aversive interactions. Our approach to depression emphasizes an active rather than a passive model of the person and leans heavily on an interactional view of personality. Within this approach, social interpersonal behavior, cognitive factors, and self-regulatory mechanisms play important roles.

Strategy

Research studies (e.g., Zeiss et al., 1979) to investigate the social learning theory of depression and clinical experience in applying the theory during treatment have generated a set of procedures useful for work with depressed patients. The guiding assumption in our treatment of depressed patients is that the restoration of an adequate schedule of positive reinforcement is essential to the amelioration of dysphoria. Alterations in the frequency, quality, and range of the patient's activities and social interactions are the most common foci for achieving such a change in the schedule of reinforcement. The events that are reinforcing are variable among different patients, and so are the factors that may result in a reduced rate of reinforcement.

Moreover, diverse sets of accompanying problems (e.g., insomnia, somatic difficulties, obsessive thinking) are found among patients who are diagnosed as being depressed. Therefore, there is no single intervention strategy that is useful for all depressed patients, nor is one likely to be discovered. Instead, several different treatment techniques have evolved, each designed to achieve a specific treatment goal. These procedures are still evolving. Indeed, it is hoped that this chapter will facilitate contributions to these developments from other therapists by assisting them in reaching a carefully specified set of goals for each patient.

Conceptualization of Problems

Patients usually enter therapy with conceptualizations or definitions of their problems. Depressed patients often see themselves as victims of their moods or of environmental forces. Rarely do patients see their behaviors and/or their interpretations of their behaviors and/or the behaviors of others as causes for the depression. To complicate things further, fairly substantial numbers of the professional community are convinced that there is a biogenic cause of unipolar depression. This is often meant to imply the insignificance of psychological variables as causal factors. Thus depressed patients often initially assume a passive stance; that is, they believe that something analogous to a physical disease has happened to them. Although they may emphasize specific behavioral problems (e.g., sleeplessness, lack of social involvement, obsessive thoughts), typically the focus is on "depression." Thus it usually takes a considerable amount of work to move patients from a construct usage of the term "depression" to a recognition of the importance of specific problematic behavioral events that may be related to their dysphoria.

One goal of the initial phase of treatment is for therapist and patient to redefine the patient's problems in terms that will give the patient a sense of control and a feeling of hope, especially in terms that will lead to specific behavioral interventions. Thus the therapist tries to understand the patient's description and definition of the problem, but the therapist does not uncritically accept the patient's view of the problem. Instead, therapist and patient attempt to redefine the problem in terms that are acceptable to both of them. It is this reformulation or conceptualization phase that sets the stage for behavioral change. We see it as important for successful treatment that the patient and the therapist evolve a common conceptualization with common expectations. This conceptualization should lead naturally to specific behavioral changes that will benefit the patient in real life situations.

There are numerous ways in which the patient and the therapist can evolve a common conceptualization. Some therapists are very directive, forcing on the patient a particular conceptualization by the power of personality, jargon, or position. In some cases such a hard-sell approach may prove successful. A preferred way to proceed is to have the patient and the therapist evolve a common conceptualization that will increase the patient's feelings of being an active participant and making a contribution. The manner in which the therapist discusses the presenting problem, the kinds of questions asked, the type of assessment procedures employed, the content of the therapy rationale, and the kinds of homework assignments given are all used to evolve a common patient-therapist conceptualization.

It is important to do a great deal of "structuring" in the initial phase of treatment of depressed patients so that there will be a clear mutual understanding of expectations, goals, time commitments, and other conditions. The beginning phase of treatment is clearly defined for the patient as a diagnostic phase. During this period, information is obtained about the patient and the patient's behavior. Following this diagnostic phase, the findings are shared with the patient, and mutually acceptable treatment recommendations are made.

Explicit Diagnostic Phase

This section will detail the strategies we use for differential diagnosis, functional analysis, and outcome evaluation. Table 2.1 presents the steps used as part of our treatment strategy.

Differential Diagnosis

In spite of the fact that there is no single generally accepted typology for depression, and in spite of the fact that depression not only occurs in "pure" form but also is present in a large number of patients suffering from other psychiatric and medical disorders, these uncertainties do not pose a serious obstacle, because on the basis of descriptive studies (e.g., Grinker et al., 1961; Lewinsohn & Lee, 1980) the symptoms and the key behavioral manifestations that constitute the depression syndrome are quite well known. Therefore, by use of the existing assessment instruments it is possible to describe a patient in regard to depression severity, to delineate the specific constellation of symptoms shown by that patient, and to evaluate the absence or presence of other psychiatric symptoms and conditions. The subtypes of depression that on the basis of past research are deemed to be important (unipolar vs. bipolar, primary vs. secondary, endogenous vs. situational, agitated vs. retarded, neurotic vs. psychotic) have been incorporated into the Schedule for Affective Disorders and Schizophrenia (SADS) (Endicott & Spitzer, 1978) and the Research Diagnostic Criteria (RDC) (Spitzer et al., 1978), by means of which it is possible to assign patients to these categories with considerable reliability. The initial step is to ascertain whether or not depression is the problem (or at least a problem) for the patient. We use a multistage screening process. The person seeking treatment first completes the MMPI and Health Questionnaire[1] and

Table 2.1 Oregon Depression Unit Strategy

Differential diagnosis
  Self-report questionnaires
    MMPI
    Health questionnaire
  Clinical interview using the Schedule for Affective Disorders and Schizophrenia (SADS)
    Grinker ratings
    Research Diagnostic Criteria (RDC)
Functional analysis
  Pleasant Events and Unpleasant Events Schedules (PES and UES)
  Daily monitoring
    Personalized activities schedule
    Depression Adjective Checklist (DACL)
  Behavioral interviewing
  Behavioral observations
Outcome evaluation
  Daily monitoring
    Personalized activities schedule
    Depression Adjective Checklist (DACL)
  Termination
    Measure of depression, e.g., Beck Depression Inventory (BDI)
    Pleasant Events and Unpleasant Events schedules (PES and UES)
  Follow-up (1 month and 6 months)
    Measure of depression
    Pleasant Events and Unpleasant Events Schedules (PES and UES)

then participates in a semistructured interview intended to provide us with an overview of the person's life situation. On the basis of the interview, the interviewer rates the person on the items in the Feelings and Concerns Checklist (Grinker et al., 1961). These items are summed and averaged to derive factor scores representing the major symptom clusters associated with depression (dysphoria, material burden, guilt, and social isolation). Summing the items rated by the interviewer yields a measure of the intensity of depression. The use of the Feelings and Concerns Checklist is facilitated by following an outline of general questions that elicit information about the various manifestations of depression and the history of previous problems. We have found the outline presented in Table 2.2 useful. In addition to this outline, we also follow the guidelines of the extensive interview provided by the Schedule for Affective Disorders and Schizophrenia (SADS) (Endicott & Spitzer, 1978).

An interview conducted along the lines suggested will last approximately 50 minutes. At the end of it, the interviewer usually has a good overview of how depressed the patient is and how the depression

Table 2.2 Interview Outline

1. Interviewer begins by probing for the patient's feelings concerning the interview situation. Has the patient ever been in a similar situation before? Conditions responsible for the patient coming to the therapist.
2. Patient is asked to describe immediate family: degree of closeness; concern about members of family.
3. Patient is asked to describe interests: hobbies; occupation; specific goals; life goals; expected success; satisfaction with goals; plans for the coming year.
4. Occupation—academic: How is it going? Do you feel good or bad about it? Worried? Pressured? By whom?
5. Concentration and/or motivation: Problems?
6. Worries: specific; general.
7. Do you have problems in taking action, making decisions and acting on them?
8. What do you do during a normal day?
9. Emotionality: Are you the kind of person who tends to be tense vs. relaxed? Calm vs. excitable? Moody? Jittery?
10. Ideas of suicide: What is the worst you have felt over the past year or two? When you felt that bad, did you feel that life was not worth living, etc.?
11. Perceived sociability: dates and/or relationships with opposite sex; sexual relations; numbers of close and casual friends; feelings of social adequacy/inadequacy; participation in social organizations.
12. Religious background and present feelings.
13. Present physical condition: On any medication? "Retarded"? Weight loss? Visceral symptoms? Insomnia? Early morning awakening?
14. Perception of major responsibilities: Burdened by? Failure in?
15. Major happenings during past year: best; worst (elicits information about environment, interest in life, self-pity).
16. Self-description: your good points; your weak points.
17. Self-description by significant others: How would they describe you?
18. Major aspects of self that you wish were different.
19. Anything you might want to add.

manifests itself. On the basis of the information provided by the interview and the health questionnaire, the interviewer assigns a diagnosis using the categories of the Research Diagnostic Criteria (RDC) (Spitzer et al., 1978).[2]

We have found that people who meet all of the following criteria have depression as their major problem and are likely to benefit from our program: (1) MMPI D-scale score ≥ 80, or ≥ 70 with D > other clinical scales; (2) mean symptom ratings on all Grinker checklist factors $\geq .7$; (3) dysphoria score on Grinker checklist ≥ 1.0; (4) RDC diagnosis of major, minor, or intermittent depressive disorder.

There are other convenient, short, and easy-to-use interview and self-report measures of depression level, such as the Beck Depression Inventory (BDI) (Beck et al., 1961), the Self-rating Depression Scale (SDS) (Zung, 1965), and the Center for Epidemiologic Studies Depression Scale (Radloff, 1977). We usually use the BDI in addition to the measures discussed earlier. The BDI has 21 items with four or five alternative statements for each item. The alternatives indicate increasing severe levels of distress that are weighted accordingly in the scoring. The sum of all items gives a total score.

During the initial diagnostic phase it is important to obtain diagnostic data and treatment-relevant data, such as mood ratings, relevant medical information, and information on type and frequency of activities, marital adjustment, occurrences of stressful life events, and suicidal risk, which have been described in greater detail elsewhere (Lewinsohn, Biglan, & Zeiss, 1976).

The diagnostic phase is followed by one or more review sessions. The patient is told at the initial interview that the therapist will meet with the patient at the end of the diagnostic phase to try to pull everything together and to make recommendations. At these review sessions, specific etiologic hypotheses are presented to the patient. Behavioral terms, graphs, and other visual aids are used to present a "behavioral diagnosis" as clearly as possible. The end product is a mutually acceptable understanding as to the nature of the patient's problems and the proposed treatment goals and procedures.

Functional Diagnosis: Identification of Targets for Intervention

Behavioral Problems Functionally Related to Depression Functional diagnosis involves pinpointing specific person-environment interactions and events related to a particular patient's depression. This part of the diagnostic process is needed to guide the formulation of a treatment plan designed to change the events contributing to the patient's depression. In order to pinpoint specific person-environment interactions related to the person's depression, we make extensive use of home observations and of the Pleasant Events and Unpleasant-Events schedules (Lewinsohn, 1975; MacPhillamy & Lewinsohn, 1971).

Use of Home Observations Clinical experience and the research literature (e.g., Chamberlin & Lewinsohn, 1979; Weissman & Paykel, 1974) suggest that many depressed patients have serious marital problems that are relevant to their depression. These problems often can be delineated through home observations. The home visit becomes a focal point for discussion between therapist and patient, and it requires the patient to communicate and to plan with the other members of the family. The manner in which this is accomplished usually results in important diagnostic information. Home visits, lasting about an hour, should be scheduled around mealtimes, when all members of the family are present. Detailed case descriptions illustrating the use of the home visit as a part of the initial assessment are available elsewhere (Lewinsohn & Shaffer, 1971). On the basis of the home observation, it is often possible to identify interpersonal behavior patterns that the therapist hypothesizes to be causally related to the depression. If, for practical reasons, the therapist is unable to conduct home observations, it might be advisable to schedule an interview with the spouse.

Home visits appear to have the following beneficial consequences: First, they immediately focus the therapist-patient interaction on behavioral and interpersonal problems. This is especially important for the many depressed patients who start out by defining themselves in a medical way (i.e., as having some kind of disease that they expect someone to treat). The home observations communicate to the patient in a powerful manner that the therapist sees the patient's problem as being interactional (i.e., intimately related to the patient's relationships with other people). Second, home observations provide an easy way to involve a significant part of the patient's environment in the treatment process. The necessity of arranging for the home observation provides a natural opening for relating to the spouse, children, etc., in ways that usually are more productive than an information-gathering social history interview with a relative.

Pinpointing Key Events   In order to pinpoint specific person-environment interactions related to the patient's depression, we make extensive use of the Pleasant-Events Schedule (PES) (MacPhillamy & Lewinsohn, 1971) and the Unpleasant-Events Schedule (UES) (Lewinsohn, 1975). The PES consists of 320 items assumed to represent an exhaustive sampling of environmental interactions that most people find pleasant. We assume that events subjectively experienced as pleasant have positive reinforcement value. The patient first rates the frequency of occurrence of each event during the past month on a 3-point scale: 0 indicates that this has not happened in the past 30 days; 1, this has happened a few times (1 to 6) in the past 30 days; 2, this has happened often (7 or more times) in the past 30 days. The patient then rates the subjective enjoyability of the events on another 3-point scale: 0 indicates that this was not or could not be pleasant; 1, this was or could be somewhat pleasant; 2, this was or could be very pleasant. The frequency ratings are assumed to measure the patient's rates of engagement in the person-environment interactions on the list during the past month. The subjective enjoyability ratings are assumed to indicate the patient's potential for positive reinforcement. The cross-product scores of the frequency and enjoyability ratings are assumed to reflect the total amount of positive reinforcement obtained by the patient. In addition to the total scores based on all items, the PES also provides subscale scores for sexual interactions, solitude, outdoor activities, and social activities (MacPhillamy & Lewinsohn, 1975).

The UES consists of 320 items assumed to represent an exhaustive sampling of environmental interactions that most people find unpleasant. We assume that events subjectively experienced as unpleasant act as punishments (i.e., they are likely to leave the patient feeling distressed). Using 3-point rating scales analogous to those used with the PES, the patient rates the items first for their frequency and then for their aversiveness. Again, the frequency scores are assumed to reflect the rates at which the events occurred, the aversiveness ratings are assumed to reflect the potential punishment values of the events, and the sums of the cross-product scores are assumed to reflect the amount of aversiveness experienced during the past month. In addition to frequency, aversiveness, and cross-product scores, the UES provides subscale scores for the following items: events related to health and welfare; material and financial events; sexual, marital, and friendship events; achievement-academic-job items; legal items; social-exits items; most-discriminating items; mood-related items (Lewinsohn & Chaplin, 1979).

Normative data on both schedules allow evaluation of the patient's scores relative to the scores of others of the same sex and age. PES scores below the norms and UES scores above the norms on the various subscales suggest kinds of reinforcing and punishing events that may be related to the patient's depression. Patterns among scores are often important. For example, a patient may have a low score for pleasant sexual events and a high score for marital-distress events. This immediately suggests possible reasons for the patient's depression and even some possible treatment tactics. We share these working hypotheses with the patient and use them to formulate some intermediate treatment goals. In particular, many depressed patients show low PES cross-product scores and high UES cross-product scores. If this is the case, therapist and patient can derive useful information by examining the score pattern. There are three possible patterns that can produce low cross-product scores in PES and UES.

PES scores: Pattern 1, low frequency and low enjoyability: The patient is not engaging in many of the activities on the schedule and is not deriving much pleasure from the ones engaged in. Pattern 2, low frequency and average or above-average enjoyability: The patient is not engaging in the kinds of activities that are believed to be potentially enjoyable for this particular patient. Pattern 3, average or above-average frequency and low enjoyability: The patient is doing many things but is not deriving much enjoyment from these activities.

The score-pattern information can assist the therapist and the patient in designing a specific treatment plan. If the patient demonstrates pattern 1, the first goal might be to enhance the enjoyment derived from the patient's activities; then, after this goal has been accomplished, the aim should be to increase the number of pleasant activities. If the scores match pattern 2, the goal can be simply to increase the number of pleasant activities. If the patient demonstrates pattern 3, the goal might be to increase the patient's enjoyment of the activities already being pursued.

UES scores: Pattern 1, high frequency and high aversiveness: The patient has many unpleasant interactions, and they are experienced as very distressing. The goal might be to work concurrently on reducing the frequency of occurrences and reducing the negative subjective impact of the events. Pattern 2, high frequency and average or below-average aversiveness: The patient experiences many unpleasant events, but the patient's emotional reactions to these are similar to the reactions of most people who are confronted by such events. The goal might be to reduce the frequency of occurrences of such events. Pattern 3, average or below-average frequency and high aversiveness: The patient is excessively sensitive to certain events. The goal might be to reduce the subjective negative impact of a few especially aversive events.

The information obtained from the PES and UES scores assists the patient and the therapist in setting specific strategic goals and in pinpointing specific pleasant activities to be increased and unpleasant activities to be decreased.

In addition to contributing to the generation of etiologic hypotheses, the PES and the UES ratings provide the basis for constructing a personalized activity schedule to be used for daily monitoring. Each patient's activity schedule consists of the 80 items the patient rated as most pleasant on the PES and the 80 items the patient rated as most unpleasant and most frequent on the UES. The role the activity schedule plays in the evaluation of the functional diagnosis and in treatment will be described later. In Appendix A we present an all-purpose activity schedule consisting of 80 pleasant items and 80 unpleasant items found to be related to mood in the general population (Lewinsohn & Amenson, 1978). The items in this list overlap heavily with the items in the individualized lists we have constructed for depressed patients. Therapists who do not wish to take time to construct an individualized list will find this list quite adequate.

Daily Monitoring As soon as possible after entry into the treatment program, patients should begin rating their moods and monitoring the occurrences of the pleasant and unpleasant activities on their activity schedules on a daily basis. They should continue this daily monitoring for the duration of treatment. Daily mood ratings are made on the Depression Adjective Checklists (DACL) (Lubin, 1965). The latter constitute a series of seven alternative lists of adjectives designed to provide a measure of the patient's mood. Each evening the patient is asked to check all those adjectives that describe how the patient felt that day. The number of positive adjectives not checked plus the number of negative adjectives checked constitute the mood score. The higher the score, the more depressed the patient felt. The DACL score gives a measure of daily fluctuations in mood, and often this permits the therapist to spot particular days of the week during which the patient becomes noticeably more depressed or less depressed and to explore reasons for these changes. Another means of tracking daily mood involves the use of the 9-point scale (1 indicates very happy; 9 indicates very depressed) shown in Appendix B.

The main purpose of daily monitoring of activities and mood is to enable the patient and the therapist to become aware of the covariance that typically exists between mood and the rates of occurrences of pleasant and unpleasant activities.

To monitor occurrences of events, patients use a 3-point scale for each of the 80 pleasant events on their personalized schedules: 0 indicates the event did not occur today; 1, the event occurred but was neutral; 2, the event occurred and was pleasant. Patients mark a similar scale for the 80 unpleasant events on their schedules, except that they indicate whether the event was neutral or unpleasant if it occurred. This easily provides scores for the pleasant and unpleasant events experienced that day. The mean pleasant-events score for daily monitoring in a normal population is 17.6, with a standard deviation of 10.35. The mean unpleasant-events score in a normal population is 5.1, with a standard deviation of 3.9. The daily frequencies of various events provide immediate feedback regarding the impact of treatment in meeting the intermediate treatment goals of changing the overall rate of reinforcing and punishing events. This continuous feedback permits therapist and patient to continually adjust the treatment tactics according to their success in meeting the strategic goals of therapy.

The covariance of certain pleasant and unpleasant events with changes in mood permits evaluation of the functional diagnosis and further specification of the person-environment interactions influencing the patient's mood. Inspection of a graph of the daily mood and events scores provides an easy means of estimating concomitant changes in the levels of these three variables. Computer analysis provides a means of pinpointing precisely the specific events most highly correlated with mood fluctuations. The therapist and patient can use this information to fine-tune the diagnosis and the associated therapy goals.

The previously mentioned comprehensive and data-based diagnostic procedures will pinpoint a small number (typically two or three) of important person-environment interactions that are hypothesized to be related to the patient's depression. Therapist and patient make use of the diagnostic information to negotiate a mutually agreeable therapy contract specifying in some detail the goals of treatment. We make every effort to involve the patient in these treatment decisions. For example, we make extensive use of charts and graphs and other visual aids to help the patient understand the results and the implications of the diagnostic procedures. The focus is always on making the feedback relevant to important aspects of the patient's life.

Termination and Follow-up Assessments At the end of therapy, and again 1 month later and 6 months later, the patient repeats the various intake questionnaires, including the PES and the UES, as well as some measure of depression level (e.g., the BDI). Comparison of pretreatment scores and posttreatment scores allows assessment of the directions and amounts of change in person-environment interactions and depression level.

Time Limit for Treatment The treatment approach we use is designed to be applied within a prespecified number of moderately well structured sessions. A time limit for treatment is always part of the initial contract. Time limits have ranged from 4 weeks to 3 months, typically involving 12 treatment sessions. The time limit should be determined for each patient on the basis of the period of time that likely will be required to achieve the treatment goals. The existence of a time limit makes it essential for both therapist and patient to define and accept treatment goals that can reasonably be expected to be accomplished during the allotted time.

Contracting and Self-reinforcement Schedules Both the assessment and the treatment of the depressed patient require effort on the patient's part. For example, the patient may be asked to fill out the PES, to keep track of mood variations, to monitor activities on a daily basis, etc., throughout the course of treatment. Moreover, the patient may be asked to take steps that involve substantial changes in daily activities. It has been found useful to take advantage of various contingencies that may motivate the patient to engage in treatment-relevant activities. We advise patients to make specific agreements with themselves to give themselves rewards, but only if they perform the specifics of the agreements. The purpose of the contract is to arrange in advance a specific positive consequence (reinforcement) to follow the achievement of a goal. For example, a contract might state that the patient will have dinner at a favorite restaurant if and only if baseline observations are faithfully carried out for 1 week. We recommend the inclusion of contracting because it has been our experience that it makes the accomplishment of goals easier for many patients.

Reinforcers may take many forms: (1) material rewards that are available in the patient's environment (e.g., favorite meals, magazines, books, clothes, records, and other objects requiring money); (2) time (e.g., earning time to do things the patient likes to do but rarely has time for, such as taking a relaxing bath, sleeping late, sunbathing, talking on the phone, or just "wasting time"); (3) mental (verbal-symbolic) rewards (e.g., self-praise for a completed task, a pat on the back, thinking about one's own good points and accomplishments, good relationships with others) or mental "treats" (e.g., daydreaming about pleasurable things, meditating, listening to music). A patient's responses on the PES often suggest appropriate reinforcers.

Other motivational tactics we have used include the following: making the next appointment contingent on completion of certain tasks; reducing patients' fees for keeping appointments and for completing assignments; using progress points. The latter involves patients rewarding themselves with progress points for engaging in and completing treatment-relevant activities. The patient is initially asked to generate a "reward menu" consisting of 5 or 10 potentially pleasurable rewards. The reward menu will consist of events the patient would like to do and is capable of doing. The patient then specifies the number of progress points needed to earn each reward.

In summary, we use contingency contracts and self-reinforcement schedules in ways that are consistent with the overall goal of the treatment, which is to increase the amount of response-contingent reinforcement. Contingency contracting also serves to clarify progress toward the accomplishment of goals.

Tactics

Within the context of a social learning approach to the treatment of depression, a wide range of tactics can be used to accomplish the goals that have been pinpointed during the diagnostic process. The most commonly used tactics are shown in Table 2.3. In general terms, our treatment tactics focus on teaching depressed patients skills they can use to change detrimental patterns of interaction with their environment, as well as the skills needed to maintain these changes after the termination of therapy. Specific interventions depend on the strategic goals for the particular patient. For example, a patient might be depressed because of having few rewarding interactions with other people (PES scores confirmed by patient self-report). More detailed exploration of the situation might suggest that the patient has difficulty in expressing opinions and emotions and consequently feels uncomfortable and inhibited in intimate relationships. Therapy could then focus on assertion training (Alberti & Emmons, 1974; Sanchez et al., 1980). Another patient might be depressed because interactions with the children in the family are unpleasant. Failure to discipline the children appropriately might be the problem. Therapy could then focus on training in parenting skills (Patterson & Gullion, 1968).

Table 2.3 Social Learning Tactics

Environmental interventions
  Environmental shifts
  Contingency management
Skills training
  Self-change methods
    Specifying the problem
    Self-observation and "baselining"
    Discovering antecedents
    Discovering consequences
    Setting a helpful goal
    Self-reinforcement
    Evaluating progress
    Time planning
  Social skills
    Assertion
    Interpersonal style of expressive behavior
    Social activity
  Relaxation
  Stress management
  Cognitive skills
    Decreasing negative thinking by thought interruption, premaking, worrying time, blowup technique, self-talk procedures, identifying and disputing irrational thoughts
    Increasing positive thinking by priming, noticing accomplishments, positive self-rewarding thoughts, time projection

---

These tactics can be classified into three general categories: those that focus on changing environmental conditions; those that focus on teaching depressed patients skills they can use to change detrimental patterns of interaction with the environment; those aimed at enhancing the pleasantness and decreasing the aversiveness of person-environment interactions.

Environmental interventions are especially useful when the patient's environment is highly impoverished and/or aversive or when the patient has few personal resources. One kind of environmental intervention involves changing the physical and social setting by assisting the patient to move to a new environment. The literature is remarkably sparse regarding the use of an environmental shift in the treatment of depression, perhaps because its therapeutic value is often so obvious. However, its implementation is often difficult.

Contingency management is another kind of environmental intervention. Contingency management involves changing the consequences of certain behaviors. For institutionalized patients, token economies can be set up and used to reinforce positively constructive (i.e., nondepressed) behaviors and reinforce negatively depressive behaviors (Hanaway & Barlow, 1975; Hersen et al., 1973; Reisinger, 1972). For outpatients, the therapist can instruct the family members to make attention, praise, and physical displays of affection contingent on the patient's adaptive behaviors, while ignoring depressed behaviors (Liberman & Raskin, 1971). The willingness of family members to become involved in this manner may in itself constitute an important prognostic sign. McLean and Hakstian (1978) found that regardless of treatment modality, patients whose spouses were willing to become involved in the treatment were much more likely to improve.

Skills training tactics focus on teaching depressed patients skills they can use to change detrimental patterns of interaction with the environment, as well as the skills needed to maintain these changes after the termination of therapy. Specific skills training interventions will vary from case to case, ranging from highly structured and standardized programs to individually designed ad hoc procedures. Training typically involves the following: didactic introduction to the skills involved; modeling and coaching by the therapist; role playing and rehearsal; practice by the patient during and after treatment sessions; application of the skills in the real world.

In our choice of self-management methods we have made considerable use of procedures and techniques described by Goldfried and Merbaum (1973), Mahoney and Thoresen (1974), and Watson and Tharp (1972). Lakein's *How to Get Control of Your Time and Your Life* (1974) is also useful because it presents a systematic format for organizing one's time and activities so as to be able to meet one's responsibilities and still have time for pleasant activities.

Tactics aimed at enabling the patient to change the quantity and quality of interpersonal relationships typically cover three aspects of interpersonal behavior: assertion, interpersonal style of expressive behavior, and social activity. For assertion, we have used a covert modeling procedure based on Kazdin's work (1974, 1976) in a sequence involving instruction, modeling, rehearsal, and feedback (Zeiss et al., 1979). After the concept of assertion is presented, the patient reads *Your Perfect Right* (Alberti & Emmons, 1974), and a personalized list of problem situations is developed by the patient and the therapist. The therapist may model some assertive possibilities for the patient; after that, the patient is encouraged to take over and to rehearse assertiveness using the covert modeling procedure. Transfer to real life situations is planned and monitored during later sessions.

Work aimed at improving the patient's interpersonal style or social impact (Coyne, 1976; Youngren & Lewinsohn, 1979) follows the same format: instruction, modeling, rehearsal, and feedback. Patient and therapist together set goals, usually small and easily attained goals, based on preassessment and on the patient's preferences. Typical goals might include responding to others with more positive interest, reducing the patient's complaints and "whining," increasing the patient's activity level during discussions, and changing other aspects of the patient's behavior or appearance.

Finally, patients are encouraged to increase their social activities. Patient and therapist set goals for an increase based on an assessment of the patient's pretreatment level of social activities. Goals are gradually increased over several sessions. For this phase of treatment, a manual prepared by Gambrill and Richey (1976) is useful for specific help in areas such as initiating conversations and finding out about activities available in the area.

Developing the patient's cognitive skills is intended to facilitate changes in the way the patient thinks about reality. The locus of control over thoughts clearly resides with the patient, because thought patterns can be monitored only by the thinker. The patient is taught to monitor thoughts every day and to discriminate between positive and negative thoughts, necessary and unnecessary thoughts, and constructive and destructive thoughts. Details of the tactics involved have been discussed elsewhere (Lewinsohn, Munoz, Youngren, & Zeiss, 1978).

We have used a number of cognitive self-management techniques, including thought interruption and premaking of positive thoughts, as described by Mahoney (1974), as well as Meichenbaum's (1975) self-instructional procedure. Rational emotive concepts may be used, and the patient should be taught a procedure for disputing irrational thoughts (Ellis & Harper, 1961; Krantzler, 1974). All of these techniques are presented as skills to be learned and practiced to become maximally useful.

Stress management skills may include relaxation training (Benson, 1975; Rosen, 1977). In relaxation training we begin by identifying three or four specific situations or interactions that are potentially stressful for the patient, making extensive use of the techniques and procedures described by Novaco (1977) and Meichenbaum and Turk (1976). Stress management training also involves teaching the patient to recognize objective signs of dysphoria early in the provocative sequence. After the patient is made aware of pending aversive situations and the effects that they can produce, the patient can begin to pinpoint specific irrational beliefs, automatic thoughts, expectancies, negative self-statements, and negative appraisals. Other components of this process of cognitive preparation involve teaching the patient specific skills needed to deal with an aversive situation, preparation for aversive encounters, self-instruction, relaxation, assertion techniques, more effective communication skills, problem solving, and other task-oriented skills.

Treatment Modules

Each depressed patient is unique, and hence treatment tactics must be flexible. Nevertheless, we have found it useful to develop several therapist manuals (treatment modules) to assist the therapist with the implementation of specific tactics. One of the manuals we are currently using is called "Decrease Unpleasant Events and Increase Pleasant Events."[3] As the title implies, the first part of the treatment is devoted to assisting the patient to decrease the frequency and the subjective aversiveness of unpleasant events encountered, and the second phase concentrates on increasing pleasant encounters. Although the module is relatively specific in suggesting what should be done, it is meant to serve as a flexible guide, not as a rigid schedule.

Daily Monitoring

We first teach patients to graph and interpret the data from their daily monitoring. Patients seem to understand intuitively that unpleasant events can affect mood, but the correlation between pleasant events and mood elevations is usually a revelation to patients. Seeing these relationships on a day-to-day basis clearly demonstrates to patients that the quantity and quality of their daily interactions have important impacts on their depression. The depression is no longer seen as a mysterious force but as a reasonable experience. The graphing and interpretation steps provide patients with a framework for understanding their depression and suggest ways of dealing with it. The monitoring of specific events can help patients to focus on coping with particular unpleasant aspects of daily life and, equally important, make them aware of the range of pleasant experiences potentially accessible to them. In a very real sense, patients learn to diagnose their own depression. Figure 2.2 shows an example of a self-monitoring graph. It can be seen that as therapy progressed, this patient's unpleasant-events score decreased, her pleasant-activities score increased and became less variable, and her mood improved.

Managing Aversive Events

The focus of therapy next moves to teaching patients to manage aversive events. Patients often overreact to unpleasant events, allowing these events to interfere with their participation in pleasant activities and their enjoyment of pleasant activities. Therefore, relaxation training is introduced early in the treatment process, with the goal of teaching patients to be more relaxed generally and especially in specific situations in which they ordinarily feel tense.

Therapy to decrease the unpleasant-events component then proceeds to the pinpointing of a small number of negative interactions and

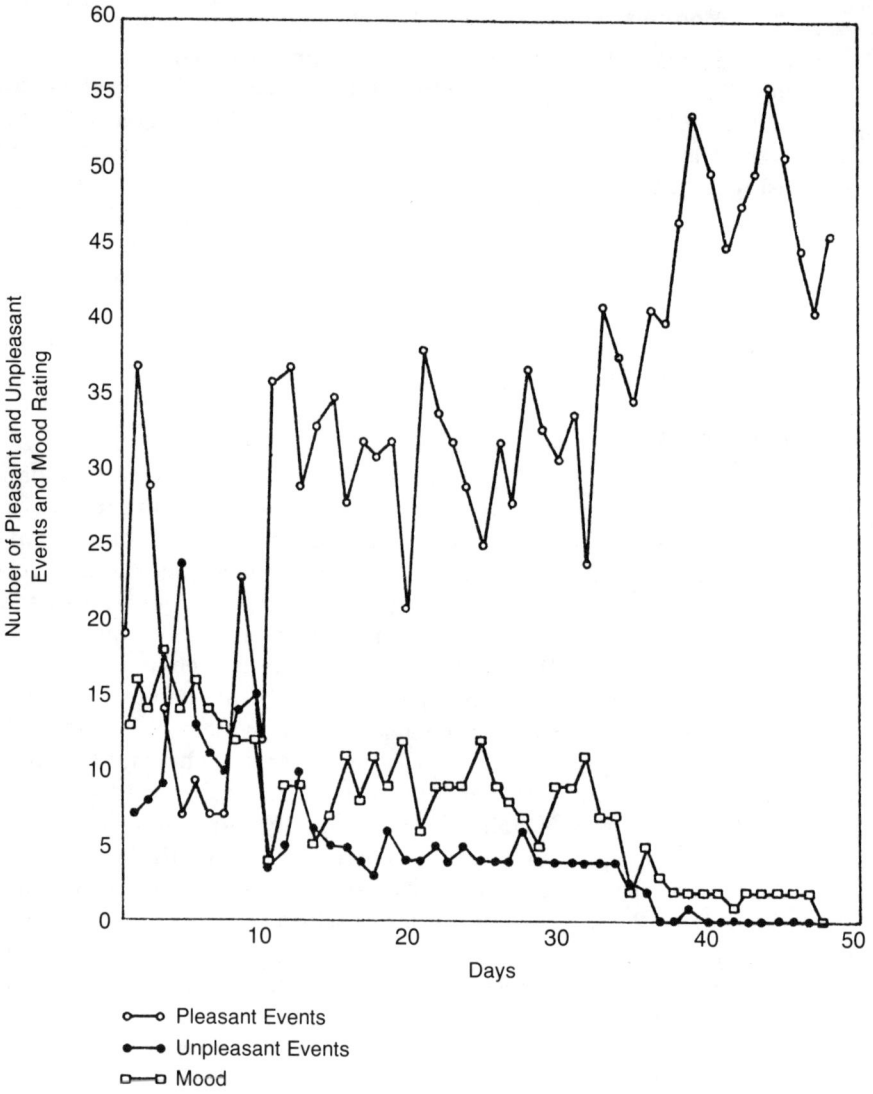

Figure 2.2. Daily monitoring of pleasant and unpleasant events and mood

situations that trigger a patient's dysphoria. To reduce the aversiveness of these situations the therapist has available a whole range of tactics, including the following: teaching the patient to deliberately interpose positive and constructive thoughts between the activating event and the subsequent development of dysphoria; teaching the patient not to take things too personally; teaching the patient to prepare for aversive encounters; teaching self-instuction; teaching constructive preparation for failure; teaching the patient other ways of dealing more adaptively with aversive situations. These tactics have been described in greater detail by Beck (1976), Ellis and Murphy (1975), Krantzler (1974), Mahoney (1974), Meichenbaum and Turk (1976), and Novaco (1977).

Time Management

Daily training in planning and time management is another general tactic included in the module. In this training we have patients read and make considerable use of selected chapters from *How to Get Control of Your Time and Your Life* (Lakein, 1974). Depressed patients typically make poor use of their time. They tend not to plan ahead, and therefore they usually have not made the necessary preparations to take advantage when opportunities arise to participate in pleasant events. This training is also aimed at assisting patients to achieve a better balance between those activities in which they want to participate and those activities in which they feel obligated to participate. By means of a daily time schedule, the patient is asked to preplan each day and each week. Initially this planning is done in therapy sessions with the therapist's assistance, with a gradual transition to having the patient do the planning at home.

The daily planning is also used for the purpose of scheduling specific pleasant events during the next phase of treatment. In helping the patient to increase the frequency of participation in pleasant activities and to decrease occurrences of unpleasant events, the emphasis is on setting concrete goals for these increases and decreases with development of a specific plan for those things the patient will do.

Relaxation Training

Relaxation training is provided because feelings of anxiety and tension tend to make unpleasant events more aversive and to reduce the patient's enjoyment of pleasant activities. Anxiety and tension also tend to impair the clear thinking required for making decisions, planning, and learning new skills.

In our experience in the treatment of depressed patients, relaxation training has become a multipurpose tactic. It is a procedure that is easy to master, and patients tend to become particularly involved with it. Without exception, our patients have reported benefiting from the skill of being able to relax themselves, and they realize the long-term value of this skill. Relaxation training (in particular, the practice sessions with the therapist) also seems to enhance certain nonspecific but positive components in the therapeutic process (e.g., feelings of liking, respect, and trust toward the therapist) and thus increase mutual communication and openness between the therapist and patient and make the patient more amenable to persuasion. This, in turn, should produce a more significant change in the patient's outlook.

The relaxation methods we use in our clinic represent a modified version of the technique developed by Jacobson (1929) for inducing deep muscular relaxation. Following the traditional method in progressive relaxation training, the patient learns to identify the feeling of muscular relaxation by alternately tensing and relaxing different muscle groups. We also give the patient the assignment of reading a book (e.g., Benson, 1975; Rosen, 1977) that presents all the rules one needs to know and follow when practicing progressive muscular relaxation. The procedures are relatively easy to learn and are readily adaptable to a self-administered program.

During the first relaxation training session it may be helpful for the therapist to practice the relaxation procedure with the patient so that the patient can see how to perform particular steps. It is important that the therapist pace the presentation to the patient's facility in performing the steps. It is also important to stress that progressive relaxation is a skill, and like any other skill it can be learned only through practice. The patient is asked to schedule practice sessions once or twice each day at a regular time and place, in addition to the therapist-assisted relaxation training.

We recommend that patients collect baseline data on how tense they are each day and how frequently they experience tension-related symptoms. By keeping records each day for 1 week, patients are able to accomplish two important preliminary steps: (1) They will have baselines against which to compare progress as they learn to relax more effectively. (2) They can identify particular situations that make them more tense and particular times of the day when they are more tense. In doing this baselining, we suggest that patients use the daily monitoring form shown in Appendixes C and D. Each day the patient records three scores on this form: (1) the average relaxation score for the day (how relaxed the patient felt most of the time that day); (2) the score for the time that the patient felt the least relaxed during that day and a brief description of what the patient was doing at that time; (3) the score for the time that the patient felt most relaxed during the day. As with all of our procedures, we present a rationale, and we also stress their importance and potential value. In addition to recording these three scores each day, the patient is instructed to keep track of any specific tension-related symptoms (e.g., headaches) that occurred.

Applying the Relaxation Procedure to Specific Situations

After collecting baseline data for about a week and practicing relaxation procedures, the patient is encouraged to start using relaxation in specific tension-arousing situations. This step requires innovation on the part of the patient. The importance of regular practice sessions must be continually emphasized.

The first step in making specific applications is for the patient to determine the most effective time to use the relaxation technique. One aid in making this decision is to examine, with the patient, the daily monitoring forms, trying to identify particular times of the day or particular situations that make the patient feel most tense. The patient is then encouraged to schedule practice sessions just prior to these times of high tension. It may not be practical for the patient to carry out a full-fledged relaxation practice at these times, but the patient may be able to use a modified version of the technique, such as doing breathing exercises augmented by self-instruction techniques designed to cope with stress (Meichenbaum, 1975; Novaco, 1977).

Evaluating Progress

Continual quantitative evaluation and pinpointing are integral parts of our approach to treatment. Earlier in this chapter we indicated that the patient is asked to examine the previously completed daily monitoring forms in order to identify particular times of the day and particular situations that seem to produce the most tension. When the patient has identified these situations, they should be written down on a form (Appendix E), with the descriptions being neither too specific (e.g., turning down Joe's request for a salary increase) nor too general (e.g., turning down requests). Ideally pinpointed problem situations should strike a balance (e.g., dealing with an employee's request). Of course, the patient may change the list of problem situations as treatment progresses to make sure that it includes situations that are currently producing the most tension. At the end of each week the patient computes the average relaxation score on the form (Appendix C) and makes comparisons with the previous week and with the baseline data. This system allows for continual evaluation of progress and permits necessary adjustments (e.g., changes in time or place for relaxation session, new ways of modifying the relaxation method, trying other on-the-spot techniques).

General Considerations

There are several general considerations that we believe to be important. We are always concerned about providing the patient a rationale for what we are doing (the daily monitoring, graphing, relaxation training, daily planning, etc.), and the rationale must be acceptable to the patient. The treatment program is presented to the patient as being oriented toward solving problems and accomplishing tasks, as well as long-range educational goals. We believe it to be important that the patient be clearly informed on all aspects of the program and participate actively in the selection of specific tactics and goals. The treatment is correctly perceived by the patient as being highly structured, but it is designed to ensure that the therapist and the patient will be able to find time to discuss problems that may be particularly pressing.

Throughout treatment we make an ongoing effort to keep the intermediate treatment goals mutually meaningful and specific. It has been our experience that our unsuccessful cases have been those in which the therapist and the patient have been unable to pinpoint some relatively specific goals for change.

Finally, toward the end of treatment, therapist and patient develop a maintenance/prevention program for the patient to implement after the termination of treatment. This may include making an active effort to continue behaviors and skills learned during treatment, as well as periodic checks (through daily monitoring) of pleasant and unpleasant events and the level of daily mood. Often the last few sessions are spaced out over several weeks in order to produce gradual withdrawal of therapist support and make the transition to self-sufficiency easier for the patient.

By the end of the treatment period the patient should have a good understanding of which activities are experienced as especially enjoyable and are correlated with feeling good, as well as those events that are especially aversive and are correlated with depressed mood. In addition, the patient should have developed skills that will facilitate mood control through an increase in the number of pleasant activities and a decrease in the rate of occurrence of unpleasant events. The patient also should have developed a plan to maintain facility with the new skills after the termination of treatment.

Summary

In this chapter we have tried to present a rationale, a strategy, and some tactics for the treatment of depressed patients within a social learning framework. Our aim has been to present the approach in a manner that will facilitate its use by therapists working with depressed patients. The relationship between depression and reinforcement is central to our approach. Depressed patients are assumed to be functioning with a low rate of response-contingent positive reinforcement. Diagnostic procedures are used to pinpoint specific person-environment interactions related to a given patient's depression. Finally, specific tactics aimed at enhancing the quantity and quality of the patient's reinforcement-related interactions are introduced. The main virtue of this approach is that it provides a structured setting in which a few clear-cut functional relationships can be pinpointed and defined as targets for intervention. Table 2.4 lists the major features of our treatment paradigm.

Summarizing, the major goals of this treatment program are to help the patient (1) decrease the rate of occurrence of unpleasant events, (2) lessen the perceived aversiveness of unpleasant events, (3) increase the rate of participation in pleasant activities, (4) enhance the enjoyment of pleasant activities, and (5) design a maintenance/prevention program to enhance the patient's ability to maintain an improved mood level and prevent future depression.

There are several practical concerns that should be addressed. The patient's compliance with these procedures is critical. The approach we use requires considerable effort on the part of the patient and is dependent on the patient's ability to keep accurate records and willingness to learn how to chart the daily monitoring data on a graph, as well as willingness to carry out other assignments from time to time. Many therapists have reservations regarding the ability of depressed patients to carry out such assignments. We have not found this to be a problem. Patients typically are quite cooperative as long as they are convinced that

Table 2.4   Treatment Paradigm

General features
 1. Clear structuring and design of rationale
 2. Explicit diagnostic phase
 3. Clear treatment contract
 4. Treatment phase, with prespecified number (12) of moderately well structured sessions (time-limited therapy)
 5. Small number of specific goals, aiming to decrease unpleasant events and increase pleasant activities
 6. Preassessment and postassessment of depression level and target behaviors
 7. Gradual withdrawal of the therapist; emphasis on maintenance in last one or two sessions

Details
 1. Diagnostic phase focuses on assessment of depression level and behaviors hypothesized to be functionally related to depression; may include interview with spouse and home observations
 2. PES and UES (and, later, daily monitoring of activities and mood) used to provide patient with feedback and to define specific goals; patient is shown how to graph and is provided with visual and computer feedback
 3. Treatment follows the manual (decrease unpleasant events and increase pleasant activities), meant to be used flexibly, but definitely provides framework
 4. Specific strategies vary, but they include relaxation training, time-management skills, and specific social and other coping skills, including cognitive strategies

the procedures are an important part of a treatment program that will be of benefit to them. The crucial factor in eliciting a patient's cooperation is the therapist's ability to present a convincing rationale for the procedures. This is absolutely vital. The therapist must be able to generate in the patient a true conviction that the self-monitoring and other assignments are integral parts of a treatment program that relies heavily on the patient's ability to pinpoint specific goals, to learn specific self-management techniques for depression, and to evaluate progress. In order to be able to present a convincing argument, the therapist must first accept the rationale and believe that it is a potentially sound way of working with a particular patient.

Adaptations and simplifications are often necessary. Our strategy and tactics follow the social learning paradigm presented in this chapter, but specific implementation and content must always be tailored to the specific situation of a given patient.

Last, but not least, the question of the therapeutic efficacy of the treatment approach must be addressed. As is well known, the question whether psychological treatment X is superior to psychological treatment Y is difficult to answer. Studies, including our own (Zeiss, Lewinsohn, & Munoz, 1979), have indicated that it is difficult to reject the null hypothesis of no differences between treatments. Perhaps more important to the clinician is to have some idea of the average clinical improvement that can be expected. Information relevant to this question is provided in Table 2.5, which shows the changes in depression levels for three cohorts of patients we have treated. As can be seen, the amounts of clinical improvement were substantial and in all instances were highly statistically significant.

New Directions

As part of our long-term program to develop systematic and replicable psychological treatment tactics for depressed patients, we are currently evaluating the efficacy of a course (i.e., an explicit educational experience) dealing with the treatment of depression (Brown & Lewinsohn, 1979). The course, entitled "Coping with Depression," consists of 12 sessions of 2 hours each and is being offered regularly (Figure 2.3) by the Psychology Clinic at the University of Oregon. A textbook (Lewinsohn, Munoz, Youngren, & Zeiss, 1978) and a participant workbook (Brown & Lewinsohn, 1979) have been developed for the course. In the first session we present, and try to personalize, the social learning approach to depression (i.e., that persons learn to act, to feel, and to think depressed, and that they can systematically learn new skills to cope with their depression). Session two is devoted to teaching participants how to design a self-change program. We teach experiences

TABLE 2.5 Intake, Termination, and Follow-up Depression Scores for
Three Treatment Groups

Treatment Group	Module	Measure	Intake	Termination	Follow-up
Group I ($N = 14$)	Increase pleasant activities	MMPI D scale	90	68	65
Group II ($N = 21$)	Increase pleasant activities	MMPI D scale BDI	93 25	71 8	77 6
Group III ($N = 12$)	Decrease unpleasant events and increase pleasant activities	BDI	26	12	10

designed to help the participant learn the basic steps one needs to work through to the development of a systematic self-change plan and apply this plan to alleviate specific problems. The next eight sessions involve techniques aimed at teaching self-control procedures relevant to relaxation, pleasant activities, thoughts, and interpersonal interactions. The final two sessions are devoted to assisting the participants to develop a "life plan" by choosing from among the techniques they have learned in the course those they intend to continue to use in order to maintain their gains and to prevent future depressive episodes. The course has been taught in three modes: classroom instruction (enrollment about eight), individual tutoring, and minimal contact (home study, with regular telephone consultation). Preliminary results (Brown & Lewinsohn, 1979) have suggested that all three methods produce significantly more improvement than the no-treatment condition (waiting control)

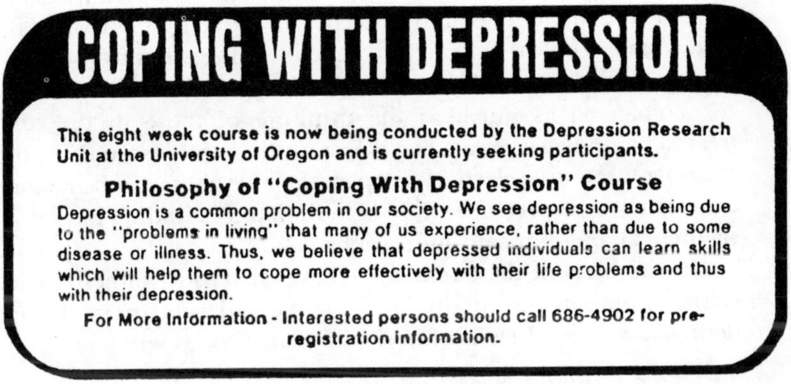

COPING WITH DEPRESSION

This eight week course is now being conducted by the Depression Research Unit at the University of Oregon and is currently seeking participants.

Philosophy of "Coping With Depression" Course

Depression is a common problem in our society. We see depression as being due to the "problems in living" that many of us experience, rather than due to some disease or illness. Thus, we believe that depressed individuals can learn skills which will help them to cope more effectively with their life problems and thus with their depression.

For More Information - Interested persons should call 686-4902 for pre-registration information.

Figure 2.3 Advertisement used in a local newspaper to recruitment of participants.

and that the results obtained with the classroom and individual tutoring methods are as good as those we have obtained with other treatments in the past. The "Coping with Depression" course represents a community-oriented outreach approach aimed at the large proportion of depressed persons who are not reached by current mental health services. The educational focus reduces the stigma involved in seeking psychiatric or psychological help, and this is especially important with elderly depressed persons. Another important feature of the course is that participants meet in groups to assist one another in overcoming their depression. With relatively few exceptions, the treatment of depression has traditionally employed individual therapy. In our work to date (11 classes) we have been impressed with the ability of depressed persons to work together toward shared goals within the structure provided by the course.

Final Comments

Early clinical applications of the social learning approach at the University of Oregon were reported as case studies of patients treated individually and in groups (Lewinsohn & Atwood, 1969; Lewinsohn & Schaffer, 1971; Lewinsohn & Shaw, 1969; Lewinsohn, Weinstein, & Alper, 1970; Lewinsohn, Weinstein, & Shaw, 1969; Libet & Lewinsohn, 1973; Robinson & Lewinsohn, 1973), followed by systematic studies of treatment outcome (e.g., Sanchez, Lewinsohn, & Larson, 1980), the most recent of which (Zeiss, Lewinsohn, & Munoz, 1979) has strongly influenced our thinking about the treatment of depression. In this study, three treatments (cognitive training, pleasant-activities training, and social skills training) were compared. Half the patients were assigned to an immediate-treatment group, and treatment of the other half were delayed by a month. The results indicated that whereas the three treatments were equally effective in reducing the level of depression, changes on the intervening dependent measures were not specific to the treatment (i.e., the thinking of the patients in social skills treatment changed as much as the thinking of those in the cognitive treatment, and vice versa). The major finding of this study (i.e., that the treatments did not selectively impact the relevant target behaviors) was completely unexpected, and we believe that this finding has important theoretical and clinical implications.

On the basis of these results we have tried to hypothesize what the critical components might be for successful short-term therapy for depression (Zeiss, Lewinsohn, & Munoz, 1979), to wit:

1. Therapy should begin with an elaborated, well-planned rationale. This rationale should provide an initial structure to guide patients

to the belief that they can control their own behavior and, thereby, their depression.
2. Therapy should provide training in skills that patients can use to make themselves feel more effective handling their daily lives. These skills must be of significance to the patients and must fit with the rationale that has been presented.
3. Therapy should emphasize independent use of these skills by patients outside of the therapy context, and it must provide enough structure so that attainment of the independent skills is possible.
4. Therapy should be such that it will encourage patients to attribute their improvement in mood to their own increased skills, not to the therapist's skill.

NOTES

1. These and other materials may be obtained from Peter M. Lewinsohn, Department of Psychology, University of Oregon, Eugene, Oregon 97403.

2. The research diagnostic criteria (RDC) were originally developed to enable clinicians and research investigators to apply a consistent set of criteria for the description or selection of samples of subjects with "functional psychiatric disorders." The purpose of this approach to diagnosis is to obtain relatively homogeneous groups of subjects who meet specified diagnostic criteria. Accordingly, the Schedule for Affective Disorders and Schizophrenia (SADS) was developed to reduce information variance in both descriptive and diagnostic evaluations of a subject. This instrument is designed as a form to record information regarding a subject's functioning and symptoms. The SADS is unique among rating scales in that it provides for (1) detailed description of the features of the current episode of disorder when they were at their most severe, (2) a description of the levels of severity of the major dimensions of psychopathologic manifestations during the week preceding the evaluation, (3) a progression of questions and criteria that provide information for making diagnoses and a detailed description of past psychopathologic manifestations and functioning relevant to diagnosis and evaluation of overall severity of disturbance. The RDC permits current and past life-history diagnoses for a given subject, with the durations of current and previous episodes of disorder noted in weeks. The RDC and SADS have, in part, resolved one of the long-standing problems of psychiatric diagnosis: interrater reliability. Research studies (Amenson & Lewinsohn, 1979) using the SADS-RDC system have shown interrater reliability to be very high.

3. This material may be obtained from Peter M. Lewinsohn, Department of Psychology, University of Oregon, Eugene, Oregon 97403.

REFERENCES

Alberti, R.E., and Emmons, M.L. *Your perfect right.* San Luis Obispo, Calif.: Impact, 1974.
Amenson, C.S., & Lewinsohn, P.W. *An investigation into the observed sex*

difference in prevalence of depression. Mimeograph, Department of Psychology, University of Oregon, 1979.
Bandura, A. *Social learning theory.* Englewood Cliffs, N.J.: Prentice-Hall, 1977.
Beck, A.T. *Cognitive therapy and the emotional disorders.* New York: International Universities Press, 1976.
Beck, A.T., Ward, C.H., Mendelson, M., Mock, J., & Erbaugh, J. An inventory of measuring depression. *Archives of General Psychiatry,* 1961, *4*, 561-571.
Benson, H. *The relaxation response.* New York: William Harrow, 1975.
Brown, R.A., & Lewinsohn, P.M. *Coping with depression.* Mimeograph, Department of Psychology, University of Oregon, 1979.
Chamberlin, T., & Lewinsohn, P.M. *Relationships between marital status, marital adjustment and depression.* Mimeograph, Department of Psychology, University of Oregon, 1979.
Coyne, J.D. Depression and the response of others. *Journal of Abnormal Psychology,* 1976, *85*, 186-193.
Ellis, A., & Harper, R.A. *A guide to rational living.* Hollywood, Calif.: Wilshire, 1961.
Ellis, A., & Murphy, R. *A bibliography of articles and books on rational-emotive therapy and cognitive-behavior therapy.* New York: Institute for Rational Living, 1975.
Endicott, J., & Spitzer, R.L. A diagnostic interview, the Schedule for Affective Disorders and Schizophrenia. *Archives of General Psychiatry,* 1978, *35*, 837-844.
Gambrill, E., & Richey, C.A. *It's up to you. The development of assertive social skills.* Millbrae, Calif.: Les Femmes, 1976.
Goldfried, M.R., & Merbaum, M. (Eds.). *Behavior changes through self-control.* New York: Holt, Rinehart, 1973.
Grinker, R.R., Miller, J., Sabshin, M., Nunn, R., & Nunally, J.C. *The phenomena of depressions.* New York: Paul B. Hoeber, 1961.
Grosscup, S.J., & Lewinsohn, P.M. Unpleasant and pleasant events, and mood. *Journal of Clinical Psychology,* 1980, *36*, 252-259.
Hanaway, T.P., & Barlow, D.H. Prolonged depressive behaviors in a recently blinded deaf-mute: A behavioral treatment. *Journal of Behavior Therapy and Experimental Psychiatry,* 1975, *6*, 43-48.
Hersen, M., Eisler, D., Alford, G., & Agras, W.S. Effects of token economy on neurotic depression: An experimental analysis. *Behavior Therapy,* 1973, *4*, 392-397.
Jacobson, E. *Progressive relaxation.* Chicago: University of Chicago Press, 1929.
Kazdin, A.E. Effects of covert modeling and model reinforcement on assertive behavior. *Journal of Abnormal Psychology,* 1974, *83*, 240-252.
Kazdin, A.E. Effects of covert modeling, multiple models, and model reinforcement on assertive behavior. *Behavior Therapy,* 1976, *7*, 211-222.
Krantzler, G. *You can change how you feel.* Eugene: University of Oregon Press, 1974.
Lakein, A. *How to get control of your time and your life.* New York: New American Library, 1974.
Lewinsohn, P.M. The behavioral study and treatment of depression. In

M. Hersen, R.M. Eisler, & P.M. Miller (Eds.), *Progress in behavior modification*, New York: Academic, 1975.

Lewinsohn, P.M., & Amenson, C. Some relations between pleasant and unpleasant mood related activities and depression. *Journal of Abnormal Psychology*, 1978, *87*, 644-654.

Lewinsohn, P.M., & Atwood, G. Depression: A clinical research approach; the case of Mrs. G. *Psychotherapy: Theory, Research and Practice*, 1969, *6*, 166-171.

Lewinsohn, P.M., Biglan, T., & Zeiss, A. Behavioral treatment of depression. In P. Davidson (Ed.), *Behavioral management of anxiety, depression, and pain*, New York: Brunner/Mazel, 1976.

Lewinsohn, P.M., & Brown, R.A. *Learning how to control one's depression: An educational approach*. Presented at a meeting of the American Psychological Association, New York, 1979.

Lewinsohn, P.M., & Chaplin, W. *Manual for the Unpleasant Events Schedule*. Mimeograph, Department of Psychology, University of Oregon, 1979.

Lewinsohn, P.M., & Lee, W.M.L. Assessment of affective disorders. In D.H. Barlow (Ed.), *Behavioral assessment of adult disorders*. New York: Guilford Press, 1980.

Lewinsohn, P.M., & Libet, J. Pleasant events, activity schedules, and depression. *Journal of Abnormal Psychology*, 1972, *79*, 291-295.

Lewinsohn, P.M., Mischel, W., Chaplin, W., & Barton, R. Social competence and depression: The role of illusory self-perceptions. *Journal of Abnormal Psychology*, 1980, *89*, 203-212.

Lewinsohn, P.M., Munoz, R.F., Youngren, M.A., & Zeiss, A.M. *Control your depression*. Englewood Cliffs, N.J.: Prentice-Hall, 1978.

Lewinsohn, P.M. & Shaffer, M. Use of home observations as an integral part of the treatment of depression: Preliminary report and case studies. *Journal of Consulting and Clinical Psychology*, 1971, *37*, 87-94.

Lewinsohn, P.M., & Shaw, D. Feedback about interpersonal behavior as an agent of behavior change: A case study in the treatment of depression. *Psychotherapy and Psychosomatics*, 1969, *17*, 82-88.

Lewinsohn, P.M., & Talkington, J. Studies on the measurement of unpleasant events and relations with depression. *Applied Psychological Measurement*, 1979, *3*, 83-101.

Lewinsohn, P.M., Weinstein, M., & Alper, T. A behavioral approach to the group treatment of depressed persons: A methodological contribution. *Journal of Clinical Psychology*, 1970, *26*, 525-532.

Lewinsohn, P.M., Weinstein, M., & Shaw, D. Depression: A clinical-research approach. In R.D. Rubin & C.M. Frank (Eds.), *Advances in behavior therapy, 1968*. New York: Academic, 1969.

Lewinsohn, P.M., Youngren, M.A., & Grosscup, S.J. Reinforcement and depression. In R.A. Depue (Ed.), *The psychobiology of the depressive disorders*. New York: Academic, 1979.

Liberman, R.P., & Raskin, D.E. Depression: A behavioral formulation. *Archives of General Psychiatry*, 1971, *24*, 515-523.

Libet, J., & Lewinsohn, P.M. The concept of social skill with special references to the behavior of depressed persons. *Journal of Consulting and Clinical Psychology*, 1973, *40*, 304-312.

Libet, J., Lewinsohn, P.M., & Javorek, F. *The construct of social skill: An empirical study of several measures on temporal stability, internal structure, validity, and situational generalizability.* Mimeograph, Department of Psychology, University of Oregon, 1973.

Lubin, B. Adjective checklists for the measurement of depression. *Archives of General Psychiatry*, 1965, *12*, 57-62.

MacPhillamy, D.J., & Lewinsohn, P.M. *Pleasant Events Schedule.* Mimeograph, Department of Psychology, University of Oregon, 1971.

MacPhillamy, D.J., & Lewinsohn, P.M. Depression as a function of desired and obtained pleasure. *Journal of Abnormal Psychology*, 1974, *83*, 651-657.

MacPhillamy, D., & Lewinsohn, P.M. *Manual for the Pleasant Events Schedule.* Mimeograph, Department of Psychology, University of Oregon, 1975.

Mahoney, J.J. *Cognition and behavior modification.* Cambridge, Mass.: Ballinger, 1974.

Mahoney, M.J., & Thoresen, C.E. *Self-control: Power to the person.* Monterey, Calif.: Brooks-Cole, 1974.

McLean, P.D., & Hakstian, A.R. *Clinical depression: Comparative efficacy of outpatient treatments.* Mimeograph, Department of Psychology, University of British Columbia, 1978.

Meichenbaum, D. Self-instructional techniques. In F.H. Kanfer & A.P. Goldstein (Eds.), *Helping people change,* New York: Pergamon, 1975.

Meichenbaum, D., & Turk, D. The cognitive-behavioral management of anxiety, anger, and pain. In P.O. Davidson (Ed.), *The behavioral management of anxiety, depression, and pain.* New York: Brunner/Mazel, 1976.

Novaco, R.W. Stress inoculation: A cognitive therapy for anger and its application to a case of depression. *Journal of Consulting and Clinical Psychology*, 1977, *45*, 600-608.

Patterson, G.R., & Gullion, M.Z. *Living with children: New Methods for parents and teachers.* Champaign, Ill.: Research Press, 1968.

Radloff, L.S. The CES-D scale: A self-report depression scale for research in the general population. *Applied Psychological Measurement*, 1977, *1*, 385-401.

Reisinger, J.J. The treatment of "anxiety-depression" via positive reinforcement and response cost. *Journal of Applied Behavioral Analysis*, 1972, *5*, 125-130.

Robinson, J.C., & Lewinsohn, P.M. Behavior modification of speech characteristics in a chronically depressed man. *Behavior Therapy*, 1973, *4*, 150-152.

Rosen, G.M. *The relaxation response.* Englewood Cliffs, N.J.: Prentice-Hall, 1977.

Rotter, J.B. *Social learning and clinical psychology.* Englewood Cliffs, N.J.: Prentice-Hall, 1954.

Sanchez, V.C., Lewinsohn, P.M., & Larson, D. Assertion training: Effectiveness in the treatment of depression. *Journal of Clinical Psychology*, 1980, *36*, 526-529.

Spitzer, R.L., Endicott, J., & Robins, E. Research Diagnostic Criteria. *Archives of General Psychiatry*, 1978, *35*, 773-782.

Watson, D.L., & Tharp, R.G. *Self-directed behavior: Self modification for personal adjustment.* Belmont, Calif.: Wadsworth, 1972.

Weissman, M.M., & Paykel, E.S. *The depressed woman: A study of social relationships.* Chicago: University of Chicago Press, 1974.

Youngren, M.A., & Lewinsohn, P.M. *The functional relationship between depression and problematic interpersonal behavior.* Mimeograph, Department of Psychology, University of Oregon, 1979.

Zeiss, A.M., Lewinsohn, P.M., & Munoz, R.F. Nonspecific improvement effects in depression using interpersonal, cognitive and pleasant events focused treatments. *Journal of Consulting and Clinical Psychology,* 1979, *47,* 427-439.

Zung, W.W. A self-rating depression scale. *Archives of General Psychiatry,* 1965, *12,* 63-70.

A Self-Control Therapy Program for Treatment of Depression

Lynn P. Rehm

My intent in this chapter is to accomplish four goals. First, I want to discuss some problems related to the nature of depression as they apply to attempts to construct theoretical models of the disorder. Second, I want to describe a model that I have been using both to direct research concerning the psychopathologic manifestations of depression and to serve as an outline for a psychotherapy program. Third, I want to describe the therapy program in sufficient depth to provide the reader with an understanding of the therapeutic techniques involved. This description will provide the basis for the fourth part of the chapter, which will review evidence evaluating the effectiveness of the therapy program.

The Complex Nature of Depression

Depression is a complex set of phenomena. It is usually thought of as a syndrome made up of many individual symptoms. However, there is less than perfect agreement as to which symptoms should be included

This research was supported in part by NIMH Grant 2R01 MH27822.

in the list. Characterizations of the symptoms vary, and it is generally acknowledged that individual cases involve different patterns or subsets of the total symptom list.

Levitt and Lubin (1975) presented lists of 38 symptoms cited in psychiatric texts as belonging to the syndrome of depression and 54 symptoms that are included as items on depression rating scales. The complexity of the construct of depression is illustrated by its verbal-cognitive manifestations. Depression goes far beyond the report of sad affect. It includes a wide variety of attitudes and beliefs about oneself and the world (e.g., pessimism, helplessness, hopelessness, low self-esteem, and guilt). The usual symptom list includes a number of so-called neurovegetative signs, such as sleep disturbance, eating disturbance, loss of libido, and fatigability. Each of these can be assessed in terms of verbal-cognitive phenomena, overt motor phenomena, and physiologic-somatic phenomena. An added dimension of complexity in assessing depression is that the symptom picture may vary with the perspective of the evaluator. That is, self-report instruments may reflect cognitive distortions of experience and may therefore be at variance with the perspective of the clinician and with objective observations, as well as the observations of significant others. One tactic that has been used in attempts to reduce the complexity of the phenomena is to search for meaningful subtypes of depression. Neurotic-psychotic, endogenous-reactive, primary-secondary, and unipolar-bipolar dichotomies have all been suggested, with varying degrees of functional validity.

There are several implications of this state of affairs in depression research. In the area of research on psychotherapy it has led to problems of lack of comparability between research populations (Rehm & Kornblith, 1979; Rehm, 1979). In the assessment area there has been a similar lack of comparability, leading to an overabundance of dissimilar and poorly correlated instruments (Rehm, 1976, 1978a).

Another important implication of the complexity of depression is that there is considerable theoretical disagreement as to the core symptoms of depression. Among current psychological theories, Lewinsohn's behavioral theory (Lewinsohn, 1974; Lewinsohn, Biglan, & Zeiss, 1976) postulates that the core symptom is a low rate of behavioral output, which leads to other symptoms, including cognitive symptoms. Beck's cognitive theory (Beck, 1972, 1974) postulates that cognitive distortions lead to other symptoms of depression, including low rates of behavior.

A pragmatic solution to some of the problems presented by the complexity of depression is to consider it a multivariate phenomenon. That is, although it is important to set some boundaries as to what depression is and what it is not, it is also important within this construct to recognize that it consists in numerous distinct behaviors that are imperfectly correlated. Taking such a view allows one to define a finite replicable population and yet look within that group at correlates of specific symptoms and behaviors. The recent development of the Research Diagnostic Criteria (RDC) (Spitzer et al., 1978) is consistent with this idea. One of its criteria for depression is that the patient must manifest five of eight specific symptoms. The purpose of the RDC is to bring consistency to definitions of research populations, but as these criteria are constructed they also allow one to look at the relationship between specific symptoms or patterns of symptoms and external variables. Multivariate assessment methods are much needed in depression research (Rehm, 1976, 1978a). For instance, specific symptoms or patterns of depression may respond to different treatments. Weissman and associates (1976) concluded that although amitriptyline produced remissions in neurovegetative signs, psychotherapy led to better social adjustment.

Similar logic holds for theories and research models of depression. The model to be presented here was developed in part in response to the need for a framework that would allow one to consider depression as a multivariate phenomenon. A model of depression should provide for the possibility of considering different core symptoms that may be individually related to one another and to different etiologic, maintenance, and treatment variables. The self-control theory of depression presented here is an attempt to provide such a model.

A Self-control Model of Depression

The self-control model of depression borrows from a more general model proposed by Kanfer (Kanfer, 1970, 1971; Kanfer & Karoly, 1972a, 1972b). Kanfer's model was intended to describe those self-regulatory processes in which a person engages to alter the probability of a response in the relative absence of immediate external support. Self-control processes are engaged when a person becomes aware of an adverse situation involving a loss of reinforcement or lack of reinforcement. Thus the model describes adaptive processes for coping with a particular form of stress: loss or lack of reinforcement. The model postulates input, processing, and output phases in a feedback loop. These processes are referred to as self-monitoring, self-evaluation, and self-reinforcement. It is assumed that the manner in which these processes are performed varies from one person to another as a function of learning experiences, and thus a person may be described as having more or fewer skills in self-control behavior.

As applied to depression, the model suggests that depressed persons may be described as having specific kinds of deficits in self-control behavior. The model has been used in a heuristic manner for describing self-regulated behavior and as an outline for designing treatment programs for persons with habit problems, such as smoking, overweight, or alcohol or drug abuse. Its application to depression is similarly intended to provide a heuristic framework that will be helpful in outlining research issues, defining research questions, and designing treatment programs. The model does suggest terms with which to describe and interrelate certain aspects of depressed behavior.

The model was proposed in an earlier report (Rehm, 1977), and it postulates six identifiable depressive deficits within self-control terminology. Two deficits are hypothesized within each of the three phases of self-control behavior. The self-monitoring behavior of depressed persons can be characterized by (1) a tendency to attend to negative events to the exclusion of positive events and (2) a tendency to attend to the immediate consequences of behavior as opposed to the delayed consequences. In the self-evaluation phase, depressed persons (3) set stringent self-evaluative criteria for their behavior and (4) make self-attributional errors consistent with expectations of a negative outcome. In the self-reinforcement phase, depressed persons (5) self-administer insufficient rewards and (6) self-administer excessive punishment. What follows is a more detailed description of each of the deficits, together with a brief review of research evidence related to each deficit.

Self-monitoring of Negative Events

Self-monitoring involves strategies by which people observe their own behaviors, including antecedents and consequences, and thus construe their performances. Selective attention to negative events is the phenomenon whereby depressed persons appear to be particularly oriented toward events in their experience that either are aversive or are potential cues for aversive events. The clinical symptom that this characterizes is the pessimism that is manifested by depressed persons. Clinically, depressed persons are observed to make negative interpretations of their experiences and pessimistically anticipate negative events in the future. Conceptually, this idea is closely related to Ferster's description (1973) of depressed persons as devoting a disproportionate amount of time to the avoidance of or escape from aversive events. Such behavior precludes attention to more productive "adjustive behavior" and precludes working toward long-term positive goals. Beck (1972, 1974) described processes of cognitive distortion in depression, including the concepts of "selective abstraction" and "arbitrary inference." Each of these processes can be described in terms of selective attention to negative events. Selective abstraction involves focusing on a detail taken out of context and using it as a basis to conceptualize the entire context. In depression, the detail on which attention is focused is usually an aversive event embedded within an array of more positive events. Arbitrary inference involves a personal interpretation of an ambiguous or personally irrelevant event. In depression, arbitrary inferences are made about irrelevant aversive events in the environment. Inappropriate attributions of causality can also be involved in this latter process.

In the last couple of years, considerable research has been done on the monitoring processes of depressed persons. The primary focus of this research has been the distortions of memory that are evident in depression. Wener and Rehm (1975) found that at the end of an experimental task, depressed students tended to underestimate the amount of positive feedback they had been given. Nelson and Craighead (1977) similarly found that depressed subjects recalled less positive feedback and more negative feedback than did controls, although this was significant only at high rates of positive feedback and low rates of negative feedback. There is another interesting finding from this study: At low rates of punishment, depressed subjects were more accurate in estimating the actual rate than were nondepressed subjects who underestimated negative feedback. Buchwald (1977) found a correlation between depression and underestimation of the number correct on another laboratory task; correlations were $-.32$ for females, $-.07$ for males, and $-.20$ overall. The correlations for males only were nonsignificant. An additional partial replication of these effects was provided by DeMonbreun and Craighead (1977), who tested depressed psychiatric patients as compared with nondepressed psychiatric and nondepressed nonpsychiatric control groups. In the high-positive-feedback condition only, depressed subjects recalled less positive feedback. Craighead and associates (1979) failed to find any distortion of recall associated with depression for neutral feedback information. Thus the most consistent finding for memory distortion is underestimation of positive feedback when it is given at high rates. Overestimation of negative feedback may be only relative. Gotlib (1979a, 1979b) found that distortion can also occur in other psychiatric conditions.

It is notable that in all of these studies of memory distortion the memory task was essentially an incidental learning task; that is, after working on what was usually a verbal learning task of some form, subjects were then asked to recall the portion or rate of positive or negative feedback they received. None of these studies examined selective memory directly. Roth and Rehm (1980) asked subjects to select those adjectives that best described themselves, using long lists of positive and negative adjectives. Later, on both recall and recognition assessments or memory, no differences were found between depressed and nondepressed psychiatric patients. Further evidence is needed to clarify this point, but it may be that memory distortion occurs only in the process of reconstructing or estimating frequencies of positive or negative events to which the subject's attention was not focused. If so, aspects of depression such as negative expectations may influence estimates of the past as well as estimates of the future.

Memory is not the only means of assessing self-observation behavior in depression. A second method is to assess the distribution of time spent attending to positive feedback and negative feedback. One way of implementing this is to give subjects a choice of exposure to positive feedback or negative feedback. For instance, Roth and Rehm (1980) presented depressed and nondepressed patients the task of guessing the most common associates of a series of ambiguous words. After they had completed the task with no feedback, they were then given the choice of seeing one of the words they supposedly had gotten wrong or one of the words they supposedly had gotten right as a choice on a series of trials. Depressed patients more frequently chose negative feedback, whereas nondepressed patients more frequently chose positive feedback.

A third method for assessing self-monitoring behavior in depression is to assess vigilance in detecting positive and negative events. This can be seen in a kind of signal-detection format whereby one assumes that depressed subjects use conservative response strategies in detecting positive events and broad and vigilant strategies in detecting negative events. Miller and Lewis (1977) performed a signal-detection analysis of recognition memory in elderly patients with depression or dementia and normal controls. They determined that the poor performances of the depressed patients on a memory task were not due to memory deficit per se but to a conservative response strategy; that is, they were relatively unwilling to guess. Roth and Rehm (1980) had depressed and nondepressed psychiatric patients view themselves on a videotape recording of a role-playing interaction with an experimenter. The patients were instructed to tally the occurrences of certain carefully defined positive and negative behaviors on their part in the videotapes. Relative to nondepressed patients, depressed patients underestimated their positive behaviors and overestimated their negative behaviors. This was true with actual rates of occurrence covaried out. The most probable explanation for this finding is that the depressed patients and nondepressed patients had different criteria for distinguishing positive and negative behaviors.

One of the questions raised by the self-control point of view is whether overestimation of negative events and underestimation of positive events can be attributed to selective attention or to actual distortion in perception of the event. Beck (1972) suggested that a distortion process does occur. A study by Weintraub and associates (1974) provided evidence in support of this contention in the form of a greater frequency of negative interpretations of projective test stimuli being associated with depressed mood in college students. However, it is questionable that projective test stimulus interpretations can be described as distortions. By definition they are ambiguous and open to a variety of interpretations, depending on the state of the subject. Craighead and associates (1979) and DeMonbreun and Craighead (1977) assessed the accuracy of their subjects' immediate perceptions of feedback on a trial-by-trial basis and found no evidence of distortion. Distortion occurred only in recall of high rates of positive feedback.

The self-control model of depression predicts that manipulations of self-monitoring strategies can influence later phases of the self-control process, and mood as well; that is, if subjects are instructed to monitor negative events versus positive events, this should influence their self-evaluation and mood. Kirschenbaum and Karoly (1977) instructed half of their subjects who were doing practice mathematics problems to tally the problems they got wrong (monitoring of negative events), whereas the other half of the subjects were instructed to tally the numbers of problems they got right (monitoring positive events). On completion of the task, those subjects who monitored errors had fewer self-evaluations and gave themselves less favorable self-reinforcement. O'Hara and Rehm (1979b) attempted to manipulate the self-monitoring strategies of normal subjects in their daily lives. Subjects monitored their daily moods and in addition were instructed to monitor (1) positive events, (2) negative events, (3) both classes of events, or (4) neither class of events. It was hypothesized that over a period of 4 weeks the monitoring of negative events would have an adverse effect on mood. However, no differences were found for the monitoring variable. It may be that some stronger manipulation is needed to influence selective attention on a daily basis. In that study the manipulation was one of recording either positive or negative events, and recording alone may not have influenced attention.

In the area of self-monitoring of negative events, many questions remain unanswered: What are the antecedents of different monitoring strategies? How are these strategies best characterized—as selective attention, as differential criterion setting, or as perceptual distortions? Are there particular circumstances under which depressive self-monitoring strategies occur? How can self-monitoring strategies be effectively modified? The function of the model is to suggest that these constitute a subset of questions that should be looked at in relation to a larger context of self-control deficits in depression.

Self-monitoring of Immediate Outcome

The second self-monitoring deficit postulated by the model is a tendency for depressed persons to attend to the immediate outcome of behavior rather than to the long-term outcome. The effect of this strategy of self-observation is that depressed persons are more likely to choose response alternatives with immediate positive consequences (including escape and avoidance) in preference to alternatives with even greater positive consequences that are delayed. The clinical phenomenon that reflects this deficit is the tendency for depressed persons to be self-indulgent and to experience difficulty in sustaining efforts toward delayed goals. Similar conceptualizations were offered by Lewinsohn (1974), who speculated that depressed behavior functions to elicit immediate reinforcement from the social environment at the expense of more important forms of delayed reinforcement. Lazarus (1968, 1974) suggested that depressed persons lose their perspective of future time and seem able to consider only the present. Both of these conceptualizations can be rephrased in terms of attention to immediate outcome at the expense of delayed outcome.

Relatively little research has been directed at this problem. Rehm and Plakosh (1975) asked depressed and nondepressed college students to respond by indicating their degrees of agreement or disagreement with a series of statements (e.g., "I would rather get $10 right now than have to wait a whole month and get $30 then"). Depressed subjects expressed a greater degree of preference for immediate rewards as opposed to delayed rewards. O'Hara and Rehm (1979a) attempted to replicate this finding with an actual choice, rather than a hypothetical choice, between an immediate reward and a delayed reward. Subjects who had participated in another experiment and had been promised payment of $20 at its completion were given a choice between the $20 immediately and a larger sum (as much as $30) 4 weeks later. The subjects were divided approximately equally in terms of their choices, but choice was not correlated with depression score. On inquiry, a wide variety of circumstances seemed to be more influential in the choice than did mood.

Further research will be necessary to determine the importance of this variable in depression. It is indeed questionable that self-indulgence and lack of persistence are best described in terms of selective attention. These problems would be predicted as overall effects of poor self-control behavior. That is, persons whose self-control is poor should show deficits in the ability to sustain efforts toward delayed goals. The self-control model pertains to this form of behavior particularly.

Setting Stringent Criteria

The self-evaluation phase of the self-control model involves primarily a comparison process in which an estimate of performance obtained from self-monitoring is compared to a standard. In depression, stringent standards are set. Clinically, depressed persons often are described as perfectionistic. Standards can be stringent in a variety of ways. First, they can be stringent in terms of the absolute level at which they are set. People may derive standards from a variety of sources and set them in a number of ways (e.g., in absolute terms, in comparison to another person, in comparison to a reference group). Standards can be set so high that they are virtually never met. Often, among depressed persons, minor accomplishments and intermediate steps toward a long-term goal are given no credit. Only accomplishment of the final goal is considered success. For most people, criteria for success and criteria for failure are set independently. A performance can be less than a complete success and yet not be considered a failure. For depressed persons these criteria may be reciprocal. That is, performance is either a smashing success or an abject failure, with no in-between possibilities.

Only a few studies have examined criterion setting in depression directly or indirectly. Golin and Terrell (1977) found that depressed college students set elevated levels of aspiration for performance on tasks (especially skilled tasks), although there were no differences in expectations. In a related experiment they concluded that the high level of aspiration set by depressed subjects resulted in average performance being perceived as unsuccessful. Loeb and associates (1967) found that depressed psychiatric patients rated their performances as poor, even though actual performances were identical with those of a nondepressed group. High criteria are implied by this finding. Examining some related variables, Warren (1976) found a correlation (for males only) between low self-esteem and a high discrepancy between estimated performances and performance standards for success. Further research is needed to establish antecedents and effective means of modifying stringent self-evaluative criteria in depression.

Self-attribution in Depression

Depressed persons are hypothesized to make self-attributions that are consistent with negative expectancies. More specifically, depressed persons are likely to attribute success to external, unstable, specific causes and failure to internal, stable, global causes.

The inclusion of self-attribution in the self-control model is a modification of Kanfer's conceptualization. The assumption made in amending the model here is that self-attributions act as modifiers of self-evaluation. Success or failure has self-evaluative importance only if it is internally attributed. That is, a positive event that is purely externally caused may have a positive effect on mood and behavior, but it cannot occasion positive self-evaluation (i.e., pride). Similarly, when the cause of an aversive event is attributed externally, it may produce sadness, but it is not a cause for negative self-evaluation (i.e., guilt). Attributions of causality usually are considered to occur along several dimensions. Attributional research has dealt primarily with internality-externality and stable-unstable dimensions (Weiner et al., 1971).

Seligman and associates (Abramson, Seligman, & Teasdale, 1978) have added the dimension of globality-specificity. Stability and globality judgments may also influence self-evaluation. Outcomes that are judged to be internal, stable, and global will have higher self-evaluative impact. The clinical result of these patterns of self-attribution in depression is what Seligman has described as helplessness (Seligman, 1974, 1975). The evidence concerning the relationship between attributions and depression has recently been reviewed elsewhere (Abramson, Seligman, & Teasdale, 1978; Rehm & O'Hara, 1980) and thus will only be summarized here. There have been various attempts to correlate depression with the Rotter scale of internal-external locus of control (Rotter, 1966). The results have generally been mixed. This is probably to be expected, because the assumption that depression is related to externality is an oversimplification. Seligman and associates have demonstrated a number of effects that are consistent with helpless attributions, such as lack of change in expectancy on skilled tasks following failure by depressed subjects (Abramson, Garber, Edwards, & Seligman, 1978). Direct assessment of helpless attributions has only recently demonstrated the predicted deficits (Seligman et al., 1979).

A number of major questions remain to be resolved in this area. One question is whether or not helpless attribution per se is a primary aspect of depression. The alternative interpretation is that helpless attributions follow from negative expectations. Seligman's model (Abramson, Seligman, & Teasdale, 1978) states that helpless attributions produce an expectancy of a negative outcome. Thus, in the helplessness model, attributions precede and determine expectancies. On the other hand, attribution research has suggested that expectancies also influence attributions (Weiner et al., 1971). Results that are discrepant with expectancies often are attributed to external, unstable, specific causes. Thus, if a depressed person expects failure, then success will be attributed to external, unstable, specific causes, and failure will be attributed to internal, stable, global causes. Several of Seligman's studies have reported no initial expectancy differences among subjects, but estimates of expectancy in these cases may be determined more by naive understandings of chance or average outcomes than by mood. Interrelationships among attributions, expectancies, and behavior need further study.

Self-reinforcement in Depression

In the self-control model, self-reinforcement is postulated as the mechanism by which persons influence their own behaviors. There is an implied analogy between the way one controls one's own behavior and the way one might control the behavior of another. That is, the assumption is that people are capable of responding as if they were two organisms, a responding organism and a controlling organism. Positive self-evaluation may result in contingent self-reward, and negative self-evaluation may result in self-punishment. The magnitudes and frequencies of rewards and punishments and how they are related to self-evaluations may vary from one person to another. The model assumes that depressed persons contingently self-reward insufficiently and self-punish excessively. The result, in terms of the clinical phenomena of depression, is a reduced rate of overt behavior, particularly initiations of behavior. The behaviors of depressed persons are influenced by external reinforcement in the same manner as those of nondepressed persons. However, self-reinforcement supplements external reinforcement and increases the effectiveness of delayed external reinforcement.

Rozensky and associates (1977) evaluated the self-reinforcement behaviors of depressed and nondepressed psychiatric patients in a general medical hospital. Depressed patients self-reinforced themselves less and self-punished themselves more on a memory task, despite the fact that there were no actual differences between the two conditions in performance. Two studies with college students partially replicated this finding. Nelson and Craighead (1977) found that depressed college students rewarded themselves less, but they found no differences in self-punishment. Roth, Rehm, and Rozensky (1980) found the reverse pattern of results. That is, depressed persons were not significantly different in terms of self-reward, but they self-punished more frequently. Task differences may explain the discrepancy.

An interesting effect was recently reported by Sacco (1979), who found that depressed persons self-rewarded less in a public setting (i.e., with the experimenter observing), but when the task was performed in private, depressed persons increased in terms of self-reward, and nondepressed persons decreased. In the private condition, nondepressed persons gave themselves fewer rewards than did depressed persons. The author suggested that self-reward rates in public may be under the control of the effects they produce on others. This phenomenon deserves further study.

General Features of the Model

There are several comments that should be made about the model as a whole. The varied symptom picture in clinical depression can be seen as a function of different subsets of the self-control deficits proposed earlier. The symptoms themselves are descriptions of either self-control deficits or their consequences. Most of the cognitive symptoms reflect self-control behavior per se. That is, cognitive symptoms represent "readouts" or descriptions of self-control behaviors and processes. For example, pessimism reflects negative self-monitoring strategies; perfectionism and low self-esteem reflect stringent standard setting; helplessness reflects self-attributional errors; self-deprecation reflects self-punishment. The overt symptoms of depression mostly involve a reduced level of activity (i.e., reduced participation in previously enjoyable activities, lack of initiation, and inertia). These are the consequences of lack of contingent self-reward and excessive self-punishment. Sad mood probably can best be described as an expression of the overall state of a person with regard to the sufficiency of reinforcement experienced. That is, when the pattern of reinforcement (internal and external contingent rewards and punishments) a person is receiving is insufficient to maintain rates of behavior necessary for functioning in a given environment, this state is experienced as aversive and is described as depressed affect. The overt signs of depressed affect (e.g., sad demeanor, weeping) are functional means of communicating this state.

The pattern of deficits in self-control, and thus the pattern symptoms, may vary from one person to another. For example, one might monitor one's own behavior with relative accuracy but set very stringent standards for oneself. This person would not necessarily be pessimistic but would show low self-esteem. Another person might set fairly realistic standards but self-monitor negative events in a distorted fashion. Both persons would end up self-administering little reward, but for different reasons.

The model is not intended to suggest that self-control behavior is totally lacking in depressed persons, only that it is impaired, dysfunctional, or deficient in certain respects. To begin with, each of the deficits postulated can exist in varying degrees. Also, the self-control efforts of many persons susceptible to depression may be successful. In most cases, depressed persons do manage to overcome depressive episodes adaptively, given sufficient time and perhaps with sufficient external support.

In general, the model predicts that certain classes of behavior will be most susceptible to deterioration during depressive episodes. Those behaviors most likely to be disrupted are those requiring persistence toward long-range goals, especially if immediate consequences are aversive and immediate external cues and rewards are minimal. Adaptive behavior, effective problem solving, and initiation of new behavior will be rare during depressive episodes unless external cues and contingencies are quite compelling. The behavior most resistant to deterioration during depression is behavior that has been well practiced or is under strong and immediate external control. It is not unusual for a depressed person to discontinue hobbies, social interaction and housework while still maintaining sufficient performance at work. Depression is considered most severe when well-practiced habits and behaviors with strong external supports begin to deteriorate.

The model suggests that self-control deficits are relatively stable aspects of behavior that are acquired and modified as a person develops and matures. Thus deficits do exist and can be assessed prior to depressive episodes. The occurrence of a depressive episode is a joint function of the degree of stress (i.e., the magnitude of reinforcement loss) and the self-control skills available to cope with the stress. External supports may diminish the stress or supplement efforts to adapt. Biological predispositions may also play a role. A susceptible person may avoid depression if that person's environment is stable and provides sufficient reinforcement to maintain behavior. A consistently improverished and punishing environment will produce chronic depression in a susceptible person.

Overall, the model serves as a framework for relating multiple aspects of depressive behavior. In addition, it makes its own contribution by indicating specific directions that can be taken by inquiring into the nature of depressive disorders.

Self-control Therapy Program

Another important function of the self-control model is to serve as an organizing rationale for a behavioral psychotherapy program. The therapy program attempts to remedy the various deficits specified in the model in a systematic sequence. It presents a sequence of self-monitoring, self-evaluation, and self-reinforcement modules that deal with the depressive behaviors associated with the phase of self-control.

The program is generally didactic in nature, with the therapist presenting a rationale for each segment in the program. This presentation blends into a discussion of how the concepts apply to each participant. In most cases, exercises are provided within the session by which participants gain practice in applying the concepts. Finally, each segment ends with a therapeutic homework assignment that is brought back and discussed at the next session. Each segment builds on the previous segment, as do course units in a sequentially organized class. Indeed, it has been common for participants to refer to the program as "class" rather than "therapy."

A group format has been used in the research program. Although there is no inherent reason that the program could not be used in individual therapy, the group format has certain advantages. It is more efficient for dealing with large numbers of participants in a research context, and it is generally a cost-efficient format. In addition, the group format appears to facilitate cohesiveness among participants, who can empathize with one another's problems, offer realistic suggestions, model improvements, and offer support for efforts. This is counter to the usual clinical lore, which suggests that group therapy with a homogeneous depressed population is inadvisable because participants will only reinforce one another's depressive complaining. It may be that the didactic structure provided by the therapist avoids problems that might occur in more traditional and less structured therapies and, instead, employs group similarities toward more therapeutic ends. The groups have been time-limited, varying with different studies from 6 to 12 weekly 90-minute sessions.

To date, the program has been used primarily in a research context. For research purposes, participants have been depressed women solicited from the community and screened by stringent criteria. The screening procedures will be described in more detail later. Suffice it to say at this point that the research population has approximated a clinical outpatient population in severity and pattern of psychopathologic manifestations and in demographic characteristics.

Thus far the program has been tested only with women, because the incidence of depression among women is considerably higher than that among men. For research design purposes, a decision was made to deal with only one sex in order to simplify the balancing of groups in regard to a variety of characteristics. Feedback from the groups has suggested that the participants like the all-female makeup of the groups, and the format has been retained partly for this reason.

Therapy manuals have been written as part of the research protocol of each outcome study. As a result, they have varied in length and have been added to and modified in a gradual process of refining the techniques. The manuals also contain much that is relevant only to the research protocol (i.e., assessment procedures). Thus, what follows is a description of the basic therapy techniques abstracted from a series of manuals, together with a commentary on our experience with the procedures.

Self-monitoring

The first session in the program begins with a review of a number of issues and ground rules typical of any structured group therapy. Confidentiality is discussed, the schedule is clarified, and instructions are given for contracting the therapist concerning absences or other problems. The therapist then begins to introduce the program with an overview stressing the didactic format in which ideas will be presented and discussed and in which homework assignments will be given on specific aspects of depression. The therapist offers the first didactic presentation by making the general argument that mood is related to activity and that gaining control over activity is a means to the end of controlling depression. Positive activities are those that are associated with reward, satisfaction, or pleasure or that will lead to reward, satisfaction, or pleasure in the future. These positive activities lead to positive mood changes. Negative activities, which are associated with punishment, frustration, or displeasure, lead to negative mood shifts. There is a body of research (e.g., Grosscup & Lewinsohn, 1980; Lewinsohn & Graf, 1973; Lewinsohn & Libet, 1972; Rehm, 1978b) demonstrating that both positive and negative events correlate with mood on a day-to-day basis. Although they are not always obvious, these correlations become apparent when data are carefully recorded. Recognizing this basic relationship and observing its functioning on a day-to-day basis are basic steps toward gaining control over depression. This idea is fundamental to the rest of the program.

This basic concept is accepted by participants to varying degrees. On the one hand, people can readily see that adverse events can produce depression, and they can come up with examples from their own lives. Accidents, deaths of loved ones, arguments, bad news, etc., are often cited as examples. The participants generally have a little more trouble in citing examples of positive events that influence mood, but some examples of good news and successes (promotions, births, reunions, etc.) usually can be elicited. Nevertheless, depressed participants may feel that these positive events are exceptions and that their experience more generally is that depressions come on them seemingly from nowhere and are constant and unvarying with the day's events. This discussion generally leads naturally to the second major point presented during this session: the idea that people who are depressed tend to focus on negative events to the neglect of positive events. Being depressed orients people toward negative events. Attention must be focused on the unpleasant events that occur from day to day in order to learn to avoid or minimize them. When people are depressed, few things seem pleasurable. Ordinary pleasant events such as an enjoyable meal or nice weather may go unnoticed or may seem unimportant compared with certain unpleasant events to which undue importance is attributed. When a person is depressed, both positive and negative events and activities continue to occur, but the negative ones get all the attention. Positive events may seem trivial, but even trivial positive events can contribute to mood elevation if they are recognized and attended to. Accurate direction of one's attention is essential for overcoming depression. The concept of attending to trivial or minor events is stressed as a means of recognizing factors that truly influence mood.

This point is likely to elicit further reservations from participants, including doubt that many or any positive events, major or minor, actually occur in their lives. The basic response to this on the part of the therapist is that the participants are being asked to take a somewhat experimental attitude toward these ideas, not accepting them on the word of the therapist, but rather trying them out in their own lives and basing their conclusions on this experience.

The homework assignment at the end of the first session is to record daily mood and daily participation in positive activities. Participants are given copies of a positive-activities list (Table 3.1) and a sufficient number of self-monitoring logs (Appendix F) to last until the next session. For convenience, the positive-activities list may be printed on the back of the log. The idea of the positive-activities list is that it contains categories of rewarding or potentially rewarding activities. Participants use it as a checklist to be reviewed several times a day as a way of reminding themselves of events that occurred that were indeed positive. Thus the list is intended as a group of categories, not a list of specific events. The categories are intentionally overlapping, but they are meant to suggest various ways in which events can be pleasurable or rewarding. The items stress active involvement or activity on the part of the participant. The only exception to this is the final item (receiving praise, compliments, attention).

Participants are instructed to keep the log and positive-activities list with them as much as possible during the day, and whenever they can (at least two or three times) they record their activities. Each activity is recorded on the self-monitoring log (Appendix F) as a brief phrase descriptive of the event (e.g., had lunch with Mary, got report in at work, got the book I wanted to read from the library). In order to promote the use of the positive-activities list, participants are asked to record the category number from the list that corresponds to the activity being described. Participants usually find that more than one category from the positive-activities list can apply, and in such cases they are encouraged to fill in more than one number.

Participants are asked to record the day's mood at the end of each day. It is recognized that mood varies even from hour to hour within a given day, but participants are asked to estimate an average of moods for the entire day. The scale used is the simple 0–10 scale, where 0 stands for "the worst mood you have ever experienced for a day" and 10 stands for "the happiest mood you have ever experienced for a day." Participants are encouraged to use the points of the scale to record even small changes from one day to the next. The importance of keeping up with the homework assignments is stressed, as is the idea that the information collected in these assignments will provide the basis for subsequent aspects of the program.

The participants' experiences with this week of keeping self-monitoring logs are discussed at the beginning of the second session. A number of reactions are typical. In our experience, participants often have expressed surprise at the results of this 1-week "experiment." They are surprised to see how many pleasant events actually occur during the week. There is always variation among participants in terms of the

TABLE 3.1 Positive-Activities List

1. Planning something you will enjoy
2. Going on an outing (e.g., a walk, a shopping trip downtown, a picnic)
3. Going out for entertainment
4. Going on a trip
5. Going to meetings, lectures, classes
6. Attending a social gathering
7. Playing a sport or game
8. Spending time on a hobby or project
9. Entertaining yourself at home (e.g., reading, listening to music, watching TV)
10. Doing something just for yourself (e.g., buying something, cooking something, dressing comfortably)
11. Spending time just relaxing (e.g., thinking, sitting, napping, daydreaming)
12. Caring for yourself, making yourself attractive
13. Persisting at a difficult task
14. Completing a routine task or unpleasant task
15. Doing a job well
16. Cooperating with someone else on a common task
17. Doing something special for someone else, being generous, going out of your way
18. Seeking out people (e.g., calling, stopping by, making a date or appointment, going to a meeting)
19. Initiating conversation (e.g., at a store, party, or class)
20. Discussing an interesting or amusing topic
21. Expressing yourself openly, clearly, or frankly (e.g., opinion, criticism, anger)
22. Playing with children or animals
23. Complimenting or praising someone
24. Physically showing affection or love
25. Receiving praise, compliments, attention

---

numbers of events recorded, and sometimes it is helpful for those who recorded few events to hear the lists reported by participants who recorded many events. This often has the effect of making them realize that more events occurred in their own lives than they recorded and that they had failed to recognize minor events and activities. Participants sometimes feel that there is something vaguely inappropriate about recording only positive activities. In one instance, a woman brought in a parallel list she had felt compelled to keep listing the negative activities that occurred during the week, even though this had not been assigned. Many participants also find it surprising that there has been discriminable variation in their day-to-day moods. All of these experiences can be used by the therapist to emphasize the original concept of selective attention to negative events in depression-prone persons.

To further illustrate and consolidate this idea, the therapist presents the participants with a mood and activity exercise (Appendix G). The intent of the exercise is to demonstrate in the participant's own experience that mood and activity do correlate. Using the scale on the left, the mood rating for each day is graphed, producing a line for the week. Using the scale on the right, another line is constructed from the number of activities for each day. The therapist should take an active part to ensure that the participants learn to do the graphing, because people vary considerably in facility with such abstractions. When the graph is finished, in most cases the correlation will be quite clear. There will be a rough correspondence between the two lines, with days of many positive activities corresponding to best moods and days of few positive activities corresponding to worst moods. In instances in which the parallels are less clear, the point usually can be made by the second part of the exercise. Here participants are asked to look at the 2 or 3 days during which moods were the highest and lowest during the week and to look at the average number of activities at these extremes. In general, more activities will have occurred on the high mood days. If, at this point, differences have not become clear, it may be because of monitoring inaccuracies. It is advisable for the therapist to look over the logs that do not show a good correlation. The therapist can point out instances of specific events that did correlate with positive mood and discuss with the participant the possibility that some events may have been overlooked and whether or not those that were listed were truly rewarding or pleasurable. In nearly all cases this exercise will illustrate fairly clearly to participants the relationship between mood and activity. As further evidence, they should be given additional copies of the exercise to do on their own from another week's log.

The next concept to be presented (usually at the second session) is that depressed persons tend to focus on the immediate effects of their activities rather than the long-term effects. It should be pointed out that any activity can have both immediate and long-term effects. For instance, completing an unpleasant job now may produce pleasure later on. People who are depressed may wish for future rewards, but they may fail to attend to the immediate opportunities that would result in these delayed rewards. One tactic for overcoming depression is to become more aware of the differences between the immediate effects and the delayed effects of specific activities. This idea usually can be presented in the context of helping to refine the concept of a positive activity. After the first week of monitoring, participants often come in with problems regarding whether or not certain activities should have been recorded. An example that illustrates the problem well came from a woman who recorded spending an afternoon with her grandchildren as a pleasant activity, but this was associated with the week's lowest mood. When she described the event in more detail, it turned out that she had taken them Christmas shopping. As the afternoon wore on, both she and the children became increasingly tired and irritable as they battled department store crowds of Christmas shoppers. The immediate aversive aspects of the situation obviously were much more powerful in influencing her mood than were the long-term positive aspects of her relationship with her grandchildren.

In order to teach the point more clearly, participants are given an exercise involving immediate effects versus delayed effects (Appendix H). This exercise presents tables for illustrating the positive and negative immediate and delayed effects of various activities. After going through some simple examples, participants are asked to take some representative events from the log of the previous week and to try to fill in the four quadrants. Negative activities recalled from the week can be analyzed in a similar manner. Most participants find this exercise fairly easy to understand, a tool useful for thinking about whether or not an activity is indeed pleasurable. Comparison of their subjective weightings of the four quadrants makes this decision much simpler. For some participants this is something of a revelation, and it is found to be useful as a simple problem-solving tool. The homework assignment for the next week is to continue monitoring positive activities and mood and, in addition, to make a note in the extra column on the self-monitoring log regarding a positive delayed effect of at least one positive activity per day. The intent is to encourage participants to give more attention to the delayed positive consequences of their daily activities. Discussion of this exercise at the following session usually involves simple reiteration and clarification of some of the points made.

Overall, the acceptance and the carrying out of these self-monitoring exercises are important and probably crucial steps in a therapy program. For the most part, participants do find it to have a logical and convincing rationale that is substantiated in their experience. In relatively few cases, compliance has been a problem in our use of the program. The homework assignments are structured and specific, and although they may present problems, most participants usually are able to complete them. In our recent use of the program we have attempted to enhance compliance by means of a follow-up telephone call during the week to each participant. The participant is told to expect this call, and it can be useful for answering questions about the assignment and prompting the participant to maintain the recording procedure during the week. Some participants remain skeptical that any program that does not fulfill their preconceived notions of psychotherapy can be effective. The therapist's approach is to encourage participants to maintain an experimental attitude.

Self-evaluation

The self-evaluation component of the program shifts the emphasis from an attempt simply to make participants more cognizant of their behaviors to a more active approach in which they examine the ways they make decisions and plans concerning their activities. The first principle that is presented in the self-evaluation part of the program is that people who are depressed tend to set unrealistically stringent goals and standards for themselves. Depressed persons tend to be perfectionistic in that they set goals that are distant, abstract, overly general, and often unattainable. Partial fulfillment is never satisfying, and this results in a lack of direction, a sense of hopelessness, and self-depreciation. In order to overcome depression, it is important to learn to set realistic positive standards for self-evaluation.

Standards can be inappropriate in a number of ways. Depressed persons often set goals that are too distant (i.e., goals that depend on many intermediate steps that are too easily ignored). The goals of getting a high-paying job seldom can be addressed directly apart from concern regarding education, training, experience, and effort. In such instances the focus must be shifted to a more immediate goal that will contribute to the possibility of attaining the long-range goal. Goals often are stated in ways that are overly abstract or general. A goal such as to be loved or to be successful is not one that is amenable to the defining of intermediate steps, nor can such a goal ever be clearly achieved. However, more concrete forms of the same goals can be stated. Depressed persons often set goals that are unattainable. To be beautiful and to be wealthy are goals that are beyond the capacity of most persons.

The activities that participants have been monitoring often have the positive effect of contributing to some form of long-range goal or meeting some important standard. These goals can be implicit and perfectionistic in unrecognized ways. To some extent, general discussion can bring out examples of perfectionistic goal setting. However, the self-evaluation worksheets (Appendix I) and associated assignments are particularly helpful in putting across the concepts. First, the participant is asked to define a goal. The worksheet begins with the sentence stem "I want to increase . . ." in order to introduce the idea that goals should be defined in positive ways. That is, a goal should be defined not in terms of an activity to be accomplished and then discontinued or decreased but rather in terms of an activity to be increased in frequency or duration. This is a basic rule used in behavior modification. The goal should be realistic and attainable by application of the capacities of the participant, not something that depends on external factors. For the purposes of the program, depressed participants are asked to define goals they can work on in the ensuing weeks. Each goal should be meaningful, yet limited in scope. The intent of the exercise is, again, practice and experimentation. The principles of goal setting are equally applicable and transferable to larger goals, but participants are cautioned to begin with goals with which they will feel free to experiment. Often it requires much discussion within the group to help participants define goals according to the criteria that they be positive and attainable and within one's capacities.

Once such a goal is specified, the next task is to define a series of subgoals. The general idea is to break down the overall goal into small individual activities that can be accomplished as steps toward the larger goal. At first, a participant may have to make a long list of possible steps and then select from this list the best and most orderly progression of activities. Subgoals should be defined with the same criteria as used for goals. In addition, it is stressed that goals should be defined operationally, that is, they should be defined in terms that will specify the behavior to be performed in a way that will permit anyone to recognize when it has been performed. This means that the criteria of successful completion are built into the goal. For example, if the goal is "to increase socializing with my neighbors," the subgoals might include "initiating a conversation when I see a neighbor in the yard" and "calling up a neighbor and inviting her for a cup of coffee." It will be important in the latter case that the activity be defined as making the call. Whether or not the neighbor can actually come over for the cup of coffee may depend on circumstances outside the participant's control. Making up the first self-evaluation worksheet is difficult for most depressed participants. Instances of perfectionism and stringent inappropriate standards are frequently seen. For many participants, setting goals and subgoals is a skill that must be acquired gradually.

In our program we have found that participants define a wide variety of goals. Typically they involve such things as dieting behavior, socialization, hobbies, and work-related activities. In terms of specifics, they can vary from "pursuing an interest in cats" to "learning to play the flute" to "spending more time with my husband."

Once a participant has filled out a worksheet with a goal to begin working on, the assignment is to continue the self-monitoring exercise, with special attention to the subgoals on the worksheet as a class of positive activities. On the self-monitoring logs, the participant makes a check mark in the extra column for each positive activity that is a subgoal. Refining and revising the goals and subgoals become the major foci of the next couple of sessions. Additional subgoals may have to be written, and goals and subgoals may have to be restated to develop workable and realistic plans. Participants may want to add additional goals, and a supply of additional worksheets should be provided.

Ideas concerning the attribution of responsibility are presented in subsequent sessions as part of the ongoing discussion of goal setting. One deterrent to making progress toward goals is the problem of making judgments about what activities are feasible and are within the participant's capacity. The general point is made that people who are depressed tend to make inaccurate evaluations of their control over their successes and failures. In working toward their goals, all participants encounter obstacles, and they meet them with varying degrees of success and failure. Participants who are depressed tend to believe that any successes they have fall into one of the following categories: (1) they are due to external forces, such as chance, luck, or someone else's help; (2) they are unstable, one-time occurrences unlikely to be repeated; (3) they are specific small victories not indicative of a general trend. Failures, on the other hand, often are assumed to fall into these categories: (1) they are due to internal causes, such as lack of skill, ability, or effort; (2) they are examples of stable trends, likely to be repeated over and over again; (3) they are indications of global and general failure. In order to overcome depression, it is important to make realistic interpretations of successes and failures. It is important to recognize one's contributions to successes and not be overburdened by inappropriate guilt regarding failures. Examples of inaccurate attributions are easy to find among depressed persons. For example, a depressed woman, on being hired for a job, may think that she is just lucky or that the employer was unable to find anyone else to do the work. On the other hand, if this same woman is laid off, she may conclude that she is incompetent and unable to handle responsibility. On receiving attention from a man, this depressed woman may reach the following conclusion: "I can't understand what he sees in me; he must have some ulterior motive," or "I'm just lucky; this could never happen again." If this relationship ends, this same woman may say "I always knew I was unlovable; I just can't make anyone happy." In order to give participants an understanding of these fairly subtle attributional concepts, an exercise on attribution of responsibility (Appendix J) is used. Basically, the exercise asks participants to choose a couple of recent events from the self-monitoring logs and describe the ways in which various factors (external and internal, stable and unstable, global and specific) may have influenced them. After this is done in a qualitative sense, participants are asked to make percentage estimates of the degrees to which events are attributable internally. In a similar way, estimates are made as to whether general-stable versus specific-unusual causes were responsible. Note that in the latter instance the dimensions of stability and globality have been collapsed for simplicity. A parallel exercise is used for failure, with participants being asked to recall two negative events or activities from the recent past. There is an assumption here that initially there are automatic distortions in self-attribution, but on being examined more closely, these give way to more realistic evaluations. There is also an implicit assumption that persons usually are largely responsible for the positive events that occur in their lives, whereas they are largely not responsible for negative events that occur. Certainly there are exceptions to these points, but in the long run this is generally the case. Discussion within the group of examples from each participant's worksheet usually substantiates this general idea.

The homework assignment relating to the self-attribution exercise is to continue self-monitoring of positive activities, with special reference to subgoals, and for this week to use the extra column for estimating the percentage to which the participant was responsible for each of the positive activities.

The self-evaluation components are essential to the therapy program. It is this portion of the therapy program that provides the basic impetus and direction for change. It is designed to facilitate intervention in the cognitive processes of making attributions and plans and in the behavior phase of carrying out those plans.

Self-reinforcement

The intent of this phase of the program is to increase the participant's use of contingent self-reward. It is employed as a tactic for helping participants motivate themselves to work on their goals, and it also provides correction of the assumed depressive tendency to use self-reward inadequately. The concept is presented to participants through the following series of points: (1) Behavior is controlled by rewards and punishments. If it is desired to increase, strengthen, and encourage a behavior on the part of another person, successful performance is followed by a reward. If it is desired to decrease, weaken, and discourage a behavior, that behavior is followed with punishment. This is true for training a pet, teaching a child, and influencing an adult. The important point is that the reward or punishment must be contingent. That is, the reward comes only after the desired behavior has occurred. The rule is, in effect, "eat your spinach, and then you get dessert." Rewards and punishments are the means by which behavior is motivated. (2) People can control their own behaviors by giving themselves rewards and punishments. When people do things of which they are proud or things they believe they have done well, they can treat themselves to rewards (e.g., go out to dinner), they can pat themselves on the back, or they can simply say to themselves that they have done a good job. When people do things of which they are not proud or things they believe they have done poorly, they can punish themselves (e.g., by denying themselves things) or they can repeat over and over to themselves critical statements about how they performed. Thus rewards and punishments can be tangible or verbal (e.g., the dinner versus praise). Self-rewards and self-punishments can be overt or covert (e.g., going out to a movie versus just enjoying the feeling of accomplishment). People employ these tactics all the time. For instance, a woman loses weight and rewards herself by buying a new item of clothing. (3) People who are depressed tend to punish themselves too much and reward themselves too little. People who tend toward depression often are hypercritical of themselves and are continually punishing themselves both overtly and covertly. These same people may feel that it is almost improper to do something to reward themselves or even to think something positive about themselves. The result is that they are not motivated to be more active in pursuing positive activities and goals.

Although this is an idea that most depressed persons can recognize as applicable to themselves in an abstract sense, it is a concept that nevertheless is difficult for depressed persons to accept in its specific applications. They have the feeling that covert self-reward is a form of bragging and excessive pride and that overt self-reward is selfish and self-indulgent. Self-rewards often are perceived as contrary to religious and moral conceptions of humility and selflessness. It may take considerable discussion and persuasion on the part of the therapist to foster the idea of self-reward as an accurate and appropriate means of recognition of success administered for the purpose of motivation. Rewards need not be so abundant as to imply an overestimate of one's success and coercion of praise from others, nor need they be wastefully self-indulgent.

The exercise associated with this component of the program involves having the participants make two lists. The first, referred to as the assets list, is an enumeration of true positive self-statements. Often it is difficult for depressed participants to come up with true positive statements about themselves. They can, with little trouble, enumerate at great length their faults and deficiencies, but it may take most of the therapy session to get all participants to construct lists of at least three or four positive items. The group can be helpful in suggesting items for a participant that have become apparent during earlier sessions. For instance, in one group a woman who a few weeks earlier had described her difficulties in finding time to complete an elaborate sewing project denied that she had any particular talents. When other participants in the group reminded her of her sewing ability and expressed the wish that they could sew with such skill, she attempted to minimize this ability and qualify it by citing her friends who were even better. After much discussion, she finally agreed that the statement "I am good at sewing" really was true and that she did feel good about this ability. The assignment associated with this list is to carry it during the week and read it as a form of self-reward each time a subgoal is accomplished. In addition, the participant is to attempt to add as many additional items to the list as possible during the week. Positive self-statements can also be supplemented by general statements recognizing successes. Statements such as "That was good" or "I finished that successfully" are to be employed by participants as appropriate. In running these groups, we have used various tactics for incorporating these latter general statements. However, it seems to be important to allow participants to phrase them in ways they find comfortable and appropriate for themselves.

The second list, which usually is drawn up at a later session, is a list of overt rewards that we call a reward menu. The reward menu consists of easily accomplished positive activities. The theory is that easy positive activities can be used as rewards for accomplishing difficult positive activities. Such a list can be made up of items from previously completed self-monitoring logs and can be supplemented with simple items involving rewards of favorite foods and activities. Once again, the idea is for participants to use these activities to reward themselves for their efforts in working toward their goals. The concept of contingency is stressed. In early forms of the program, participants constructed point systems whereby they earned points by completing subgoal activities and spent them for reward items from their reward menus. We found that this was unnecessarily complex. The concepts of reward and contingency are just as easily conveyed when participants self-administer rewards of their choosing following accomplishment of difficult subgoal activities as they deem appropriate.

Note that the program does not directly involve an effort to decrease punishment. The rationale for this is that decreases in self-punishment should occur as consequences of changes in self-monitoring and self-evaluation and that it is therapeutically more important to spend time teaching participants to increase their self-rewards, which is consistent with the concept of increasing one's positive goal behavior.

General Issues

In the preceding sections we described several of the more frequently encountered reactions, both positive and negative, of participants. There are several reactions relating to the overall program that deserve discussion. One frequent criticism of the program from participants is that it tends toward Pollyannaism. That is, they believe that the program ignores significant real problems, adverse life circumstances, and unpleasant events in favor of focusing on positive events and a positive interpretation of events. It is important to stress that throughout the program we try to emphasize realistic self-monitoring, realistic self-evaluation, and realistic self-reinforcement. In this program we do not attempt to deny the existence of real-life problems; rather, we attempt to develop positive ways of approaching them in a problem-solving goal-setting format.

A second common criticism was mentioned earlier in relation to self-reinforcement: Participants sometimes believe that we are teaching them to be self-centered and hedonistic; such popular phrases as "the me generation" are sometimes cited as examples of the basic orientation of our program. Such is not the intent of the program, and it is important to discuss this point. In our view, there is nothing in the program that militates against the values of unselfishness, altruism, and devotion to others; however, there is an implication in the program that this should not lead to negation of one's own rights. In the group sessions, discussions of rights similar to those used in assertion training may be necessary. The basic idea is that human interaction should be a social exchange in which there is mutual respect and benefit. Depressed patients frequently find themselves involved in relationships in which they are taken for granted and abused. A positive self-image requires the capacity to evaluate oneself in terms of one's own criteria, without excessive dependence on the judgment of others.

A third criticism of the program is that it does not mesh with the common notions of what psychotherapy should be. The program focuses on current day-to-day events and planning for the future. Some participants have complained that we fail to address the historic origins of their depression. One woman complained that her attempts to discuss the distressing events of her childhood were discouraged by the therapist. Our response is consistent with many current behavioral and phenomenological therapies: One can exert control only over the present and the future; success in dealing with problems today makes it easier to come to terms with adverse experiences in the past. In one sense this is an issue of attribution and control. One cannot control the past or set goals for changing the past, but one can set goals in the present for changing the future.

Another frequent criticism is that the program focuses on working toward insignificant goals, ignoring the participant's real problems, which are current, significant, and all-consuming. In some instances this may be true. Many depressed persons are trapped in life circumstances that are highly aversive and virtually unchangeable. In some instances, of course, psychotherapy is not the appropriate intervention. In one of our groups, a participant revealed that she had just moved out of the apartment she had been sharing with a man for a number of months, whereupon he telephoned her at work threatening to harm her if she did not come back to him. Psychotherapy was not the intervention of choice; a call to the police and contact with a women's shelter were considerably more important.

An example of this issue is provided by instances of marital discord. There are many types of marital discord for which therapy cannot hope to provide a solution. Our approach to this issue is that where marital problems exist, the participant must first make a realistic evaluation of those things that are not under her control. This decision may involve determining if the marriage is worth saving. If the decision is that there are some aspects of the marriage that can be modified and that the marriage in general is salvageable, then it may be possible to deal with some aspects of the marital problem within the context of the program. Goals such as increasing the time spent with the husband, increasing the number of nonargument conversations, and increasing the number of discussions of particular problem areas are feasible. There have been instances in which women in our groups have felt that they could derive little satisfaction from their marriages, but given their ages and the alternatives available, they did want to consider divorce. In such instances, goals concerning obtaining greater satisfaction outside the marriage through involvement in hobbies and community activities have been set. Overall, it is our belief that the program is relatively flexible, involving a form of behavioral problem solving which can be applied to many specific kinds of problems.

On the positive side, most participants have shared this view and have believed that they have acquired specific skills that they can use in dealing with depression in the future. For different participants, each of the separate elements in the program has at one time or another been cited as particularly important for a set of circumstances. Overall, the program seems to have met good participant acceptance. A more formal evaluation of its success will be provided in the next section.

Outcome Studies

This self-control therapy program has been evaluated over the last several years in a series of outcome studies. Because most of these studies have been published or presented elsewhere, they will only be summarized here. There has been an attempt in this series of studies to maintain as much comparability as possible from one study to the next, so that comparisons could be made not only within a study but also among studies. Nevertheless, there have been certain variations. There have been minor variations in participant selection criteria, assessment procedures, and parameters of therapy, such as number of sessions, etc. Also, the therapy itself has changed in minor ways as the manuals have been revised and refined from year to year. Despite these variations, the general strategies have remained the same. In all studies the participants have been solicited from the general community via announcements in various news media. Participants have been selected on the basis of psychometric and interview criteria. Assessment has involved the commonly used self-report measures of depression plus behavioral observations; in the later studies, clinician evaluations have also been used. The therapy has been presented in formats ranging from 6 to 12 sessions, but always in the same sequence of self-monitoring, self-evaluation, and self-reinforcement modules. Therefore, although there have been variations among studies, comparisons from one study to another have some validity and add interesting additional insights.

Validation Study

The first study in the series was that of Fuchs & Rehm (1977). This was an initial validation study in which the main purpose was to make comparisons among the newly devised self-control program, nonspecific group therapy, and waiting-list control conditions. Twenty-eight of 36 subjects who began the study completed the posttesting phase. These included 8 self-control subjects, 10 nonspecific therapy subjects, and 10 waiting-list controls. The mean age for all subjects was 28.8 years, with a range from 18 to 48 years. Subjects were selected on the basis of MMPI criteria adopted from Lewinsohn, Weinstein, and Alper (1970): $F \leqslant 80$, $L \leqslant 60$, $D \geqslant 70$, $D > HY$, $D > PT$. In addition, a screening questionnaire and interview eliminated any potential subject with a history of psychiatric hospitalization, serious suicidal ideation or suicide attempts, or psychoses, as well as any candidate receiving any form of concurrent psychological therapy. Subjects were assigned to one of two therapists, each of whom supervised one group in each of the two active therapy conditions. All groups were seen for six weekly 90-minute sessions.

The major dependent variables were the Beck Depression Inventory (BDI) and the MMPI D scale, probably the most frequently used and psychometrically the best depression scales available. In addition, the MMPI total elevation was used as a measure of general psychological functioning. Behavioral observation measures in this study consisted of a pair of group interaction measures taken from 10-minute segments of the first and last therapy sessions, during which the therapist was absent. The number of verbalizations from each subject was scored as a measure of interaction activity. In addition, the number of different speakers who followed a given subject was tallied, and the percentage of group members who followed each subject was used as a measure of the range of response elicitation. Both of these measures were intended to assess the activity level of the subject as an aspect of depressive behavior.

A paper-and-pencil measure of activity level was also used. This was a 49-item version (Lewinsohn & Graf, 1973) of the Pleasant Events Schedule (MacPhillamy & Lewinsohn, 1971). This instrument asks subjects to indicate the frequency and enjoyability of a number of pleasant events in the last 30 days. Measures of activity level and reinforcement potential are taken from these two dimensions. Thus the format of the instrument is self-report, but it is inquiring about activity over the past 30 days.

Three experimental measures were used to assess self-control behavior and attitudes. A self-evaluation questionnaire employed comparison of ideal-self and actual-self ratings on 18 dimensions. A common-associate task in which subjects were asked to guess the most common associates of words selected for the ambiguity of their associates (Wener & Rehm, 1975) was employed to elicit indications of self-reward and self-punishment from subjects. After each response, subjects were asked to indicate if they were "sure I'm right" (self-reward), "sure I'm wrong" (self-punishment), or "don't know." Finally, a Self-control Concepts Test was constructed of 25 statements reflecting various self-control attitudes and beliefs such as "I have extremely high standards for what I demand of myself" and "When I do something right, I take time to enjoy the feeling." Subjects indicated their degree of agreement with each statement on a 5-point scale. All of the paper-and-pencil measures except the Concepts Test were administered pretest, posttest, and at 6-week follow-up. The Concepts Test was assessed only posttest and at follow-up to avoid pretest sensitization. The group interaction measures were taken only pretest and posttest, because the group did not meet for the follow-up.

On the two self-report depression measures, both therapy groups improved significantly over time, and they were significantly less depressed than the waiting-list group posttest. In addition, there were significant differences between the therapy groups: The self-control group was more improved posttest and at follow-up. It is notable that when absolute criteria for improvement were used posttest (e.g., below 11 on the BDI and below 70 on the MMPI D), all self-control subjects were within the normal range, whereas only 3 of the 10 nonspecific subjects were in the normal range. The reduction in total MMPI elevation was also greatest for the self-control group, suggesting a fairly generalized effect on self-report measures of depression and general psychopathologic manifestations.

On the group interaction measure, there was again significantly greater improvement for the self-control subjects in terms of activity level. No significant differences were found on the response elicitation measure. The Pleasant Events Schedule measure of activity level also yielded significant differences, suggesting the greatest improvement for the self-control group and intermediate improvement for the nonspecific therapy group. Self-control subjects also improved significantly on the reinforcement potential score posttest in comparison with the nonspecific therapy subjects.

On the self-control measures, the results were somewhat less clear, but in all instances they were consistent with the idea that the self-control subjects improved the most on their self-control attitudes and beliefs.

The results of the study are viewed as fairly strong validation for the effectiveness of the therapy program. The magnitudes of the effects suggest clinical as well as statistical significance, even with relatively small numbers of subjects. This was true with a subject population that appeared to be within a clinically relevant but moderate range of depression. The effect was obtained in a relatively economical 6 weeks of therapy, and it appeared to be maintained at 6-week follow-up. The results encouraged us to continue with our evaluation of the program.

Comparison with Assertion Training

One possible weakness of the first study may have been that the control subjects, although possibly representative of those in group therapies available to patients at this level of depression, may not have provided a strong comparison. It was concluded that with a generally nondirective therapy program such as we attempted to administer in this first study, more sessions would be needed or more structure would have to be given to the sessions to make the program effective. Our belief was that the self-control program may have succeeded because it was a well-structured program with a logical behavioral rationale. We concluded that a more stringent test would be to compare the self-control program with another structured behavioral therapy program. The model we chose for comparison was assertion training (Rehm, Fuchs, Roth, Kornblith, & Romano, 1979). Assertion training had been suggested as an appropriate therapy for at least a subset of depressed patients (Lazarus, 1974; Wolpe, 1971). Several reports had appeared describing assertion training as part of larger package programs (e.g., Lewinsohn, Biglan, & Zeiss, 1976; McLean, 1976; Shaw, 1977; Taylor & Marshall, 1977).

The design of this study called for an intrasubject control condition such that each subject was seen at four times spaced at 6-week intervals: screening, pretherapy, posttherapy, and follow-up. Two pairs of therapists saw a group of subjects in each of the two treatment conditions. Male and female therapist pairs were used to enhance role-playing and modeling capabilities in the assertion training condition. Twenty-four of 27 women who began the program completed it. Fourteen subjects were seen in the assertions skills condition. Subjects were screened on the same criteria as in the first study.

The assertion skills program focused on role playing in assertion problem situations. Therapists provided scenarios covering refusing unreasonable demands, making requests, and expressing criticism, disapproval, approval, and affection. In addition, there were scenes taken from subjects' weekly logs of assertion problem situations. Training included instruction, rehearsal, group feedback, coaching, and occasional modeling. Through each scene, the group provided feedback on the subject's performance regarding the dimensions of eye contact, voice, volume, affect, expressivity, owned statements of opinion, requests for new behavior, and overall assertion.

Depression was again assessed by the BDI and the MMPI D scale. The Pleasant Events Schedule was again employed in this study as a means of assessing behavioral aspects of depression. A more elaborate behavioral observation strategy was employed whereby the subjects in the first and last sessions were asked individually to make statements concerning their current functioning. These statements were videotaped and afterward rated for a variety of measures theoretically related to depression. The overall assessment strategy of this study was to assess depression by the measures just mentioned and then independently to assess self-control behavior and assertion skills. Self-control behavior was assessed by the same three methods used in the first study. Assertion skills were assessed via self-report in the form of the Wolpe-Lazarus Assertion Scales (Wolpe & Lazarus, 1967). To assess overt assertion skill, we used an audiotaped situation test consisting of eight situations calling for assertive responses. The subjects' audiotaped responses were coded for a series of behaviors that have commonly been associated with assertion.

Overall, the MMPI D scale and the BDI indicated the following: (1) There was relatively little improvement between screening and pretherapy. (2) Both groups improved from pretherapy to posttherapy. (3) The self-control group improved to a greater degree than the assertion group at posttherapy. (4) Therapy gains were maintained at the 6-week follow-up. Once again, it was notable that when absolute criteria for improvement were used, nearly all (11 of 14 on the BDI and 10 of 14 on the MMPI D) self-control subjects were in the normal range posttest, whereas relatively few (5 of 10 on the BDI and 2 of 10 on the MMPI D) subjects in the assertion skills program ended up in the normal range. The Pleasant Events Schedule activity measure also indicated superiority for the self-control group. Behavioral observation measures during therapy yielded significant differences favoring the self-control group on overall depression, negative self-references, and negative references to others. Thus it was fairly clear on both self-report and behavioral measures that the self-control group showed greater improvement in terms of depression.

The Self-control Concepts Test yielded a significant difference in favor of the self-control group posttest. This adds some validity to the therapy rationale. That is, the self-control program was effective in changing self-control attitudes and beliefs. As to assertion measures, the self-report Wolpe-Lazarus scale showed no significant differences.

However, the assertion skills of subjects were significantly better than those of self-control subjects posttest on several specific assertion behaviors (duration of speech, requests for new behavior, statements of opinion, loudness, fluency, and overall assertion). Interestingly, the self-control subjects rated their own assertion behavior as better posttest than did the assertion skills subjects. Because the self-control program specifically incorporated attempts to reduce the stringency of subjects' evaluative criteria, this outcome is perhaps not so surprising. Nevertheless, the other findings in favor of the assertion skills group suggest that this treatment did validly modify its intended behavioral target.

This study provided a replication of the effects found in the first study. It demonstrated that for a given subject a clinically significant effect on depression can be obtained within a 6-week period, when little change in the subject's condition had occurred previously with no treatment. The study also indicated that it is not simply the behavioral orientation and structure of the program that make it effective; in addition, some aspects of therapy content may be important. At the very least it can be said that the self-control program was effective for a higher proportion of depressed subjects than was the assertion training program. Nevertheless, assertion training may be important and effective for a certain number of depressed persons.

One-Year Follow-up

The first two studies were carried out at approximately the same time. One year later, follow-up data were obtained on subjects from both studies through the mail (Romano & Rehm, 1979). The self-control subjects from the first two studies were combined and compared with the subjects receiving nonspecific therapy and assertion skills training. The waiting-list subjects had subsequently received therapy; so this condition no longer existed. Data were obtained from 29 of the 42 subjects in the first two studies. Sixteen of 22 self-control subjects responded, 6 of 10 assertion subjects, and 7 of 10 nonspecific therapy subjects. Questionnaires showed no differences among the three groups on their ratings of current mood or current mood compared with mood before or after the therapy program. A significantly greater proportion of subjects from self-control groups stated that they had not experienced recurrent episodes of depression during the year. Nearly half of the subjects in the nonspecific and assertion groups had sought additional professional help during the year, whereas none of the self-control subjects had done so. At 1-year follow-up there were no longer any significant differences between the groups on the BDI and the MMPI D scale. All groups appeared improved over pretherapy levels of depression. This lack of differences is, of course, partly confounded by the additional therapy obtained by many of the subjects in the control groups. The self-control program is intended to provide skills participants can use to cope with depressegonic situations as they are encountered. Our preferred interpretation of these data is that the self-control subjects were able to ward off depressive episodes without additional help, whereas subjects in the other groups suffered additional episodes and required additional help to arrive at approximately the same level of improvement 1 year later.

First Disassembly Study

The first two outcome studies demonstrated the efficacy of a complex package program. The program consists of major components addressing different aspects of self-control behavior. The relative values of these components were unknown. Therefore, the purpose of the next study (Rehm, Kornblith, O'Hara, Lamparski, Romano, & Volkin, in press) and later studies was to dismantle the program to evaluate the contributions of the components. The design of the study included five treatment conditions: (1) the full self-control program, including self-monitoring, self-evaluation, and self-reinforcement modules; (2) self-monitoring plus self-evaluation; (3) self-monitoring plus self-reinforcement; (4) self-monitoring only; (5) a waiting-list control program. Two therapists saw one group in each of the four therapy conditions. Treatment groups met for 90 minutes per week for 7 weeks in this study. The five conditions were replicated in two cohorts such that some of the waiting-list subjects from the first cohort served as treatment subjects in the second cohort. For the purposes of analysis, 9, 11, 12, 9 and 15 subjects were included in the study in the five respective conditions. There were some changes in selection criteria for this study. Again, women between the ages of 18 and 60 years were sought through the news media, but the selection criteria were modified such that to be included in the study the subjects needed an MMPI D score equal to or greater than 70, and then they had to satisfy Research Diagnostic Criteria (Spitzer et al., 1978) for nonpsychotic, nonbipolar, major depressive disorders based on a structured interview using a modified Schedule for Affective Disorders and Schizophrenia (Endicott & Spitzer, 1978). Thus, psychometric and interview criteria continued to be employed, but a much more elaborate interview procedure was used to establish a diagnosis of depression and to rule out a variety of other neurotic and personality disorders. As an indication of the stringency of the criteria employed, it is notable that in obtaining the final sample, telephone inquiries were elicited from 576 women, of whom 211 were screened on the MMPI and 86 were interviewed. The mean age for the final group was 39.2 years, with a range of 20 to 58 years. Subjects were fairly well educated, with a median of 13.7 years of school. Only 35.7% were currently employed, and 55.4% were married.

The assessment battery was also modified in some ways. The BDI and MMPI D were continued as primary measures of self-reported depression. An Unpleasant Events Schedule was added to the Pleasant Events Schedule. Only the Self-control Concept Test was retained as a measure of self-control behavior. A major addition was the inclusion of clinical interview ratings of depression. These included the Hamilton Rating Scale for Depression (Hamilton, 1960) and the Raskin Three-Item Scale (Raskin et al., 1967) and the Global Assessment Scale (Endicott et al., 1976). These scales were employed twice, first by an independent interviewer who saw the subjects pretest (and did the Research Diagnostic Criteria screening) and posttest, and then again by another clinician who viewed only the videotapes. These raters were blind as to the condition and pretest/posttest status of the subjects. This interview also served to provide a behavior sample, and videotapes of the first minutes of the interviews were coded for 11 categories of nonverbal and paralinguistic behaviors theoretically related to depression.

The results of this study can be summarized fairly succinctly. There was fairly consistent evidence for a general treatment effect. That is, the four treatment groups did better than the waiting-list group on the BDI, Self-control Concepts Test, and Pleasant Events Schedule, as well as on the interviews by Hamilton, Raskin, and Global scales. No consistent differences were found among the four experimental groups. That is, there was no evidence that either the self-evaluation condition or the self-reinforcement condition or their combination added any effectiveness to the program over and above the self-monitoring component alone.

These results were somewhat surprising in that we had had anecdotal evidence from subjects in earlier studies that elements of the self-evaluation and self-reinforcement modules were particularly helpful to them. In some ways, conditions in this study may not have been optimal for detecting true differences. The numbers of subjects continue to be fairly small in our studies. The overall therapy effect in this study was of somewhat lower magnitude than in the earlier two studies, such that larger numbers may have been particularly needed to detect differences. Also, it may be that therapy elements later in the sequence are inherent in the self-monitoring module. That is, once subjects have had positive activities defined and are monitoring them on a weekly basis, it is implied that they should attempt to increase these and that they should define them in operational chunks with realistic criteria. They should take responsibility for their successes. They are offered reinforcement from the therapist, and self-reinforcement is modeled by group members and reinforced by the therapist.

Second Disassembly Study

If, indeed, the further components of the therapy program were inherent in the self-monitoring-only condition in the first disassembly study, then it may be that elements within that component are of particular importance. One logical assumption would be that the therapy improvement was largely due to the instigational effects of the behavioral homework assignments. That is, the explicit assignments to monitor positive activities may be sufficient to induce higher levels of activity and thus improvement in terms of depression. The fourth outcome study in this series was designed to address this question, in addition to rectifying some of the other factors that may have hindered the obtaining of clearer results in the previous study. The second disassembly study (Kornblith et al., 1979) consisted of four conditions. The first was a full self-control package condition. The second was the full package less any explicit homework assignments (i.e., the principles were presented and discussed, but no assignments for monitoring or home practice were made). A third condition involved a self-monitoring component plus a self-evaluation component replicating the condition in the previous study. The idea was to give us a second look at the contribution of the self-reinforcement component and thus accumulate data on a larger number of subjects concerning this issue. In addition, for comparison purposes, a single group of subjects was seen in an active, problem-solving-oriented, group therapy condition that in some ways approximated Weissman's interpersonal therapy (DiMascio et al., 1978). All the therapy protocols were increased to 12 weeks on the assumption that minor additions to the therapy manual had made the procedure more complex and more difficult to deliver in a 6-week or 7-week format.

Subject selection procedures in this study were essentially the same, the only change being that a criterion of a BDI score of 20 or greater was substituted for the MMPI selection criterion in the previous study. Assessment procedures were essentially the same as in the last study. Eleven subjects were seen in the self-control condition, 11 in the no-homework condition, 12 in the self-monitoring plus self-evaluation condition, and 5 in the control therapy condition.

Again, the results can be summarized succinctly. Whereas there were overall therapy effects comparable to those obtained in the prior study, there were no significant differences among the conditions on any of the dependent variables.

This has several implications. First, once again, no effect was found for the addition of the self-reinforcement component of the program. Second, explicit behavioral homework assignments were not demonstrated to contribute significantly to the program. Third, doubling the length of the therapy program produced no difference from the prior study. Fourth, the active control group did as well as the other experimental therapy groups. It should be noted that whereas two therapists saw one group each in each of three self-control conditions, a third therapist with considerable training and experience in group therapy saw the control therapy group. Thus, the small numbers plus the confounding with possible therapist differences make conclusions regarding this group somewhat tenuous.

Comment

In some respects this series of studies raises more questions than it answers. Nevertheless, some general comments can be made. Above all, it appears clear that the self-control behavior therapy program can be effective in a high percentage of cases in ameliorating depression. The program can be administered economically (i.e., in a group format in 12 or fewer sessions), and there is some evidence that the effects are maintained up to a full year later. This effect has been replicated in four studies. Recently, an independent replication by Rothblum and associates (1979) has been reported.

This conclusion must be put in the larger context of the field of behavior therapy for depression generally (Rehm, 1981; Rehm & Kornblith, 1979). A number of therapy package programs have now been demonstrated to have some efficacy in the treatment of depression. In addition to the self-control program, this includes Beck's cognitive behavior therapy (Rush et al., 1977), McLean's behavioral depression program (McLean & Hakstian, 1979), Lewinsohn's behavior therapy modules (Zeiss et al., 1979), and perhaps Weissman's interpersonal therapy (Weissman et al., 1976). All of these programs are complex packages involving many elements, techniques, components, or modules. Their rationales and the theories behind them vary considerably. However, when the therapy operations involved are examined closely, there is considerable overlap. They have many general assumptions in common. To begin with, they are all highly structured. They are short-term didactic programs with defined sequences of steps. Second, they all have clearly communicated rationales. For the most part, the rationales present a view of depression in concrete causal language with clear implications for change. Regardless of theory, these rationales are utilitarian in providing an acceptable and functional understanding of the disorder to depressed patients. Third, they all provide mechanisms for change. That is, each outlines a clear-cut series of steps, and the therapist guides the patient along these steps in such a way that progress can be easily gauged. Fourth, all of these programs activate effort on the part of the patient. Uniformly, they are oriented toward the patient's day-to-day life, and there are clear assignments that instigate behavioral change in specific situations. This seems to be the case in our own research, with or without an implicit homework assignment. Fifth, regardless of the origin of the theory, all of these programs span both behavioral and cognitive therapy targets. That is, they explicitly attempt to modify the ways in which patients view their depressive behaviors, in addition to modifying the behavior per se.

Although there is overall evidence for the efficacy of behavior therapies for depression, and although commonalities among methods can be observed, it is equally clear that at this point we have little empirical evidence to pinpoint the essential ingredients of behavior therapy methods for depression. The studies described here are a first attempt to move in the direction of specifying the essential ingredients of one program, the self-control therapy program. Future research is needed to explore these questions in greater depth and perhaps to ask new questions. First, research should be directed at some of the factors of similarity noted earlier. More generally, there is a need to look at what have traditionally been called the nonspecific factors in psychotherapy as they relate to behavior therapies for depression. A second important direction for research may be the possibility of fitting specific techniques to specific patients. It may be that all of these package techniques are effective in that they contain elements that are relevant to the depressions of different patients. Thus the overall effect is to cover the broad range of problems presented, but the effective ingredients for various patients may be different. Our current research is turning in this latter direction. As a first approximation, we are beginning to differentiate those aspects of our program that focus on behavioral versus cognitive targets and to examine which variables predict responses to therapies differentially weighting these two sets of targets. It is clear that this and many other questions need to be addressed during future research. Models such as the self-control model should aid in directing this research.

Conclusion

In this chapter we have attempted to outline the uses of a self-control model of depression. The model is intended as a framework for considering depression as a multivariate phenomenon. Different facets of depression should be studied independently, but also in relation to one another. The model organizes this form of research strategy. It suggests a series of related deficits. Research on each of these deficits has been summarized, and some directions for future research have been suggested. A therapy program has been described that uses the model as an outline for correcting the same series of deficits. Outcome studies of the therapy program have attempted to evaluate the importance of procedures focused on specific deficits. The value of the model will depend on its utility as a framework for organizing research. It is intended as a somewhat loose framework that can be refined and developed as research findings accumulate.

The self-control model of depression is an attempt to study the phenomena of depression within a framework with wider applicability in psychology generally. The self-control model has been used for other problems and may have applicability as a model for other psychopathologic conditions. That is, other psychological disorders may consist of different patterns of self-control deficits. In recent years, psychopathologic research has been characterized by the development of limited models focusing on specific aspects of specific disorders. There is now a need to place these various models into their larger contexts.

Ultimately, psychological models must also be articulated with biological and social models. Diathesis-stress models of psychological disorders have become popular in recent years. The usual form of such models involves a biological diathesis that makes persons susceptible to certain classes of socioenvironmental stress. A more complete general model would be a diathesis-stress-coping model. Coping refers to the skills acquired during psychological development that enable persons to deal with stress with various degrees of effectiveness. A person with particularly effective skills might be able to handle stress without developing psychological disorder, despite fairly powerful stress or a high degree of biological vulnerability. Poor coping skills might make a person with some degree of biological vulnerability susceptible to even mild stress.

Depression fits well into such a model. It has fairly well established genetic and biochemical components that may act as a biological diathesis (Mendels, 1975). Depression is also clearly related to socioenvironmental stress (Brown & Harris, 1978). The self-control model is one way of looking at the skills that persons acquire in handling certain kinds of stress. It is hoped that in the future we shall see more interaction and integration among these perspectives.

REFERENCES

Abramson, L.Y., Garber, J., Edwards, N.B., & Seligman, M.E.P. Expectancy changes in depression and schizophrenia. *Journal of Abnormal Psychology*, 1978, *87*, 102-109.

Abramson, L.Y., Seligman, M.E.P., & Teasdale, J.D. Learned helplessness in humans: Critique and reformulation. *Journal of Abnormal Psychology*, 1978, *87*, 49-74.

Beck, A.T. *Depression: Causes and treatment.* Philadelphia: University of Pennsylvania Press, 1972.

Beck, A.T. The development of depression: A cognitive model. In R.M. Friedman & M.M. Katz (Eds.), *The psychology of depression: Contemporary theory and research.* New York: Wiley, 1974.

Brown, G.W., & Harris, T. *Social origins of depression: A study of psychiatric disorder in women.* New York: Macmillan, 1978.

Buchwald, A.M. Depressive mood and estimates of reinforcement frequency. *Journal of Abnormal Psychology,* 1977, *86,* 443-446.

Craighead, W.E., Hickey, K.S., & DeMonbreun, B.G. Distortion of perception and recall of neutral feedback in depression. *Cognitive Therapy and Research,* 1979, *3,* 291-298.

DeMonbreun, B.G., & Craighead, W.E. Distortion of perception and recall of positive and neutral feedback in depression. *Cognitive Therapy and Research,* 1977, *1,* 311-329.

DiMascio, A., Neu, C., Klerman, G.F., Weissman, M., Prusoff, B., & Rounsaville, B. *Manual for short term interpersonal psychotherapy (IPT) of depression.* Unpublished manuscript, New Haven-Boston Collaborative Depression Project, Yale University, January 1978.

Endicott, J., & Spitzer, R.L. A diagnostic interview: The Schedule for Affective Disorders and Schizophrenia. *Archives of General Psychiatry,* 1978, *35,* 837-844.

Endicott, J., Spitzer, R.L., Fleiss, J.L., & Cohen, J. The Global Assessment Scale: A procedure for measuring overall severity of psychiatric disturbance. *Archives of General Psychiatry,* 1976, *33,* 766-771.

Ferster, C.B. A functional analysis of depression. *American Psychologist,* 1973, *28,* 857-870.

Fry, P.S. Success, failure, and self-assessment ratings. *Journal of Consulting and Clinical Psychology,* 1976, *44,* 413-419.

Fuchs, C.Z., & Rehm, L.P. A self-control behavior therapy program for depression. *Journal of Consulting and Clinical Psychology,* 1977, *45,* 206-215.

Golin, S., & Terrell, F. Motivational and associative aspects of mild depression in skill and chance tasks. *Journal of Abnormal Psychology,* 1977, *86,* 389-401.

Gotlib, I.H. *Self-monitoring and self-reinforcement in clinically depressed psychiatric patients.* Presented at the convention of the Canadian Psychological Association, Quebec City, Canada, June 1979. (a)

Gotlib, I.H. *Self-control processes in depressed and nondepressed psychiatric patients: Self-evaluation.* Presented at the convention of the American Psychological Association, New York, September 1979. (b)

Grosscup, S.J., & Lewinsohn, P.M. Unpleasant and pleasant events, and mood. *Journal of Clinical Psychology,* 1980, *36,* 252-259.

Hamilton, M. A rating scale for depression. *Journal of Neurology, Neurosurgery and Psychiatry,* 1960, *23,* 56-61.

Kanfer, F.H. Self-monitoring: Methodological limitations and clinical applications. *Journal of Consulting and Clinical Psychology,* 1970, *35,* 148-152.

Kanfer, F.H. The maintenance of behavior by self-generated stimuli and reinforcement. In A. Jacobs & L.B. Sachs (Eds.), *The psychology of private events: Perspectives on covert response systems.* New York: Academic, 1971.

Kanfer, F.H., & Karoly, P. Self-control: A behavioristic excursion into the lion's den. *Behavior Therapy,* 1972, *2,* 398-416. (a)

Kanfer, F.H., & Karoly, P. Self-regulation and its clinical application: Some additional conceptualizations. In R.C. Johnson, P.R. Dokecki, & O.H. Mowrer (Eds.), *Socialization: Development of character and consciences.* New York: Holt, Rinehart & Winston, 1972. (b)

Kirschenbaum, D.S., & Karoly, P. When self-regulation fails: Tests of some preliminary hypotheses. *Journal of Consulting and Clinical Psychology*, 1977, *45*, 1116-1125.

Kornblith, S.J., Rehm, L.P., O'Hara, M., & Lamparski, D.M. *An evaluation of the contribution of self-reinforcement and behavioral assignments to the efficacy of a self-control therapy program for depression.* Presented at the New Mexico Conference on Behavior Therapy, New Mexico Highlands University, Las Vegas, N.M., September 1979.

Lazarus, A.A. Learning theory and the treatment of depression. *Behavior Research and Therapy*, 1968, *6*, 83-89.

Lazarus, A.A. Multimodal behavioral treatment of depression. *Behavior Therapy*, 1974, *5*, 549-554.

Levitt, E.E., & Lubin, B. *Depression: Concepts, controversies and some new facts.* New York: Springer, 1975.

Lewinsohn, P.M. A behavioral approach to depression. In R.M. Friedman & M.M. Katz (Eds.), *The psychology of depression: Contemporary theory and research.* New York: Wiley, 1974.

Lewinsohn, P.M., Biglan, A., & Zeiss, A.M. Behavioral treatment of depression. In P.O. Davidson (Ed.), *The behavioral management of anxiety, depression and pain*, New York: Brunner/Mazel, 1976.

Lewinsohn, P.M., & Graf, M. Pleasant activities and depression. *Journal of Consulting and Clinical Psychology*, 1973, *41*, 261-268.

Lewinsohn, P.M., & Libet, J. Pleasant events, activity schedules and depressions. *Journal of Abnormal Psychology*, 1972, *79*, 291-295.

Lewinsohn, P.M., Weinstein, M.S., & Alper, T. A behavioral approach to the group treatment of depressed persons: Methodological contributions. *Journal of Clinical Psychology*, 1970, *26*, 525-532.

Loeb, A., Beck, A.T., Diggory, J.C., & Tuthill, R. Expectancy, level of aspiration, performance and self-evaluation in depression. In *Proceedings, 75 Annual Convention, APA*, 1967.

MacPhillamy, D., & Lewinsohn, P.M. *The Pleasant Events Schedule.* Unpublished manuscript, Department of Psychology, University of Oregon, 1971.

McLean, P. Therapeutic decision-making in the behavioral treatment of depression. In P.O. Davidson (Ed.), *The behavioral management of anxiety, depression and pain.* New York: Brunner/Mazel, 1976.

McLean, P.D., & Hakstian, A.R. Clinical depression: Comparative efficacy of outpatient treatments. *Journal of Consulting and Clinical Psychology*, 1979, *47*, 818-836.

Mendels, J. *The Psychobiology of depression.* New York: Spectrum, 1975.

Miller, E., & Lewis, P. Recognition memory in elderly patients with depression and dementia: A signal detection analysis. *Journal of Abnormal Psychology*, 1977, *86*, 84-86.

Nelson, R.E., & Craighead, W.E. Selective recall of positive and negative feedback, self-control behaviors, and depression. *Journal of Abnormal Psychology*, 1977, *86*, 379-388.

O'Hara, M.W., & Rehm, L.P. Choice of immediate versus delayed reinforcement and depression. Unpublished manuscript, Department of Psychology, University of Pittsburgh 1979. (a)

O'Hara, M.W., & Rehm, L.P. Self-monitoring, activity levels and mood in the development and maintenance of depression. *Journal of Abnormal Psychology*, 1979, *88*, 450-453. (b)

Raskin, A., Schulterbrandt, J., Reatig, N., & Rice, C.E. Factors of psychopathology in interview, ward behavior, and self-report ratings of hospitalized depressive. *Journal of Consulting Psychology*, 1967, *31*, 270-278.

Rehm, L.P. Assessment of depression. In M. Hersen & A.S. Bellack (Eds.), *Behavioral assessment: A practical handbook*. Oxford: Pergamon, 1976.

Rehm, L.P. A self-control model of depression. *Behavior Therapy*, 1977, *8*, 787-804.

Rehm, L.P. *The assessment of depression in therapy outcome research: A review of instruments and recommendations for an assessment battery*. Report to the Psychotherapy and Behavioral Intervention Section, Clinical Research Branch, National Institute of Mental Health, November 1978. (a)

Rehm, L.P. Mood, pleasant events and unpleasant events: Two pilot studies. *Journal of Consulting and Clinical Psychology*, 1978, *46*, 854-859. (b)

Rehm, L.P. *Research recommendations for the behavioral treatment of depression*. Report to the Psychotherapy and Behavioral Intervention Section, Clinical Research Branch, National Institute of Mental Health, September 1979.

Rehm, L.P. (Ed.). *Behavior therapy for depression: Present status and future directions*. New York: Academic, 1981.

Rehm, L.P., Fuchs, C.Z., Roth, D.M., Kornblith, S.J., & Romano, J.M. A comparison of self-control and assertion training treatments of depression. *Behavior Therapy*, 1979, *10*, 429-442.

Rehm, L.P., & Kornblith, S.J. Behavior therapy for depression: A review of recent developments. In M. Hersen, R.M. Eisler, & P.M. Miller (Eds.), *Progress in behavior modification, Vol. 7*. New York: Academic, 1979.

Rehm, L.P., Kornblith, S.J., O'Hara, M.W., Lamparski, D.M., Romano, J.M., & Volkin, J. *An evaluation of major elements in a self-control therapy program for depression*. Behavior Modification, in press.

Rehm, L.P., & O'Hara, M.W. The role of attribution theory in understanding depression. In I.H. Frieze, D. Bar-Tal, & J.S. Carroll (Eds.), *Attribution theory: Applications to social problems*. San Francisco: Jossey-Bass, 1980.

Rehm, L.P., & Plakosh, P. Preference for immediate reinforcement in depression. *Journal of Behavior Therapy and Experimental Psychiatry*, 1975, *6*, 101-103.

Romano, J.M., & Rehm, L.P. Self-control treatment of depression: One-year follow-up. In A.T. Beck (Chair), *Factors affecting the outcome and maintenance of cognitive therapy*. Symposium presented at the meeting of the Eastern Psychological Association, Philadelphia, April 18-21, 1979.

Roth, D., & Rehm, L.P. Relationships between self-monitoring processes, memory and depression. *Cognitive Therapy and Research*, 1980, *4*, 149-158.

Roth, D., Rehm, L.P., & Rozensky, R.A. Self-reward, self-punishment and depression. *Psychological Reports*, 1980, *47*, 3-7.

Rothblum, E., Green, L., & Collins, R.L. A comparison of self-control and therapist control in the treatment of depression. Presented before the Eastern Psychological Association, Philadelphia, April 20, 1979.

Rotter, J.B. Generalized expectancies for internal versus external control of reinforcements. *Psychological Monographs*, 1966, *80*, 1-28.

Rozensky, R.A., Rehm, L.P., Pry, G., & Roth, D. Depression and self-reinforcement behavior in hospital patients. *Journal of Behavior Therapy and Experimental Psychiatry*, 1977, *8*, 35-38.

Rush, A.J., Beck, A.T., Kovacs, M., & Hollon, S. Comparative efficacy of cognitive therapy and pharmacotherapy in the treatment of depressed outpatients. *Cognitive Therapy and Research*, 1977, *1*, 17-38.

Sacco, W.P. *Self-reinforcement by depressives under public and private measurement conditions.* Presented before the Eastern Psychological Association, Philadelphia, April 20, 1979.

Seligman, M.E.P. Depression and learned helplessness. In R.J. Friedman & M.M. Katz (Eds.), *The psychology of depression: Contemporary theory and research.* New York: Wiley, 1974.

Seligman, M.E.P. *Helplessness: On depression, development and death.* San Francisco: W.H. Freeman, 1975.

Seligman, M.E.P., Abramson, L.Y., Semmel, A., & von Baeyer, C. Depressive attributional style. *Journal of Abnormal Psychology*, 1979, *88*, 242-247.

Shaw, B.F. Comparison of cognitive therapy and behavior therapy in the treatment of depression. *Journal of Consulting and Clinical Psychology*, 1977, *45*, 543-551.

Spitzer, R.L., Endicott, J., & Robins, E. Research Diagnostic Criteria: Rationale and reliability. *Archives of General Psychiatry*, 1978, *36*, 773-782.

Taylor, F.G., & Marshall, W.L. Experimental analysis of a cognitive-behavioral therapy for depression. *Cognitive Therapy and Research*, 1977, *1*, 59-72.

Warren, N.T. Self-esteem and sources of cognitive bias in the evaluation of past performance. *Journal of Consulting and Clinical Psychology*, 1976, *44*, 966-975.

Weiner, B., Frieze, I., Kukla, A., Reed, L., Rest, S., & Rosenbaum, R.M. *Perceiving the causes of success and failure.* Morristown, N.J. General Learning Press, 1971.

Weintraub, M., Segal, R.M., & Beck, A.T. An investigation of cognition and affect in the depressive experiences of normal men. *Journal of Consulting and Clinical Psychology*, 1974, *42*, 911.

Weissman, M.M., Klerman, G.L., Prusoff, B.A., Hanson, B., & Paykel, E.S. The efficacy of psychotherapy in depression: Symptom remission and response to treatment. In R.L. Spitzer & D.F. Klein (Eds.), *Evaluation of psychological therapies.* Baltimore: Johns Hopkins, 1976.

Wener, A.E., & Rehm, L.P. Depressive affect: A test of behavioral hypotheses. *Journal of Abnormal Psychology*, 1975, *84*, 221-227.

Wolpe, J. Neurotic depression: An experimental analog, clinical syndromes, and treatment. *American Journal of Psychotherapy*, 1971, *25*, 326-368.

Wolpe, J., & Lazarus, A.A. *Behavior therapy techniques.* Oxford: Pergamon, 1967.

Zeiss, A.M., Lewinsohn, P.M., & Munoz, R.F. Nonspecific improvement effects in depression using interpersonal, cognitive, and pleasant events focused treatments. *Journal of Consulting and Clinical Psychology,* 1979, *47,* 427–439.

Cognitive Therapy for Depression

Ronald E. Coleman
Aaron T. Beck

Depression remains ubiquitous, accounting for perhaps 75% of all psychiatric hospitalizations (Secunda et al., Note 3). Despite much initial optimism, psychobiological treatments for depression have not alleviated the problem. According to research reviews, 35% to 40% of patients do not respond to initial therapeutic trials of antidepressants (Beck, 1973). Furthermore, many of these patients refuse medication. With medication alone, depressed patients may fail to learn effective psychological methods of coping with predisposing and precipitating factors.

Our experience has been that the core of depressive illness, hopelessness and negative expectancy, can be treated effectively with a brief course of cognitive behavioral therapy. The cognitive therapy approach presented here is based on 20 years of research into the causes and treatment of depression. Evaluations of this therapy have begun to suggest that it has more immediate and longer-lasting effectiveness than antidepressant treatments (Rush et al., 1977).

In this chapter we shall present an overview of a cognitive model of depression and the key principles of its associated treatment program. The chapter will provide details of various cognitive therapy procedures and techniques.

A Cognitive Model of Depression

The formulation central to cognitive therapy is that a person's constructs and evaluations of events are basic to depression, as they are to all emotions. This cognitive model of depression states that the depressed person develops, probably in childhood, a negative view of the self, the world, and the future that affects subsequent judgments about the person's interactions with the world. This cognitive triad of negative conceptions is a determinant of associated affective, behavioral, and motivational symptoms of depression. This negative cognitive triad consists in a developing constellation of three categories of self-conceptual ideas ranging from the general ("I am no good." "The world is unjust." "Things won't work out.") to increasingly more specific attitudes and beliefs about the self ("I can't speak coherently." My memory is not what it used to be.").

Naturalistic, clinical, and experimental studies have provided substantial empirical support for this model of depression (Beck & Rush, 1977). The clinician practicing cognitive therapy will find it useful (1) in understanding the personal world view of the depressed person and (2) in organizing observations regarding the depressed person's idiosyncratic thinking and logic.

The arousal of these idiosyncratic depressive self-judgments is associated with systematic errors in the thinking of the depressed person. These errors include the following: overgeneralization, the drawing of negative conclusions from a single incident; magnification and minimization, leading to gross errors in evaluation; personalization, undue inference that external events pertain to oneself; selective abstraction, focusing on a detail of an event taken out of context; arbitrary inference, the process of drawing a conclusion without evidence to support that conclusion (Beck, 1976).

It seems useful to assume that the constellation of thoughts incorporated into the cognitive triad remains relatively dormant until a person becomes depressed. Depressed persons (depressives) are capable of logical self-evaluation when not in a depressed mood or when only mildly depressed. When depression does occur, after some stressful event or series of stressful events, the long-dormant concepts associated with the cognitive triad make their appearance. The stress that precipitates the experience of loss to the self usually is associated by the depressive with an earlier similar event (e.g., loss of a loved one at any early age). As depression develops and increases, the negative idiosyncratic thinking increasingly replaces objective thinking.

The constellation of long-dormant thoughts seems to function at a primitive illogical level. The beliefs and attitudes that make up this system (e.g., "I am inferior." "I am weak.") seem to be highly idiosyncratic crude concepts whose private meanings have little relationship to objective reality. Despite the lack of authenticity of these concepts, depressives have little opportunity to evaluate the concepts objectively prior to their depression because of the triad's unavailability. As depression increases in severity, depressives seem to accept their negative self-statements to the extent that they are unwilling or unable to evaluate themselves realistically.

Cognitive Therapy: An Overview

Cognitive therapy for depression is consistent with this cognitive model of depression; see the work of Coleman (1975) for an empirical evaluation of this relationship. First, patients are instructed in the specifics of the cognitive model. They are taught to recognize the association between their dysfunctional thoughts and their affect and behavior. Therapy is presented as a collaborative venture between patient and therapist that permits them to determine whether or not the patient's personal thoughts, attitudes, and beliefs create depression. Next, cognitive therapy techniques are presented in order to train the patient to identify, evaluate, and correct the faulty thinking that distorts reality. Thus, patients become full participants in understanding the treatment rationale and procedure.

Behavioral Treatments

Behavioral tasks frequently are used at the beginning of therapy, especially for severely depressed patients, to mobilize patients to activity. This assists patients to break out of the downward spiral of inactivity and self-deprecation. Rather than try to argue patients out of their belief in their own weakness and ineffectualness, a nearly impossible task, one should use simple behavioral tasks to help demonstrate the difference between their beliefs and their actual ability. These tasks are assigned as experiments, so that whatever the outcome, patients' responses and conclusions are grist for discussion between patients and therapist. It is often the case that patients are able to accomplish the assigned tasks and even surpass what they assumed was possible. This aids the therapist in pointing out the role that patients' expectations of failure and discouragement play in undermining their ability to mobilize themselves. Patients are then encouraged to examine, with the therapist, other areas in which negative expectancy may distort reality.

Unlike behavior therapy approaches, behavioral treatment by cognitive therapy emphasizes evaluation of negative sets that can undermine therapy, despite patients' behavioral successes. We believe that the strict behavior therapy approach of providing tasks solely as an opportunity to experience success leaves the therapist on dangerous ground. All too often, despite a positive outcome, patients reinterpret their successes as failures within their negative frame of reference, or they may discount their successes sufficiently to make them meaningless. By approaching behavioral tasks from a cognitive position, the therapist points up the patient's negative expectancy as the central issue for examination. An example cited by Beck, Rush, Shaw, and Emery (1979) illustrates the ease with which a depressed person can misinterpret a success experience within a consistently pessimistic world view: A husband was interested in reducing his wife's depression. The husband scheduled a tennis lesson for his wife, an activity they previously had enjoyed. Although she was a "different person" during the lesson, in her husband's eyes, the woman saw it differently. She believed that her skills had deteriorated to the point that she would be able to function only during lessons. A cognitive therapist might likewise have assigned a tennis lesson as a behavioral task early in cognitive therapy if this woman had been a patient in cognitive therapy, but the therapist would have taken care to determine and discuss the woman's negative beliefs about her tennis ability prior to the lesson. This would have provided an opportunity to compare her opinion with an objective assessment of her actual performance during the lesson. The behavioral task would have been carefully presented to the woman as an experiment to determine whether or not her evaluation of herself as tennis player was realistic. This would have placed the act of evaluation firmly on the woman, not the therapist. Most important, the *context* of the *experiment* would have been highlighted in the *comparison* between the woman's belief about her inability to perform versus her experience of self in that situation.

As mentioned earlier, typical targets for behavioral tasks are severely depressed patients and their passivity, avoidance, lack of gratification, and inability to express appropriate emotions. These tasks typically are employed early in therapy to provide concrete examples, rather than abstract examples, of the contrast between patients' thoughts and their experiences. This assists the therapist in breaking the vicious cycle of inactivity and self-denigration.

Later in therapy, behavioral tasks are assigned to test specific assumptions against experience. For instance, a patient who had been married for 18 years and separated for 2 years refused to go out alone and was reluctant to go out with other women if not in the company of a man. Her self-restriction added to her loneliness and sadness, but she believed that if she were seen out alone she would be thought of as inadequate intellectually and in terms of attractiveness. She agreed to test this assumption by attempting a series of tasks in which she was to count the numbers of women alone and in groups at restaurants and the theater. She reported seeing various numbers of women either dining alone or attending the theater, depending on the time of day.

She saw additional numbers of two or more women out socializing. In addition, she made the optimistic and humorous observation that she rated many of the women she saw with men as being less attractive than herself. She reassessed her point of view on the basis that her appraisal of other women who were out alone was not disparaging. She was also aided by her observation that sometimes when she was out alone to test the assumption, she unexpectedly felt satisfaction and enjoyment rather than loneliness and sadness. This challenged her assumption that she ought to feel inadequate if she were out socially without a man. Specific behavioral techniques employed in cognitive therapy will be described in a later section.

Identifying Automatic Thoughts

From the first session, patients are taught to recognize the association between dysfunctional thoughts and their effect and behavior. Once they have become accomplished at this, they can actively take over the task of observing their dysfunctional thinking. We use a variety of methods to elicit an accurate account of a patient's cognitions. Prior to the initial session, the process of cognitive therapy and the importance of automatic thoughts are explained in a brochure given to patients (Beck & Greenberg, Note 1). Patients are told that automatic thoughts are cognitive events that can take the form of thought processes or visual images. It is explained to the patients that these cognitive events may not come to our attention unless we focus on them.

Some characteristics of automatic thoughts are as follows: They are automatic; they just seem to happen; they are based on a low opinion of oneself; they are unreasonable or even inaccurate, but they seem plausible at the time, and the more one believes them, the more one will fail (Beck & Greenberg, Note 1). To further illustrate the concept to the patients, examples are provided: "Suppose you were at home alone one night and heard a noise in another room, such as a door shutting. You might think it was a burglar. The emotion you would feel would be fright or panic. But if you were expecting your husband, the emotion might be pleasure. It's the thought ('It's a burglar,' 'It's my husband.') that triggers the feeling." Patients can be asked to recall particularly happy or unhappy times from the recent past to elicit the automatic thoughts associated with these events. Patients can be asked about recent events to demonstrate further the presence of cognitions that are relevant to them. For instance, patients frequently are asked about their thoughts prior to the first therapy appointment. Most patients report thoughts about the therapist, the treatment, and concerns about receiving help.

Once patients understand the concept and are providing examples of their own, they are asked to detect the presence of automatic thoughts in their daily lives. The specific assignment may depend on the targeted problem for that patient. Patients are taught that one of the most effective ways to catch automatic thoughts is to notice when an increase in negative (or positive) feelings occurs. Patients are instructed to note the event and the associated feelings and to try to become aware of what is not so apparent: the thought, image, or memory. Following observation and reflection on the latter, the automatic thought will reveal to the patient its relationship to the patient's feelings. Changes in affect throughout the day are excellent markers or cues as to when to look for automatic thoughts. Frequently, other methods can also be used. Patients may be instructed to identify periods or life situations that are troublesome and to note automatic thoughts at those times. Another tactic has patients search for automatic thoughts with a common theme, such as rejection or the need to be liked.

Note that it is patients' verbal reports of their perceptions, conceptualizations, and attitudes that are the core data of cognitive therapy. The therapist accepts these retrospective psychological data at face value, unlike psychoanalytic and behavior therapists, who tend to distrust these processes. It is the personal or private meaning of an event that is the crucial variable for cognitive therapy, rather than purely objective descriptions of events. It is personal meaning that determines emotional response and emotional disorder.

It is acknowledged that personal meanings frequently are unrealistic, because patients frequently avoid checking or lack the opportunity to check their authenticity (e.g., "I am worthless." "Nobody likes me."). Although the therapist may assume that such patients are engaging in (1) distortion of perception, (2) distortion of conceptualization, or (3) old biased beliefs, the therapist must avoid the position of arbiter of the correctness of these cognitions. The therapist asks the patient to judge the correctness of the preceding assumption, while gathering additional facts with which to make the decision. As patients actively reevaluate their dysfunctional thinking, they learn *experientially* that perceptions of reality are not reality itself, that interpretation of reality is based on cognitive processes that are fallible, and the beliefs are hypotheses that are themselves not factual (Beck & Bedrosian, 1980).

Cognitive Strategies

As soon as patients begin to *identify* their automatic thoughts, they begin to feel less overwhelmed, becoming more familiar with these thoughts through the process of successive observations. As they begin to recognize automatic thoughts as psychological phenomena, rather than equating them with reality, they can achieve some *"distance"* from these thoughts. This allows for more thorough comparison of these thoughts with reality. The therapist aids in the reevaluation of automatic thoughts by directing patients to examine the accuracy of perceptions, logic, and conclusions. This is frequently achieved through careful and *specific* questioning by the therapist. For instance, a young lawyer was worried about his ability to function in his new job at a highly respected law firm. He was worried that he was not handling day-to-day procedure well. The therapist reviewed the lawyer's daily activities in detail. Questioning confirmed that he was doing as well as other new members of the firm; he had received feedback from others to the effect that he was doing what was expected. His concern over competency was reduced. A new area of concern uncovered by the therapist's questions was that he was returning to his superior to ask questions too frequently. This point needed further empirical evaluation, but the lawyer's initial concern was not supported by the facts.

Patients are taught to be active participants in evaluating their automatic thoughts in daily activities, with supervision provided during therapy sessions. The various additional methods of logical analysis include the following: creating experiments to evaluate a belief, conclusion, or theme objectively by collection of empirical data or by additional reality testing; alternative therapy, the consideration of alternative conceptions of events; use of the triple-column technique, a written homework procedure for evaluating automatic thoughts. These will be described in more detail in later sections.

Once patients reach the stage at which their initial symptoms are diminished, one can begin to question the basic assumptions, rules, and formulas that help maintain their depression and also predispose them to depression. For instance, the lawyer's concern that he was not competent was accompanied by other concerns involving charm, wit, intelligence, and humor. These concerns gave rise spontaneously to an underlying belief ("People will not like me if I am not likable and acceptable."). The lawyer, with aid from his therapist, began to modify this belief ("I can satisfy myself, rather than having to satisfy others.").

The Therapist in Cognitive Therapy

Cognitive therapy consists in a number of specific treatment techniques applied in a planned and orderly fashion. The therapy is brief and goal-oriented within each session. The therapist must be active, sometimes directive, and accurate about selecting appropriate target symptoms that can be translated into problem-solving tasks for the patient. Although the agenda for each session may be full, the therapist must be flexible enough to deal with a pressing issue brought up by the patient.

We believe, therefore, that applying cognitive therapy requires more than applying a hodgepodge of techniques; our therapist must have good clinical skills. Concerned as we are with the manner in which the technique is presented and the patient is accepted, we emphasize in our training of therapists those facilitative conditions, empathy, warmth, and genuineness, that we consider necessary but not sufficient conditions for successful therapy. In training therapists for cognitive therapy, we observe, frequently enough, neophyte therapists buying into the pessimism of their depressed patients. Visitors to the Center for Cognitive Therapy have made the observation more than once that the therapists there remain optimistic, a crucial factor for a therapist in the face of depressed patients' negative sets.

Logical Empiricism and Therapeutic Collaboration

A powerful method of evaluating the validity of automatic thoughts or underlying assumptions is to view them as hypotheses. Then empirical evaluations or experiments can be set up to test the hypotheses. The patient and therapist together pick appropriate hypotheses to be tested and mutually decide on a manner of obtaining additional feedback. For example, a patient who was depressed and exhausted from nursing her sick husband believed that it was wrong to take time for her own interests. She predicted dire consequences if she should do so. Because pragmatic analysis suggested that the consequences might be minimal, she was willing to test the belief as a hypothesis. An experiment to spend an evening at the movies with a neighbor resulted in a positive response from the husband and a sense of relief on the part of the wife. Note that the therapist, rather than using persuasion or argument, collaboratively created a situation in which the patient made the evaluation of her own cognition.

From the start, the therapeutic relationship is viewed as a team effort or collaboration. The job of the therapist is to guide the patient to collect the appropriate data, to aid the elicitation of introspection, to identify underlying themes, and to facilitate objective evaluation of these data. The patient's unique contribution involves thoughts, feelings, and wishes. Because the therapy is viewed as an experimental venture for patients, so that they can learn how to correct errors in thinking, their active participation is crucial to success. Feedback from patients is sought frequently each session regarding the appropriateness of between-session assignments, responses to evaluations of cognitions, etc.

The cognitive therapist must avoid an adversary role that might lead to disputing the patient's conclusion (e.g., "I am stupid." "I am worthless."). Although these negative conclusions may have little *external validity*, they have powerful *internal* consistency. The patient's personal paradigm is therefore acknowledged, but not directly attacked.

Evidence to disprove the patient's negative conclusions can begin to be marshaled only when the patient spontaneously begins to doubt their degree of certainty in the patient's own personal negative paradigm.

Typical Course of Treatment

The moderately to severely depressed patient, in our experience, does best with a therapy regimen of twice-weekly sessions, initially. For instance, in a study by Rush and associates (1977), patients received therapy twice a week for 4 weeks, on the average, and thereafter once a week for an average total of 15 therapy sessions over 11 weeks. The treatment protocol in that study called for up to 20 sessions of therapy over 10 to 12 weeks. The length of treatment and the degree of tapering off of therapy are, of course, individual matters to be determined by each patient-therapist team.

Structure of Therapeutic Sessions

Therapy is intended to achieve (1) rapid relief of symptoms and (2) prevention of their recurrence. The patient accomplishes this by learning to identify and modify faulty cognitions. The therapist explains these goals and the cognitive paradigm of depression in the first session. This is done didactically, with brochures explaining the therapy (Beck & Greenberg, Note 1) being sent to the patient prior to the initial session, as well as by providing examples of how cognitions are related to feelings and behavior in the patient's current situation.

In the first session the therapist must assess the patient's symptoms and determine which are most important and will require the most work. The therapist redefines these symptoms within the cognitive paradigm in ways that will allow them to be approached as concrete problems to be solved. Usually, in initial sessions, these are behavioral and motivational issues. Initial complaints are also discussed, and relationships are redefined, if necessary. For instance, the following complaint needs to be examined: "I'm depressed because my fiancée broke our engagement and I can't be happy without her." The therapist may redefine this in such a way that it becomes amenable to problem-solving techniques. The therapist may suggest that the patient may wish to learn to feel happy whether or not his fiancée is present. This point may be a hypothesis that the patient would be willing to test out as a crucial part of his therapy.

After the initial sessions, a shift is made from concrete behavioral and motivational issues to the content and pattern of the patient's thoughts. This involves the recognition, recording, and evaluation of dysfunctional cognitions. During the middle and late stages of therapy, more appropriate responses are determined and substituted for errors in logic, in dysfunctional thinking, and in basic assumptions that are depressogenic. Finally, supraordinate themes that are underlying dysfunctional formulas for the patient's life are ascertained, evaluated, and modified.

From the first session the therapist begins to formulate a therapy plan that is then outlined for the patient. It is reflected in each session thereafter in the form of an agenda in which targeted goals are sought in a form consistent with the stage of therapy and the progress of the patient. During each session, both patient and therapist propose topics; these may include a brief resumé of the patient's experience since the last session, feedback on homework assignments between sessions, topics on which the therapist thinks more work is needed, and topics the patient would like to talk about. The therapist must remain alert to the patient's possible "hidden agenda" and to current problems the patient says are important.

Homework

The use of homework assignments between sessions is an integral part of cognitive therapy. It is important to determine these assignments collaboratively, to explain the rationale to the patient, and to assess whether or not the patient is likely to complete the task. The therapist depends on the homework for observations and evaluations of automatic thoughts, and frequently the session agenda and strategy are based on the written record of activities and the log of dysfunctional cognitions provided by the patient. A real-life setting often is the most appropriate place to evaluate a hunch or hypothesis about the patient's dysfunctional thoughts.

Deuterolearning

Patients are encouraged to take an active role in their therapy. They are encouraged to learn to identify seemingly automatic thoughts and images, to recognize logical errors and idiosyncratic conclusion making, to test assumptions and beliefs, and to modify these beliefs. Patients are thus encouraged to learn how to think for themselves. Beck (1976, p. 230) saw the problem as one of the patient learning how "to learn from his personal experience how to solve problems." This process of learning how to learn has been labeled deuterolearning by Bateson (1942).

Specific Behavioral Techniques

The rationale and the appropriate times to use behavioral treatments were discussed in a previous section. Following are more detailed accounts of several behavioral techniques used by cognitive therapists.

Activity Scheduling

Activity scheduling is an hour-by-hour planning for each day by therapist and patient. Both depressed patients and their families tend to believe that these patients can accomplish little. Accomplishment of some of the selected activities is important in demonstrating to patients that they have control of their time as well as self-mastery. Activity scheduling provides rich feedback for patients and therapist in regard to automatic cognitions and the manner in which patients view their functioning in various activities. For instance, as part of her daily activities, a patient was asked to go shopping. Because she had formerly shopped for a month's supplies, her reaction to the request to shop for a day's supply of groceries was negative. The therapist was able to deal with this by providing the rationale that comparing this performance with her previous best performance negated the value of accomplishing one day's shopping.

As patients go through the day, they record each activity actually accomplished. Initially, patients are reassured that the purpose of the task is to *observe*, rather than *evaluate*, their performances of these activities. No emphasis is placed on failure to accomplish some tasks. We also expect patients to be flexible in following a plan, rather than viewing the schedule as something that must be strictly followed.

Mastery and Pleasure Techniques

Ratings of *mastery* (the sense of accomplishment) and pleasure (pleasant feelings associated with an activity) are given for each activity. The weekly ratings will provide the therapist information about the patient's week. Accounts of activities and their ratings provide data with which the therapist can counter negative statements ("I can't do anything." "Nothing makes me feel better."). Frequently, certain activities can be shown to relieve dysphoric feelings. Patients will notice that their depressions fluctuate with their levels of activity and the degree of pleasure a task provides. Becoming sensitized to events that provide even slight increases in pleasure may aid patients' recall of pleasurable sensations and affect.

The mastery and pleasure ratings also provide data that will enable the therapist to identify and work to modify cognitive distortions. Consider the following ratings for a severely depressed 38-year-old executive (Beck et al., 1979). Ratings for mastery (M) and pleasure (P) are on a scale of 0 to 5 points.

Saturday		M	P
8–9 A.M.	Awoke, dressed, breakfast	1	1
9–12 noon	Wallpaper kitchen	0	0
12–1 P.M.	Lunch	0	0
1–3 P.M.	Watched TV	0	0

Note that whereas dressing and breakfast provided some pleasure, wallpapering a friend's kitchen (the patient did most of the work) provided none. How did the patient manage to entirely discount this accomplishment? The patient reported that several of the many flowers in the pattern failed, by a fraction of an inch, to line up. This selective abstraction of a real but minor flaw led to a useful discussion of the patient's perfectionism. After the patient was led to assess the job from an objective position ("What would you say if someone else wallpapered your kitchen in that way?"), he had a different view of the facts of the situation.

Graded Task Assignment

A series of tasks, the graded task assignment, can be used to break a goal-directed activity into smaller tasks. This assists the patient in the completion of the overall goal. The graded task assignment can be agreed on by patient and therapist when a problem arises relating to a goal the patient feels incapable of attaining. Then the means to the goal can be examined to create a stepwise assignment of tasks ranging from the simple to the complex, ending in attainment of the goal. The opportunity to immediately observe success in achieving each subsidary objective provides continual feedback regarding the patient's self-mastery. Along the way, the patient's doubts and minimization of personal efforts can be noted. This can be compared with a realistic evaluation of the patient's performance. As the goal is achieved, the therapist can emphasize that the attainment of the goal was as the result of the patient's own operations. The patient can be encouraged to learn the process of grading tasks while attempting more complex goals.

Presenting Behavioral Tasks

It is important that patients understand the rationale for their assigned behavioral tasks. Whatever the initial behavioral task objective, it is the therapist's major responsibility to determine that patients evaluate their performances within the context of the objective. Depressed patients have a facility for reinterpreting the facts of experiments *post hoc* from a perspective more consistent with their pessimistic world view. Frequently, after successfully completing tasks, patients will make statements implying that they did not do well enough. The counter of such notions is what makes behavioral techniques useful in changing patients' dysfunctional attitudes regarding their inactivity and lack of motivation, as well as in providing crucial feelings of gratification regarding self-mastery.

Specific Cognitive Techniques

Patients are presented with the principles of cognitive therapy and from the beginning of therapy are asked to consider and elucidate their automatic thoughts and the meanings of the events in their lives. Whether or not this is the initial focus for patients depends on their activity levels, their motivation, and their ability to independently focus on their abstract psychological processes with some objectivity. Once patients are able to engage in goal-directed activities, the therapist can use specific cognitive techniques to concentrate on those events that maintain the depression: patients' cognitions. Use of these techniques avoids the problems that can arise when the therapist confronts patients with the therapist's interpretations and judgments or with attacks on patient's thinking. As mentioned in a previous section, patients are socialized into cognitive therapy by being trained to understand the importance of detecting automatic thoughts. This is done through the use of information brochures (Beck & Greenberg, Note 1), as well as didactically and by providing examples of how thoughts are related to feelings and behavior.

Triple-Column Technique

The triple-column technique is a method that involves the recording of automatic thoughts. Patients are provided with duplicating recording forms so that they can retain one copy and give the other to the therapist for discussion during sessions. Patients record each event associated with an automatic thought (whether it be an external event, memory, or daydream) in the first column. They then make note of the associated emotion in the second column and write down the intervening thought or image in the third column. They are instructed to write each thought with as much accuracy and detail as possible. Once patients are adept at this, the therapist can profitably modify automatic thoughts by suggesting more rational responses. Once this is possible, patients are encouraged to record rational responses in the fourth column.

Patients are expected to supply rational responses situationally only as a formal goal of therapy. Initially, rational responses are elucidated within sessions; then, if possible, patients can supply them some time after the events occur. During much of therapy it is the therapist's responsibility to help patients derive reasonable responses to negative cognitions. Whole sessions may be devoted to this endeavor. Rather than suggesting to patients rational alternative responses, as in rational-emotive therapy, the therapist encourages patients in logical analysis of their interpretations of events. This can be done by asking patients to review logical errors, determine empirically whether or not a thought corresponds to fact, and evaluate pragmatically the consequences of holding a belief.

Additional columns are provided so that patients can note the strength of an original emotional response and then rate the strength of the emotional response elicited subsequent to the more rational response. Over time, the provision of rational responses will lead to an increase in positive mood. Other columns are provided for ratings of the strength of belief in the original dysfunctional thought and the strength of belief in the rational response. These records can be reviewed later to demonstrate the effects of patients' efforts. After varying amounts of practice in supplying more rational responses, patients will be able (first with effort, then automatically) to provide themselves rational thoughts as events occur.

Alternative Therapy

Once patients can observe their dysfunctional thinking, they can attain some "distance" from their cognitions. They become more open to alternative responses or conclusions as opposed to their former automatic thoughts that were detrimental to the situation. The search for alternatives involves the process of switching from catastrophic automatic thinking to interpretations of events that allow for effective problem solving. The process of providing alternatives calls for patients to question and reevaluate the reality of their interpretations of situations and search for possible options. For instance, a graduate student who received a grade of C on an essay believed that her English teacher thought that she was a "reject." This proved to the student that she couldn't make it in school. The search for alternative conclusions included several possibilities ("The professor has a bias against females." "The grade was no different than those of other students." "The professor provided the comments to help with future essays because he believes that I have ability."). It became clear that more information was needed. A telephone call to the professor elicited the information that the average grade was C and that the professor found the essay's style "wanting" but the content "promising." He requested a meeting with the patient for further discussion. Note that in this illustration the use of alternative construction led to the development of testable hypotheses and additional reality testing. Also note that appropriate reality testing resulted in the patient facing her deficits realistically and beginning a problem-solving approach to those deficits, rather than only reviewing assets, which would encourage unrealistic positive thinking.

Reattribution Techniques

Depressed patients are particularly prone to self-blame. They unrealistically assign blame or responsibility for negative consequences to themselves. Reattribution is the technique of applying the rules of logic to the facts in order to make a more just assignment of responsibility. By accurate assessment of situations, patients can become better able to cope with those situations. In addition to reviewing the facts of situations to "deresponsibilize" patients, the therapist can demonstrate the different criteria patients use to assign responsibility to their own behavior as opposed to the behavior of others. The therapist can challenge patients' beliefs that they are 100% responsible for negative consequences.

The Special Problem of Suicide

Many depressed patients we have counseled also have been subject to suicidal ideation. We have found that if patients have seriously considered suicide, it is best to talk with them about the problem. Serious exploration of suicidal intent with the patient, rather than increasing the suicidal risk, as some professionals believe this process might, can lead the patient to view the situation with increased objectivity and can elicit information useful for therapeutic intervention. The fact that the therapist understands and is willing to assist with the problem can of itself provide some relief for the patient.

The assessment of suicide is crucial. The seriousness of the intent must be examined, taking into account such factors as the method contemplated, the patient's access to the means, the availability of others in the patient's environment, and the patient's control over the ideation.

The therapist should deal with suicidal intent therapeutically from the first session. The most useful starting point is to ascertain the basis for the suicidal wishes. We have found that the reasons for suicide attempts are relatively easily categorized. Among a sample of 200 patients hospitalized for attempted suicide, 56% reported that their reasons were based on the wish to escape from pain, 13% gave reasons that were manipulative (i.e., meant to produce some interpersonal change), and 31% reported a combination of the preceding reasons (Kovacs et al., 1975).

The types of motives patients report can guide the therapist's response. If the motive is surcease, escape from pain, then the patient's hopelessness would be an appropriate area for exploration. If the motive is to manipulate others, then the patient should be helped to sort out these manipulative intentions. The patient should be persuaded to adopt more effective communicative methods. In short, the therapist's job is to accept the notions of suicidal intent in order to lay the groundwork for tipping the balance away from suicide and in the direction of dealing constructively with the patient's problems. This is why it is crucial to take the patient's motive for suicide seriously. Only by accepting the patient's frame of reference can we enter a collaborative effort with the patient. The therapist must then enter into a dialogue with the patient, actually discussing the pros and cons of suicide. In this way the therapist can elicit a list of reasons for living. Such a list may even be formalized in writing.

We have found that an accurate predictor of suicidal intent (in fact, better than the degree of depression) is hopelessness (Beck, Kovacs, & Weissman, 1975). We have developed a measure of hopelessness that serves as an adjunctive measure of suicidal risk (Beck, Weissman, Lester, & Trexler, 1974). If the patient's index of hopelessness is high, the therapist must deal with this immediately. If the therapist waits, the patient may not be alive for the next session. The strategy used in dealing with hopelessness is based on the observation that hopelessness is predicated on arbitrary and fixed conclusions. As the therapist explores the evidence that can contradict these conclusions, the patient's beliefs may become more accessible to modification. For instance, a woman who broke up with her second husband was intensely suicidal. When asked why she wanted to die, her answer was "I cannot live without Peter." She believed that she could not get along without a man. When asked if she had always needed a man to be happy, she brightened somewhat and remembered that one of her happiest times had been when she had lived apart from her husband.

An additional method of reducing hopelessness is the approach of turning hopeless situations into realistic problems to be solved. In our analysis of case histories of men who have attempted suicide, we have found that the precipitating stressors frequently have been related to performance at work or school. Among women who have attempted suicide, the precipitating stressor frequently has been disruption of a relationship with another person. Thus, real-life problems often provide the basis for suicidal intent, and the therapist may begin by proposing solutions to these problems, while guarding against the pessimism likely to be encountered from these patients initially.

We have found that, for some reason, certain suicidal patients may be prone to consider suicide when they overestimate the magnitude of a problem, whereas others may make successful adaptive responses in the same circumstances. After suicidal patients have been taught how to cope with their immediate problems, it may be useful to teach them problem-solving distraction techniques to be used to counter their suicide-prone responses. When suicidal ideation is among the symptoms presented by a patient, it is crucial that it be dealt with first.

Maintaining Functioning: Modifying Underlying Assumptions

Faulty assumptions are those basic beliefs that predispose patients to depression. Therapy must shift toward modification of faulty basic assumptions during the middle and latter stages of therapy. This will enable patients to avoid future depressions. Sometimes patients will find that their symptoms are relieved after only brief treatment in several sessions; rather than have them drop out of therapy at that point, we emphasize the need to continue working on their personal rules about their assumptions.

Assumptions provide an underlying stratum from which everyday events acquire significance. These assumptions may be learned in childhood, or they may derive from childhood experiences or from the attitudes of peers or from family rules. Some assumptions that Beck (1976) found predisposing to excessive depression include the following:

1. "In order to be happy, I have to be successful in whatever I undertake."
2. "To be happy, I must be accepted by all people at all times."
3. "If I make a mistake, it means I am inept."
4. "I can't live without love."
5. "If somebody disagrees with me, it means he doesn't like me."
6. "My value as a person depends on what others think of me."

Because faulty basic assumptions provide a stratum from which erroneous conclusions are derived, the therapist must work backward carefully from everyday automatic thoughts to identify these assumptions. To confront the patient with them too early in the course of therapy can lead to rejection of their validity or, alternatively, overcompliance without real agreement by the patient. We therefore recommend that cognitive therapists avoid suggesting these faulty basic beliefs to patients until they are actively involved in identifying their own assumptions. We acknowledge that the therapist is likely to be ahead of the patient in recognizing these assumptions, but in our approach to therapy we always require validation and elicitation of assumptions from the patient. Faulty basic assumptions can be recognized in a number of ways: the use of particular rules of logic, such as overgeneralization about a particular class of events; the use of particular words, such as "stupid" or "dumb," in referring to oneself or to situations; the situation in which a patient is unusually happy about an event.

The flow of recognition of cognitive events proceeds during therapy from the specific and explicit to the general and abstract. Initially in therapy the patient recognizes automatic thoughts. A second step involves collaborative effort in identifying themes or abstractions that occur among the automatic thoughts. The final stage of therapy is attained when the patient examines and modifies central life rules or equations.

The following case illustrates the search for basic assumptions. A woman in her early thirties had been depressed since she and her husband had separated 2 years earlier. She was isolated and troubled by the separation, and she had numerous automatic thoughts about being ugly and undesirable. One of the supporting proofs she had for these beliefs was that men did not ask her out. After the therapist pointed out that there were objective bases for her isolation (the fact that she worked alone and remained at home evenings, without any opportunity to meet men), she agreed to socialize more. As she began to date, she realized that her attitude regarding her attractiveness was false. This process led to her spontaneous recognition of the importance she placed on love (or attention) from men. She believed that she was worthless without it. Once these assumptions were identified tentatively, they were discussed and empirically evaluated at length.

The relationship between this patient's automatic thoughts and basic assumptions can be presented in the following manner:

Primary assumption: Without the love or attention of a man I am worthless.

Secondary assumption: Men aren't interested in me. Life is worthless.

Automatic thoughts: I am unattractive. I am ugly.

Such an outline can be presented to the patient once the content has been at least tentatively identified. Note that in the preceding case illustration the patient was in touch with automatic thoughts first and had associated assumptions to them. As the exploration of automatic thoughts continues, the patient becomes aware of the basic assumptions that serve as themes or formulas or provide an underlying stratum of rules.

Once patients' assumptions are identified, they can be modified. At this point in therapy, patients are capable of changing their own belief systems by looking in new ways (with more objective evaluations) at concrete situations in which their basic assumptions arise. Thus, in discussions of assumptions between therapist and patient, the patient is encouraged to be active in the search for alternative conclusions, rather than being a passive recipient of the therapist's didactic interpretations. In the case of the woman mentioned earlier, she decided to place a moratorium on dating for a period to see how she felt without men. For the first time in her adult life she was able to find out if she could be happy independent of a heterosexual relationship.

Effectiveness of Treatment

Examination of our treatment procedures (Rush et al., 1977) was undertaken in a pilot study that compared cognitive therapy with antidepressant drug therapy for 41 depressed patients. By the end of active treatment, both groups showed significant decreases in depressive symptoms. Unexpectedly, cognitive therapy resulted in significantly greater improvement than did pharmacotherapy, as judged by self-reports and observers' clinical ratings of depression. At 3 and 6 months follow-up, cognitive therapy continued to show significant gains over pharmacotherapy. This was the first controlled outcome study to show superiority of psychological or behavioral intervention over drug therapy among moderately to severely depressed patients.

Follow-up at 12 months for those who completed the study showed that both groups had maintained their treatment gains up to that time. However, self-rated depressive symptoms continued to be significantly lower for patients in cognitive therapy than for those in drug therapy (Kovacs et al., Note 2).

A recent unpublished study by our group compared cognitive therapy alone with cognitive therapy in combination with drug therapy (amitriptyline). Thirty-three patients were assigned randomly to the treatment conditions, and 4 patients were discontinued because of breach of research protocol. Reductions in depression at the end of treatment were equal for the two treatment groups, based on both Beck Depression Inventory and Hamilton depression scale scores. At 6 months follow-up, these gains were partially sustained, with no difference between groups. The cognitive therapy group did as well as those in the study of Rush and associates (1977); a more detailed account of that study is provided by Beck and associates (1979). Furthermore, it appeared that the addition of drug therapy, on the average, did not add to the efficacy of cognitive therapy.

We look forward to continuing development and evaluation of our therapy and its use with depressed patients.

NOTES

1. Beck, A.T., & Greenberg, R.L. *Coping with depression.* New York: Institute for Rational Living, 1974.
2. Kovacs, M., Rush, A.J., Beck, A.T., & Hollon, S.P. *A one-year follow-up of depressed out-patients treated with cognitive therapy or pharmacotherapy.*

Unpublished manuscript, Department of Psychiatry, University of Pittsburgh, 1978.
3. Secunda, S.K., Katz, N.M., Friedman, J.J., & Schuyler, D. *Special report 1973—The depressive disorders.* Washington: U.S. Government Printing Office, 1973.

REFERENCES

Bateson, G. Social planning and the concept of deutero-learning in relation to the democratic way of life. In L. Bryson & L. Finkelstein *Science, philosophy and religion*, pp. 97. New York: Harper 1942.

Beck, A.T. *The diagnosis and management of depression.* Philadelphia: University of Pennsylvania Press, 1973.

Beck, A.T. *Cognitive therapy and the emotional disorders.* New York: International Universities Press, 1976.

Beck, A.T., & Bedrosian, R.C. Principles of cognitive therapy. In M.D. Mahoney (Ed.), *Psychotherapy process: Current issues and future directions.* New York: Plenum, 1980.

Beck, A.T., Kovacs, M., & Weissman, A. Hopelessness and suicidal behavior: An overview. *Journal of the American Medical Association*, 1975, *234*, 1146-1149.

Beck, A.T., & Rush, A.J. Cognitive approaches to depression and suicide. In G. Servan (Ed.), *Cognitive defects in development of mental illness*, pp. 235-257, New York: Brunner/Mazel, 1977.

Beck, A.T., Rush, A.J., Shaw, B.F., & Emery, G. *Cognitive therapy of depression.* New York: Guilford, 1979.

Beck, A.T., Weissman, A., Lester, D., & Trexler, L. The measurement of pessimism: The hopelessness scale. *Journal of Consulting and Clinical Psychology*, 1974, *42*, 861-865.

Coleman, R.E. Manipulation of self-esteem as a determinant of mood of elated and depressed women. *Journal of Abnormal Psychology*, 1975, *84*, 695-700.

Kovacs, M., Beck, A.T., & Weissman, A. The use of suicidal motives in the psychotherapy of attempted suicides. *American Journal of Psychotherapy*, 1975, *29*, 363-368.

Rush, A.J., Beck, A.T., Kovacs, M., & Hollon, S. Comparative efficacy of cognitive therapy and imipramine in the treatment of depressed outpatients. *Cognitive Therapy and Research*, 1977, *1*, 17-37.

Attributional Reformulation of Learned Helplessness and Depression
Therapeutic Implications

Steven R. H. Beach
Lyn Y. Abramson
Frederick M. Levine

Depression is like fever: It is a symptom complex that can result from a wide variety of biological and psychological processes. Depression has been associated with various forms of failure, loss of a loved one, metabolic disruptions, catecholamine deficiency, and allergies, to name but a few of the hypothesized causes of this symptom complex. Different models of depression may well apply to different types of the disorder. Rather than argue whether depression is biological, cognitive, or behavioral, we believe that it is more useful to break the disorder down into its functional and etiologic types. As with fever, dividing the disorder into such types can lead to more effective therapeutic interventions. In this chapter we shall focus on the therapeutic implications of one model of depression: the learned helplessness model.

Uses of Theories in Guiding Clinical Practice

Before we discuss the reformulated model of learned helplessness and its therapeutic implications, it may be useful to examine the role of theory, in general, in guiding clinical practice. From various perspec-

This research was supported by U.S. Public Health Service Biomedical Research Grant 5S07RR07067-13 to the State University of New York at Stony Brook.

tives, several prominent clinical psychologists have discussed the potential problems involved in applying theories in clinical settings (e.g., Goldfried, 1980; Lazarus, 1971; London, 1964, 1972; Rogers, 1961). Consider a recent comment from the *American Psychologist:*

> In reviewing the history of various approaches to therapy, it becomes apparent that therapists have typically operated from within a given theoretical framework, often to the point of completely blinding themselves to alternative conceptualizations and potentially effective intervention procedures (Goldfried, 1980).

In a more personal vein, Lazarus (1971) suggested that his adherence to a particular theoretical perspective blinded him to many important aspects of clinical practice:

> The reason why not all the additional procedures were clearly apparent in my previous writings was due to the false selectivity of my own perceptions. Often my interest and attention were so firmly riveted to behavior therapy that I translated nearly everything I did into post-hoc S-R terms. At other times I erroneously failed to recognize the additional procedures I employed as anything more than incidental activity (p. xi).

Both of these authors argued that rigid adherence to one particular model or perspective can blind clinicians to potentially valid alternative conceptualizations of their patients' problems and potentially useful therapeutic strategies.

Although we agree that rigid adherence to particular theories can decrease clinicians' therapeutic efficacy, we believe that clinicians risk even worse problems if they attempt to divest themselves of theories and models. As Korchin (1976) pointed out, "without such [a] framework, the clinician risks bumbling ineffectually or perhaps worse yet, acting on implicit assumptions about the nature of man which reflect more his own personal needs and biases than the qualities of his patient" (p. 49). Likewise, Kanfer and Saslow (1969) characterized the task of the clinician as an "attempt to identify classes of dependent variables in human behavior which would allow inferences about the particular contemporary controlling factors . . . of which they are a function" (p. 419).

Clearly, models and organizing principles guide the clinician in identifying classes of maladaptive behavior and cognition and allow inferences to be made about controlling or etiologic factors that then can be verified. Indeed, the application of a new model or a new set of principles to a patient's problem may be the single most important aspect of the clinician's job. It is this activity that allows the clinician to go beyond the patient's account of the problem. Models and organizing principles enable the clinician to see alternative ways of approaching the patient's problem, even though the patient sees only stalemate and dilemma. If clinicians are unable to apply new perspectives and models to their patients' problems, then they are in no better position to productively understand these problems than were the patients themselves when they came to the clinic for help in the first place (Levy, 1963).

The clinician is in a dilemma. On the one hand, rigid adherence to a particular theory or perspective can blind a clinician to important aspects of clinical reality. On the other hand, without a theory or perspective, the clinician may be no more able to usefully conceptualize patients' problems that the patients themselves. We believe the clinician's dilemma can be resolved by taking a "models approach" to psychotherapy (Levine & Lee, Note 1). This approach explicitly recognizes that a number of different models potentially might account for the production of a given syndrome of maladaptive behavior. Moreover, it is likely that any given model "fits" only some subgroup of patients with the syndrome. We define a model as a sufficient explanation of some behavior problem. In order to be clinically relevant, a model must contain one or more elements which can be influenced through clinical activity. In addition, the model must predict that manipulating these elements will result in changes in the problem behavior. Those elements of the model that potentially can be manipulated through clinical activity and that the model specifies as causal are referred to as "points of intervention." Because each model suggests different points of therapeutic intervention, the clinician's task is to determine which model best organizes the clinical data and identifies the most appropriate points of intervention for a particular patient.

Clinicians working from a models approach are unlikely to adhere rigidly to any particular model, because the approach itself compels them to examine and evaluate alternative models for any given patient. At the same time, however, the models approach retains the major advantage of a theoretical perspective in the clinic: Clinical data can be organized in a way that will suggest clear-cut points for therapeutic intervention. Thus, in the models approach the clinician constructs a "blueprint" that can identify effective points for intervention for a particular patient.

Applying the models approach to therapy for depressed patients helps to clarify its essentials. When confronted with a patient exhibiting some or all of the major symptoms of depression, the clinician working from a models approach will evaluate the existing models of depression to determine which, if any, best fits the data for this particular case. As we noted earlier, there are numerous different factors each of which may be sufficient to produce depressive symptoms. Consequently, the clinician must determine if a particular depressed patient's symptoms are best explained by an operant model (Ferster, 1973), a norepinephrine depletion model (Schildkraut, 1965), a model involving loss of interest in reinforcers (Costello, 1972), a self-control model (Fuchs & Rehm, 1977), or the helplessness model (Abramson et al., 1978; Seligman, 1975), to name some of the current models of depression. According to Abramson and associates (1978), those cases of depression that are caused by an expectation of uncontrollability and display the symptoms of passivity, negative cognitive set, depressed affect, and low self-esteem are most likely to qualify as "helplessness depressions."

Once the clinician decides which model seems to best fit the particular case, the optimal points for therapeutic intervention can be derived from the model and a treatment plan instituted. After the therapeutic regimen is instituted, the clinician must monitor the patient's depressive symptoms carefully to determine if they are changing in accordance with the predictions of the model. The degree to which clinical observations coincide with the predictions from the model constitutes an important test of the initial conceptualization of the patient's problem. If the therapeutic interventions do not produce the expected changes in the patient's depressive symptoms, it may be that the clinician has not chosen the appropriate model of depression for the particular case and should consider reconceptualizing the case in terms of an alternative model. Thus the clinician must continually test whether or not the model used to conceptualize the case provides a good fit to the clinical data.

The picture we have just presented is a tidy one, and although it is not inaccurate, it does oversimplify the functions of the clinician. For example, it is necessary that the clinician relate the specifics of a particular case to the general terms used in the relevant models. This activity requires a creative leap that is not highlighted in our presentation. Nevertheless, it is an integral part, and perhaps the hardest part, of clinical activity (Meehl, 1954). In addition, the clinician may be confronted with cases in which more than one model is applicable. For instance, a depressed patient's symptoms may have been produced initially by a chemical depletion, but currently they may be maintained, in part, by the rewards the patient receives by taking a sick role. In this case, both an operant model and a biological model would be applicable to understanding the patient's symptoms. In such situations the clinician must creatively synthesize the models to construct a unified, coherent account of the patient's problem. Thus, implementation of the models approach in the clinical setting requires a creative clinician who can relate the specifics of a given case to the general principles of relevant models.

The clinician requires three types of information for successful implementation of the models approach to therapy. First, the clinician needs to know when to apply a particular model from the armamentarium. Second, the clinician needs to know the points for intervention suggested by each model. Third, the clinician needs to know which techniques produce changes at each of these points of intervention. With these general guidelines in mind, we shall now discuss the reformulated model of learned helplessness and depression. We shall derive points for intervention from this model and turn to current clinical practice and contemporary theory and research in experimental psychology for techniques that will produce change at each of these points.

Helplessness Theories of Depression

Clinicians and experimental psychologists alike have emphasized the role of helplessness and hopelessness in depression (Abramson et al., 1978; Arieti, 1970; Beck, 1967, 1976; Bibring, 1953; Lichtenberg, 1957; Melges & Bowlby, 1969; Seligman, 1975). Central to this perspective is the idea that depressed people believe that they have little control over the important outcomes in their lives and therefore refrain from making adaptive responses. As early as the second century A.D., Aretaeus, a Greek philosopher, described the depressive as an individual characterized by hopelessness, powerlessness, and a sense of futility.

Emphasizing the similarities between helplessness produced in laboratory subjects exposed to aversive uncontrollable events and the major symptoms of human depression, Seligman (1975) proposed an explicit statement of a helplessness theory of depression. The underlying assumptions of this model are that helplessness is a major feature of the syndrome of depression and that many, though perhaps not all, of the symptoms of depression result when people expect that their responses will not control the important outcomes in their lives. In particular, the helplessness model postulates that the expectation of no control is sufficient to produce the motivational and cognitive symptoms of depression. The motivational symptom of depression consists in retardation of initiation of voluntary responses and is reflected in passivity, intellectual slowness, and social impairment. According to Beck (1967), the cognitive component of depression consists in a "negative cognitive set" that biases depressives to believe that their actions are doomed to failure. Helplessness theory further describes the cognitive component of depression and postulates that depressives have difficulty in perceiving the relationship between their own responses and the outcomes those responses produce. Finally, Abramson and associates (1978)—argued that sad affect, the emotional symptom of depression, occurs only in those cases of helplessness in which people expect that they will not be able to attain important goals.

Attributional Reformulation of Learned Helplessness and Depression

Abramson and associates (1978) proposed an attributional reformulation of the learned helplessness hypothesis. This reformulation resolves a number of the inadequacies of the original hypothesis when applied to human helplessness and depression; see the work of Abramson and associates (1978) and Wortman and Dintzer (1978) for comprehensive accounts of the inadequacies of the original hypothesis. According to the attributional reformulation, the kinds of causal attributions people make for lack of control influence whether or not their helplessness will entail low self-esteem and whether or not their symptoms of helplessness will generalize across situations and time. According to the reformulation, three attributional dimensions are crucial for explaining human helplessness and depression: internal-external, stable-unstable, and global-specific.

In brief, the reformulated model postulates that attributing lack of control to internal factors leads to lowered self-esteem, whereas attributing lack of control to external factors does not. Attributing lack of control to stable factors should lead to an expectation of uncontrollability in future situations and, consequently, helplessness deficits extended across time. Similarly, attributing lack of control to global factors should lead to an expectation of uncontrollability in other situations and, consequently, helplessness deficits extended across situations. Alternatively, attributing lack of control to unstable specific factors should lead to short-lived situation-specific helplessness deficits. It is worth pointing out that the logic of the attributional reformulation of learned helplessness and depression is very similar to the logic used in Weiner's attributional account of achievement motivation (Weiner, 1972, 1974).

At this point it is useful to spell out the flow of events leading from the perception of uncontrollability to the symptoms of helplessness (Figure 5.1). Like the original helplessness hypothesis, the attributional reformulation regards the expectation of uncontrollability as the crucial determinant of the symptoms of learned helplessness. Whereas the original hypothesis was vague in specifying the conditions in which a perception that events are uncontrollable (past- or present-oriented) is transformed into an expectation that events will be uncontrollable (future oriented), the reformulation regards the attributions that people make for noncontingency between acts and outcomes in the here and now as determinants of their subsequent expectations for future uncontrollability. These expectations, in turn, determine the generality and chronicity of a person's helplessness symptoms, as well as later self-esteem. As Figure 5.1 suggests, the inferential process figures largely in the attributional reformulation of helplessness and depression. A series of inferences bridges the gap between the initial perception of no control and the final expectation of future uncontrollability. The symptoms of helplessness (and depression) can be short-circuited by interventions aimed at any point in the inferential process prior to the onset of the symptoms themselves.

An important clinical implication of the reformulation is that people may come to expect that important goals in their lives will be uncon-

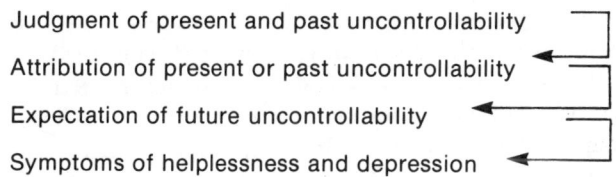

Figure 5.1. Flow of events leading to symptoms of helplessness and depression.

trollable as a result of perceiving that some relatively unimportant outcome is uncontrollable. For example, a person may perceive that regardless how hard he tries, he cannot pass a physics course. Suppose his goal is to become an English professor. If he attributes his failure in physics to intellectual incompetence, he will expect to be helpless about attaining his goal of becoming an English professor, even though he has had no direct experience in English courses. Thus, people may expect to be helpless in situations they have never experienced.

Abramson and associates (1978) summarized the implications of the attributional reformulation for the helplessness model of depression:

1. Depression consists of four classes of deficits: motivational, cognitive, self-esteem, and affective.
2. When highly desired outcomes are believed improbable or highly aversive outcomes are believed probable, and the individual expects that no response in his repertoire will change their likelihood (helplessness), depression results.
3. The generality of depressive deficits will depend on the globality of the attribution for helplessness, the chronicity of the depression deficits will depend on the stability of the attribution for helplessness, and whether self-esteem is lowered will depend on the internality of the attribution for helplessness.
4. The intensity of the deficits depends on the strength, or certainty, of the expectation of uncontrollability and, in the case of the affective and self-esteem deficits, on the importance of the outcome (p. 68).

An interesting implication of the attributional reformulation is that the symptoms of depression will not necessarily covary. For example, a person who attributes the occurrence of a positive, but uncontrollable, outcome to internal, stable, and global factors may show the cognitive and motivational symptoms of helplessness, but no depressive affect or loss of self-esteem. Alternatively, a person who attributes the occurrence of a negative uncontrollable outcome to external, stable, and global factors may show the cognitive and motivational symptoms of helplessness as well as depressive affect, but no loss of self-esteem. Finally, a person who attributes the occurrence of a negative uncontrollable outcome to internal, stable, and global factors may show the cognitive and motivational symptoms of helplessness as well as depressive affect and loss of self-esteem. In line with these implications of the attributional reformulation, Beck (1967) noted that no particular depressive symptom or symptom class is necessary or sufficient for a clinical diagnosis of depression. Instead, some clinically depressed people display all the major symptoms of depression, whereas other depressives display various subsets of the major symptoms. According to the reformulation, different etiologic factors are relevant for different depressive symptoms. The cognitive and motivational deficits result from the expectation of no control per se. The tendency to attribute uncontrollable events to stable global factors increases the likelihood that an expectation of no control will persist in the future and in new situations and thereby also contributes to producing cognitive and motivational deficits in depression. Alternatively, self-esteem deficits result from a tendency to attribute uncontrollable events to internal factors. Finally, depressive affect results from an expectation that an important goal is unattainable rather than from the expected uncontrollability of the goal. Thus the attributional reformulation predicts that persons who expect to have no control over the important goals in their lives, who attribute this uncontrollability to internal, stable, and global factors, and who expect that they will not be able to attain these goals should manifest all four major symptoms of the syndrome of depression.

It is important to emphasize that both the original helplessness hypothesis and the attributional reformulation regard the expectation of no control as a sufficient condition, but not a necessary condition, for depression. Physiological states, postpartum conditions, hormonal states, loss of interest in reinforcers, chemical depletions, and so on, can produce the symptoms of depression in the absence of an expectation of uncontrollability. The term "depression," like "mental retardation," can be used to refer to a number of distinct syndromes with similar symptoms but different causes. According to helplessness theory, there exists a subset of depression (helplessness depression) that is caused by an expectation of response-outcome independence and displays the symptoms of passivity, negative cognitive set, depressed affect, and low self-esteem. We emphasize that the reformulation model is still in the process of being validated and we present relevant validation data when appropriate.

A hypothetical clinical vignette will illustrate the development of a helplessness depression. Suppose a woman is rejected by a man she loves. She perceives that regardless of what she does, she cannot regain his love. If she attributes this rejection to a general inability on her part to get along with other people, she is likely to feel helpless about ever achieving a satisfactory relationship with any man, and she may expect to fail in all situations involving interpersonal relations, such as work. The woman should develop the cognitive, motivational, emotional, and self-esteem symptoms of depression. Alternatively, if the woman attributes her rejection to her lover's own idiosyncratic insecurity about being around attractive women, she will be unlikely to develop expectations of no control about other situations involving men or interpersonal relations. Consequently, her symptoms of depression will be predicted to be less severe than if she attributes the rejection to her general inability to get along with people.

It is worth pointing out that the attributional reformulation of helplessness and depression bears a significant similarity to Beck's cognitive model of depression (Beck, 1967, 1976). Beck emphasized that depression-prone persons are characterized by certain primitive, rigid cognitive "schemas" that are activated automatically during environmental stress (failure, loss, etc.). These schemas consist of pervasive negative beliefs about oneself, the future, and the world (Beck's "cognitive triad"). Once activated, these schemas become prepotent and dominate the cognitions of depressed people, leading to systematic distortions in perception and interpretation of information. Although Beck implicated numerous maladaptive cognitive schemas in depression, he assigned particular importance to primitive and egocentric schemas concerning causality (Beck & Greenberg, 1974). According to Beck, the depressed person attributes bad outcomes to internal factors such as incompetence and good outcomes to external factors such as luck. Beck's cognitive theory regards the cognitive, motivational, and affective symptoms of depression as direct consequences of depressives' inferences that they are unworthy, that the future is hopeless, and that interactions with the environment are characterized by defeat and deprivation.

Therapeutic Implications

According to the reformulation, the cognitive, motivational, and affective symptoms of helplessness depression occur when people expect that they will not be able to exert control and attain important goals. In addition, if these people believe that relevant others can exert control and can attain such goals, they will show loss of self-esteem. Any therapeutic strategy that undermines the expectation that important goals are uncontrollable and unattainable should be effective in reversing the current depressive episode. Similarly, undermining the person's expectation that relevant others can exert control and attain goals, whereas the person cannot, should be therapeutic. Thus, four points for intervention in a depressive episode can be derived from the reformulated helplessness model: (1) Reverse the patient's expectations of having no control over important goals. (2) Facilitate a change from unrealistic goals to more realistic goals. (3) Decrease the importance of unattainable goals. (4) Reverse the patient's expectations that other people do have control over their important goals, whereas the patient does not (i.e., change an internal attribution for uncontrollability into an external attribution).

A major advantage of the reformulation is that it not only suggests points for intervention for reversing current depressive episodes but also suggests points for intervention for decreasing one's *vulnerability* to future depressive episodes (Hollon & Garber, 1979). The logic of the reformulation suggests that individual differences may exist in cognitive styles and that particular cognitive styles may be "depressogenic." See the work of Beck and associates (1979) for a discussion of depressogenic cognitive styles. Insofar as the reformulation specifies a number of inferential steps leading to an expectation of no control over an important goal (Figure 5.1), three cognitive styles emerge as potential vulnerability factors for depression: (1) a bias toward judging that outcomes are uncontrollable; (2) a bias toward attributing negative outcomes to internal, stable, and global factors; (3) a bias toward subscribing to unrealistic and unattainable goals and viewing these goals as very important.

Reversing Current Depressive Episodes *Modifying Expectations of No Control.* According to the reformulation of learned helplessness, an expectation of no control over outcomes directly produces cognitive and motivational symptoms of depression. An expectation of no control indirectly contributes to loss of self-esteem by providing an occasion for the negative social comparison that is hypothesized to produce loss of self-esteem. Finally, an expectation of no control will contribute indirectly to the production of negative affect if it decreases the subjective probability that an important goal will be attained. Thus, changing a patient's expectation of no control to an expectation of control is likely to lead to reductions in a wide variety of depressive symptoms, and consequently it should be a major goal of therapy with patients who currently are depressed.

The logic of the reformulation of learned helplessness and depression suggests that the depressed patient's expectation of no control over the attainment of certain important goals is a joint product of the environmental feedback or data the patient receives about the relationship between responses and outcomes and the interpretive or inferential processes the patient applies to that feedback. Accordingly, techniques relevant to reversing a depressed patient's expectation of no control can be organized into two major classes: (1) techniques aimed at changing the depressed patient's interpretation of the available environmental feedback; (2) techniques aimed at changing the nature of the feedback the patient is receiving. The two approaches are potentially complementary and may be used simultaneously if necessary.

Beck and associates (Beck, 1976; Beck et al., 1979) have made important contributions to developing techniques for combating depressogenic interpretations of the available environmental feedback. The essence of Beck's approach is summarized in his emphasis on helping depressed patients systematically investigate their own depressogenic interpretations: "The overall strategy of cognitive therapy may be differentiated from other schools of therapy by its emphasis on the *empirical investigation* of the patient's automatic thoughts, inferences, conclusions, and assumptions" (Beck et al., 1979, p. 7). Thus, Beck's approach centers on encouraging the patient to formulate interpretations and conclusions as *testable hypotheses* and then motivating the patient to test these hypotheses in a systematic way. For example, suppose a depressed patient expects that no matter what she does, everyone meeting her will turn away in disgust. In this case, Beck and associates (1979) would suggest that the therapist help the woman set up a system for judging the reactions of other people and then encourage her to make objective assessments of the facial and bodily movements of other people. The theme here is that given the available environmental information or data, the depressed woman may not be forming realistic expectations about control. In taking an empirical approach, the therapist helps the patient to generate those data that will have the greatest power to disconfirm the patient's expectations if they actually are faulty: data generated from the patient's own experience.

Contemporary work in social psychology has suggested that some difficulties may be encountered in using Beck's empirical approach to disconfirming expectancies. Ross (1977, 1978) pointed out that when patients encounter information or data that do not fit their expectations, beliefs, or theories, they often tend to dismiss such data as unreliable, erroneous, or unrepresentative or as being the product of contaminating third-variable influences. Ross's analysis implies that therapists taking an empirical approach to disconfirming patients' depressogenic expectancies must be careful to make the disconfirming nature of the evidence salient and battle against patients' attempts to discount it. Indeed, Ross (1977) argued that disconfirming evidence can actually end up strengthening a patient's preconceptions if the normal tendency to dismiss data that don't fit one's preconceptions is allowed.

In fact, Beck and associates (1979) did emphasize the importance of having the therapist highlight success for the depressed patient and evaluate the results of the patient's investigations jointly with the patient. Thus, Beck's approach can be viewed as an attempt to change patients' expectations by encouraging them to test those expectations or the beliefs on which they are based and by doing everything possible to prevent the new evidence from being discounted by the patients.

According to the attributional reformulation of learned helplessness, patients' causal attributions for previous failures and their perceptions of no control strongly influence whether or not they will develop current expectation of no control. Thus, to the extent that the therapist can bring these previous attributions into question, the therapist undermines patients' expectations of no control. Beck and associates (1979) have provided a technique that appears ideal for this enterprise. They suggested eliciting possible alternative attributions for events from patients. These alternative explanations can be rated by patients according to degree of plausibility. Then patients can be encouraged to search for more information relevant to deciding between alternatives. Having the alternative explanations available can help to make depressed patients amenable to reconsidering their previous attributions. More important, this procedure allows patient and therapist to develop empirically testable hypotheses. In this way, a method for disconfirming the debilitating attributions becomes available. In addition, after the data have been collected, patients can again rate the plausibility of alternative attributions to see if they previously overrated the alternatives with the worst consequences. Of course, it is possible that the evidence will favor an attribution that reflects negatively on the patient or bodes ill for the future. When appropriate in such cases, the therapist may turn to techniques aimed at skill building or environmental enrichment in an effort to modify the data base from which the patient is drawing conclusions.

Lewinsohn (1974) and his colleagues have provided evidence that depressed patients may suffer social skills deficits and thereby may be basing their conclusions on a limited data base. They have found that in social situations, depressed patients initiate fewer social acts toward others and are less adept at timing the social responses they do make. As a result, the actions of depressed patients have less favorable social impacts on others. Thus, when appropriate, social skills training may be one important way to modify an expectation of no control.

As we shall point out later, there is evidence to suggest that in both interpersonal settings (Gotlib & Asarnow, 1979) and achievement settings (Abramson et al., Note 2) depressed patients may be deficient in generating alternatives to solve problems. Consequently, depressed patients currently expecting that they cannot control outcomes may have failed to consider many of the potentially effective means for controlling the relevant outcomes. In such cases the therapist should focus on helping patients to generate alternative successful strategies for controlling outcomes and thereby reverse these patients' expectation of no control.

Modifying Unrealistic Goals. In general, the more unrealistic the goals to which patients subscribe, the more likely they are to expect that the goals are unattainable and uncontrollable. This expectation of no control and nonattainment will directly produce the cognitive and motivational symptoms of helplessness depression and possibly will indirectly contribute to the development of sad affect and loss of self-esteem. Thus, in a case of depression in which the patient's subscription to unrealistic goals is facilitating an expectation of no control, an appropriate point for intervention is modification of these goals.

Goal setting has been discussed by Rehm (1977) and Bandura (1971) as a central problem in depression. Similarly, clinical observation has suggested that depressed patients may be setting unrealistic goals. An examination of Ellis's list (1962) of irrational beliefs and Beck's list (1976) of dysfunctional assumptions has uncovered a number of unrealistic goals. Thus, according to Beck (1976), attitudes that predispose people to excessive sadness or depression include the following: "In order to be happy, I have to be successful in whatever I undertake." "To be happy, I must be accepted (liked, admired) by all people at all times." Ellis (1977a) identified similar beliefs as predisposing people to excessive emotional upset: "I must have sincere love and approval almost all the time from all the people I find significant." "I must prove myself thoroughly competent, adequate, and achieving, or at least have real competence or talent at something important." Thus, both Ellis and Beck identified unrealistic goals as one cause of emotional upset and depression. Finally, empirical evidence supporting the hypothesis that unrealistic goals are associated with depression was found by Golin and Terrell (1977). They found that depressed students typically set higher goals on laboratory tasks than did nondepressed students. Similarly, Diggory (1966) found that depressed inpatients set their levels of aspiration higher than their previous levels of performance warranted. Although none of this evidence unequivocally supports the claim that unrealistically high goals can cause depression, it is consistent with the identification of unrealistic goals as an important point for intervention in depression.

One approach to modifying unrealistic goals is to redirect the patient's attention away from them and toward more realistic goals. In this type of approach, the original unrealistic goals will not need to be attacked directly. Instead, the clinician can work at increasing the salience of new goals that are more realistic. Rehm (1977) suggested a technique that appears to work in this manner. He suggested that patients' standards of evaluation can be altered by aiding them to construct specific behavioral goals that they can then be encouraged to pursue actively. In this manner, patients' attention can be focused on goals that are more realistic and more readily obtainable without having to consider explicitly their previous unrealistic goals.

A similar technique that also may work by redirecting patients' attention to new and more realistic goals is the graded-task assignment advocated by Beck and associates (1979) and Goldfried (personal communication). Essentially, this technique consists in assigning patients a number of specific tasks. As the patients master these tasks, more complex tasks can be assigned. Beck and associates (1979) emphasized that the tasks should be devised in collaboration with the patients, making sure that the tasks address problems or test dysfunctional beliefs of the patients. In addition, throughout the process, patients should be helped to evaluate their performances and note the positive consequences for their lives that are resulting. Following these suggestions would seem to be important for effectively redirecting and maintaining patients' attention on the new goals that have been provided.

The next group of techniques that normally would be included in this section are the "cognitive" techniques suggested by Beck and associates (1979), Ellis (1977a), and others. However, a review of these techniques has suggested that they are normally used to modify the unrealistic goals espoused by patients and simultaneously to decrease the importance patients attach to these goals. Consequently, these cognitive techniques will be outlined in the next section, which will address the problem of decreasing the importance attached to a goal.

Decreasing the Importance of Unattainable Goals. According to the reformulation of learned helplessness and depression, the intensity of the sad affect resulting from an expectation of no control and nonattainment of a goal is determined by the importance of the goal. Consequently, if depressed patients attach excessive importance to unattainable goals, their negative affective reactions should be intensified. Likewise, if depressed patients can decrease the importance they attach to unattainable goals, the negative effective responses they suffer should no longer be as intense, even if they continue to have expectations of no control and nonattainment of their goals.

Clinical observations seem to support the claim that depressed patients attach excessive importance to unattainable goals. For example, Ellis (1977a) contended that depressed patients may be increasing their suffering by exaggerating the significance and importance they attach to the attainment of certain goals. Similarly, in his list of dysfunctional attitudes, Beck (1976) characterized his patients as believing that the attainment of certain goals was crucially important.

Research studies also have supported the claim that depressives may attach excessive importance to the attainment of their goals. Nelson (1977) found that a strong correlate of depression in an undergraduate population was the belief that it is terrible when things are not the way one would like them to be, one of Ellis's (1962) "irrational beliefs." Similarly, Munoz (1977, cited by Zeiss et al., 1979) found that depressed patients endorsed more irrational beliefs relevant to guilt, failure, and the sources of unhappiness than did nondepressed psychiatric patients and normal controls. Presumably these beliefs included beliefs about attaching excessive importance to the attaining of certain goals. Once again, this evidence does not unequivocally support the claim that attaching excessive importance to the attainment of certain goals causes affective reactions to be intensified. However, it is consistent with the identification of decreasing the importance depressed patients attach to the attainment of certain goals as an important point for intervention in depression.

Klinger's analysis (1977) of the role of instrumentality in determining value suggests one way to manipulate the importance attached to a goal. Klinger pointed out that one can rapidly increase or decrease the value one places on attaining a goal if one's view of its instrumentality in attaining another goal changes. This observation suggests that when patients see particular goals as instrumental in the attainment of other highly desired goals, such as happiness or effective functioning, the therapist can decrease the importance attached to the particular goals by disputing the assumed instrumentality of the particular goals for attaining the highly desired goals. To the extent that a patient decreases the instrumentality assigned to a particular goal, the importance attached to the attainment of that goal should also decrease.

Beck and associates (1979) proposed a technique that appears to work in the manner just outlined. Beck suggested that after a patient's automatic thoughts have been identified, it should be possible to identify a theme. This theme may be a depressogenic assumption: "Without a man I can't be happy." This assumption can then be tested. In one case Beck described, the therapist told the woman she was fortunate in that she was currently in a situation in which she could run an experiment to test this assumption. Beck proposed to the patient that this goal was important to her because it seemed instrumental in attaining happiness. Then Beck suggested that the goal was not really instrumental, and he proposed an experiment to test the belief that it was. This should constitute powerful evidence that the goal is not instrumental in producing happiness. Thus, this procedure should be effective in reducing the importance the patient is attaching to the goal.

Ellis (1977a) proposed a technique similar to that of Beck for decreasing the importance patients attach to goals. Like Beck, Ellis suggested identifying the disturbance-creating assumption, which may be placing excessive importance on the attainment of some goal. The therapist then takes a Socratic, questioning role, challenging the patient's assumptions and asking for evidence supporting the assumptions. This appears to undermine the patient's uncritical acceptance of the belief that certain goals must be attained. The therapist then can suggest more "rational" alternative beliefs. When accepted and used by the patient, the more rational assessment of a goal's importance should short-circuit the patient's extreme negative reactions in the face of nonattainment of the goal.

Goldfried and Davison (1976) also suggested a basically Ellisonian approach to dealing with the irrational assumptions patients make. However, on the basis of social psychological literature (e. g., Brehm &

Cohen, 1962) they suggested that having the patient offer arguments to refute these assumptions may be more effective in producing change than having the therapist argue with the patient. Thus, Goldfried and Davison proposed that the therapist play the role of devil's advocate, encouraging the patient to openly refute irrational assumptions.

Another technique suggested by both Ellis (1977a) and Beck and associates (1979) is the use of humor. For example, Beck and associates (1979) suggested using a hypothetical example to exaggerate a particular position the patient is taking. The use of this technique may dramatize how unreasonable or inappropriate the patient's thinking is. Of course, as Beck and associates (1979) hastened to add, humor should be used with caution. The target of the humor should be the patient's thoughts or ideas, not the patient. In addition, potential negative misinterpretations of the humor should be sought out and corrected. Finally, if the patient is strongly convinced of the validity of the ideas in question, humor may weaken the therapeutic relationship rather than highlight the unreasonable nature of the beliefs.

Reversing Internal Attributions for Uncontrollability. The reformulation of learned helplessness and depression states that depressed patients suffer loss of self-esteem if they attribute their helplessness to internal factors rather than external factors. That is, depressed patients will suffer loss of self-esteem if they believe that they cannot control the attainment of goals that relevant others can control. Therefore, when appropriate, changing patients' attributions for uncontrollability from internal factors to more external factors will help alleviate self-esteem deficits, according to the reformulation. It is important to note that it is not predicted that making patients' attributions for uncontrollability more external will necessarily alleviate cognitive, motivational, or affective deficits. Thus, techniques aimed only at reversing internal attributions for uncontrollability may enhance patients' self-esteem but leave them helpless and distressed.

Before discussing therapeutic strategies for modifying attributions, it will be useful to examine the empirical evidence on the relationship between self-esteem and causal attributions. Do people who have low self-esteem make internal attributions for uncontrollability or negative outcomes as compared with people who have high self-esteem? Several studies have suggested that making internal attributions for negative outcomes is associated with low self-esteem. For example, Fitch (1970) found that subjects with high self-esteem more frequently attributed failure to external causes than did subjects with low self-esteem; also see the work of Maracek and Mettee (1972). Similarly, Ickes and Layden (1978) measured subjects' negative outcomes across a range of achievement and nonachievement situations. These investigations revealed that high-self-esteem subjects were more likely to attribute positive outcomes to internal factors than were low-self-esteem subjects, whereas low-self-esteem subjects were more likely to attribute negative outcomes to internal factors than were high-self-esteem subjects.

In devising techniques for altering patients' internal attributions for negative or uncontrollable outcomes, it is useful to bear in mind the suggestion of a number of investigators (e.g., Metalsky & Abramson, 1980; Ross, 1977, 1978) that attributions are functions of both the available environmental evidence and the interpretive system that guides the person's information processing. Thus, attributional change techniques may focus on either modifying the available evidence or modifying the person's interpretive system or both.

Because social psychologists have devoted considerable attention to the study of attributional processes, we shall turn to their work for information relevant to altering internal attributions for uncontrollability. According to Kelley (1967), certain configurations of situational information compel internal attributions, whereas other configurations compel external attributions. In particular, Kelley (1967) argued that people attribute outcomes to the factors with which they covary. In Kelley's view, people should be more likely to make internal attributions for negative outcomes that happen to themselves but not to other people. Alternatively, people should be more likely to make external attributions for negative outcomes that happen both to themselves and to others. Thus, Kelley's analysis suggests that when a depressed patient makes an internal attribution for a negative outcome, the clinician should encourage the patient to seek additional information about the performance of relevant others in the situation to determine if the patient's attribution is unrealistically biased in the internal direction.

Indeed, Beck and associates (1979) presented an example of "collaborative empiricism" that is congruent with Kelley's analysis. A 22-year-old depressed graduate student was convinced that her English professor thought she was a "reject" because she had received a grade of C on a paper along with two pages of critical comments. At the therapist's urging, she called the professor for more information. On the telephone she found out that the average grade in the class was C and that the professor thought that although the style of the essay was "wanting," the content was "promising." Beck and associates (1979) reported that as a result of this new information this patient became more animated and cheerful.

Of course, the evidence gathered in the search for more information may corroborate the patient's initial internal attribution for failure. Although this can be distressing, such evidence can be helpful in charting the future course of therapy. If indicated, the therapist can teach the patient social skills or problem-solving skills to increase the patient's effectiveness.

According to the reformulation, people compare themselves with relevant others in deciding whether to make internal or external attributions for uncontrollability. Some depressed patients who make internal attributions for their helplessness may be comparing themselves with an inappropriate group of relevant others. For example, a beginning graduate student might berate himself if his first paper is returned with numerous red marks and critical comments in the margins. Perhaps the graduate student would be less harsh on himself if he were to compare his work with the work of other beginning graduate students rather than with papers published in professional journals. Thus, when appropriate, the therapist may encourage a patient to find a new and more appropriate reference group.

In this section we have highlighted two major approaches for altering internal attributions for negative outcomes. In a later section on modifying attributional styles we shall explore more fully the techniques for modifying general attributional patterns that can predispose a person to depression.

Decreasing the Vulnerability to Depression *Modifying the Bias to Judge Outcomes as Uncontrollable.* According to the logic of the attributional reformulation of learned helplessness, people who show a bias toward judging that outcomes are uncontrollable should be vulnerable to depressive episodes. When attempting to obtain a desired outcome or avoid an aversive outcome, people who are biased to judge that they have no control will be less likely to learn and perform those responses that can control the outcome of interest and will give up more readily than will people who are not biased to judge that they have no control over outcomes. Abramson and associates (Note 2) specified two conditions that can bias people toward judging that they have no control over outcomes. First, people can fail to learn about control because they have low rates of initiation of voluntary responses and are less likely to perform the appropriate controlling response in a given situation. Consequently, such people will fail to sample the potential contingency between this response and the outcome. That is, a low rate of initiation of voluntary responses indirectly biases people toward judging that they have no control by limiting the amount of contact they have with the response–outcome contingency. Second, people can fail to learn about control even when they do perform the controlling response if they exhibit an "associative" deficit (Seligman, 1975) or difficulty in actually perceiving the relationship between the controlling response and the outcome.

In a recent set of experiments, Alloy and Abramson (1979) and Abramson and associates (Note 2) examined depressed and nondepressed students' judgments of control in contingency learning problems in the laboratory. These investigators found no evidence for an associative deficit in depression (Alloy & Abramson, 1979), but they did find that depressed students underestimated their control over environmental outcomes when they had to generate a complex hypothesis in order to exert control (Abramson et al., Note 2). Abramson's findings are in line with clinical observations (Beck, 1967) suggesting that depressives may be less likely to initiate voluntary covert responses as well as voluntary overt responses. That is, depressed persons may be less likely than nondepressed persons to engage actively in a number of cognitive strategies (e.g., hypothesis generation, attention focusing, memory search, and rehearsal).

In similarity to the findings of Abramson and associates (Note 2), Gotlib and Asarnow (1979) found that both mildly depressed and clinically depressed university students showed impaired performance in an interpersonal problem-solving task (means-ends problem-solving procedure) relative to nondepressed students. When confronted with hypothetical interpersonal problem situations in which they were required to describe the actions they would take in order to bring about a given resolution, depressed students generated fewer means or actions relevant to obtaining the given resolution than did nondepressed students. However, depressed students did not show a deficit on an anagrams task.

It is important to note that Abramson and associates (Note 2) and Gotlib and Asarnow (1979) assessed problem solving and the generation of hypotheses among students who were depressed at the time of testing. Further studies will be necessary to determine whether deficits in problem solving are the causes or results of depression. Do some persons show enduring deficits in initiating covert and overt responses in problem-solving situations and thereby exhibit a bias toward judging that they have little control over outcomes? Further, are such persons especially vulnerable to depression?

Insofar as individual deficits in problem solving tend to increase vulnerability to depression, therapies aimed at building problem-solving skills should be effective in reducing a patient's risk for developing depression. Within the behavior therapy tradition, clinicians have developed relatively clear-cut techniques for helping patients acquire more effective problem-solving skills (e.g., D'Zurilla & Goldfried, 1971; Goldfried & Davison, 1976). The major objectives of problem-solving therapy include teaching the patient how to generate alternative solutions to a problem and how to choose the most effective solution from among these alternatives. Along these lines, Beck and associates (1979) emphasized problem-solving techniques that induce depressed patients to search for alternatives. The suggestion of Goldfried and Davison (1976) that problem-solving therapy may be construed as a form of self-control or independence training is particularly relevant to the issue of vulnerability to depression. As Goldfried and Davison (1976) pointed out, the use of problem-solving principles has potential for training patients to function as their own therapists. Once a depressed patient has recovered from a depressive episode, training in effective problem solving can decrease vulnerability to future depressions.

Modifying the Bias to Attribute Negative or Uncontrollable Outcomes to Internal, Stable, and Global Factors. Abramson and associates (1978) speculated that individual differences should exist in attributional style, and they postulated the existence of a depressogenic attributional style. People who tend to attribute negative or uncontrollable outcomes to internal, stable, and global factors should be more likely to develop general and chronic depressive reactions with lowered self-esteem than should persons who tend to attribute negative or uncontrollable outcomes to external, unstable, and specific factors. Seligman and associates (1979) recently developed an attributional style scale that consists of both positive and negative affiliation and achievement hypothetical situations. Subjects are asked to name the one major cause of each situation that they have experienced and to rate each cause on a 7-point scale for degree of internality, stability, and globality. Compared with nondepressed college students, depressed college students attributed bad outcomes to internal, stable, and global causes as measured by the scale. In addition, relative to nondepressed students, depressed students attributed good outcomes to external, unstable causes. Likewise, grade-school children exhibiting depressive symptoms showed a "depressive attributional style" as compared with nondepressed children (Alloy et al., Note 3). Raps and associates (Note 4) recently examined attributional patterns among psychiatric patients in a Veterans Administration hospital. These investigators reported that unipolar depressives exhibited the depressive attributional style observed in depressed college students and depressed grade-school children, whereas nondepressed schizophrenics and nondepressed medical patients exhibited the attributional style observed in nondepressed college students and grade-school children. See also the work of Klein and associates (1976), Kuiper (1978), and Rizley (1978) for similar evidence about attributional style and depression.

In similarity to the work on problem solving and depression, the studies examining attributional patterns in depressed and nondepressed people have demonstrated only a correlation between attributional style and depression; they have not distinguished between the possibility that particular attributional styles function as vulnerability factors for depression and the alternative possibility that depression itself causes people to attribute negative outcomes to internal, stable, and global factors. We currently are conducting studies designed to assess the directionality of the relationship between attributional style and depression. Our preliminary findings support the hypothesis that attributional style predisposes to depression, rather than the reverse. For example, Mukherji and associates (Note 5) reported that inducing depressive mood states in characteristically nondepressed people in the laboratory did not alter their attributional styles. Similarly, Alloy and associates (Note 3) used causal modeling statistics with their sample of schoolchildren and found that the correlation between attributional style for negative events at time 1 and depressive symptoms at time 2 ($r = .54$) exceeded the correlation between depressive symptoms at time 1 and attributional style for negative events at time 2 ($r = .34$), supporting the prediction that the bias to attribute negative events to internal, stable, and global factors puts one at risk for depressive symptoms. Further longitudinal studies are needed to determine whether or not attributional styles modulate emotional responses to stressful events.

Although the attributional differences between depressed and nondepressed people are robust, clinically oriented researchers are only just beginning to devise techniques aimed specifically at modifying depressive attributional styles. There are cognitive therapy approaches to depression (e.g., Beck et al., 1979) that include explicit techniques for modifying *particular* attributions depressed persons might make, but these approaches have not yet generated explicit techniques for modifying depressive attributional *styles*.

One study conducted by two social psychologists, Ickes and Layden (1978), has suggested that the kind of attributional style exhibited by depressed people may be somewhat difficult to modify. Ickes and Layden (1978) reported that people with low self-esteem attributed bad outcomes to internal factors and good outcomes to external factors, whereas people with high self-esteem attributed bad outcomes to external factors and good outcomes to internal factors. Reasoning in a fashion similar to the attributional reformulation of learned helplessness, Ickes and Layden hypothesized that low-self-esteem people might experience enhancement of self-esteem if their attributional styles were modified to resemble those of high-self-esteem people. Consequently, a therapy regimen was instituted for a 5-week period during which low-self-esteem people were instructed to list as many plausible causes as they could for three good and three bad outcomes each week. Subjects were restricted in the types of causes they could list. Subjects in group 1 were asked to list only internal causes for good outcomes and external causes for bad outcomes. Subjects in group 2 were allowed to list any type of cause for good outcomes but were required to list only external causes for bad outcomes. Finally, subjects in group 3 were required to list only internal causes for good outcomes but were allowed to list any type of cause for bad outcomes. Of course, the goal of therapy was to induce low-self-esteem subjects to make attributions somewhat inconsistent with their characteristic attributional style and consistent with the style of high-self-esteem subjects. Unfortunately, the therapy technique was unsuccessful. At the end of the 5-week therapy period, the low-self-esteem subjects showed no change in attributional style; they continued to attribute bad outcomes to internal factors and good outcomes to external factors. In passing, it is interesting to note that those subjects whose attributional styles became more similar to the attributional styles of high-self-esteem subjects also showed an elevation in self-esteem.

Work in experimental psychology has also suggested that attribution styles might be resistant to change. Beginning with Bartlett (1932), cognitive psychologists have emphasized the importance of "cognitive structures" or "schemas" in guiding people's interpretations and comprehensions of information (Abelson, 1976; Bobrow & Norman, 1975; Bransford & McCarrell, 1975; Harris & Monaco, 1978; Minsky, 1975; Schank & Abelson, 1977). Although the term "schema" has been defined in a number of ways by cognitive psychologists, the term generally is used to refer to an organized representation of prior knowledge that guides the processing of current information (e.g., Neisser, 1967; Ross, 1978).

Because the quantities and varieties of information at any time are greater than any person could process or attend to, people must be selective in what they notice, learn, remember, or infer in any situation (Neisser, 1967). Prior knowledge or schemas can facilitate selective processing of information in nonrandom ways. Information that is inconsistent with the general organization of the schema is often dropped out, and other aspects of the information are elaborated to be consistent with the activated schema (e.g., Bartlett, 1932; Bransford & Johnson, 1972; Bruner & Postman, 1979). Thus, although schemas facilitate perception, comprehension, recall, and problem solving, important consequences of their operation are bias and distortion.

Recently, a number of social psychologists have recognized the utility of applying the concept of schemas to the processing and interpretation of information in the social world (e.g., Cantor & Mischel, 1977, 1979). Of particular relevance to this chapter, social psychologists (e.g., Ajzen, 1977; Ross, 1977, 1978; Tversky & Kahneman, 1978) have extended this general perspective to the study of causal inferences and have argued that in making causal inferences, people not only rely on relevant situational or statistical information but also rely on their knowledge or schemas. In fact, Ajzen (1977) has shown that people are more likely to use information that is statistically relevant to making judgments about the likelihood of events when that information is consistent with their causal schemas than when it is not. Because people frequently assimilate what they observe to their preconceptions, their interpretations of information often are biased, and they may make unwarranted causal attributions. For example, suppose a person holds a perception that he is socially incompetent. The social psychological view suggests that such a person may make internal attributions for interpersonal negative events even when such inferences are unwarranted in a particular situation. This person might attribute the bad time he had on a date to his own lack of social skills, in spite of the fact that many of his friends also had unpleasant dates with the particular woman, suggesting that something about the woman herself is responsible for the unpleasant date.

A major therapeutic implication of the view that causal inferences are "schema-driven" or "theory-driven" is that people's attributional styles may not be easily changed through mere exposure to contradictory information (Ross, 1977). The logic of this implication is straightforward. Because the information is selectively interpreted in accordance with the person's beliefs or schemas, it is unlikely to provide strong disconfirmation of those schemas that are guiding the causal attributions the person makes. Thus, simply exposing depressed people to information suggesting that they attribute negative outcomes to external, unstable, and specific causes may produce attributional style changes only very slowly.

Does contemporary work in social psychology provide any insights about which techniques might produce powerful and rapid changes in attributional style? Although it is only suggestive at this point, a study by Ross and associates (1975) on the effects of debriefing has provided some reason to believe that personal insight concerning one's attributional biases may facilitate changes in these attributional tendencies. The subjects in Ross's experiment received false feedback about their performances and abilities in a novel discrimination task in which they were required to distinguish authentic suicide notes from fictitious notes. After the subject's perceptions of their own abilities for the task had been manipulated by the false feedback, the experimenter totally discredited the "evidence" on which these perceptions had been based. That is, subjects were fully debriefed and were told that their performance feedback had been totally unrelated to their actual performances. Surprisingly, in spite of the debriefing, subjects' ratings of their abilities for the task on a subsequent postexperimental questionnaire were congruent with the prior false feedback they had received. Although the debriefing completely discredited the evidence on which the subjects' initial impressions of their abilities had been based, those subjects who had received false feedback that they had failed at the task rated their abilities lower than did the subjects who had received false feedback that they had succeeded at the task. Thus, subjects' initial self-perceptions persevered and survived even the complete negation of their original evidential basis (Valins, 1974; Walster et al., 1967).

Although the standard debriefing in which subjects simply were made aware of the bogus nature of the prior feedback they had received was ineffective in reversing their initial self-perceptions, Ross and associates (1975) reported that a special "process debriefing" was quite effective in reversing these perceptions. In the special process-debriefing condition, subjects also were given an explicit account of the perseverance phenomenon and of the cognitive mechanisms that might lead them personally to retain inappropriate self-perceptions.

Although it is speculative, an implication of the study of Ross and associates (1975) is that informing depressed people that they exhibit a particular attributional style and that the operation of this style may lead them to experience more negative affect than nondepressed people might facilitate modification of this style. In this regard, it is noteworthy that in their cognitive therapy for depression, Beck and his colleagues (e.g., Beck et al., 1979) have reported that they devote a considerable portion of the initial therapy sessions to developing a common conceptualization of cognitive therapy with the depressed patient. Beck and associates (1979) reported the course of cognitive therapy with a typical depressed patient. Prior to the first treatment session, the therapist sent the patient the booklet *Coping with Depression* (Beck & Greenberg, 1974) with the request that the patient read the book in order to assist the treatment. During the first therapy session the therapist presented a rationale for cognitive therapy and discussed the patient's reaction to the model. In the early therapy sessions the therapist often used the patient's own experiences to demonstrate the relationship among cognition, behavior, and affect. Later in therapy, after the patient showed significant improvement, the therapist and patient discussed how her basic assumptions made her vulnerable to depression. Thus, the special process-debriefing manipulation in the Ross study has a counterpart in Beck's cognitive therapy for depression.

Previously we mentioned that exposing depressed people to information that contradicts their depressive causal inferences may produce changes in attributional style relatively slowly because the depressives may interpret the information in line with their beliefs or schemas. The experiment of Ross and associates (1975) suggested that exposure to disconfirming information may be a more powerful technique when it is paired with giving depressives an explicit account of their attributional styles. It is interesting that work in the area of the history of science also supports this suggestion. In his analysis of scientific revolutions, Kuhn (1970) argued that it is only against the backdrop of a well-articulated theory that the implications of an anomaly can be appreciated fully. So depressives may be most able to utilize information that contradicts their typical attributional patterns when they have insight about the operation of these attributional patterns.

A final implication for the modification of depressive attributional styles comes from the distinction between belief-based and evidence-based attributional styles (Metalsky & Abramson, 1980). A belief-based attributional style is a tendency to make particular causal inferences (rather than other possible inferences) by consistently relying on the same or similar generalized beliefs or knowledge about oneself, other people, and the world to resolve causal ambiguity. Alternatively, an evidence-based attributional style is a tendency to make particular causal inferences (rather than other possible inferences) by consistently relying on the same or similar patterns of situational information to resolve causal ambiguity. Whereas people displaying belief-based attributional styles may be quite insensitive to environmental information, people displaying evidence-based styles are quite sensitive to environmental information. See the work of Ross (1978) for a distinction between theory-driven and data-driven assessments of covariation. Metalsky and Abramson argued that cognitive-oriented therapy (e.g., Beck et al., 1979) will be most therapeutic for people exhibiting strong belief-based styles. This will be the case particularly for people who consistently rely on beliefs or schemas that are not congruent with the situational information they typically confront in making causal attributions. In contrast, more direct behavioral interventions, such as assertiveness training and social skills training, may be most effective for people displaying evidence-based attributional styles. This is particularly true for those people who in making causal attributions consistently rely on the negative situational information they generate by their own actions. For example, consider a depressed man who is lacking in social skills and who typically receives hostile gestures from others. Such an individual may justifiably attribute the rejections he receives from others to his own lack of ability, and he may come to therapy quite distressed. This patient might be helped most by a training and education program in which he could learn to express his feelings and concerns to others without eliciting negative responses from them (Hersen & Eisler, 1976). According to Metalsky and Abramson (1980), as patients change their stylistic ways of interacting with others, the situational information they rely on to resolve causal ambiguity should begin to point to more benign attributions as being most plausible. Thus, both cognition-oriented and behavior-oriented approaches may be helpful in modifying depressive attributional styles (Hollon & Garber, 1979).

Modifying the Bias to Subscribe to Unrealistic Goals. All other things being equal, people who are biased to subscribe to unrealistic goals will be more likely to develop expectations of no control than will people who are biased to subscribe to more realistic goals. Consequently, people biased to subscribe to unrealistic goals may be especially prone to helplessness depressions. Moreover, people who are biased to attach high importance to unrealistic goals should be especially prone to bouts of depressive affect, according to the logic of the reformulation of learned helplessness and depression.

Drawing on their clinical experience, psychotherapists (e.g., Beck et al., 1979; Ellis, 1977a) have argued that individual differences exist in the degrees to which people subscribe to unrealistic goals and that people showing a propensity to subscribe to such goals are at high risk for depressive affect. Recently, researchers have begun empirical testing of clinicians' intuitions about the relationship between subscribing to unrealistic goals and the development of depressive affect. Weissman and Beck (Note 6) developed the Dysfunctional Attitude Scale (DAS), which measures a number of "dysfunctional" attitudes hypothesized to predispose to depression. A careful inspection of the items on the scale suggests that many of them tap into the degree to which a person subscribes to and attaches high importance to unrealistic goals. For example, people are asked to what extent they agree or disagree with such statements as the following: "A person should do well at everything he undertakes." "I cannot be happy unless most people I know admire me." "It is difficult to be happy unless one is good looking, intelligent, rich, and creative." These are only some of the test items. In a preliminary investigation, Weissman and Beck (Note 6) reported that there were individual differences in the degrees to which people endorsed the "dysfunctional" attitudes, that subjects' scores on the DAS correlated highly with their scores on the Beck Depression Inventory (BDI) ($r = .65$), and that subjects' scores on the DAS were relatively consistent over an 8-week period (scores on the two administrations of the test correlated .71). In addition, a cross-lagged panel correlation design (e.g., Campbell, 1963; Crano et al., 1972) was implemented in order to compare the BDI scores and the DAS scores at times 1 and 2 (8 weeks apart) and possibly to allow inferences about causal relationships from the correlation data. The results tended to suggest (they fell just short of a .05 level of statistical significance) that DAS scores at time 1 were more predictive of BDI scores at time 2 ($r = .64$) than were BDI scores at time 1 predictive of DAS scores at time 2 ($r = .35$). Thus, although the data are only suggestive, the study of Weissman and Beck supports the idea that there are individual differences in the degrees to which people subscribe to and attach high importance to unrealistic goals and that these individual differences are predictive of a person's vulnerability to depression. To substantiate the initial findings of Weissman and Beck, further longitudinal studies will be necessary.

Ellis and his associates (e.g., Ellis & Grieger, 1977) and Beck and his associates (e.g., Beck, 1976; Beck et al., 1979) have been influential in developing therapeutic techniques aimed at modifying patients' biases to subscribe to and attach high importance to unrealistic goals. As we pointed out earlier, Ellis's approach, Rational-Emotive Therapy (RET), consists in the use of logical and empirical methods of scientific questioning, challenging, and debating. Once patients recover from current depressive episodes and terminate their RET, they can act as their own therapists by continuing to identify and challenge their unrealistic goals. Presumably, such self-help procedures will decrease their vulnerability to future depressions. Of particular importance for vulnerability issues, RET practitioners have begun to stress the importance of "rational-emotive education" for children (e.g., Knaus, 1977).

Emphasizing that subscribing to unrealistic goals increases one's vulnerability to depression, Beck and his colleagues (e.g., Beck et al., 1979) often warn depressed patients that although their depressive symptoms may have abated, they will be particularly prone to relapses until they are able to refrain from subscribing to these unrealistic goals. Once the unrealistic goals have been identified, patients are encouraged to evaluate their adaptiveness by listing the advantages and disadvantages of subscribing to such goals. Although no therapy studies have examined this technique in isolation from other techniques, Beck and associates (1979) have speculated that listing the advantages and disadvantages of a given assumption is one of the most effective procedures for long-term modification of the way one handles a problem.

Clinical Efficacy of Therapeutic Strategies

It is important to emphasize that this chapter is not intended to constitute a therapy manual for the treatment of depression. On the contrary, we have chosen a particular model of depression, the helplessness model, and presented techniques that may be effective in producing changes at the points for intervention we have derived from the model. Although some of these techniques have already been incorporated into existing therapy regimens for depression (e.g., Beck et al., 1979; Ellis, 1977a; Fuchs and Rehm, 1977), other techniques have been suggested by experimental work in cognitive and social psychology and thus have not been examined in clinical trials with depressed patients. Further research will be necessary to determine if the techniques do, in fact, produce changes at the appropriate points for intervention. Also, we recognize that a number of factors not specific to the points for intervention we derived may nonetheless be important for producing therapeutic change.

Although the existing studies examining the clinical efficacies of various therapies for depression have not, in the main, examined the utility of particular techniques in isolation from other techniques, it is useful to examine their results, because many of the techniques featured in our analysis are also incorporated in these other therapies. In a recent review, Hollon and Garber (1979) concluded, that in controlled outcome studies in which the combination of cognitive and behavioral procedures was tested against alternative therapy procedures, the cognitive-behavioral procedures were superior in treating depression, as compared with the alternatives (Hollon, Note 8; Hollon & Beck, 1978). Cognitive-behavioral procedures were more efficacious than strictly cognitive procedures (Taylor & Marshall, 1977), strictly behavioral procedures (Shaw, 1977; Taylor & Marshall, 1977), strictly pharmacotherapy procedures (McLean & Hakstian, 1979; Rush et al., 1977), and nonspecific and/or dynamic procedures (Fuchs & Rehm, 1977; McLean & Hakstian, in press; Shaw, 1977; Shipley & Fazio, 1973). Future studies of therapy for depression must use more highly refined assessment devices to determine which particular techniques are exerting which predicted effects on the various psychological processes associated with depression. In addition, subsequent therapy studies must determine which techniques are useful in reversing current depressive episodes and which techniques are useful in decreasing one's vulnerability to depression.

Cognitive Biases and Illusions in Nondepressed People: Implications for the Psychotherapy of Depression

Whereas cognitive accounts of depression have emphasized depressives' cognitive distortions and biases in interpreting their environments and behaviors (e.g., Beck, 1967, 1976; Beck et al., 1979), growing numbers of empirical studies have demonstrated the existence of cognitive biases and illusions in nondepressed people. For example, Alloy and Abramson (1979) reported that depressed students' judgments of the degree of control their responses exerted over outcomes were not influenced by the hedonic valences of the outcomes. Nondepressed students, on the other hand, overestimated the degree of control their responses exerted over objectively uncontrollable outcomes that occurred with high frequency or that were desirable. Alternatively, nondepressed students underestimated the degree of control their responses exerted over objectively controllable but undesirable outcomes. Finally, nondepressed students accurately judged their degree of control over neutral, controllable outcomes. In line with the results of Alloy and Abramson (1979), Golin and associates (1977) found that depressed students did not show an "illusion of control" (Langer, 1975) in an objective chance task in which elements typically associated with skills tasks (e.g., practice) had been introduced, whereas nondepressed students did succumb to the illusion of control. Golin and associates (1979) extended these studies to a clinical setting and reported that in similarity to mildly depressed college students, depressed inpatients did not show the illusion of control, whereas nondepressed schizophrenic inpatients showed a robust illusion of control.

In a study of selective recall of positive and negative feedback, Nelson and Craighead (1977) found that depressed college students accurately recalled the frequency of negative feedback on a laboratory task, whereas nondepressed students underestimated the frequency of negative feedback (DeMonbreun & Craighead, 1977). Similarly, Rozensky and associates (1977) reported that nondepressed control patients rewarded themselves to a greater degree than their objective performances would warrant. Although depressed patients also tended to overreward themselves, they were more accurate with their self-rewards than were the nondepressives.

Lewinsohn and associates (1980) examined the relationship between subjects' own perceptions of their social competence and observers' perceptions of their social competence for depressed patients, psychiatric control patients, and a normal control population. Surprisingly, depressed patients saw themselves as others saw them, whereas both groups of control subjects perceived themselves more positively than other people saw them. Instead of supporting Beck's contention (1967) that depressives are characterized by unrealistically negative views of themselves, the results of Lewinsohn and associates suggest that nondepressives may be characterized by unrealistically positive views of themselves. Similarly, Mischel and associates (1973, 1976) have found that positive experiences and expectations for future success lead people to remember and pay more attention to their strengths relative to their weaknesses. Finally, nondepressed college students (Klein et al., 1976; Kuiper, 1978; Rizley, 1978; Seligman et al., 1979; Mukherji & Abramson, Note 8), nondepressed children (Alloy et al., Note 3), nondepressed medical patients (Raps et al., Note 4), and nondepressed schizophrenics (Raps et al., Note 4) exhibited the attributional pattern characterized as "self-serving" by social psychologists (i.e., attributing negative outcomes to external factors and positive outcomes to internal factors), whereas depressed college students (Klein et al., 1976; Kuiper, 1978; Rizley, 1978; Seligman et al., 1979; Mukherji & Abramson, Note 9), depressed children (Alloy et al., Note 3), and unipolar depressives (Raps et al., Note 4) did not.

Taken together, these studies show that at times nondepressed people succumb to cognitive biases or illusions that enable them to see themselves and their environment with a rosy glow. Freud (1917/1957) also was aware of "depressive realism" (Mischel, 1979) when he wrote *Mourning and Melancholia*:

> When in his [the depressive's] heightened self-criticism he describes himself as petty, egoistic, dishonest, lacking in independence, one whose sole aim has been to hide the weakness of his own nature, it may be, so far as we know, that he has come pretty near to understanding himself; we only wonder why a man has to be ill before he can be accessible to a truth of this kind (p. 246).

In light of these studies demonstrating nondepressive biases and illusions, it is interesting that the professed goal of cognitive therapy for depression is to encourage depressives to process information more realistically. As Mischel (1979) has speculated, the assumption that realism is the crux of appropriate affect may have to be seriously questioned. See the work of Ellis (1977b) for a discussion of when ego-enhancing defense mechanisms may not be necessary for psychological well-being. The preceding discussion raises an important and intriguing question for psychotherapy in depression: Should therapy focus on helping depressives process information more realistically, or should therapy focus on helping depressives acquire the benign illusions and biases that characterize nondepressed people?

REFERENCE NOTES

1. Levine, F.M., & Lee. *Models of psychotherapy*. Unpublished manuscript, Department of Psychology, State University of New York at Stony Brook, 1981.
2. Abramson, L.Y., Alloy, L.B., & Rosoff, R. *Depression and the generation of complex hypotheses in the judgment of contingency*. Unpublished manuscript, Department of Psychology, State University of New York at Stony Brook, 1980.
3. Alloy, L.B., Abramson, L.Y., Seligman, M.E.R., Tanenbaum, R.L., Kaslow, W.J., Peterson, C., Semmel, A., & Miller, S. *Depression in children: Problem solving, attributional style, and parent's attributional style*. Unpublished manuscript, Department of Psychology, Northwestern University, 1980.
4. Raps, C.S., Reinhard, K.E., Seligman, M.E.P., & Abramson, L.Y. *Attributional style in unipolar depressives and schizophrenics*. Unpublished manuscript, Northport Veterans Administration Medical Center, Northport, N.Y., 1980.
5. Mukherji, B.R., Abramson, L.Y., & Martin, D.J. *Induced depressive mood and attributional patterns*. Unpublished manuscript, Department of Psychology, State University of New York at Stony Brook, 1980.
6. Weissman, A.N., & Beck, A.T. *Development and validation of the Dysfunctional Attitude Scale: A preliminary investigation*. Presented at the annual meeting of the American Educational Research Association, Toronto, Ontario, 1978.
7. Hollon, S.D. *Status and efficacy of behavior therapies for depression:*

Comparisons and combinations with alternative approaches. Presented at the NIMH-sponsored conference "Research Recommendations for the Behavioral Treatment of Depression," L.P. Rehm, chairman, University of Pittsburgh, Pittsburgh, Pa., April 1979.

8. Mukherji, B.R., & Abramson, L.Y. *Causal inferences in depressed and nondepressed people: Evidence for a nondepressive bias.* Unpublished manuscript, Department of Psychology, State University of New York at Stony Brook, 1980.

REFERENCES

Abelson, R.P. Script processing in attitude formation and decision making. In J.S. Carroll and J.W. Payne (Eds.), *Cognition and social behavior.* Hillsdale, N.J.: Erlbaum, 1976.

Abramson, L.Y., Seligman, M.E.P., & Teasdale, J. Learned helplessness in humans. Critique and reformulation. *Journal of Abnormal Psychology,* 1978, *87,* 49-74.

Ajzen, I. Intuitive theories of events and the effects of base-rate information on prediction. *Journal of Personality and Social Psychology,* 1977, *35,* 303-324.

Alloy, L.B., & Abramson, L.Y. Judgment of contingency in depressed and nondepressed students: Sadder but wiser? *Journal of Experimental Psychology: General,* 1979, *108,* 441-485.

Arieti, S. Cognition and feeling. In M.B. Arnold (Ed.), *Feelings and emotions,* New York: Academic, 1970.

Bandura, A. Vicarious and self-reinforcement processes. In R. Glaser (Ed.), *The nature of reinforcement,* New York: Academic, 1971.

Bartlett, F. *Remembering.* Cambridge: Cambridge University Press, 1932.

Beck, A.T. *Depression: Clinical, experimental, and theoretical aspects.* New York: Harper & Row, 1967.

Beck, A.T. *Cognitive therapy and emotional disorders.* New York: International Universities Press, 1976.

Beck, A.T., & Greenberg, R.L. *Coping with depression.* New York: Institute for Rational Living, 1974.

Beck, A.T., Rush, A.J., Shaw, B.F., & Emery, G. *Cognitive therapy of depression.* New York: Guilford, 1979.

Bibring, E. The mechanism of depression. In P. Greenacre (Ed.), *Affective disorders,* New York: International Universities Press, 1953.

Bobrow, D.G., & Norman, D.A. Some principles of memory schemata. In D.G. Bobrow & D.A. Norman (Eds.), *Representation and understanding,* New York: Academic, 1975.

Bransford, J.D., & Johnson, M.K. Contextual prerequisites for understanding: Some investigations of comprehension and recall. *Journal of Verbal Learning and Verbal Behavior,* 1972, *11,* 717-726.

Bransford, J.D., & McCarrell, N.S. A sketch of a cognitive approach to comprehension: Some thoughts about understanding. What it means to comprehend. In W.B. Weimer & D.S. Palermo (Eds.), *Cognition and the symbolic processes,* Hillsdale, N.J.: Erlbaum, 1975.

Brehm, J.W., & Cohen, A.R. *Explorations in cognitive dissonance.* New York: Wiley, 1962.
Bruner, J.S., & Postman, L. On the perception of incongruity: A paradigm. *Journal of Personality,* 1979, *18,* 206-223.
Campbell, D.T. From description to experimentation: Interpreting trends as quasi-experiments. In C.W. Harris (Ed.), *Problems in measuring change,* Madison: University of Wisconsin Press, 1963.
Cantor, N., & Mischel, W. Traits as prototypes: Effects on recognition memory. *Journal of Personality and Social Psychology,* 1977, *35,* 38-48.
Cantor, N., & Mischel, W. Prototypes in person perception. In L. Berkowitz (Ed.), *Advances in experimental social psychology* (Vol. 12), New York: Academic, 1979.
Costello, C.G. Depression: Loss of reinforcers or loss of reinforcer effectiveness? *Behavior Therapy,* 1972, *3,* 240-247.
Crano, W.D., Kenny, D.A., & Campbell, D.T. Does intelligence cause achievement? A cross-lagged panel analysis. *Journal of Educational Psychology,* 1972, *63,* 258-275.
DeMonbreun, B.G., & Craighead, W.E. Distortion of perception and recall of positive and neutral feedback in depression. *Cognitive Therapy and Research,* 1977, *1,* 311-329.
Diggory, J.C. *Self-evaluation: Concepts and studies.* New York: Wiley, 1966.
D'Zurilla, T.J., & Goldfried, M.R. Problem solving and behavior modification. *Journal of Abnormal Psychology,* 1971, *78,* 107-126.
Ellis, A. *Reason and emotion in psychotherapy.* New York: Lyle Stuart, 1962.
Ellis, A. The basic clinical theory of rational-emotive therapy. In A. Ellis & R. Grieger (Eds.) *Handbook of rational-emotive therapy,* New York: Springer, 1977. (a)
Ellis, A. Research data supporting the clinical and personality hypotheses of RET and other cognitive-behavior therapies. In A. Ellis & R. Grieger (Eds.), *Handbook of rational-emotive therapy,* New York: Springer, 1977. (b)
Ellis, A., & Grieger, R. *Handbook of rational-emotive therapy.* New York: Springer, 1977.
Ferster, C.B. A functional analysis of depression. *American Psychologist,* 1973, *28,* 857-870.
Fitch, G. Effects of self-esteem, perceived performance and choice on causal attributions. *Journal of Personality and Social Psychology,* 1970, *16,* 311-315.
Freud, S. Mourning and melancholia. In J. Strachey (Ed. and Trans.), *The complete psychological works of Sigmund Freud* (Vol. 14), London: Hogarth, 1957 (originally published 1917).
Fuchs, C., & Rehm, L.P. A self-control behavior therapy program for depression. *Journal of Consulting and Clinical Psychology,* 1977, *45,* 206-215.
Goldfried, M.R. Toward the delineation of therapeutic change principles. *American Psychologist,* 1980, *35,* 991-999.
Goldfried, M.R., & Davison, G.C. *Clinical behavior therapy.* New York: Holt, Rinehart, 1976.
Golin, S., & Terrell, F. Motivational and associative aspects of mild depression in skill and chance tasks. *Journal of Abnormal Psychology,* 1977, *86,* 389-401.

Golin, S., Terrell, F., & Johnson, B. Depression and the illusion of control. *Journal of Abnormal Psychology*, 1977, *86*, 440-442.

Golin, S., Terrell, F., Weitz, J., & Drost, P.L. The illusion of control among depressed patients. *Journal of Abnormal Psychology*, 1979, *88*, 454-457.

Gotlib, I.H., & Asarnow, R.F. Interpersonal and impersonal problem solving skills in mildly and clinically depressed university students. *Journal of Consulting and Clinical Psychology*, 1979, *47*, 86-95.

Harris, R.J., & Monaco, G.E. Psychology of pragmatic implication: Information processing between the lines. *Journal of Experimental Psychology: General*, 1978, *107*, 1-22.

Hersen, M., & Eisler, R.M. Social skills training. In W.E. Craighead, A.E. Kazdin, & M.J. Mahoney (Eds.), *Behavior modification: Principles, issues, and applications*, Boston: Houghton Mifflin, 1976.

Hollon, S.D., & Beck, A.T. Psychotherapy and drug therapy: Comparisons and combinations. In S.L. Garfield & A.E. Bergin (Eds.), *The handbook of psychotherapy and behavior change*, New York: Wiley, 1978.

Hollon, S.D., & Garber, J.G. A cognitive-expectancy theory of therapy for helplessness and depression. In J. Garber & M.E.P. Seligman (Eds.), *Human helplessness: Theory and application*, New York: Academic, 1979.

Ickes, W., & Layden, M.A. Attributional sytles. In J. Harvey, W. Ickes, & R. Kidd (Eds.), *New directions in attribution research* (Vol. 2), Hillsdale, N.J.: Erlbaum, 1978.

Kanfer, F.H., & Saslow, G. Behavioral diagnosis. In C.M. Franks (Ed.), *Behavior therapy: Appraisal and status*, pp. 417-444. New York: McGraw-Hill, 1969.

Kelley, H.H. Attribution theory in social psychology. In D. Levine (Ed.), *Nebraska symposium on motivation* (Vol. 15), Lincoln: University of Nebraska Press, 1967.

Klein, D.C., Fencil-Morse, E., & Seligman, M.E.P. Depression, learned helplessness, and the attribution of failure. *Journal of Personality and Social Psychology*, 1976, *85*, 11-26.

Klinger, E. *Meaning and void: Inner experience and the incentives in people's lives*. Minneapolis: University of Minnesota Press, 1977.

Knaus, W.J. Rational-emotive education. In A. Ellis & R. Grieger (Eds.), *Handbook of rational-emotive therapy*, New York: Springer, 1977.

Korchin, S.J. *Modern clinical psychology: Principles of intervention in the clinic and community*. New York: Basic Books, 1976.

Kuhn, T.S. *The structure of scientific revolutions* (Vol. 2). Chicago: University of Chicago Press, 1970.

Kuiper, N.A. Depression and causal attributions for success and failure. *Journal of Personality and Social Psychology*, 1978, *36*, 236-246.

Langer, E.J. The illusion of control. *Journal of Personality and Social Psychology*, 1975, *32*, 311-328.

Lazarus, A.A. *Behavior therapy and beyond*. New York: McGraw-Hill, 1971.

Levy, L.H. *Psychological interpretation*. New York: Holt, Rinehart, 1963.

Lewinsohn, P.M. A behavioral approach to depression. In R.J. Friedman & M.M. Katz (Eds.), *The psychology of depression: Contemporary theory and research*, pp. 157-178. Washington D.C.: Winston, 1974.

Lewinsohn, P.M., Mischel, W., Chaplin, W., & Barton, R. Social competence and depression: The role of illusory self-perceptions? *Journal of Abnormal Psychology*, 1980, *89*, 203-212.

Lichtenberg, P. A definition and analysis of depression. *Archives of Neurology and Psychiatry*, 1957, *77*, 516-527.

London, P. *The modes and morals of psychotherapy*. New York: Holt, Rinehart, 1964.

London, P. The end of ideology in behavior modification. *American Psychologist*, 1972, *27*, 913-920.

Maracek, J., & Mettee, D. Avoidance of continued success as a function of self-esteem, level of esteem certainty and responsibility for success. *Journal of Personality and Social Psychology*, 1972, *22*, 98-107.

McLean, P.D., & Hakstian, A.R. Clinical depression: Comparative efficacy of outpatient treatments. *Journal of Consulting and Clinical Psychology*, 1979, *47*, 818-836.

Meehl, P.E. *Clinical versus statistical prediction: A theoretical analysis and a review of the evidence*. Minneapolis: University of Minnesota Press, 1954.

Melges, F.J., & Bowlby, J. Types of hopelessness in psychopathological process. *Archives of General Psychiatry*, 1969, *20*, 690-699.

Metalsky, G.I., & Abramson, L.Y. Attributional styles: Toward a framework for conceptualization and assessment. In P.C. Kendall & S.D. Hollon (Eds.), *Cognitive-behavioral interventions: Assessment methods*, New York: Academic, 1980.

Minsky, M. A framework for representing knowledge. In P.H. Winston (Ed.), *The psychology of computer vision*, New York: McGraw-Hill, 1975.

Mischel, W. On the interface of cognition and personality: Beyond the person-situation debate. *American Psychologist*, 1979, *34*, 740-754.

Mischel, W., Ebbesen, E., & Zeiss, A.R. Selective attention to the self: Situational and dispositional determinants. *Journal of Personality and Social Psychology*, 1973, *27*, 129-142.

Mischel, W., Ebbesen, E., & Zeiss, A.R. Determinants of selective memory about the self. *Journal of Consulting and Clinical Psychology*, 1976, *44*, 92-103.

Neisser, U. *Cognitive psychology*. New York: Appleton-Century-Crofts, 1967.

Nelson, R.E. Irrational beliefs in depression. *Journal of Consulting and Clinical Psychology*, 1977, *45*, 1190-1191.

Nelson, R.E., & Craighead, W.E. Selective recall of positive and negative feedback, self-control behaviors, and depression. *Journal of Abnormal Psychology*, 1977, *86*, 379-388.

Owens, J., Bower, G.H., & Black, J.B. The "soap opera" effect in story recall. *Memory and Cognition*, 1979, *7*, 185-191.

Rehm, L.P. A self-control model of depression. *Behavior Therapy*, 1977, *8*, 787-804.

Rizley, R. Depression and distortion in the attribution of causality. *Journal of Abnormal Psychology*, 1978, *87*, 32-48.

Rogers, C.R. *On becoming a person*. Boston: Houghton Mifflin, 1961.

Ross, L. The intuitive psychologist and his shortcomings: Distortions in the attribution process. In L. Berkowitz (Ed.), *Advances in experimental social psychology* (Vol. 10), New York: Academic, 1977.

Ross, L. Some afterthoughts on the intuitive psychologist. In L. Berkowitz (Ed.), *Cognitive theories in social psychology*, New York: Academic, 1978.

Ross, L., Lepper, M., & Hubbard, M. Perseverance in self-perception and social perception: Biased attributional processes in the debriefing paradigm. *Journal of Personality and Social Psychology*, 1975, *32*, 880-892.

Rozensky, R.H., Rehm, L.P., Pry, G., & Roth, D. Depression and self-reinforcement behavior in hospitalized patients. *Journal of Behavior Therapy and Experimental Psychiatry*, 1977, *8*, 35-38.

Rush, A.J., Beck, A.T., Kovacs, M., & Hollon, S.D. Comparative efficacy of cognitive therapy versus pharmacotherapy in outpatient depressives. *Cognitive Therapy and Research*, 1977, *1*, 17-37.

Schank, R., & Abelson, R.P. *Scripts, plans, goals and understanding: An inquiry into human knowledge structures.* Hillsdale, N.J.: Erlbaum, 1977.

Schildkraut, J.J. The catecholamine hypothesis of affective disorders. *American Journal of Psychiatry*, 1965, *122*, 509-522.

Seligman, M.E.P. *Helplessness: On depression, development, and death.* San Francisco: Freeman, 1975.

Seligman, M.E.P., Abramson, L.Y., Semmel, A., & von Baeyer, C. Depressive attributional style. *Journal of Abnormal Psychology*, 1979, *88*, 242-247.

Shaw, B.F. Comparison of cognitive therapy and behavior therapy in the treatment of depression. *Journal of Consulting and Clinical Psychology*, 1977, *45*, 543-551.

Shipley, C.R., & Fazio, A.F. Pilot study of a treatment in psychological depression. *Journal of Abnormal Psychology*, 1973, *82*, 372-376.

Taylor, F.C., & Marshall, W.L. Experimental analysis of a cognitive-behavior therapy for depression. *Cognitive Therapy and Research*, 1977, *1*, 59-72.

Tversky, A., & Kahneman, D. Causal thinking in judgment under uncertainty. In B. Butts & J. Hintikka (Eds.), *Logic, methodology, and philosophy of science.* Dordrecht, Holland: D. Reidel, 1978.

Valins, S. Persistent effects of information about internal reactions: Ineffectiveness of debriefing. In H. London & R.E. Nisbett (Eds.), *Thought and feeling: Cognitive modification of feeling states*, Chicago: Aldine, 1974.

Walster, E., Berscheid, E., Abrahams, D., & Aronson, V. Effectiveness of debriefing following deception experiments. *Journal of Personality and Social Psychology*, 1967, *6*, 371-380.

Weiner, B. *Theories of motivation: From mechanism to cognition.* Chicago: Rand-McNally, 1972.

Weiner, B. (Ed.). *Achievement motivation and attribution theory.* Morristown, N.J.: General Learning Process, 1974.

Wortman, C.B., & Dintzer, L. Is an attributional analysis of the learned helplessness phenomenon viable? A critique of the Abramson-Seligman-Teasdale reformulation. *Journal of Abnormal Psychology*, 1978, *87*, 75-90.

Zeiss, A.M., Lewinsohn, P.M., & Munoz, R.F. Nonspecific improvement effects in depression using interpersonal skills training, pleasant activity schedules, or cognitive training. *Journal of Consulting and Clinical Psychology*, 1979, *47*, 427-439.

Clinical Behavioral Treatment of Depression

PART III

Multimodal Therapy and the Problems of Depression

**Allen Fay
Arnold A. Lazarus**

For the clinician dealing with depression, it is clear that not all patients manifest a homogeneous set of external behaviors and symptoms. There are many different symptoms in the depression spectrum (Goodwin & Guze, 1979, p. 9), and polar opposites such as hyperphagia-anorexia, hypersomnia-insomnia, and agitation-retardation can be found in various cases. Skinner (1953) viewed depression as a hypothetical construct and defined it simply as a general weakening of one's behavioral repertoire. Of course, a multitude of clinical entities can be associated with global response deficits. Also, a clinician observing only a person's behavior cannot determine with any degree of reliability if that person is "feeling" depressed.

When a person states "I am feeling depressed," what does this imply? Is the person sad? Is the person harboring a low-grade infection, latent malignancy, or endocrinopathy? Is this the operant response of a person searching for sympathy and comfort? Is the person manifesting normal fatigue? Or do we indeed have someone suffering from what we might call "pathological dysphoria"? One of the problems with nosological broadsides is that they obscure attention to detail and befog the range of inner and outer behaviors and the specific variables that affect them.

Because the various depressive intensities constitute a continuum and there is a broad clinical spectrum ranging from sadness to grief to "neurotic" depression to a syndrome of profound biological and psychological alteration, confusion arises when generalizations are made about "depressives" without reference to the degree and also the type of depression under discussion. And because most depressive episodes are self-limited, there are as many different treatments for depression as there are for the common cold.

Apart from those who favor a pharmacological approach, we have the behavioral emphasis of Lewinsohn (1974), Beck's cognitive theories and therapies (Beck, 1976; Beck et al., 1979), the learned helplessness model of Seligman (1975), the self-control techniques of Fuchs and Rehm (1977), and the interpersonal orientation of McLean and associates (1973), to mention but a few different psychological viewpoints. Undoubtedly, many different theories can readily accommodate and integrate the existing data, and the empirical evidence can be used to support several different positions.

In our daily practices we frequently are consulted by people who complain that they are depressed. These people manifest various combinations of the following (in most instances, these phenomena constitute a departure from a premorbid status):

Behavior. The patient may manifest the following: reduced work performance; impaired sexual activity; diminished food intake; neglect of grooming and personal appearance; motor retardation; statements of dejection, pessimism, and self-reproach; poverty of action and decisions; complaining (e.g., somatic), crying, and suicidal threats, gestures, or attempts.

Affect. There are reports of few or no feelings. The "mirth response" is absent. The patient seems especially prone to fatigue ("I find everything an effort."). Sadness usually dominates the affective range, but self-directed anger may also be present. Guilt is often prominent. There is diurnal variation in mood (usually improving later in the day).

Sensation. A conspicuous absence of sensory pleasure dominates this modality. Negative sensations prevail: dizziness, burning sensations, pain, indigestion, and other somatic complaints. In more severe disorders it is not uncommon to find auditory hallucinations, especially a voice that denigrates the patient.

Imagery. Visions of doom, loneliness, abandonment, illness, failure, and helplessness are most evident. There is inability to form positive images of oneself in pleasurable situations or to picture oneself feeling better in the future. Positive past experiences frequently are blocked out as well.

Cognition. There are pervasive ideas of self-worthlessness, as well as low self-esteem and high self-blame. There are negative expectations ("Things will always be bad for me.") and negative self-attributions ("I am to blame." "I am a terrible person." "I'm no good at anything." "I am a burden to my family, friends, to everyone.").

Interpersonal. There is decreased social participation (generally less communicative and more withdrawn); social activities are seldom initiated. There is a general lack of assertiveness and a loss of interest in personal obligations and responsibilities, despite protestations of guilt.

Biological. The following manifestations may be seen: weight loss as a consequence of anorexia; insomnia and fitful sleep patterns, especially early morning awakening; dry mouth; constipation; decreased libido. "Depression" may be the result of a variety of medical illnesses (e.g., hypothyroidism, malignancies, infections), as well as therapeutic or nonmedical use of various substances (e.g., reserpine, oral contraceptives, alcohol).

Conspicuously absent from the literature are long-term systematic follow-up studies. Most of the research has involved follow-up periods extending over a few months to perhaps a year or 2 years at best. It is well documented that depressive conditions tend to be recurrent. Moreover, what research evidence we have seems to indicate that unimodal interventions, no matter how impressive initially, tend to produce only short-term improvement. Shaw (1977) compared cognitive restructuring and a behavioral approach for the treatment of depression, and he added two controls: an attention-placebo group and a nontreatment group. The cognitive restructuring group experienced significantly superior results, but after only 1 month the differences between the cognitive group and the behavioral group were no longer statistically significant. We have serious doubts about any long-term superiority of most unimodal therapies. The use of lithium carbonate in the treatment and prevention of bipolar affective disorders is a notable exception, assuming an absence of negative cognitions, sensations, affects, images, and interpersonal reactions (poor relationship with therapist, pressures from family) that would preclude taking the drug (Fay, 1976). It is worth noting that Taylor and Marshall (1977) found that a bimodal therapy (a combined cognitive-behavioral approach) was more effective than either a cognitive method or a behavior modification method and also more effective than the no-treatment condition. Our own work on multimodal interventions points to a synergistic effect that not only yields positive outcomes but also promotes durable results (based on 2- and 3-year follow-up).

Multimodal Orientation

Personality, according to the multimodal orientation (Lazarus, 1973, 1976, 1981), is made up of the interactions among a person's overt behaviors, affective responses, sensory reactions, images, cognitions, and interpersonal dealings, all of which rest on a biological matrix. It cannot be overemphasized that each of the seven modalities is essentially interactive. Affective responses, for instance, result from ongoing biological processes, sensory stimuli, images and cognitions, overt behavior, and interpersonal dealings, but they, in turn, influence each and every one of the other modalities, thus producing a continuous flow or ripple effect. Yet, for purposes of assessment and intervention, we can treat the seven interactive modalities as discrete and specific entities. Comprehensive assessment from a multimodal standpoint implies that every modality will be carefully examined, and thorough therapy entails devoting specific attention (training and retraining) to each modality in which problems arise.

Whereas cognitive therapists consider the source of depression "a hypervalent set of negative concepts" and regard "the correction and damping down of these concepts" as a necessary and sufficient treatment for depression (Rush et al., 1977), therapists with a multimodal orientation strongly disagree with this unimodal position. It is inaccurate to speak of depression (singular); rather, there are depressions. Some depressions are predominantly biological in nature, and even among these, biological markers may discriminate subtypes (Maas, 1978; Schildkraut et al., 1978). Others may be caused primarily by biological and sensory interactions (e.g., chronic pain). Some may be the outgrowth of behavioral deficits. Again, it must be emphasized that regardless of its points of origin, any problem will influence and be influenced by each and every modality. Thus, even if a patient's depressive reaction is largely the result of biogenic amine depletion, a multimodal therapist will nevertheless recommend dealing with the patient's behaviors, affective responses, sensations, images, cognitions, and interpersonal relationships, in addition to prescribing the necessary pharmacological ingredients. The major reason for advocating multimodal therapy is that long-term benefits seem to be in direct proportion to the range of modalities employed in treatment.

The multimodal orientation rests on the assumption that there is no unitary cause or single cure for most problems encountered by the clinician. Human conditions are multileveled and multilayered. Certainly, "depressions" are multidetermined. Although medication, social skills training, activity charting, cognitive restructuring, electroconvulsive therapy, behavioral training, pleasant-events training, and many other approaches have achieved positive outcomes, only rarely are singular methods or approaches both necessary and sufficient for a long-range benefit. A case history may clarify most of the foregoing points.

Case History

Leon, a 32-year-old architect, had been hospitalized twice during his twenties for "agitated depression." His mother had suffered postpartum depressions and had been treated for "involutional melancholia" during her late forties. Leon complained that during the preceding 2 or 3 months his powers of concentration had deteriorated, he was sleeping poorly, he had no appetite, and he felt fatigued and disheartened. A psychiatrist had prescribed a tricyclic antidepressant that was not helping.

An initial interview followed by a detailed life-history questionnaire indicated clear-cut problems in his interpersonal, cognitive, imagery, and affective modalities. Interpersonally, Leon was generally unassertive and inclined to suppress his feelings. The latter tendency seemed closely linked to unexpressed anger, which led to feelings of agitation from time to time. Cognitively, he was perfectionistic and inclined to denigrate himself. His imagery was replete with visions of failure and personal humiliation.

Some of the foregoing reactions probably were secondary to his feelings of depression per se. In his premorbid state, Leon had been somewhat less likely to suppress his feelings and resort to self-critical thoughts and catastrophic images. Nevertheless, even when he had not been depressed, he had certain chronic deficits and excesses that probably will make him vulnerable to relapse. Thus, Leon's perfectionism and lack of social assertiveness called for specific interventions, quite apart from his acute depressive state.

After the fourth session, he was handed a large index card with the following instructions:

Behavior. Increase doing, moving, exercising, and other activities.

Affect. Channel unexpressed anger into direct and appropriate assertiveness.

Sensation. Expose yourself to pleasant sensations at least twice daily (e.g., listening to music, taking a hot shower).

Imagery. Practice using success and mastery images (e.g., picture yourself succeeding at various tasks, real or imagined).

Cognition. Challenge and dispute false cognitions. Monitor negative thoughts. For example, avoid "I can't." Change "I am a failure" to "I have failed in some specific situations."

Interpersonal. Deliberately seek out new people, even when least in the mood for company. Practice assertive skills when appropriate.

Biological. Comprehensive medical evaluation.

This initial treatment plan was also typed out and given to Leon for ready reference. He was advised to keep a copy in his wallet and to place another copy in some conspicuous place at home.

Parnate (10 mg b.i.d.) was prescribed. Concurrently, imagery exercises (Lazarus, 1978), cognitive restructuring, and social assertiveness regimens were introduced. Within 3 weeks he reported feeling nondepressed and much more optimistic (probably as a result of the medication more than anything else), but the cognitive, behavioral, imagery, sensory, and interpersonal training continued.

Three months later, Leon's new assertive skills resulted in (or coincided with) a job promotion and finding a girl friend, whom he subsequently married. But problems arose between Leon and his mother. After an initial family consultation (with Leon, his older brother, and his parents), several additional sessions were held with Leon and his mother to permit resolution of major differences that had troubled both of them for years.

We successfully pinpointed the major conflict areas and managed to work out an acceptable modus vivendi that augurs well for the future.

Leon gradually reduced his medication and was off medication entirely after 5 or 6 months. It has been more than 3 years since Leon was treated. A personal follow-up interview with Leon and his wife revealed that his gains have been maintained.

Discussion

The foregoing case history is not intended to prove anything about the alleged superiority or efficacy of multimodal therapy; it is presented simply to demonstrate the way we work with such problems. From a scientific standpoint, we are unable to say whether or not Leon would have derived the same benefit from the Parnate alone, but clinically it seems likely that his general lack of assertiveness, his tendency to suppress anger, and his perfectionism, as well as the troublesome relationship with his mother, were likely to undermine his psychological integration unless specific corrective measures were instituted.

The stability of the treatment outcome seems to be closely tied to the thoroughness with which clearly identifiable excesses and deficits across a patient's seven modalities are specifically and systematically resolved. Strong emphasis is placed on teaching requisite coping skills. We believe that everyone has acquired certain inappropriate or excessive responses; likewise, we all have specific deficits in at least one or two modalities. The greater the number of dysfunctional or undeveloped responses, the greater the degree of subjective inconvenience or suffering.

In multimodal therapy we are interested in specific difficulties within a given modality as well as the interactive effects of this modality with each of the six others. For example, a 55-year-old man learns that he is diabetic. Although the biological modality takes precedence over the other vectors of personality (we know that he will be required to adhere to certain dietary rules and restrictions and that he may require daily oral medication or even insulin injections), from a multimodal standpoint we will want to examine the rest of his BASIC ID (behavior, affect, sensation, imagery, cognition, interpersonal, drugs-biological). We will ask, for instance, what impact his diabetic condition is likely to have on his general behavioral repertoire, affective responses, sensory experience, self-image, cognitive appraisals, interpersonal dealings, and other biological functions. To what extent will compliance with the medical regimen depend on his functioning in all of the modalities? We regard this as an operational definition of what is typically called "treating the whole person."

In our practices we have encountered numerous chronic cases of so-called characterologic depression that have not responded to several unimodal or bimodal treatments but have responded with substantial benefit following multimodal interventions. The following is a typical illustration.

Case History

A 41-year-old woman, a freelance artist whose work was not well received, reported being depressed fairly consistently for 18 years, with periods of exacerbation lasting many months at a time. Therapy with four different clinicians over the years had been unsuccessful. The multimodal profile was as follows:

Behavior. Minimal job seeking; procrastination with new projects; little physical activity; poor grooming and unstylish clothing.

Affect. Depressed affect; crying at times, with expressions of anger about what parents did to her and about friends who are nonsupportive; fear response when contemplating failure or rejection; diurnal mood variation (less depressed, more energy late in day).

Sensation. Physical discomfort; muscular tension; a variety of abdominal complaints; dysphoric effects from tricyclic antidepressants.

Imagery. Pictures self as unattractive, growing old, and being totally alone; crowds out positive memories of self in the past; nonexistent positive images of the future.

Cognition. Bright, with a potentially good sense of humor. Self-talk: "The past was damaging; I will never overcome the hurt; the scars [metaphor suggests permanence] will never be erased; I have tried everything, and nothing works; I can't help the way I feel; I can't function; nobody cares; nobody understands me." Guilt about mother being old and infirm.

Interpersonal. Withdraws from social interaction; unassertive, especially with regard to seeking dates, but also does not pursue friendships and other contacts; unassertive with mother, who is clinging, demanding, and highly critical; in the past, has formed intense relationships with men and then been devastated when rejected; patient herself is clinging and demanding with friends.

Drugs-biological. Constipation; various aches and pains; no response to two tricyclic antidepressant drugs and several antianxiety drugs; appetite not impaired; no sleep disturbance at present time, but has had intermittent insomnia, especially onset and early morning types; mild obesity.

Multimodal Interventions

Behavior. Structure time. Set up work interviews. Take courses with an eye toward possible career change. More attention to hair grooming. Force self to engage in formerly pleasurable activities (e.g., tennis). Weight-control techniques, running, walking long distances. Practice approach behavior with men, using role playing in office sessions and with friends outside.

Affect. Convert anger into assertive responses toward mother and others; practice exaggerated anger responses (in the consulting room, shout imprecations, vilifying people who are feared); use of humor in therapy sessions to tap rich potential for positive affect.

Sensation. Promote noneating sensory experiences, self-touching exercises, use of massage and whirlpool in local gym.

Imagery. Practice picturing self not depressed, having fun; picture mother and other feared persons in devil's attire with horns; sensitization exercises to control/intake food.

Cognition. Bibliotherapy (Ellis, 1975; Lazarus & Fay, 1977); repeatedly challenge irrational, defeating, pessimistic self-talk.

Interpersonal. Encourage assertive responses; bring mother and friends to session. [Patient would not ask mother, but did bring friends. They treated her in a patronizing manner as a sick person, and she responded in a clinging, demanding manner. Patient was encouraged not to whine and demand; friends were coached in operant and paradoxical strategies (Fay, 1978)].

Drugs-biological. Physical examination for a variety of somatic complaints; fitness program as part of weight-control efforts.

After weeks of relentless negativity about herself, the present, and the future, accompanied by abundant expressions of self-pity, and following predominantly cognitive and behavioral exercises, there was a transient lifting of the patient's lugubrious mood. A recrudescence of symptoms lasted 4 to 5 weeks before durable improvement occurred. Dating activity was resumed. Her hair and clothing were consistently neat. She became a jogging enthusiast. Her weight decreased to a level that pleased her. Although she was securing more work, she enrolled in a training course to become a stockbroker. Sixteen months later she was still free from her "characterologic" depression.

Discussion and Conclusions

The purpose of presenting these cases is simply to demonstrate the application of the multimodal orientation. Our favorable experiences with many patients who previously had undergone 5 to 20 years of unsuccessful therapy involving one or two modalities have demonstrated the value of the multimodal approach. We recognize that whatever difficulties there are in rigorously demonstrating the efficacy of unimodal therapies are compounded for multimodal therapy.

Treatises on diagnosis may cover the full range of symptoms, signs, and biochemical parameters of depression, but nowhere does the clinician find a systematic investigation of all modalities and particularly a therapy that embraces all modalities. We find that invariably there is lack of attention to the full modality spectrum; in addition, many patients have not even derived the full benefit of a unimodal approach. This may occur because the necessary information is unavailable or because many clinicians are not sufficiently trained. The "D modality" provides classic examples. To illustrate, many bipolar patients still do not receive lithium carbonate, especially in the so-called bipolar II cases, in which mania is less prominent than depression. Many classic agoraphobic patients who have severe panic attacks are still treated with benzodiazepines (e.g., Valium) and do not receive tricyclics or monoamine oxidase (MAO) inhibitors. Rarely do patients with refractory depressions receive drug combinations such as tricyclics and MAO inhibitors. Undertreatment is common, and blood levels are seldom determined in refractory cases. Concerning the cognitive therapies, Beck (personal communication, 1979) raised questions about determining the efficacy of this approach when many practitioners are inadequately trained.

What is distinctive about the multimodal approach is precisely that it attempts in a systematic way to be comprehensive in assessment and exhaustive in intervention. It is not sufficient to espouse one school or orientation or to work with a limited number of techniques. Nor is it satisfactory for us to pay lip service to the idea that traditional divisions are archaic. Rather, it is essential to search out the deficits or excesses in all modalities and draw on the available techniques or devise new remedies. It is not possible for every clinician (in fact, any clinician) to be expert in all modalities. We therefore recommend consultation and even collaboration with colleagues in unresponsive cases.

Sometimes a patient will insist on unimodal therapy, or even no therapy at all, as in the following instance: A 51-year-old woman was in the throes of a classic unipolar affective episode. The various therapeutic approaches were suggested, including antidepressant medication, which she adamantly refused. During the initial session she expressed the view that she would be this way for the rest of her life. We emphasized that most of these episodes are self-limited and that recovery was highly likely within a period of months regardless of therapy. She was advised that therapy could maximize the likelihood of recovery, shorten the duration of the episodes (probable relief in 10 days to 2 weeks), and decrease the probability of recurrence. She came for a second appointment, but cancelled the third and did not resume. Four months later she called to express her thanks and to report great satisfaction that our prediction about spontaneous remission had been correct. Although we offer the full spectrum of multimodality to all patients, ultimately they will select what they believe is acceptable and useful.

In some cases, cognitive interventions will facilitate acceptance of what formerly was unacceptable. Simply offering factual information will help in other instances. Several patients have refused to consider MAO inhibitors because physicians had told them that the drugs were "dangerous." We provide our patients with literature about drugs as part of a bibliotherapy program. The educated consumer concept is as important in multimodal therapy as in other approaches that view therapy as education.

REFERENCES

Beck, A.T. *Cognitive therapy and the emotional disorders.* New York: International Universities Press, 1976.

Beck, A.T., Rush, A.J., Shaw, B.F., & Emery, G. *Cognitive therapy of depression.* New York: Guilford, 1979.

Ellis, A. *How to live with a neurotic.* (2nd ed.). New York: Crown, 1975.
Fay, A. The drug modality. In A.A. Lazarus (Ed.), *Multimodal behavior therapy,* New York: Springer, 1976.
Fay, A. *Making things better by making them worse.* New York: Hawthorn, 1978.
Fuchs, C.Z., & Rehm, L.P. A self-control behavior therapy program for depression. *Journal of Consulting and Clinical Psychology,* 1977, *45,* 206-215.
Goodwin, W., & Guze, S.B. *Psychiatric diagnosis* (2nd ed.). New York: Oxford University Press, 1979.
Lazarus, A.A. Multimodal behavior therapy. Treating the BASIC ID. *Journal of Nervous and Mental Disease,* 1973, *156,* 404-411.
Lazarus, A.A. *Multimodal behavior therapy.* New York: Springer, 1976.
Lazarus, A.A. *In the mind's eye.* New York: Rawson, 1978.
Lazarus, A.A., & Fay, A. *I can if I want to.* New York: Warner, 1977.
Lazarus, A.A. *The practice of multimodal therapy.* New York: McGraw-Hill, 1981.
Lewinsohn, P.M. A behavioral approach to depression. In R.J. Friedman & M.M. Katz (Eds.), *The psychology of depression: Contemporary theory and research,* New York: Wiley, 1974.
Maas, J.W. Clinical and biochemical heterogeneity of depressive disorders. *Annals of Internal Medicine,* 1978, *88,* 556-563.
McLean, P.D., Ogston, K., & Grauer, L. A behavioral approach to the treatment of depression. *Journal of Behavior Therapy and Experimental Psychiatry,* 1973, *4,* 323-330.
Rush, A.J., Beck, A.T., Kovacs, M., & Hollon, S.D. Comparative efficacy of cognitive therapy and pharmacotherapy in the treatment of depressed outpatients. *Cognitive Therapy and Research,* 1977, *1,* 17-36.
Schildkraut, J.J., Orsulak, P.J., Schatzberg, A.F., Gudeman, J.E., Cole, J.O., Rohde, W.A., & LaBrie, R.A. Toward a biochemical classification of depressive disorders. *Archives of General Psychiatry.* 1978, *35,* 1427-1433.
Seligman, M.E.P. *Helplessness.* San Francisco: Freeman, 1975.
Shaw, B.F. Comparison of cognitive therapy and behavior therapy in the treatment of depression. *Journal of Consulting and Clinical Psychology,* 1977, *45,* 543-551.
Skinner, B.F. *Science and human behavior.* New York: Macmillan, 1953.
Taylor, F.G., & Marshall, W.L. Experimental analysis of a cognitive-behavioral therapy for depression. *Cognitive Therapy and Research,* 1977, *1,* 59-72.

Remediation of Skills and Performance Deficits in Depression
Clinical Steps and Research Findings
Peter McLean

Depression and Its Treatment

The most characteristic feature of depression is negative mood. Depressed persons variously describe their moods as hopeless, frustrated, unmotivated, self-critical, and gloomy. What is responsible for the induction of these moods? Biochemistry? As yet there is no impressive evidence that biochemical factors are casually related to depressed mood states, although presumably they are interactive with these states, particularly as severity increases. On the other hand, there is a wide range of findings strongly suggesting that psychosocial factors figure prominently in the causes and treatment of depression. Even the casual observer will note that depressed persons manifest rather remarkable performance deficits, as compared with nondepressed persons and with themselves when they are not depressed. These performance deficits interact with negative mood in the development and maintenance of depression, and they provide a logical focus for treatment efforts.

This chapter will outline a treatment approach that attempts to reverse performance deficits as a primary objective. Performance deficits may be the causes of depression or only contributing factors, but in either case they are almost always in the top two on the list of presenting complaints. More important, direct intervention in the area of a person's performance deficits, rather than in some other area or other assumed cause, is a parsimonious approach to treatment that has produced good results in clinical trials.

A Model of Depression

The theoretical model to which one subscribes to account for the phenomena of depression usually is determined by the presumed cause (e.g., noncontingent reinforcement, irrational cognitive processes) of the depression. From this point of view, the model presented here must be considered atheoretical, because no single factor within the psychosocial realm is considered to be both necessary and sufficient to cause depression. There are two main reasons for this. First, for every theoretical explanation for the onset of depression there are simply too many clinical exceptions to the theory, and thus far no theory has accounted for the impressive amount of case variation in regard to etiology. This is not to berate the importance of theory construction and testing, but to point out that adherence to any one theoretical paradigm to account for the development of depression, at this time, is not clinically very useful. Second, if we forget theoretical explanations for a moment and look at the procedural recommendations for intervention offered by the divergent theoretical schools of thought within the broad range of psychosocial explanations for depression, a great similarity becomes apparent. In practice, if content analysis is carried out to identify treatments deriving from the learned helplessness model, cognitive theory, and social learning theory, for example, it is unlikely that the interventions will prove to be distinguishable. Why have theoretically distinct schools converged in terms of treatment to a relatively common pool of techniques? Most likely because depression itself can result from many different causes and because, regardless of theory, there are some treatment techniques that are more successful than others in abolishing depression. This suggests that nonspecific factors play more powerful roles in the treatment of clinical depression than has generally been thought. These factors compromise theories and represent the realities of the clinical task.

Depression seems to be a common side effect of a large variety of problems (e.g., marital discord, unemployment, physical illness) that, when severe enough, becomes functionally autonomous as the symptoms and their effects stimulate more depressed cognitions and behaviors. Specifically, there seems to be a four-stage serial process that is followed by persons who become depressed: (1) repeated goal frustrations in a variety of significant areas over time; (2) feelings of having little control over the outcomes of important events, particularly interpersonal behavior; (3) anticipation of chronic failure in efforts to change oneself or to constructively influence other people and important events; (4) appearance of depression symptoms. Cognitive, behavioral, motivational, and physiological factors are interactive in clinical depression, and different schools of thought align themselves with one or more of these modalities for the purpose of treatment in the belief that improvement of functioning in one area (e.g., cognitive) will generalize to other modalities as well.

Our work tends to focus on the performance or behavior component of personal functioning for several reasons. We believe that successful performance is a powerful antidepressant that easily lends itself to personal and social recognition. Also, we believe that behavioral performance is relatively easy to quantify from the point of view of accountability and assessment. Finally, there is recent evidence (McLean & Hakstian, 1974) indicating that therapeutic effect is independent of treatment modality. Behavior therapy, in that study, produced improvement not only in the areas for which it was targeted (e.g., social functioning and behavioral productivity) but also in the areas of mood and somatic complaints. Similarly, drug therapy patients improved in the area of social functioning. These findings, contrary to those of earlier work (Friedman, 1975; Klerman et al., 1974; Weissman, 1978) and contrary to the selective-effect hypothesis, suggest that if a treatment works, it works across all modalities. Consequently, if depressed patients can improve their performance levels, there is reason to believe that improvements in cognitive, physiological, and motivational functioning will follow.

A person's functional performance may be inadequate because of lack of either motivation or skill, and it is important to identify the correct deficiency in order to target treatment in a meaningful manner. For example, in Vancouver several years ago the real estate market entered a prolonged tailspin, with the result that a number of realtors became clinically depressed, were unable to function professionally, and ended up in our treatment program. There was no question that these realtors possessed the social skills that so many depressed persons lack, and in this case a social skills training program would have been inappropriate. These sales people knew how to interact socially, but their capacities in this area were dormant. The thesis is that chronic inadequate performance in the face of task or goal demands mediates depression. The therapeutic task is to mobilize significant goal-directed performance. To do so may require a problem analysis of the coping process that has proved to be insufficient, a reconceptualization of the problem, the development of new goals, social skills training, marital treatment, etc., or it may require a broad-based approach using a combination of specific behavioral treatment strategies, serially arranged, to meet the needs of individual patients (Biglan & Dow, 1981, McLean, 1976). Successful performance provides therapeutic leverage by which the therapist can then guide the momentum of treatment. That is, without the mobilization of goal-directed performance that can be attributed to the treatment effort, no matter how little the performance gain is, it is doubtful that verbal treatment will have a therapeutic impact. Thus, from the point of view of treatment, depression is a performance disorder in which the rate of adaptive functioning across a wide range of domains is suppressed, thereby reducing the opportunity for personally and socially recognized goal attainment.

At this point a question arises: What comes first, depressed affect and reduced motivation, or reduced performance? From the treatment viewpoint, this question is irrelevant, because the task remains the same (to increase goal-directed performance) and because the most efficient means of influencing the cognition-performance-affect interaction seems to be through accelerating goal-directed performance.

The relationship between depressed affect and performance is illustrated in Table 7.1, which shows the results for subjects depressed at a moderate clinical level before treatment [⩽ 23 on the Beck Depression Inventory (BDI) (Beck, 1967)], the results for these subjects after 3 months of treatment (average BDI = 11), and the results for normal subjects having no history of clinical depression (BDI before and after treatment = 3 and 2.9, respectively). Although the individual differences are large within groups, it can be seen that depressed mood correlates directly with performance on all measures except watching TV, where (presumably because watching TV represents social withdrawal or avoidance behavior or both) it correlates indirectly with depressed mood. Of particular interest is the relative lack of involvement of depressed subjects in social activities. Table 7.1 shows that the depressed subjects in this study elected to become reclusive when they were most depressed. Such action permits much more time for personal rumination and negative self-evaluation and decreases the likelihood of social reinforcement. In fact, our studies have shown that even after successful treatment, at which time formerly depressed subjects are indistinguishable from nondepressed subjects on the basis of mood scores (both having BDI scores of 7 or less), those formerly depressed subjects who are less active socially (even though they are not depressed) are significantly more likely to become depressed 3 months later.

In practice, it has been our experience that all depressed patients are deficient in important skills areas (usually social skills, but also, almost universally, in skills involving how to conceptualize the experience of normal depression and what actions to take as a result).

It is evident that other investigators within the broad range of behavior and cognitive therapies also focus primarily on improving performance and skills deficits, despite claiming diverse theoretical positions. For example, the useful distinction between cognitive therapy and behavior therapy is increasingly diminishing as behavioral procedures

TABLE 7.1 Self-report of Selected Performance Measures before and after Treatment in Normal ($N = 161$) and Clinically Depressed ($N = 196$) Populations

Measure	Before Treatment				After Treatment			
	Depressed		Normal		Depressed		Normal	
	Mean	SD	Mean	SD	Mean	SD	Mean	SD
Social activities								
Elective time (hours) spent with friends per day	0.95	(1.78)	2.52	(3.34)	1.34	(1.47)	2.93	(2.31)
Number of times in past week:								
Had a friend over	0.57	(0.92)	1.33	(1.52)	0.85	(1.15)	1.36	(1.84)
Went out with a friend	0.84	(1.17)	1.73	(1.64)	1.49	(1.51)	1.81	(1.58)
Telephoned a friend	0.97	(1.26)	1.66	(1.36)	1.37	(1.33)	1.42	(1.51)
Verbally praised someone	1.59	(1.57)	3.06	(1.99)	2.14	(1.86)	3.26	(2.10)
Personal activities								
Number of times in past week or 2 days:								
(2 days) worked on hobby	0.62	(1.05)	0.87	(1.14)	0.69	(1.05)	0.68	(1.19)
(week) wrote letters	0.74	(1.31)	1.27	(1.57)	0.90	(1.34)	0.96	(1.41)
(2 days) watched TV	1.84	(1.68)	1.50	(1.31)	1.72	(1.58)	1.36	(1.30)
(week) paperwork (e.g., bills)	0.92	(1.31)	1.70	(1.66)	1.53	(1.45)	1.53	(1.56)
(week) home/car improvements	0.59	(1.12)	1.05	(1.52)	1.04	(1.54)	0.94	(1.35)
Time utilization								
Number of hours in last 2 days that were (by personal standards):								
Wasted	15.35	(9.54)	4.32	(4.56)	10.15	(9.45)	4.43	(5.36)
Productive	7.92	(6.11)	17.26	(8.61)	11.96	(8.57)	16.83	(10.06)

figure more prominently in cognitive therapy studies (e.g., Rush et al., 1977) and virtually all depression treatment programs employ graduated task assignments, in some form, to accelerate adaptive functioning.

Individual Differences and Diagnostic Subtypes

Ideally, clinicians would match client and treatment characteristics to produce optimal treatment results. The problem is that there are no reliable criteria by which to make such matches, primarily because the scope of research required to identify optimal combinations is enormous. There have been two multivariate studies published to date in this area. In the first study (Paykel et al., 1973), four groups of patients (psychotic depressives, anxious depressives, hostile depressives, and young depressives with personality disorders) previously classified by multivariate cluster analysis (Paykel, 1971) were shown to have predictable responses to tricyclic medication. The second study (McLean & Hastian, 1974) taxonomized 196 depressed patients into four clusters using a data base of information of patients' characteristics that was relatively large as compared with that in the study of Paykel and associates, which focused on psychopathologic variables. These clusters of patients proved to be different from those in the Paykel study, and this clustering did not result in a main effect across treatment groups, nor did it interact with treatment (treatment effects were significant). Further, at the end of treatment, patients were rank-ordered according to treatment response, and the high and low responders were compared (treatment groups collapsed, $N = 196$). A Hotelling T^2 analysis was completed based on 24 patient characteristics, followed by a discriminant function analysis that was used to classify patients into high and low response categories. The subsequent classification of patients based on discriminant function scores (i.e., the "hit rate") was 68%. Therefore, even with a large pool of patients, a relatively large number of patient variables, and a multivariate statistical procedure, the correct classification (i.e., high or low treatment outcome) represented only an 18% improvement beyond chance. Using the same approach, but classifying high and low treatment responses up to 15 months after treatment and using the nine most discriminating variables [sex, marital status, number of suicide attempts, a life events score, the psychoticism score from Eysenck's EPQ (Eysenck & Eysenck, 1976), number of depressed persons in the family, average satisfaction, cognitive functioning, and personal activity rate], the hit rate was improved to 81%.

In summary, the use of empirical means to determine treatment group selection based on patients' characteristics is a promising technique that has a long way to go. In practice, chance factors and patients' preferences (based on what they have heard about the efficacy of specific treatment approaches or what they have experienced directly) usually determine treatment assignments.

Another approach (indeed, the traditional approach) to matching patients' characteristics to the proper treatment is through diagnostic classification. Diagnostic subtype classification within depression assumes differential causes and treatment responses. However, there is little empirical evidence to support this approach, despite the fact that it has a wide following, particularly in the psychiatric community. The difficulties are familiar: low reliability in subtype diagnostic classification; inconsistent predictions of treatment responses based on subtype classifications that vary from one study to another. Research designed to identify biological and psychological markers is a relatively young field, and it is hoped that these will soon be of help in classifying the clinical population into empirically derived subgroups. In the meantime, almost all investigators use a two-step process to reduce the heterogeneity of their patient populations. First, bipolar depressives, schizophrenics, drug-dependent patients, and brain-syndrome patients typically are screened out. Second, severity usually is regulated psychometrically for admission-to-program purposes. The result is that most studies involve patients who are heterogeneous in terms of diagnostic subtype classification. This state of affairs is probably an advantage inasmuch as it will encourage investigators to derive empirical subtype classifications rather than rely on traditional diagnostic subtype groupings, which have produced classification-by-default categories (i.e., endogenous depression is assumed to have biological determinants, although there is no impressive evidence).

Depressed patients receiving behavior-based broad-spectrum package treatment (Biglan & Dow, 1981; McLean, 1976) have their hierarchy of treatment components arranged as a function of their apparent needs. This approach to dealing with patients' individual differences by designing individually tailored series of treatment components has become increasingly popular. The basis for matching treatment components and patients' characteristics resides in the natures and apparent causes of patients' performance deficits. For example, Wolpe (1979) identified four types of reactive depressions (conditioned anxiety, self-devaluative cognitions, negative interpersonal interactions, excessive responses to bereavement) and prescribed a behavioral treatment for each. Similarly, the treatment procedure outlined in this chapter is designed to increase the performance levels of patients in standard skills areas (e.g., communication, assertive behavior, rate of social interaction) as a function of the treatment goals identified during assessment.

Sources of Personal Stress

Depression is a specific response to stress. Often the source of stress is evident, as in the case of bereavement, illness, loss of employment, and the like; but what is by far the most common form of personal stress leading to depression is not at all obvious to the external observer. These stressors are the high-frequency losses and disappointments that occur at the rate of 10 to 80 per day, each having little effect alone, but taken together (and in the absence of compensating positive events) produce a major and chronic negative impact. Little things said or not said between family members, critical looks between married couples, constant self-appraisal resulting in negative conclusions, the routine realization that life-styles so alluringly portrayed by the advertising industry and attractively modeled in magazines are beyond one's grasp—these are the kinds of routine stressors whose effects can accumulate at astonishing rates. What these minor stressors, or irritants, lack in dramatic value, as compared with major life stress events, they make up for in terms of their rate of accumulation. Nondepressed persons also report high rates for these kinds of stressors, but the critical difference is that, on the average, nondepressed persons experience compensating numbers of positive events and outcomes within the same time period that effectively offset the negative impact of the routine stressors. It is the ratio between negative and positive events and outcomes that is decisive for mood determination.

The following four areas account for the most frequent sources of stress experienced by clinically depressed patients who have received treatment in our unit over the years.

Unrealistic Goals and Performance Criteria If goals are unrealistically formulated from the outset, goal frustration is inevitable. Many depressed people seem to have internalized the expectations others have for them (e.g., family); they have developed goals and standards that are not subjected to routine and realistic (i.e., probability of attainment) review, and they appear to spend inordinate amounts of time engaged in wishful thinking. Rather than moving in a graduated fashion toward goals, depressed persons often have an all-or-nothing standard, being willing to accept only the most desirable outcome. For example, a 38-year-old divorced woman who was functionally almost a social recluse wanted desperately to meet a potential husband, a tall, tweed-jacketed, foreign-accented professor, and almost no one else would do. This woman also had a somewhat snobbish attitude toward men who did not closely approximate her ideal. She consequently did herself the great disservice of social withdrawal. To have remained socially active would have increased the possibility of meeting her professor, as well as the opportunity to alter her standards.

The manner in which depressed persons formulate their personal performance criteria, as compared with the manner of normal control subjects, is striking. Basically, the problem here seems to be a combination of lack of experience, poor organization skills, and acute sensitivity to negative stimuli (Teasdale & Bancroft, 1977) and potential failure. Planning a goal requires that a series of active steps be taken on some schedule. The steps toward the goal must be graduated so that successes with the early steps will be recognized as small but important gains, and one must be prepared to incur setbacks en route to goal attainment. Because of lack of experience and poor organizational skills, which can be manifested in poor action plans, a low tolerance for failure, or faulty expectations, depressed patients usually must be "walked through" the process of construction and review of plans.

It is of interest to note the relatively high proportion of introverted goals pursued by depressed patients. Literary composition, listening to one's record collection, reading philosophical works, and other soul-searching attempts to understand the meaning of life and express one's own inner odyssey are flatly discouraged in our treatment program. No value judgement is intended in doing so; rather, it is recognized that these activities should be pursued later, when depressive cognitions are not predominant and the patient can engage in these weighty endeavors from a position of strength. The rationale for this is straightforward: Introverted searches for meaning when patients are in a depressed mood are virtually always counterproductive by any standard. Spending time alone detracts from time that could profitably be spent socially to increase the possibility of enhanced self-esteem (e.g., social recognition, plus less opportunity to engage in negative self-appraisal).

Personal Disuse and Lack of Goals A significant difference between depressed patients and normal persons readily becomes apparent when we consider the topic of personal goals. Studies have shown that normal control subjects are able to articulate a range of personal goals with a relative ease that makes it clear that they devote considerable attention to the planning of personal goals. In marked contrast, depressed patients frequently are at a complete loss when asked to identify goals they have set for themselves, indicating that they have been more absorbed in their problems than in goal setting; even when they are able to make an effort to identify their goals, they find the process difficult and foreign. The following exchange during an assessment interview with a depressed patient is not atypical: "Mrs. Higgans, what are some of the goals that you would like to accomplish if you were feeling better?" "I'm sorry, I really haven't thought about it much." "If things were definitely going much better for you, say in 6 months time, what are some of the things you might be doing differently?" "Oh, I don't know, I suppose I'd be happier." "What would you do if you were happier?" The point here is that depressed people are not goal-oriented. They are problem-oriented and crisis-oriented. In effect, many depressed people have no good way to assess their own personal accomplishments; their daily agendas are not well planned, and they seem to be carried along by events rather than attempting to determine the events that affect them.

The consequence of not routinely setting, planning, and reviewing goals is most often a sense of personal disuse, a feeling reported by the majority of our depressed patients.

Life Stress Events Subsequent to the pioneering work of Holmes and Rahe (1967) in quantifying stress associated with social adjustment, others have used this approach for measurement of stress concentrations experienced by subjects who have become depressed shortly thereafter. Paykel and associates (1969) categorized the life-stress events (LSE) experienced by 185 hospitalized depressed patients during the 6 months prior to the onset of symptoms and compared the rate of occurrence of these LSEs with those for 185 matched controls. Overall, depressed patients reported experiencing three times the number of LSEs experienced by control subjects. Additionally, when these data were construed in terms of "exits" (e.g., divorce, child married, death of close relative) and "entrances" (e.g., birth of a child, gaining a son-in-law or daughter-in-law), it was found that depressed patients had experienced significantly more exits from their social fields than had the control subjects, whereas there was no difference in the numbers of entrances. Subsequently, Brown and associates (1973) demonstrated a causal link between the experience of a relative excess of LSEs and the probability of depressive disorder.

In our own work we found that only those LSEs that were perceived as negative could be used to make statistical distinctions between normal and depressed populations (i.e., negative household, health, work/financial, social changes), and here the most dramatic difference was in the social area, where depressed patients reported experiencing 5.5 times more negative changes in their social lives than normal subjects.

Inadequate Coping Techniques There are no qualitative differences apparent in the kinds of problems that beset depressed and non-depressed persons (marital interactions, child management, and social interactions in general). Given the same problems, albeit more of them, people who become depressed differ from those who do not on two grounds: (1) They have relatively fewer positive experiences to compensate for their negative experiences; (2) They seem to manage, or cope, less skillfully with problems. As a group, depressed people tend to look for causes rather than remedies to problems, and they appear to be relatively unskilled in establishing priorities, detailing step-by-step action plans, and developing alternative plans should the original plans fall through. Presumably, the requisite problem-solving skills have not been fully mastered. Coopersmith (1967) found that self-management skills are associated with preadolescent mastery experiences, and this may account for some of the deficits in skills noted here. However, one feature that we have noticed repeatedly in interviewing depressed patients and normal control subjects is that normal subjects report acquiring their coping skills by watching others, whereas depressed patients report such learning experiences much less frequently. It is common for our normal subjects to state that when they see someone handle a difficult situation well, they make a practice of remembering the approach in order to try it themselves when an opportunity arises. On the other hand, our depressed patients, when asked if they acquire coping ideas by watching others, often state that they believe it is more important to be original.

Certainly the fact that depressed persons are relatively withdrawn socially exacerbates problem solving, because they have fewer opportunities to assess other ways of dealing with problems. Weissman and Klerman (1973) found that when women in psychotherapy sessions for depression were allowed to determine the topics of conversation, they tended to bring up pragmatic problems of coping (typically involving family members) more often than any other topic. Similarly, during clinical interviews with more than 200 depressed patients, we asked patients to identify the main problems that brought them to seek treatment. A content analysis of 23 problem categories indicated that problems in socializing were at the top of the list by a considerable margin.

All things considered, when depressed people are compared with nondepressed people, it seems reasonable to conclude that depressed people experience more stress, deal less effectively with the causes of stress, and experience a lower ratio of positive events to negative events. For both groups, the greatest single source of stress is reported to be the problem of dealing effectively with other people.

Roles of Personal and Social Skills

In our treatment experience with depressed patients, six skills areas have been found to be essential for a nondepressed life-style. The first three of these (interpersonal communication, behavioral productivity, and social interaction) are universal in that all patients automatically receive treatment aimed at building skilled performance levels in these three areas. The remaining three skills areas (assertion, decision making/problem solving, and cognitive self-control) are optional, depending on the specific problems, goals, and abilities of individual patients. These six treatment components form the basis of our treatment program, which has been evaluated as a package in comparison with two other treatments and one control group. This evaluation has been presented elsewhere (McLean & Hakstian, 1974) and will be summarized only briefly here. The study involved 178 clinically depressed patients who were randomly assigned to four groups for 10 weeks of outpatient treatment: psychotherapy; behavior therapy; drug (amitriptyline) treatment; relaxation (attention-control condition). Differential dropout rates were observed among the treatment groups during the course of treatment, and at the end of treatment it was found that behavior therapy had produced superior results for 9 of 10 outcome measures. The results for the behavior therapy group remained marginally superior at the 3-month follow-up evaluation.

The first three of these skills areas are considered to be essential, because we have observed performance deficits in these areas of functioning for virtually all clinically depressed patients. It must be determined on an individual basis whether or not these performance deficits represent a lack of skills. If so, remedial skills building must be employed. If a patient has skills in these areas, the therapist and patient should design a program to mobilize goal-related activities in each area. The objective of functional goal-directed performances in these six skills areas is to increase the ratio of positive outcomes to negative outcomes in the patient's daily life experiences.

Communication Skills Verbal communication is one of the most important skills to be maintained in the event of depression, and it is equally important in preventing depression altogether. Communication is a vehicle for positive feedback, which enhances self-esteem, and it competes with negative thought intrusions. Problems arising from poor communication habits generally fall into two categories: (1) aversive marital interchanges; (2) constricted quantity and range of one's interaction sources. These are distinct problems that will be discussed separately.

Aversive marital interchanges result from frustrated attempts by spouses to influence one another's behavior constructively. These interchanges are relevant to depression because malfunctioning marriages probably constitute the most important single source of clinical depression in Western cultures, and even when a marriage is harmonious it can easily become strained when one spouse becomes depressed. Paterson and Hops (1972) presented a useful model of how married couples inadvertently train one another to become destructive through increasingly coercive interchanges: If a request made by one spouse to another is not complied with, it will escalate into a demand, which if not complied with will further escalate to include a negative personal remark. This interaction pattern is reciprocated until avoidance behavior is established and the couple's communication becomes increasingly estranged in terms of contestable topics, eventually reaching the point that the familiar complaint is heard: "We don't talk anymore."

In a previous study (McLean et al., 1973), tape recorders were sent home with couples, (one member of each couple was clinically depressed) so that the quality of verbal interchanges could be recorded during the course of routine conversations. Ten of 20 couples were given feedback cue boxes designed to signal positive and negative feedback during ongoing conversation. A green light was flashed when one considered one's spouse to be positive during the planned discussion times (e.g., complimentary, showing interest, laughing with), and a red light was flashed when one considered one's spouse to be negative (e.g., contemptuous, critical, indifferent, sarcastic). The feedback procedure was effective in significantly reducing the proportion of negative feedback cues (feedback boxes included built-in frequency recorders) given by both members of each couple. When the home tape recordings (before and after treatment) were assessed (Lewinsohn, Note 1) to determine the rates of positive and negative interchanges, it was found that couples in the behavior therapy group had significantly decreased their use of negative interchanges, whereas the couples in the comparison treatment had not. The feedback procedure, along with training in the use of behavioral contracts and social learning principles, resulted in significant improvements in targeted complaints for the behavior therapy group but not the comparison treatment group.

The powerful role of negative cueing became apparent in this study when further analysis showed that those in both treatment groups responded negatively 76% of the time when they were themselves negatively cued. Furthermore, this microanalysis revealed that "constructive criticism," defined as an attempt to change spouse behavior by faulting it, invariably resulted in negative reactions.

In order to ensure routine verbal interaction, we ask all couples to (1) ritualize a daily conversation time by setting aside 20 minutes of undisturbed "talk time" at a prearranged time of mutual convenience; (2) review with one another how each person's day went (otherwise; content is elective); (3) ensure that spouses contribute equally to the conversation; (4) premediate and monitor their individual interactions to ensure that their contributions are constructive and positive rather than negative; (5) engage in constructive criticism only when invited.

We also evaluated the communication patterns of married couples who were having no marital conflict, as well as those of patients who lived alone (47% of our patients lived alone). If couples are already spending the equivalent of 20 minutes in constructive conversation to consolidate their day, and if they value the opportunity to learn the views of their spouses, or if a person who lives alone already has a vibrant social life, several close confidants, and no complaints about ability to communicate meaningfully to others, then these people will have no need for skills development in this area. But this is rarely the case. Couples who do not experience conflict often have life-style demands or habits that preclude conversation on a routine and meaningful level. Work schedules, child-care demands, and TV all compete for time that might be spent in marital conversation. In this situation, our couples are asked to engage in the daily talk-time assignments plus contract with one another during shared activities (e.g., social, recreational, interest-area activities). Our patients who live alone (as well as married couples who wish to develop greater communication links between spouses and with friends, work colleagues, and others), but who feel awkward about their conversational skills, are instructed to focus on the practices of initiating and maintaining conversations, making small talk with strangers, making requests of both friends and strangers, making self-disclosures, and giving compliments. These conversational skills are integrated on a time-sharing basis with the rest of the program and involve daily task assignments.

Other social skills programs such as those of Argyle and associates (1974) and Zeiss and associates (1979), also provide specific training in verbal interaction skills. The exact contribution made by the teaching and practicing of verbal interaction skills in the alleviation of depression is unknown, because there have been no large-scale dismantling studies to determine the individual contributions made by particular components of multicomponent treatment programs.

Behavior Productivity We stated earlier the belief held by many that successful performance is a powerful antidepressant. The origins of this position lie in the law of effect and in self-efficacy theory (Bandura, 1977). Procrastination becomes dramatically evident in most cases of clinical depression. Procrastination mediates negative self-evaluation by precluding opportunities for self-reinforcement and social recognition. It is interesting that most depressed patients view their reduced behavioral productivity as a case of depleted motivation induced by dysphoric mood, and they believe that motivation will spontaneously return to energize their behavior once the dysphoric mood lifts. Whereas this may well be true in part or in whole, it does not occur to most patients that successful performance will improve mood, and they use dysphoric mood as a rationalization for inaction.

Behavioral productivity is a main building block in a behavioral program; it promotes accomplishment and facilitates the identification of obstacles to successful performance. The therapist's task is to elicit relevant goals in accordance with the patient's criteria for feeling better; these goals are then defined operationally and are integrated into graded assignments. Specifically, it is necessary to (1) break performance goals down into explicit units small enough to ensure successful performance, (2) work on no more than four performance goals at a time and ensure that these goals are relevant to the needs of the patient, (3) establish daily task assignments and ask the patient to monitor daily goal attainment, (4) focus attention on the task and on what has been accomplished already, rather than worry about what has yet to be done,

(5) make positive recognition (preferably social recognition) contingent on performance.

Social Interaction Evidence from diverse sources indicates that social factors play the major role in the causation, maintenance, and resolution of clinical depression. Social interaction serves to moderate the experience of depression by providing a response that is incompatible with depressive withdrawal and by providing a source of increased self-esteem through social reinforcement (approval, acceptance, recognition, support, etc.).

A major problem in the resocialization process is that depressed patients are less skilled in social interactions (Libet & Lewinsohn, 1973) and are aversive to others (Coyne, 1976; Hammen & Peters, 1978) because of their pessimism and self-absorption. Consequently, depressed patients in our program are prompted to avoid depressive conversation styles and to role-play standard situations (e.g., talking to strangers at parties, introducing themselves to the parents of their children's friends) to learn how to keep the conversation content focused on the other party. Although this possibility is often overlooked, spouses can constitute a major resource in mobilizing the social interactions of depressed patients. Spouse participation is strongly encouraged in our program, and intervention is targeted at the couple in a symmetrical fashion so that both are involved in between-session assignments. In this manner, communication and support can be increased, any tendency to exacerbate the condition of the depressed spouse can be minimized, and spouses can be taught how to recognize constructive behavior and ignore negative ruminations.

Next to family conflict interactions, the social problem most frequently reported by depressed patients is inability to meet new people and engage in an active social life. We have found it necessary to point out to depressed patients that friendships and social activities alike evolve from shared interests. Thus the initial step is to complete an interest survey with the patient to identify recreational, personal development, cultural, and other interests, followed by a discussion of how best to pursue these interests through community organizations and other social outlets. Once patients become involved with an organization, class, or group, it becomes easier to help them plan and rehearse social encounters, because then they have the opportunity to practice in real situations.

The standard sequence of events for facilitating social interaction is as follows: (1) Survey the patient's social and life-style interests; (2) Review existing and potential social resources available to the patient; (3) Promote increased social involvement by use of graduated task assignments; (4) Rehearse troublesome social interactions to the point that the patient feels satisfactorily in control, and review progress afterward; (5) Increasingly encourage patients to choose and initiate their own social interactions in a wide variety of areas.

Assertive Action This treatment component is optional and is reserved for those patients whose rights and legitimate preferences are frequently violated by others. Unassertive interactions constitute a special case of social interaction skills, deficiency for which a large minority of depressed patients require structured training to help them better influence the outcome of interpersonal encounters. A wide variety of well-developed assertiveness training programs have been described in the professional literature, and the assertive component used in our program is not unique. However, we devote special attention to identifying situations in which assertive action is called for and determining the form that the assertive response should take. A number of assertion programs recommend self-disclosures of a personal nature in the name of being "honest" (e.g., "When you treat me like that, I feel as if you take me for granted."). We consider such complaintive behavior to be counterproductive and ill-advised. Instead, we advise patients to request specific and positive changes in the behavior of other people in order to resolve problems (e.g., "If you're going to be more than half an hour late for dinner, will you call me before 5 to let me know?").

Our assertiveness training procedure involves the following steps: (1) Review the patient's unassertive behaviors in the context of specific situations that represent stressful interactions (e.g., talking to boss, requesting behavior changes of relatives, offering personal opinions), and arrange these into a hierarchy according to challenge; (2) Rehearse constructive assertive alternatives to avoidance reactions, compliant reactions, and aggressive reactions on a situation-by-situation basis; (3) Use graded task assignments to engage the patient in routine assertive behavior in stress areas, and practice instigating and maintaining conversations (e.g., using self-disclosure, "canned" questions, and bridging words and phrases when necessary); (4) Assess performance records in detail, and construct alternative strategies as necessary; (5) Encourage the patient to generalize newly acquired assertion skills in self-management (i.e., patient sets own tasks, records and reviews progress).

Decision Making and Problem Solving Patients who have difficulty in making routine decisions (e.g., what to wear in the morning) and solving ordinary problems (e.g., car breakdown) are relatively few, and these problems can be handled by minimizing the importance the patient attaches to the making of "errors" in judgment when deciding a course of action. The things that produce greater stress in patients are strong double-avoidance conflicts (e.g., whether or not to remain in an unhappy marriage). In these cases, patients respond well to procedures that will help them organize their approaches to their decisions and problems. The five procedural steps we use in both problem solving and decision making are the following: (1) Specify the problem in detail to avoid overgeneralization; (2) Determine what information will be helpful in making a decision within a specified time period, and gather this information; (3) Consider the different solutions available, specifying the procedural steps involved in each; (4) Compare the anticipated outcomes of the possible solutions in terms of critical variables (e.g., who is affected; cost; short-term and long-term effects); (5) Encourage the use of organizational aids to help with long-term planning and to teach crisis management (e.g., budget; holiday, child-care, and work-planning calendars).

Cognitive Self-control Depressed patients have high rates of negative thoughts (Beck, 1974) that mediate their dysphoric mood and avoidance behavior. Many patients believe (often as a result of experience with other treatment orientations) that it is important to explore the casual roots of their negative affect, and accordingly they are prone to introspective journeys in search of solutions to current dilemmas. Our experience indicates that this is always a depression-inducing exercise. Negative thoughts, particularly those involving self-evaluation, tend to stimulate further negative thoughts, and if this pattern is not interrupted, it can quickly escalate into catastrophic thinking. This process is illustrated by an incident involving one of our patients. On her way to a treatment session by bus, and otherwise in a relatively good frame of mind, she noticed a young woman with a baby sitting several seats ahead. She began to think how lucky that woman was to have a man who loved her (patient's assumption entirely) and, given their apparent age difference (the patient was about 5 years older), how unlikely it was that anyone would find her attractive, and so on.

It is our belief that the most effective way to compete with these automatic negative thoughts and irrational assumptions and conclusions is to involve the patient in meaningful social interactions. In this process, these negative thoughts are largely blocked by the task demands presented, and other people can provide a sounding board to help redirect irrational ideas and unrealistic standards and expectations. However, clearly there are times when social solutions will not be available, and self-control will be necessary. In this case we use the following techniques: (1) Teach patients to recognize and label depressive thought patterns before they develop momentum; (2) Teach patients to disrupt depressive thoughts and substitute task-oriented coping thoughts or positive scanning (i.e., quick inventory of opportunities, personal assets, strengths, and behavioral accomplishments); (3) Model the verbal feedback that should accompany cognitive coping strategies (i.e., teach patients to pace performance by talking supportively to themselves); (4) Ask patients to avoid unscheduled personal evaluation and program evaluation; (5) Instruct patients to follow a geographic stimulus-control procedure (e.g., faithfully go to a predetermined area, such as a particular chair or a particular position in the room, to have their depressive thoughts) when they are unable to suppress their depressive cognitions through the processes of thought substitution or interruption.

Treatment Assembly

In outlining the preceding three standard and three optional treatment components we have described briefly the rationale and the treatment steps involved in our multicomponent treatment program. However, aside from these formal ingredients, the treatment can succeed or fail depending on the attention paid to the logistics of treatment planning.

Identification of Problems and Treatment Goals The first step is to construct an operational definition of the problems that brought the patient to treatment, then define treatment goals that are sufficiently specific to permit measurement of progress. Although problems and goals often are the reciprocals of one another, this is not always the case, and each set should be identified and defined separately. In practice, most patients present with three or four complaints (e.g., social withdrawal, domestic conflict, work procrastination, sleep disturbance, lack of ambition), and three to five treatment goals are identified. It should be noted that it is not intended that the problem list be exhaustive; it is intended only to sample a small range of more important problem areas. The primary purpose of the problem identification is to provide the therapist with clinical background material and data for use in monitoring treatment responses as measurable changes in problem states (McLean & Craig, 1975). Goal identification is also used for treatment evaluation, but this is a therapeutic exercise that determines the direction that treatment is to follow.

Development of a Behavioral Focus To mobilize performance and provide the basis for program accountability, the therapist must establish a behavioral focus from the outset and reinforce this position throughout the program. Often it can be difficult to sell this orientation to patients, because depressed patients usually are preoccupied with mood and thought patterns, assuming behavioral inaction to be a perfectly understandable consequence. It is necessary to emphasize the point that thoughts and feelings are important consequences of behavior that can most effectively be influenced through behavior changes. We explain to patients that their depressed mood is normal given their disengagement from goal-directed activities.

Development of Serial Treatment Targets A common error, particularly by novice therapists, is to overload patients with assigned tasks in deficient performance areas and with excessive behavioral recording duties. The therapist's task is to ensure proper volume and distribution of assignments. The tasks assigned to patients for homework should be selected on the basis of their probability of completion, because the therapist must help engineer a series of small successes that will have impact in a patient's life. Our treatment program lasts, on the average, 10 weeks. The homework assignment for the first week always involves some form of behavioral productivity, and the other two essential components (communication and social interaction) are gradually incorporated during succeeding sessions. Only when the three cornerstone treatment components are functional are any of the last three treatment components introduced as they are needed.

Graduated Attainment of Goals This deceptively simple treatment concept always requires careful attention in planning treatment delivery, primarily because depressed patients are so inaccurate in estimating their performance capabilities. There are two rules of thumb. The content of each goal must be clearly relevant to the patient's needs, so that the patient cannot easily dismiss task completion as unimportant. Second, the therapist must help the patient keep the scheme of graduated steps in mind so that the end point is clearly visible, and the therapist must ensure that the steps are practical, attainable, and measurable.

Personal and Social Recognition of Gains In the absence of the optimism and self-confidence that usually serve to maintain motivation when one is confronted with negative feedback or no feedback at all, every effort must be made to ensure that depressed patients' fragile performance gains are duly recognized, both by themselves and, more important, by others, because depressives often consider the opinions of others to be more credible. It is all too easy to end up in a debate with depressed patients as to the value of their accomplishments, with the therapist taking the positive viewpoint. This can be avoided by determining the relative importance of a task at the time the patient makes a commitment to it (i.e., in advance).

We always explain the rationale for self-reinforcement, contrasting the examples of "internal dialogue" used by depressed persons, normal persons, and highly accomplished persons (e.g., athletes, survivors). However, there is no good way of determining the degree to which patients use such principles in practice. Because of this, it is important to steer patients toward those social interactions in which positive recognition is most likely. Spouse involvement and training can prove beneficial in this regard.

Tapering Treatment Treatment gains can be endangered by abrupt termination of treatment. The objective is to move the patient through dependence on the therapist early in treatment to complete self-management by the end of the treatment. To help patients generalize their constructive treatment efforts across time and place, treatment should be tapered from once a week (at the seventh or eighth week of treatment) to every other week, and the last treatment session should be spaced a month later. This schedule works well for reactive depressions, but if the nature of the depression is that of a depressed life-style (sometimes referred to as endogenous depression or depressed personality), monthly review sessions may have to be extended over a 6-month period. In either case, it is important that the responsibility for conceptualization and management gradually be transferred to the patient over the course of treatment. By definition, patients' coping styles are deficient at the beginning of treatment. For example, toward the latter part of treatment, when a patient brings up a problem that has arisen, the therapist should be in a position to pose this question: "Knowing what you now know about how best to handle this sort of situation, how would you recommend dealing with it?"

Redundant but Important Therapeutic Tasks

Depression is a habit complex of overt and covert behavior. Changing patients' habits always involves repetitive efforts on the part of the therapist. The following four areas are considered by therapists in our program to be those in which it is most important for the therapist to be consistent and insistent.

Role of Normalization Patients benefit immediately and measurably from the knowledge that their thoughts, behaviors, and feelings differ only in degree from those of other people. Depressed patients react strongly and negatively to their belief that they are abnormal and are on the brink of indescribable and uncontrollable catastrophes, variously described as "going completely mental," "falling into a dark hole," or "going completely insane." They clearly have little understanding of the natural limits of thoughts, physiology, and behavior. Such thoughts mediate anxiety and depressive ideation and disrupt goal-oriented behavior. It is important that the therapist make repeated efforts to normalize such evaluations throughout treatment.

Focus on Behavioral Productivity Depressed patients have a tremendous inclination to try to solve their problems with thoughts rather than through actions. Of course, some thoughts (e.g., excessively high standards) need to be discussed, but the fact remains that the easiest way to change depressed mood and cognitions is to increase the patient's goal-directed behavior. We always take every opportunity to rationalize patients' negative moods in terms of their relative inactivity. When patients complain of motivational, thought, or mood problems, they should be directed to the present and future time frames, and the focus should be on corrective, goal-oriented behavior.

Descriptive Integration of the Program Behavioral approaches to depression necessarily deal with details, and one is always in danger of having the patient lose sight of the gestalt of the treatment rationale, goals, and procedures. Furthermore, a number of important concerns of the patient must necessarily be postponed while more basic goals are pursued in the process of bringing about behavioral changes. Accordingly, it seems to be helpful to patients if the therapist spends a few minutes at the beginning and end of each session to place the objectives of the session into perspective. There is evidence to show that a social learning explanation for occurrences of psychological disturbances, as opposed to a mental illness conceptualization, fosters self-help behaviors on the part of patients (Farina et al., 1978). This finding underscores the importance of ensuring that patients maintain an integrated understanding of the rationale and methods of treatment.

Promotion of an Active Social Network Because of the social learning emphasis of the approach described in this chapter, it is obvious that we consider it important to promote an active social network. Depressed patients, typically introverted in personality to begin with, withdraw socially when beset by depressed thoughts and mood, in order to "get myself sorted out." Such withdrawal soon compounds the experience of depression, rather than providing a sanctuary for improvement. We consider active social involvement critical for the development and maintenance of an antidepressant life-style, and we expend considerable treatment effort in this area. Our data show that after depressive episodes, when patients are "back to normal," their rates of social activities are intermediate between the norms for a depressed population and a normal population with no history of depression. This signals a need for social "prophylaxis" to help prevent recurrences of depressive episodes.

Nonspecific Factors

Traditionally, treatment studies have been presented and interpreted in terms of procedures derived from the theoretical models on which they have been based (the assumed active ingredients of treatment), and nonspecific effects have been confused with remission. (In treatment evaluation studies of clinical depression, a nontreatment control group of depressed subjects is not really possible if subjects are depressed at a clinical level. They simply are not in a position to wait for treatment.

As a result, the only practical design seems to be a treatment comparison format.) It is now clear that the majority of treatment effects in treatment programs within the behavioral/cognitive framework are nonspecific treatment effects. This does not mean that these treatments are ineffective. Those in the behavioral treatment group in our recent study (McLean & Hakstian, 1974) significantly outperformed those in the short-term psychotherapy group, for example, but those in the treatment control condition (relaxation training) were intermediate between these two treatment groups. Nonspecific effects deserve close investigation so that their determinants can be put to clinical use in a planned manner. Goal setting and monitoring, for example, have been shown to be therapeutic measures in themselves (Hart, 1978). We have found that patients in both our behavioral and relaxation treatment groups appreciate the concreteness of the program (knowing what is coming up in future sessions, homework assignments, having rules and procedures to follow when anticipated events take place, etc.). This suggests that the treatment structure provides a positive nonspecific treatment effect.

The magnitude of the influence that nonspecific effects have on treatment outcome can be estimated by contrasting the before–after treatment effect of the worst-performing treatment with the difference in treatment effects between the best treatment and worst treatment (i.e., nonspecific improvement versus treatment-specific improvement). Reviews of most studies will quickly show that nonspecific treatment effects are of greater magnitude than specific treatment effects. Zeiss and associates (1979) were able to find no treatment-specific effects in a comparison of interpersonal skills treatment, cognitions treatment, and pleasant-events treatment, even though significant pretreatment–posttreatment changes were evident in all cases. Similarly, whereas our treatment comparison study (McLean & Hakstian, 1979) showed significant between-group treatment differences, no group had significantly better results than those for the treatment control condition (relaxation training).

Unfortunately, there has been little research on nonspecific effects in the area of mood disorders. However, highly structured treatment was associated with the best treatment outcome and the lowest dropout rate (dropout rates: psychotherapy, 30%; drug therapy, 36%; relaxation therapy, 26%; behavior therapy, 5%) in our recent treatment comparison study. These findings, combined with practical experience, suggest that treatment compliance can be enhanced by means of a well-explained logical treatment rationale and by increasing the structuring in the treatment (e.g., generally involve the patient, provide a program curriculum, encourage self-management, and use a social learning orientation delivered in an educational format).

Common Complications

There is a small number of high-frequency complications associated with behavioral treatment programs. Although all clinicians evolve their own means of dealing with these complications, the following is a brief description of how we approach these problems in our treatment unit.

Program Noncompliance Due to Symptoms

Preoccupation with physical symptoms and mood symptoms is routine for depressed patients, and these symptoms frequently are used as the basis for rationalization for noncompliance with a treatment commitment previously agreed on (e.g., "I would have gone out, but I began to feel so down."). We explain to patients that they can expect to have such symptoms until they begin doing more of the things that are important for them to do. That is to say, we normalize the complaints. Further, we attempt to teach patients to be increasingly tolerant of negative mood cues and associated physiological complaints, much as they would do for the symptoms of the common cold or a hangover. Accountability for committed behavioral performance is always foremost.

Loss of Goal Orientation

It can happen that a patient will lose interest in a goal during the course of treatment or that because of external factors the goal will no longer be relevant. Under these circumstances, the treatment effort expended by the patient can quickly cease, in which case new goals must be identified and broken down into logical sequences. Typically, the therapist must suggest at least some goals to patients by prompting in selected life-style areas (love relationships, friendships, employment, self-improvement, leisure-time interests, etc.). Developing personal goals is an important skill in which most patients are deficient and in which they will require repeated tutoring.

Suicidal Ideation

One-quarter of our patients have made at least one suicide attempt, and over 50% report frequent suicidal ideation. Suicide screening before treatment and ongoing monitoring for the seriousness of the suicidal intent in the case of selected patients constitute our active suicide-watch procedures. We ask patients to inform us of any serious suicide intent during the course of treatment. More troublesome is the mild suicidal ideation that disrupts a patient's ability to function for 1 to 3 days. At the beginning of treatment, we discuss suicide with patients who have had suicidal ideation. We express the view that suicide is a civil right that requires an informed decision on the patient's part, but until the treatment program is completed, the patient cannot know what its outcome will be, unless the patient prejudges the program. Suicidal ideation is thus identified as an illicit and premature evaluation. Patients are asked to postpone such considerations until the scheduled discussion of the topic at the end of treatment; they are asked to refocus attention on their program goals. We have never found suicidal ideation to be an issue at the time of treatment termination.

In Search of Causes

Patients frequently become preoccupied in an attempt to understand the causes of their depressed mood. This does not mean that they engage in a constructive analysis of the circumstances under which their depressed mood occurs. It usually entails a critical life-history analysis in which a host of circumstances and events (e.g., breech birth, alcoholic father, too many family moves, overachievement or underachievement in school) all become candidates for the cause of the current malaise. Almost invariably such reviews result in increased self-preoccupation, self-devaluation, and social withdrawal, to say nothing of frustration and the problems associated with task avoidance. Early in the course of treatment we attempt to have patients identify the thought sequences that lead them into these reviews; then we encourage them to practice thought control. When patients in treatment raise questions relating to the causes of their depression, such questions are used to cue a review of remedies that can be tried instead.

Conflicting Hypotheses

Whether stated or not, most patients have a number of conflicting hypotheses for the occurrence of depression, acquired from a variety of sources (friends, relatives, TV, *Reader's Digest*, newspapers, magazines). Therapists are artifacts in the lives of their patients; typically, therapist and patient spend only 1 hour per week in treatment together (i.e., 1 of approximately 116 waking hours per week). It is unreasonable to assume that patients will easily see the "wisdom" of our treatment rationales beyond those of competing rationales they have acquired on their own. To enhance treatment compliance, it is often necessary for the therapist to discuss, defend, and reinforce the social competence (i.e., social skills) treatment rationale.

Confusion of the Relationships among Mood, Thoughts, and Behavior

The relationships among thought content, personal behavior, mood, and social interaction are not well understood by most patients; even when they are explained they are soon confused. Understanding these relationships is absolutely fundamental to successful treatment and prevention. The innovative therapist will have any number of illustrations, stories, and means to make these distinctions and interactions clear.

REFERENCE NOTE

1. Lewinsohn, P. M. *Manual of instructions for the behavior ratings used for the observation of interpersonal behavior.* Unpublished manuscript, Department of Psychology, University of Oregon, 1968.

REFERENCES

Argyle, M., Trower, P., & Bryant, B. Explorations in the treatment of personality disorders and neuroses by social skill training. *British Journal of Medical Psychology*, 1974, *47*, 63-72.

Bandura, A. Self-efficacy: Toward a unifying theory of behavioral change. *Psychological Review*, 1977, *84*, 191-215.

Beck, A.T. *Depression.* New York: Harper & Row, 1967.

Beck, A.T. The development of depression: A cognitive model. In R.J. Friedman & M.M. Kutz (Eds.), *The psychology of depression: Contemporary theory and research.* New York: Wiley, 1974.

Biglan, A., & Dow, M.G. Towards a "second generation" model of depression treatment: A problem specific approach. In L.P. Rehm (Ed.), *Short-term psychotherapies for the depressed patient: Cognitive, behavioral, interpersonal and Psychodynamic approaches,* New York: Academic Press, Inc., 1981.

Brown, G.W., Harris, T.O., & Peto, J. Life events and psychiatric disorders. Part 2: Nature and causal link. *Psychological Medicine*, 1973, *3*, 159-176.

Coopersmith, S. *The antecedents of self-esteem.* San Francisco: Freeman, 1967.

Coyne, J.C. Depression and the response of others. *Journal of Abnormal Psychology*, 1976, *85*, 186-193.

Eysenck, H.S., & Eysenck, S.B.G. *Eysenck personality questionnaire.* San Diego: Educational and Industrial Testing Service, 1975-1976.

Farina, A., Fisher, J.D., Getter, H., & Fisher, E.H. Some consequences of changing people's views regarding the nature of mental illness. *Journal of Abnormal Psychology*, 1978, *87*, 272-279.

Friedman, A.S. Interaction of drug therapy with marital therapy in depressive patients. *Archives of General Psychiatry*, 1975, *26*, 57-63.

Hammen, C.L., & Peters, S.D. Interpersonal consequences of depression: Response to men and women enacting a depressed role. *Journal of Abnormal Psychology*, 1978, *87*, 322-332.

Hart, R.R. Therapeutic effectiveness of setting and monitoring goals. *Journal of Consulting and Clinical Psychology*, 1978, *46*, 1242-1245.

Holmes, T.H., & Rahe, R.H. The social readjustment rating scale. *Journal of Psychosomatic Research*, 1967, *11*, 213-218.

Klerman, G.L., DiMascio, A., Weissman, M.M., Prusoff, B., & Paykel, E.S. Treatment of depression by drugs and psychotherapy. *American Journal of Psychiatry*, 1974, *131*, 186-191.

Libet, J., & Lewinsohn, P.M. The concept of social skill with special references to the behavior of depressed persons. *Journal of Consulting and Clinical Psychology*, 1973, *40*, 304-312.

McLean, P. Therapeutic decision-making in the behavioral management of depression. In P.O. Davidson (Ed.), *Behavioral management of anxiety, depression and pain*, New York: Brunner/Mazel, 1976.

McLean, P.D., & Craig, K.D. Evaluating treatment effectiveness by monitoring changes in problematic behaviors. *Journal of Consulting and Clinical Psychology*, 1975, *43*, 105.

McLean, P.D., & Hakstian, A.R. Clinical depression: Comparative efficacy of outpatient treatments. *Journal of Consulting and Clinical Psychology*, 1974, *47*, 818-836.

McLean, P.D., Ogston, K., & Grauer, L. A behavioral approach to the treatment of depression. *Journal of Behavior Therapy and Experimental Psychiatry*, 1973, *4*, 323-330.

Patterson, G.R., & Hops, H. Coercion, a game for two: Intervention techniques for marital conflict. In R.E. Ulrich & P. Mountjoy (Eds.), *The experimental analysis of social behavior*. New York: Appleton-Century-Crofts, 1972.

Paykel, E.S. Classification of depressed patients: A cluster analysis derived grouping. *British Journal of Psychiatry*, 1971, *118*, 275-288.

Paykel, E.S., Myers, J.K., Dienelt, M.W., Klerman, G.L., Lindenthal, J.J., & Pepper, M.P. Life events and depression: A controlled study. *Archives of General Psychiatry*, 1969, *21*, 753-760.

Paykel, E.S., Prusoff, B.A., Klerman, G.L., Haskell, D., & DiMascio, A. Clinical response to amitriptyline among depressed women. *Journal of Nervous and Mental Disease*, 1973, *156*, 149-165.

Rush, A.J., Beck, A.T., Kovecs, M., & Hollon, S.D. Comparative efficacy of cognitive therapy and behavior therapy in the treatment of depressed outpatients. *Cognitive Therapy and Research*, 1977, *1*, 17-36.

Teasdale, J.D., & Bancroft, J. Manipulation of thought content as a determinant of mood and corrugator electromyographic activity in depressed patients. *Journal of Abnormal Psychology*, 1977, *86*, 235-241.

Weissman, M.M. Psychotherapy and its relevance to the pharmacotherapy of affective disorders: From ideology to evidence. In M. Lipton, A. DiMascio, & K. Killam (Eds.), *Psychopharmacology: A generation of progress*. New York: Raven, 1978.

Weissman, M.M. & Klerman, G.L. Psychotherapy with depressed women: An empirical study of content themes and reflection. *British Journal of Psychiatry*, 1973, *123*, 55-61.

Wolpe, J. The experimental model and treatment of neurotic depression. *Behavior Research and Therapy*, 1979, *17*, 555-565.

Zeiss, A.M., Lewinsohn, P.M., & Munoz, R.F. Nonspecific improvement effects in depression using interpersonal skills training, pleasant activity schedules, or cognitive training. *Journal of Consulting and Clinical Psychology*, 1979, *47*, 427-439.

Clinical Behavior Therapy for Depression

Herbert Fensterheim

8

A patient presents with depression as a primary symptom. The logic of behavior therapy requires that specific target behaviors be selected and that systematic attempts be made to change these behaviors. If these attempts are successful, the depression is then reevaluated to determine the extent to which this symptom has been relieved. The major problem facing the therapist is the selection of the appropriate target behaviors. The field of behavior therapy, in general, offers few guidelines for making this determination. Although there is increasing concern with the measurement and assessment of specific behaviors, often the selection of the target behaviors must be made on the basis of expediency, common sense, or clinical lore (Kanfer & Phillips, 1970).

In approaching the problem of target behavior selection, we assume that a careful and thorough clinical examination has already been conducted. For the purposes of this discussion, we rule out the endogenous depressions, the depressions that are side effects of medications, and those depressions that are the consequences of other maladaptive behaviors. We are concerned here with those patients for whom neurotic depression is the primary problem.

Behavior therapists have formulated a number of paradigms for depressive behaviors (Beck et al., 1979; Lewinsohn, 1974; Rehm, 1977; Seligman, 1975). The thinking appears to be that because depressions have phenotypic characteristics that differentiate them from other clinically important behavior patterns, they must therefore have a different underlying psychological organization than these other behaviors. Indeed, each theorist tends to think in terms of a unitary model for depression, a concept recently challenged by Craighead (1980). He suggested that the various components of depression may vary from patient to patient, that these components should be evaluated in each case, and that this evaluation should then be used as a basis for determining the extent to which the various models can be applied to the patient in question. This, of course, helps to determine target behaviors and treatment strategies.

Although Craighead's formulation is a new approach more in accord with clinical experience, it does not go far enough. It tends to limit the therapist's choice of intervention strategies because of two fallacious assumptions:

1. It tends to maintain the belief that because the depressive behaviors themselves tend to be unique, the variables with which we must concern ourselves must also be unique. Wolpe (1979) directly challenged this assumption. He argued that depression is a function of conditioned anxiety, that the experimental neuroses provide a sufficient model for this disorder, and that the usual behavioral treatments used in reducing conditioned anxiety are effective when used with depressions. Wolpe thus disclaimed the need for unique models for depressive behaviors. However, although he did describe different triggers for depressions, his is basically another unitary model centering around the conditioned anxiety and the means for reducing it. We find clinically that many of the behavioral principles that apply to other disturbances also apply to depression. However, we also find great variation from patient to patient and a need for flexible consideration of many potential variables.

2. In the behavioral paradigms of depression, little attention is paid to distinguishing between precipitants, maintainers, and by-products of depression. Many of the depressed patients we see do show an insensitivity to positive reinforcers, a lack of assertiveness, or any of the other behaviors that characterize the main models of depression. However, as we work with these patients, such characteristic behaviors turn out to be essentially by-products of the depression, appearing neither to precipitate nor to maintain the depressive state. If the therapist attempts to treat these behaviors as the main thrust of treatment, any change that comes about is, at best, transitory.

Case History 1

A 28-year-old depressed man was referred by his (traditional) therapist "for assertive training." His depression appeared to stem from a great concern about losing his job; his fears appeared to be justified because of extremely poor interpersonal relationships in his work situation. Assertiveness training to improve his job-related social skills appeared to be the logical approach. However, a behavioral evaluation revealed that the necessary social skills were already in this repertoire and, indeed, had been used effectively in the past. Rather, he presented a picture of "learned helplessness." He was resigned, and he believed that nothing he could do would really make any difference. The consequences that befell him, be they good or bad, be they on or off the job, were matters over which he had but minimal control. He had recently become involved in astrology, and he "proved" by citing several instances that his fate truly stemmed from the stars.

A treatment program was designed to counter his learned helplessness. A major part of the program was that he was to perform deliberate assertive acts on the job and to keep note of these, their consequences, and their effects on his mood. He performed his tasks well, and at the end of 2 weeks his depression was gone, as was his belief in his own helplessness. At the end of a further 2 weeks there was some backsliding; there was a decrease in the assertive behavior and some return of the depression and the feelings of helplessness. At the end of a further 2 weeks he was back to where he had been at his first interview, except that now he was completely unable to perform any deliberate acts of assertion. At this point his case was reformulated.

From the beginning it had been noted that he had a ruminative obsessive fear of losing his job. However, this obsessive fear had been considered to be a consequence of his depression and his sense of helplessness. It was believed that as these disappeared, the obsessive fear would also be relieved. In the reformulation, this fear was considered to be the precipitant of the depression rather than its consequence. The fear was treated directly through aversion-relief desensitization during office visits and by means of thought stoppage in life situations. During the next 6 weeks there was definite diminution of the obsession and a gradual but sustained increase in assertive behavior on the job. At the end of this period, the depression and feelings of helplessness were completely relieved. At a 1-year follow-up examination it was found that these changes had been maintained, and he had received a major promotion at work.

In this case, selection of the correct target behavior was critical, as it so often is. When helplessness was selected as the target behavior, no sustained change was possible, despite dramatic initial results. When his obsessive fear was selected as the target, the desired changes were brought about. It was vital to distinguish between the precipitants and the consequences of the depression. It was the obsessive fear that precipitated and maintained the depression; the sense of helplessness and the lack of assertion were the consequences of the depression. Again we come back to the problem of selecting the target behaviors for change.

Target Behaviors

To aid in the selection of target behaviors, a number of areas must be systematically investigated. We have previously described several of these areas (Fensterheim, 1972), each requiring a different treatment strategy. Those most relevant to the treatment of depressions are general tension, automatic emotional reactions, obsessions, unwanted behaviors, and assertiveness. Many aspects of the most important models formulated for depression can be viewed as special cases in one of these areas. It is through investigation of each area in its own right that the therapist can be alerted to target behaviors that fall outside the scope of a given model.

General Tension

Different people, probably because of differing temperamental characteristics of their nervous systems (Eysenck, 1970), tend to experience their tensions differently. Although most people experience tension as tension or "nervousness," other modes are not uncommon: irritation; feelings of withdrawl. Although it is not frequent, we have seen several patients who have experienced their tensions as depression. With such patients, the onset of depression is usually gradual, with the depressive feelings building over a period of time; muscle tensions are obvious, and frequently there are sleep disturbances that take the form of difficulty in falling asleep, rather than early waking. At times when tensions might be expected to decrease, such as during vacations, these patients experience some decrease in their depression. At times when tensions might be expected to increase, such as at the end of a day's work or in a stressful situation, the depression will be exacerbated.

Several of the epiphenomenal characteristics of tension tend to exacerbate the depressive aspects. As the tension increases, so does the tendency to obsession. In this situation the obsessive thoughts may contain depressive content, such as negative views of oneself, the world, and the future. Second, patients become aware of their inability to control these tensions. This leads to feelings of helplessness that may generalize to other situations. Another derivative aspect concerns the screening effect of the tension. Masters and Johnson (1970) described how anxiety can screen out the natural sexual stimuli. In much the same manner, tension can screen out the impact of positive experiences, and patients can become insensitive to the positive reinforcers that do exist in their lives. Finally, patients label themselves as depressed and begin to act in accordance with the expectancies this label imposes on them.

For successful treatment, depressive behavior must be treated as an anxiety or tension equivalent. Treatment aimed at the epiphenomenal aspects, the negative world view, the helplessness, the insensitivity to reinforcers, at best will have only slight and temporary success. The main thrust of treatment must be through some form of relaxation training. The Jacobson-type relaxation exercises and/or biofeedback training in relaxation often can be helpful. Coping desensitization (Goldfried, 1971), in which patients are trained to lower their tension responses to specific stimuli, also should be considered. When medication is considered, the tension-reducing drugs are more effective than the antidepressants. As control of the tension is achieved and the tension itself is lowered, the depressive state and the other characteristics noted may be expected to disappear without being treated specifically.

Habitual mild chronic hyperventilation (HMCH) may be considered within the category of general tension (Lum, 1976). This HMCH condition can arise when one picks up incorrect habits of breathing. This can result in major changes in the biochemistry and physiology of the body and can precipitate both physical and psychological symptoms. Beyond this, because the body chemistry is already slightly askew, any increase in hyperventilation, from whatever cause (anxiety, enthusiasm), can produce extremely large effects. It differs from the well-known acute type of hyperventilation in that whereas the rate of breathing may or may not be important, the critical variable is the differential of expansion of the upper thorax and lower thorax. In normal breathing, the lower thorax expands about twice as much as the upper thorax; in HMCII the reverse is true.

This form of hyperventilation can lead to depression in several ways. Gibson (1978) suggested that it can directly precipitate depressive reactions. There is some experimental evidence suggesting that continued overbreathing can lead to chemical changes similar to those encountered in depressed patients (Damas Mora, et al., 1977). Second, as with general tension, the reactions that some people experience as anxiety or panic can be experienced by others of different temperament as depression. Finally, the common HMCH symptoms of fatigue and exhaustion may limit one's activities so that a depressive life-style is established and depression follows. Or, more directly, the fatigue and exhaustion can lead one to label oneself as depressed, and then one begins to act as if depressed. In all these instances the main target behavior to be treated is the breathing pattern, rather than the characteristics of the depression.

This type of hyperventilation can also have indirect effects that can lead to depression. We have seen several patients who have had moderate degrees of HMCH and have been constantly in a state of anxiety. However, when they would become depressed, their breathing patterns would change, and they would feel more comfortable; they had learned to precipitate and prolong their depressions in order to secure this relief. As one of these patients stated: "It seems that depression is my natural state." Again, the major target behavior is the breathing pattern, rather than the depressive behaviors.

Case History 2

A 31-year-old highly obsessive salesman suffered from periodic depressions that 10 years of treatment (including medication) had been unable to relieve. Each episode would last from 3 to 6 months, and he would be so disabled during these periods that he would be unable to work, being supported by his mother.

He was able to identify a number of situations that precipitated his depression, but one set of events repeatedly stood out. He called these "fear of success combined with compulsive gambling." He would be on the point of making a big sale but would do something peculiar (such as yelling at the customer) that would spoil it at the last minute. He would then go to the racetrack and lose far more money betting than he could afford to lose. He would ruminate about his foolish behavior and become depressed. During the subsequent period of time, whenever he began to feel the depression lifting, he would deliberately recall his gambling losses and, once again, deepen his depression. He was aware of doing this, and he labeled it as a need for self-punishment.

Examination during his first visit (he was not depressed at the time) showed a marked state of HMCH. His breathing rate in a relaxed position was 24 respirations per minute, with marked involvement of the upper thorax and a number of typical hyperventilation sighs. Overbreathing for a period of 3 minutes led to feelings of intense panic. The depression-producing pattern noted earlier was reinterpreted in the light of these findings. Because of the HMCH, he was in a constant state of anxiety. When he was on the point of making a big sale, he would become not anxious but excited. The excitement would increase the hyperventilation to the extent that it would give rise to feelings of panic. These feelings, in turn, led to the peculiar actions that spoiled his sales. This led to further feelings of anxiety (not depression) that maintained the hyperventilation, and hence the panic, at a high level. He had learned a number of methods, including losing money gambling, that would precipitate a depression. When depressed, his breathing would change, the hyperventilation would be minimal, and he would feel more comfortable. As the depression would lift, the hyperventilation would return, and he would once again experience the discomfort. He had learned to prolong the depression as a means of avoiding the aversive anxiety.

The target behavior for this problem was the breathing pattern. After 6 weeks of training in diaphragmatic breathing, the general feeling of discomfort was gone in his everyday life, and he did abort several panic reactions in the early stages. Several months later he had a relapse. He became extremely upset, went to the track and lost a large sum of money, and became depressed. However, he realized what had happened; he worked on his breathing with renewed vigor and relieved his own depression within several days. He has now been free of depression for close to a year, and treatment for other aspects of his obsessive state (a separate problem) is being conducted.

Note that in this instance the epiphenomenal aspects of the depression, particularly a strongly negative view of himself and the future, would be inappropriate target behaviors. The breathing pattern was the behavior that needed to be modified. This was determined by producing symptoms through overbreathing for 3 to 4 minutes and observing such breathing characteristics as rate, relative movement of upper and lower thorax, and the presence of hyperventilation sighs. A further diagnostic criterion, not used here, would have been an arterial partial pressure of carbon dioxide less than 40 mm Hg. Training to counter this condition involves exercises in diaphragmatic breathing performed twice a day, deliberate periodic diaphragmatic breathing during the course of the day in order to change the general breathing habit, and deliberate use of diaphragmatic breathing to counter symptoms as they appear (Lum, 1976).

Automatic Emotional Reactions

Depression can be a phobialike reaction to a specific stimulus. "Phobia" is not really the proper term, because it tends to restrict our attention to those reactions characterized by fear or by anxiety. As used by behavior therapists, the concept is far wider than this. It is basically a conditioned response of the autonomic nervous system to a given stimulus or class of stimuli. It can be experienced as any kind of disturbed feeling besides fear or anxiety. Anger, rage, hopelessness, and depression all fall into this category (Fensterheim, 1972). Recently, we have argued that this category can even include excited sexual feelings that lead to variant sexual behaviors (Fensterheim & Kantor, 1979). If these sexual feelings are treated as if they are phobic reactions (i.e., with desensitization procedures), fairly rapid changes in the variant behavior can be obtained.

It is the organization of the behavior rather than its content or the subjective experience it creates that is important. The reaction (1) is automatic, (2) is emotional, and (3) is elicited by specific stimuli; hence the term automatic emotional reaction (AER) to be substituted for the more limiting phobic response. It is preferred to Wolpe's term "conditional emotional response" because (1) it stresses the automatic nature of the reaction without making any assumption as to the manner in which it comes about, conditioned or otherwise, and (2) Wolpe tended to confine the use of his term almost exclusively to anxiety and fear, whereas we are aiming for a far broader spectrum of emotions.

The most common depressive AER we have encountered involves loss of some kind. It can be the loss of some cherished or important object, such as a home, loss of a job, or, most likely, loss of some significant person. The onset of the depression usually is sudden and often is unexpected. The depressive reaction itself may be mixed with sharp feelings of anger or guilt. It appears to be maintained through cues (including thoughts) that constantly remind the depressed person of the loss. As the depression continues, more cues take on the property of being associated with the loss. In this way the depression deepens and prolongs itself.

Treating such depressions with desensitization methods as if they were phobias often yields quick results. A formal hierarchy (Wolpe, 1973) is not necessary; a nonsystematic desensitization (Fensterheim, 1972) can be conducted. First the patient must be relaxed and then instructed to think about or to imagine anything in the phobic area. The patient signals the very first sign of any disturbed sensation, regardless of quality, and then is relaxed again. This is repeated 15 to 25 times in a single session; sessions should be frequent during the initial phase of treatment to prevent resensitization. Some definite sign of change should be evident by the third such session; if it is not, a more systematic desensitization should be attempted.

Our limited experience with the flooding method for treatment of this kind of depression suggests that the flooding procedure be avoided. The few people with whom we have tried flooding have become extremely depressed and upset to the point that they have refused to continue or to repeat the experience.

A second and very different kind of depressive AER has been observed in several patients. These patients are in unfortunate life situations (for several, this has involved physical injury or illness) and are angry about it. However, these patients have long histories not so much of not expressing anger as of not experiencing it. In this situation the anger is experienced as depression that tends to prolong itself until it becomes constant. Usually it is accompanied by severe muscle tension in specific areas of the body. The forehead and facial muscles appear to be the most frequent (but not exclusive) sites for this tension, but relaxing these muscle groups does not appear to bring about any change in the depression. Physical aches and pains and feelings of exhaustion often accompany the depression.

Desensitization to "unfair things" is often the best approach to treating such depressions. Despite the muscle tension, often the nonsystematic desensitization with relaxation described earlier can be used. However, the therapist must keep extremely alert for the possibility that the disturbed response to the stimulus scenes is increasing. Should this happen, the procedure must be discontinued at once. Aversion-relief desensitization is a good alternative method. With these depressions, the aversive stimulus used in such a desensitization should be kept at a moderate level. Having the stimulus too highly aversive has in several instances exacerbated the depression.

Case History 3

A 40-year-old woman suffered moderate but disfiguring injuries in an automobile accident, and several operations were necessary. The predicted outcome was that the disfigurements would be barely noticeable, if at all. Soon after the accident she became depressed to the extent that she no longer experienced satisfactions in life; she avoided pleasurable activities and performed the bare minimum of functions required by her home and her job. She slept a lot and constantly felt tired. She often cried quietly, and the crying was set off by her thoughts: "Why me?" "How unfair!"

She had previously been an active and energetic woman. She had raised two children, who were now teenagers, had built a career, and had an essentially good marriage. She was generally firm and directive with her children, but rarely she would become upset or angry with them. She would have arguments with her husband, but rarely was she really angry. The only time she would get really angry was when she had had too much to drink. At the time of her initial examination, although she felt and acted depressed, she stated that she was periodically aware of feeling angry at the unfairness of it all.

When first examined, she was about to be hospitalized for further surgery. There was just enough time for the examination, to prepare a formulation on which to base treatment, and to decide that a desensitization approach was the logical first step. However, there was no time for office visits before she entered the hospital. Therefore, a desensitization tape was prepared for her to use during her hospital stay and at home afterward. The aim was to have her think of "unfair things" while she was in the context of relaxation. However, because of her muscle tensions and the lack of time in which to train her in relaxation procedures, our usual Jacobson-type relaxation method was not feasible. Instead, sensory image relaxation was used. This method consists in presenting questions that evoke images or sensations at a steady rate. Following the model of emotive imagery (Lazarus & Abramowitz, 1962), the disturbing stimuli were periodically introduced within this context of relaxation. Six times during the 8-minute tape we had inserted this question: "Can you think about unfair things that are going on?"

She listened to the tape three or four times a day during the next 3 weeks and then with decreasing frequency as the depression disappeared. In slightly more than a month the depression was completely relieved, although an appropriate concern about her physical condition persisted. Several times, when she was confronted by "unfair" situations, the depression began to return: once when there was an unexpected complication with one of the medical procedures; another time when there was some difficulty at work brought about by her absences for medical care. On each such occasion she resumed listening to the tape. Each time the depression remained mild and was short-lived. It was suggested that treatment possibilities for her problem with her anger in general be explored, but she felt no need for this.

A third type of AER associated with depression is more truly phobic and follows a model that has been applied to agoraphobia and to obsessions. In this situation the patient is phobic to the depressive symptom itself. The patient constantly anticipates depression ("I wonder if I'll feel depressed when I get up tomorrow.") and constantly engages in self-examination for signs of depression. When signs of depression are present, the patient becomes anxious and concerned over them and pays them undue attention. All this attention acts as a reinforcer, increasing the probability of depression; in essence, one is training oneself to be depressed. Beyond that, the patient begins to avoid situations and activities that may bring on depression or call attention to the depression ("If I go to that party, I won't enjoy it. That will prove how depressed I am. I had better not go."). In this way, pleasurable activities are neglected, life becomes increasingly restricted, and a depressing life-style accentuates and maintains the depression.

This phobic reaction to the depressive symptoms is best treated through a desensitization procedure using a hierarchical approach: A series of life situations (getting up in the morning, on the way to work, arriving at the office, at lunch, etc.) is imagined, and one adds to these scenes the input that one is feeling very slightly (mildly, moderately) depressed. Any disturbance elicited by the image is countered with relaxation procedures. Desensitization tapes have been found to be extremely helpful with this phobia, and detailed instructions for constructing a tape of this kind have been published (Fensterheim & Baer, 1977, p. 308). The tape is played in the morning using situations in which the patient may feel depressed during the coming day. It is also used in the evening, with the patient imagining situations that tended to produce feelings of depression during the course of the day. A typical self-report when this method works: "I started to feel depressed but just ignored it, and it soon went away." In a successful course of treatment, these depressive feelings may be as strong as ever when they emerge, but the durations of the feelings become shorter and the frequency decreases until they completely disappear.

Although many other patterns of automatic depressions could be described, some of them highly idiosyncratic, one last fairly common pattern will be discussed. This is the automatic reaction to thoughts of lack of self-worth. These patients ruminate about all the things they have done wrong, about how inadequate they have been in various situations, and each such thought brings on a surge of depression. If they cannot find something wrong with what they did in specific situations, they begin to dwell on thoughts that they are bound to do things to spoil even their earlier successes, and these thoughts, too, bring on the depressive reaction. With such patients, superficially there may appear to be an assertiveness problem; they just do not speak up, nor do they stand up for themselves. However, the assertiveness problem turns out to be derived from the thoughts; if these patients do speak up, they may reveal how inadequate they are.

The automatic nature of the depressive response leads to a poor prognosis when attempts are made to deal with the contents of thoughts directly. For example, attempts were made to teach several such patients the differences between Aristotelian and Galilean thinking and to have them quantify the extent of their inadequacies in the two areas. However, in each instance the patient was aware of the illogical nature of his thought but was helpless to do anything about it. One patient stated: "I know that I am 90% right 95% of the time and that this is a lot better than either of my business partners. But then I start thinking that I am going to mess it up and this angry depression comes on."

Successful treatment must be focused on the reactions to thoughts rather than on the thoughts themselves. Although aversion-relief desensitization usually works best, different desensitization procedures can be tried. With several patients, desensitization has brought unusual results: Different procedures were tried. Each procedure worked initially, bringing about a definite change in the depression. Then each procedure stopped working, and the depression deepened. In all instances, as patients noted that changes were coming about, they began to think that they were certain to do something to spoil the situation. This thought brought a high level of disturbance into the procedure, and the result was that patients became sensitized rather than desensitized to the thoughts. Aversion-relief desensitization to these "spoiling" thoughts did away with their disruptive effects.

Obsessions

The correct diagnosis of obsessive states that precipitate depressions is the one with which we have the greatest difficulty. On the one hand, they must be differentiated from the automatic emotional reaction to the thoughts as stimuli that was described earlier. On the other hand, they must be differentiated from the incorrect cognitions so fully described by Beck and associates (1979). Such a differentiation is important to the treatment strategy. If there is an AER to the thoughts, the specific class of thoughts involved must be delimited and explored for a possible hierarchical approach. If they are cognitive distortions, the thoughts must be clarified and challenged through the methods of Beck and associates (1979) or those of Ellis and Harper (1973). However, if there is truly an obsessional disorder, then, following Rachman (1976), the content of the thought and its possible rationality are not discussed. When patients insist on evaluating the possible rationality of their obsessions, we refuse to do so, stating the following position: "Look, you are not psychotic, so of course there is a reality basis for your obsessions. But do not confuse this kind of thinking with true thinking. It can never lead to constructive solutions, only to anxiety and depression." In actuality, the content of the depression may influence the degree of the depression, but we have noted depression in patients whose obsessions have been mainly pleasant sexual fantasies ("moping," they call it). Elsewhere (Fensterheim, 1975) we have argued that because of the lack of control over the obsessive thoughts, the patient feels a loss of mastery. This, in turn, leads to lowered self-esteem and, hence, often to depression.

Besides the usual diagnostic methods of differentiating between the phobic, the cognitive, and the obsessive variables, our own clinical experience suggests certain indications:

1. A history of obsessive episodes or a family history of obsessiveness (Slater & Cowie, 1971) is helpful in making the diagnosis. However, more extended verbal exploration to make the differential usually is not very helpful at this point and often can be misleading.

2. Should a patient present during an acute phase of depression, the probability is that we must first deal with either a phobic disorder or an obsessive disorder. It is only when these are reduced that a cognitive approach, if still indicated, can be instituted to prevent recurrence of

the depression. If a patient presents between depressive episodes and the patient's style of thinking appears to be related to past depressions, then direct intervention with cognitive methods may be considered.

3. There is one observation that must be noted, but it may not stand the test of further experience or more systematic experience. This concerns the feelings, besides depression, that are also present. When guilt is present along with the depression, we usually find an obsessive state to exist; when the secondary feeling is anger, usually there is a phobic state.

4. Activity assignments between treatment sessions often provide useful information. By examining the thoughts that impede or facilitate performance of the assignment, a distinction between phobic and obsessive processes can sometimes be made.

5. Therapeutic action usually is the most important method for making the necessary differential diagnosis. What we do is to take any of the depression-eliciting thoughts the patient has had during that day and attempt to desensitize them. Two or three sessions may be required for this. If a decrease in the disturbance is obtained by this procedure, one of two results may be observed: (1) With the lowering of the general level of disturbance, specific and clearly demarcated areas that elicit the automatic depressive response may appear. In this instance, we are dealing with a phobic reaction, and we can consider formulating more systematic desensitization procedures. (2) As the disturbance decreases in connection with one thought, other equally disturbing thoughts come to mind. It is almost as if depression and disturbance were in search of a triggering thought. The content of the new intrusions may be quite different from the original thought. Here we are most probably dealing with an obsessive state.

Once the diagnosis is made that an obsessional state underlies the depression, a variety of treatment methods become available (Beech, 1974). Often we have found thought stoppage to be helpful with milder depressions and flooding to be helpful with more severe depressions, expecially if there is a strong guilt component. In many cases we construct flooding tapes for patients. This is a 20-minute tape made by the therapist in close collaboration with the patient in which an attempt is made to capture in words the essence of the memories, incidents, and thoughts that best reflect the spirit of the depression-producing ruminations. The patient listens to the tape daily, attempting to pay full attention and to minimize escapes. The goal of the treatment is not to extinguish the ruminations completely, for this is rarely achieved at this stage of treatment; rather, the goal is to reduce the paralyzing depressive reactions to these obsessions so that other counter-depressive behaviors can be undertaken. Patients with this type of depression invariably need further treatment in other areas.

Unwanted Habits

There are depressions, whatever their origin, that are being maintained as habits. These habits may be reinforced by other people, they may have a reinforcing consequence for the depressed patients themselves, or they may persist simply as blind habits. In these instances, patients usually present with a long history of either continuous or intermittent depression and a long history of varied but unsuccessful treatment. If these habits are reinforced by other people, patients usually arrive for their first visits accompanied by concerned spouses or parents. Except for the case of the blind habit, the depression usually is moderate to severe in intensity, accompanied by strong feelings of helplessness and much crying, and the patient has a severely restricted lifestyle.

In the situation in which habits are reinforced by others, it would be expected that a pattern would be found in which others would pay great attention (through concern or through irritation) to the patient's depression. The treatment would be to withdraw these reinforcements, to ignore the depressive aspects, and to pay much attention to any nondepressed acts that are emitted. It would be expected that despite a possible inital increase in the depressive behavior, the depression would gradually disappear over a period of weeks. Unfortunately, rarely is it that simple.

Perhaps the most common such pattern we have seen is the situation in which the patient is depressed, and the other person is concerned, caring, and protective. When the patient starts to improve, the other person suddenly becomes aversively demanding and argumentative. This change may be rationalized as being completely appropriate ("I've been under a tremendous burden when he really needed me. Now that he's getting better, let him do more things for himself and do something for me for a change."). However, discussion with the reinforcing person will sometimes reveal a stake in the patient's depression. For instance, a man had severe social anxieties, and so long as his wife was depressed, their social life was minimal. In another instance a woman was afraid that her son would leave home. So long as he was too depressed to work, there was no danger of his leaving. The strangest such stake we have seen was that of a woman who was having an extramarital affair and had strong feelings against having sexual relations with two different men. For several years her husband was sufficiently depressed that he was uninterested in sex, but not so depressed that he couldn't work. In each of these instances the other person was only minimally aware of this stake in the patient's depression, and not at all aware of the relationship between this stake and the other person's inability to follow the reinforcement withdrawal procedures that had been learned.

Sometimes there is no stake, but the other person is unable to follow the withdrawal program because of an automatic emotional reaction. In this instance the patient's depressive behavior is the trigger stimulus, feelings of anxiety and concern are the automatic emotional responses, and some form of attention is the overt response. It is under control only to the extent that any phobic response can be under control, and it must be treated in the same manner. Just as a phobic patient must learn to relax out the feelings of fear and refrain from avoidance and escape behaviors, so must the reinforcing person learn to relax out the feelings of anxiety and concern and refrain from attention-paying behaviors. Desensitization is often helpful.

The desensitization procedures not only change automatic emotional reactions but also, in so doing, can change interpersonal reactions. It has been reported that changing a patient's behavior has led to a change in another person's symptoms. In one instance, desensitization of a woman to her husband's cross-dressing preceded the disappearance of transvestite behavior in the husband (Fensterheim, 1974). In another case, desensitization of a woman to her lover's sexual impotence led to the disappearance of his impotence (Fensterheim & Kantor, 1979). So, although desensitization may be performed primarily as an aid in maintaining the reinforcement withdrawal program, sometimes it has a more direct effect. We have seen several instances in which such desensitization of a reinforcing person has led to an immediate decrease in the depression of the spouse. In one such instance, a woman mental health professional with a long-standing depression that had been highly refractory to any treatment explained her dramatic change by saying that suddenly her husband had become so understanding and empathic that she no longer "needed" the depression. In this instance, treatment probably was discontinued too soon. The depression returned some 6 months later, but because she went elsewhere for further treatment, there was no way we could determine what was involved.

Thus, in cases in which a significant other person appears to reinforce a patient's depression (especially in cases of long-standing and apparently refractory depression), treatment must focus for a while on the reinforcing person rather than on the depressed patient. There are situations in which the interaction is so complex that they must be seen as a couple. We have even had several instances in which the depressed person has not been seen at all.

Case History 4

A woman in her early thirties, mother of two children, presented with what she labeled as a marital problem. For the past several months her husband had been quite withdrawn, sulky, no fun, not even interested in sex, participating only minimally in social and other pleasurable activities, ignoring the children. After work and on weekends he would only sit and watch television, paying no attention to anything else. She described his appetite as being poor, but she did not know if any sleep disturbance was present. He sounded as if he were depressed. Also, he refused to participate in any psychological treatment. The woman was sufficiently disturbed by the situation that she was considering separation, much as she did not want to do so.

The husband's refusal of consultation was indeed an obstacle in planning treatment. The first target selected was to attempt to relieve some of her discomfort. It was hoped that in doing so, her perceptions of the situation might change, and some strategy for coping with the situation might be formulated. A chief source of her disturbance was the trigger stimulus of her husband sitting in front of the television set, and desensitization to this was conducted. An almost immediate result of this was that the husband stopped watching television and once again became involved with the family, and his depressive behavior disappeared.

Several months later, the husband did appear for a consultation, and the following story emerged. He had a long-term behavioral pattern concerning pressure. Whenever he felt pressured, automatically he would resist it without any regard to his own desires and goals. When the difficulty with his wife had started, he had felt mildly depressed because of some difficulty at work. To relax himself, he spent a weekend morning watching television, but he did not explain to his wife why he was doing so. She reacted to this by becoming upset and angry, which reaction he experienced as a pressure. Following his characteristic pattern, he resisted the supposed pressure by increasing his television watching. This upset his wife even more; he experienced increased pressure and therefore further increased his television watching. So the spiral continued. He really did not like himself for watching television. He really did want to do other things. However, he could not break the pattern, and he became increasingly depressed. Following the desensitization of his wife, he experienced relief from the pressure and became able to do what he had wanted to do anyway. Thus, desensitizing his wife changed a pattern of interpersonal interactions, and this, in turn, led to the relief of his depression.

Patterns similar to these have been observed when the depression has had consequences that have been reinforcing to the depressed patients. These consequences may occur through the subtraction of anxiety-provoking situations or potentially anxiety-provoking situations from the patient's immediate environment. Or they may occur through the addition of some desired stimulus. Case history 2, cited earlier, illustrates the situation of a patient who prolonged his depressions as a means of avoiding the disturbed feelings brought on by habitual mild chronic hyperventilation. Sometimes, however, the pattern can be far more complex and subtle.

Case History 5

A young woman presented with the symptom of obesity plus a marked depression of moderate severity. The basis of the depression appeared to be the obesity. She was constantly thinking about her appearance, and each such thought set off a surge of depression and self-hate. The basis of her inability to keep to a diet or a weight-control program was her depression. The more successful her diet, the more depressed she became. The only way she had learned to control her depression was through the comfort derived through eating. She was depressed because she ate, and she ate because she was depressed. A variety of treatment interventions aimed at both symptoms brought only temporary relief, followed by a return to the initial status.

Further investigation revealed severe anxiety concerning social and sexual relations with men; this had existed since high school. Although this had been noted during the initial interview, its importance in maintaining the current problem was not realized until her case was reformulated following the initial failure of treatment. In this reformulation it was hypothesized that the depression-overeating interaction allowed her to avoid this anxiety-laden area. Treatment (through assertiveness training, desensitization, covert rehearsal, and deliberate formation of exciting fantasies) was aimed at this new target area. When she noted increased enjoyment of both heterosocial and heterosexual fantasies, she stated that she felt some hope in regard to resolving her problems with men, and she suggested that we attempt to treat the depression and overeating again. It was at this point that desensitization to the thoughts concerning her appearance was successfully maintained and she became able to keep to a weight-control program.

Patients with such reinforced depressions often appear to be (and actually are) very manipulative. Threats of suicide may be used in attempts to manipulate the therapist, as well as others. Here the therapist must walk the fine line between taking the threat seriously (as one must always do) and yet not reinforcing it. The reinforcers gained through the manipulations must be uncovered, and alternative methods of obtaining these reinforcers must be taught. At times, the manipulation is used to cope with a feeling of powerlessness in the face of controlling others (often parents, even for 30- or 40-year old patients who have their own families); at other times, it may be a way of waging disagreement without a direct dialogue on the relevant subject. Often a combination of assertiveness training and desensitization is required.

Unlike the previously cited reinforced depressions, the blind habit depressions we have been able to identify usually are low-grade depressions, but, again, they last a very long time (often years) and apparently are refractory to any kind of treatment. Whatever the original precipitant of the depression, the patient has become passive in the face of the feelings. These patients take no active measures to reduce these feelings, but rather allow them to wax and wane without any attempt at control of either the feelings themselves or the actions (or lack of actions) to which they lead. The helplessness, the negative thoughts about oneself, and the other characteristics of depression appear to be epiphenomenal; treating them does not result in any change. No reinforcers for these depressions can be observed, even after intensive search. It appears that these patients are simply passively going along with an already established habit of feeling depressed.

The first step in treatment is to explain the situation to these patients and tell them that they must be trained in the counterhabit of feeling not depressed. Self-monitoring is one effective way of establishing new habits. These patients are to keep charts of the amount of time each day they feel not depressed. Specific reinforcers may be earned for increases in the desired direction, but usually such changes are sufficient reinforcement by themselves. It is difficult for these patients to describe just what they do to bring on the nondepressed feeling, but several have described it as "a sort of summoning up of energy" when they feel the deadness. Nevertheless, over a period of several months, the time each day one of these patients feels depressed tends to diminish and eventually disappear completely. With such patients, further exploration should be carried out to determine if the passive orientation has deleterious effects in other life areas.

Assertiveness

There are perhaps as many definitions of assertiveness as there are behavior therapists who use assertiveness training methods. We relate this area to legitimate feelings of mastery characterized by behavior that has three characteristics: (1) The behavior is deliberate. One can make a specific decision to perform or not perform a given act, and one has the ability to carry through one's decision. (2) The aim of the behavior, taking all the circumstances into consideration, is to increase one's own self-respect. Given the fact that there is indeed a reality, one cannot always be certain of winning. Given the fact that other people have their own individualities, one cannot always be certain of their approval. One can, however, be certain that one is trying to act in a way that will maximize one's own self-respect in that given situation. (3) Behavioral difficulties in this area can result from either lack of necessary skills or inability to mobilize those skills that do exist. Behavioral inhibitions caused by high levels of anxiety, by automatic emotional reactions, or by obsessive thought patterns are not properly included here.

The feeling of lost mastery, whether justified or not, or the consequences of the actual loss of mastery often can bring on a depression. Many psychological symptoms bring on secondary depression for just that reason. With compulsive variant sexual behavior, with a variety of phobic reactions, and with many other symptoms, the patient feels a loss of mastery in those areas and hence the depression. It is interesting to note the superficial similarity of this formulation to a psychoanalytic formulation of Bibring (1953) that involves the ego's recognition of its own powerlessness. However, Bibring based his formulation on childhood trauma, whereas we stress the current status of the patient. The loss of mastery may be based on reality, and although one's personal developmental history may influence one's reaction to this loss, the goal is not to "resolve" the childhood trauma but rather to restore legitimate mastery in the present.

Actual loss of mastery can come about because of external or internal (psychological) changes. Some of the depressive reactions among the elderly represent the latter. Elderly patients may have undergone certain intellectual changes, such as some loss of recent memory or some loss in abstract ability. Even though the actual loss may be relatively slight, the reaction to it may be great. They are aware that they no longer have the mastery they formerly had. They may continue to try to cope as they had done in the past, which will sharpen their sense of helplessness and also expose them to catastrophic reactions, and thus they become depressed. Or, in their attempts to avoid the catastrophic reactions, they may unrealistically limit their life situations, depriving themselves of potential sources of reinforcement, and depression follows. Treatment is aimed at teaching these patients the realities of these new limitations and how to function most effectively within them.

A loss of mastery leading to depression can also come about through choices of inappropriate and unobtainable goals. Clinical observation has led to the identification of two common forms of such incorrect goal choices:

1. Patients set long-term goals but formulate no intermediate short-term goals. This is found in obsessive patients who think in Aristotelian terms. They either achieve a goal or do not achieve it. Because long-term goals cannot be achieved on a short-term basis, and because no subgoals have been recognized, there is no reinforcement for actual accomplishments. This quite understandably is followed by a decrease in this activity, often labeled as procrastination. These patients feel angry with themselves, worthless and helpless. This is followed by depression.

A slightly different form of this behavior involves inappropriate standards, usually standards of perfection to be achieved immediately at one fell swoop. These patients pay great attention to the slightest deviation from their standards, ruminate about it, and completely ignore their actual accomplishments and their actual movement toward their goals. Feelings of unworthiness and helplessness increase, and these patients are indeed helpless to achieve their unrealistic goals.

2. The second common goal-setting error that often leads to depression concerns the actions of other people. For instance, a patient's goal may be to have other persons like him, be friendly, not get angry, do what they are asked to do. This is an area of minimal control, for the other persons are individuals in their own right, with their own needs, styles, and problems. Lazarus (1971) conceptualized assertion not just

as recognition of one's own rights and standing up for them but also as recognition of the rights of others and respecting them. Certainly other people have the right to have their own needs and problems. However, because of the impossible goals set, when other people do not respond in the desired manner, the patient feels powerless, helpless, and inadequate. Depression often follows.

In this way, the choice of unobtainable goals does lead to a lack of mastery and to depression of greater or lesser intensity. Because the goal-setting difficulty usually is a general problem, these patients keep facing situations in which they feel no mastery. Hence, these depressions tend to be constant and to last for very long periods of time. Should there be some intermittent relief, the depression tends to return as soon as the patient is in a new problem situation.

The treatment for this type of depression is first to make these patients aware of their incorrect goals choices and the relationship between these choices and the depression. Then these patients must be taught how to choose more appropriate goals. In some cases this may involve teaching patients to formulate subgoals and to monitor their achievement of the subgoals, or it may involve teaching them to quantify their actual progress or achievement ("It is 80% good. What do I have to do to bring it up to 90%?") to counter the Aristotelian thinking. However, the major core of the reeducation usually is to have patients center their goals in the area of self-respect.

1. First, self-respect is discussed with patients as the area of maximum control. They are taught that there is indeed a reality and that they cannot always win or get what they want. They are taught that other people are indeed independent of them and that they cannot always control what other people do and feel. It is amazing how many patients have misconceptions in this area (Ellis & Harper, 1973). Given these limitations, what patients can do is attempt to act in a manner that will increase or maintain their own self-respect.

The concept of self-respect is not defined by the therapist except in the vague terms of becoming the kind of person the patient would most like to be. Rather, patients are told to discover for themselves through their actions what they mean by the term. Few patients have more than a slight initial difficulty with this idea; indeed, often they tend to become intrigued by the discovery project. Even more rare is the appearance of destructive concepts of self-respect. The worst of such concepts ("I would respect myself most if I committed suicide." "I would respect myself most if I killed him.") have never come up in our experience.

2. Models can be used in determining self-respect goals. One helpful model is an internal model, the idealized self-image (Susskind, 1970). Another model can be a respected person whom one would like to emulate: What would the model person do or say (not think or feel,

because he would not be in that situation) if he realized his work was not up to his standard? What would the model person do or say if the patient became angry, acted unfriendly, refused the request? The patient attempts to react as the model person would. This furnishes a structure for the formation of self-respect goals in specific situations. As training in this area progresses, feelings of mastery develop, and the depression recedes.

Of course, this training program will not be immediately effective. There will be many situations in which patients will not think of the self-respect goals or will be unable to perform the necessary behaviors. Patients will react to these failures much as they reacted to their previous failures. They will berate themselves, feel worthless and helpless, and become depressed. The depression may even be stronger than usual, for the future will seem even more hopeless (here they are failing in the very things that are supposed to help them to change). The treatment of this reaction is to teach patients to turn their failures into constructive training exercises.

The treatment in this context is based on Suinn's visual motor behavior rehearsal (Suinn, 1972) using a coping model (Kazdin, 1973; Meichenbaum, 1971). For instance, one first formulates what one's self-respect behavior in the failed situation might have been. One then briefly relaxes oneself. Under the conditions of relaxation, one imagines a scene with the following characteristics: (1) the failed situation, including one's own disturbed feelings; (2) successful coping with the disturbed feelings; (3) successful performance of the self-respect act. This image is repeated several times. If successful, it will increase the probability of self-respect behaviors in future situations.

3. Special exercises in self-respect behavior can be devised. There is one such exercise that, although it has never been tested experimentally, does appear to be clinically useful. It is similar to one reported by Beck and associates (1979), but it differs in that the performance of the act is deliberate. The instructions given are as follows: "Each day, deliberately (premeditatedly) do something, preferably something trivial, that will give you even a momentary feeling of increased self-respect. As soon as feasible after you have done it, make a note of what you have done. If it increased your self-respect at all, regardless of what else you felt, put a check next to it. Do one a day; no repeats." In this way, patients are trained to know the sources of their self-respect, to become more aware of (and so to reinforce) the feelings of self-respect, and, most important, to attain the legitimate feelings of being in command of their self-respect behaviors. It is this last that most effectively counters the feelings of helplessness and lack of mastery.

The stress is on the deliberate aspect of the act. Activity qua activity often is not the crucial variable in depression. We have seen any number of patients leading most active lives: They work at challenging jobs, and their personal relationships on the job are good. They lead active social lives, are involved in many recreational activities, have close friends and good communication with spouses. Still they are depressed ("I do all these things, but I just do not enjoy them. I always feel down.") With such patients the diagnosis often is "passivity." They are carried along by events outside of themselves and have no feeling of command over these events. The treatment is to establish the legitimate feeling of being able to act deliberately to achieve specific goals, usually self-respect goals.

From this perspective, the treatment approach of increasing the patient's activity (Rehm, 1977) has as its major variable the deliberate activity it brings into play. The acts of record keeping, self-monitoring, and self-reinforcement are all deliberate acts. Even the construction of fantasy (Lazarus, 1968) is a deliberate act that can start to reverse the depression.

This distinction is not mere academic hair splitting, for it does have implications for treatment. Many of the depressed patients we see do engage in very few activities. For many of them, it is important to increase their rates of doing things. However, we run into a difficulty in getting them to follow such a program: Most often there is no one with whom they can do things, and the idea of doing things alone makes them anxious, more aware of their isolation, and exacerbates the depression. If the therapist attempts to set up a program in which the presence of other people is not important (such as doing things in one's own home), this may be rejected as trivial and meaningless. To counter this, the therapist must explain the importance of deliberate performance of acts, no matter how trivial. As the patient accepts this and does begin to perform deliberate acts, there may be a decrease in the depression. At that time, either some social contacts can be established or the doing of things alone can be approached as a separate problem.

Lack of assertiveness can have consequences that can lead to depression. Lack of the skills involved in open and appropriate communication can lead to lack of truly close relationships. Inability to stand up for oneself can lead to feelings of being exploited and to actual exploitation. The absence of social skills can lead to an inadequate social network and to loneliness. A depressing life-style comes into being, and depression is an appropriate reaction. The recognition of one's helplessness tends to exacerbate the depression. Proper treatment of such depressions is, of course, assertiveness training used to change one's life style.

Conclusions

The material presented in this chapter obviously is based on the observations of one therapist. No careful measurements are presented; there are no graphs of progress to support these observations; no overall rates of cure and failure are reported. Hence, better that the word "conclusion" would be the word "opinion," a conclusion based on admittedly inadequate evidence. Despite this, and despite certain caveats that must be stated, some general statements can be made:

1. We have noted no great need for a special theory of depression in order to treat the majority of depressed patients we have seen. Depression, like any other behavioral disorder, usually can be formulated through the customary variables in general use in behavior therapy. Usually it can be treated through the behavioral techniques already in general use in this area.

2. Despite the phenotypic similarities of the depressions, the psychological organizations that underlie them can be quite different. Each such organization calls for a different strategy of treatment and the application of different techniques. A thorough behavioral evaluation is essential for each patient.

3. Although inquiries into the models of depression do add to our knowledge and hence to our therapeutic flexibility, these contributions appear to be peripheral. In the current atmosphere of behavior therapy, they involve the risk of limiting the therapist's formulations to these models and thus decreasing the therapist's flexibility and effectiveness.

4. Not only are the reported observations those of a single therapist; they are based on a highly select group of patients. They derive from an office practice in New York City, with the treatment group being composed mainly (but not exclusively) of patients of middle-class and upper-middle-class socioeconomic status. Other therapists, working with different patients, may report different clinical experiences.

5. These observations are not presented in raw form, but are organized. The clinical material presented is to illustrate these observations. Hence, some of the material presented as "pure" was instead part of a more complex structure involving a number of the variables discussed. Pure cases (those involving only a single variable where treatment of that variable leads to a change in the depression) have indeed been observed and are not uncommon. Others have been observed that are pure in one variable (e.g., general tension) at one stage of treatment and pure in another variable (e.g., assertion) at a different stage of treatment. Many, however, are found to be mixed from the outset, and a multiple-thrust treatment must be formulated from the beginning.

These, then, are the highly individualistic observations of a single therapist who, over many years, has attempted to treat a great many patients with neurotic depressions through the behavioral approach.

REFERENCES

Beck, A.E., Rush, A.J., Shaw, B.F., & Emery, G. *Cognitive therapy of depression.* New York: Guilford, 1979.

Beech, H.R. *Obsessional states.* London: Methuen, 1974.

Bibring, E. The mechanism of depression. In P. Greenacre (Ed.), *Affective disorders*, New York: International Universities Press, 1953.
Craighead, W.E. Away from the unitary model of depression. *Behavior Therapy*, 1980, *11*, 122-128.
Damas Mora, J., Patel, M.K., & Jenner, F.A. The effect of mild hyperventilation on red cell sodium. *British Journal of Psychiatry*, 1977, *130*, 459-462.
Ellis, A., & Harper, R.A. *A guide to rational living*. North Hollywood, Calif.: Wilshire, 1973.
Eysenck, H.J. The classification of depressive illness. *British Journal of Psychiatry*, 1970, *117*, 241-250.
Fensterheim, H. The initial interview. In A.A. Lazarus (Ed.), *Clinical behavior therapy*, New York: Brunner/Mazel, 1972.
Fensterheim, H. Behavior therapy of the sexual variations. *Journal of Sex and Marital Therapy*, 1974, *1*, 16-28.
Fensterheim, H. The case of Marion: Behavior therapy approach. In C.A. Loew, H. Grayson, & G.H. Loew (Eds.), *Three psychotherapies*, New York: Brunner/Mazel, 1975.
Fensterheim, H., & Baer, J. *Stop running scared*. New York: Rawson Associates, 1977.
Fensterheim, H. & Kantor, J.S. The behavioral approach to sexual disorders. In B.B. Wolman & J. Money (Eds.), *Handbook of human sexuality*, Englewood Cliffs, N.J.: Prentice-Hall, 1979.
Gibson, H.B. A form of behavior therapy for some states diagnosed as "affective disorder." *Behavior Research and Therapy*, 1978, *16*, 191-195.
Goldfried, M.R. Systematic desensitization as training in self-control. *Journal of Consulting and Clinical Psychology*, 1971, *37*, 228-234.
Kanfer, F.H. & Phillips, J.S. *Learning foundations of behavior therapy*. New York: Wiley, 1970.
Kazdin, A.E. Covert modeling and the reduction of avoidance behavior. *Journal of Abnormal Psychology*, 1973, *81*, 87-95.
Lazarus, A.A. Learning theory and the treatment of depression. *Behavior Research and Therapy*, 1968, *6*, 83-89.
Lazarus, A.A. *Behavior therapy and beyond*. New York: McGraw-Hill, 1971.
Lazarus, A.A. & Abramowitz, A. The use of "emotive imagery" in the treatment of children's phobias. *Journal of Mental Science*, 1962, *108*, 191-195.
Lewinsohn, P.M. A behavioral approach to depression. In R.J. Friedman & M.M. Katz (Eds.), *The psychology of depression: Contemporary theory and research*, New York: Winston-Wiley, 1974.
Lum, L.C. The syndrome of habitual chronic hyperventilation. In O. Hill (Ed.), *Modern trends in psychosomatic medicine* (Vol. III), Boston: Butterworth, 1976.
Masters, W.H. & Johnson, V.E. *Human sexual inadequacy*. Boston: Little, Brown, 1970.
Meichenbaum, D. Examination of model characteristics in reducing avoidance behavior. *Journal of Personality and Social Psychology*, 1971, *17*, 298-307.
Rachman, S. The modification of obsessions—a new formulation. *Behavior Research and Therapy*, 1976, *14*, 437-444.
Rehm, L.P. A self-control model of depression. *Behavior Therapy*, 1977, *8*, 787-804.

Seligman, M.E.P. *Helplessness: On depression, development and death.* San Francisco: Freeman, 1975.

Slater, E., & Cowie, V. *The genetics of mental disorders.* London: Oxford University Press, 1971.

Suinn, R.M. Removing emotional obstacles to learning and performance by visual-motor behavioral rehearsal. *Behavior Therapy,* 1972, *3,* 308–310.

Susskind, D.J. The idealized self-image (ISI): A new technique in confidence training. *Behavior Therapy,* 1970, *1,* 538–541.

Wolpe, J. *The practice of behavior therapy* (2nd ed.). Elmsford, N.Y.: Pergamon, 1973.

Wolpe, J. The experimental model and treatment of neurotic depression. *Behavior Research and Therapy,* 1979, *17,* 555–565.

A Social-Behavioral Analysis of Suicide and Parasuicide Implications for Clinical Assessment and Treatment

Marsha M. Linehan

At one time or another most psychotherapists are faced with the possibility of having a patient commit suicide or attempt suicide. The likelihood that suicidal behavior will be encountered during the course of therapy is especially high if the therapist works primarily with seriously disturbed or depressed patients. The frequency of suicidal behavior makes it a phenomenon that cannot be ignored by any mental health professional. Each year more than 25,000 persons in the United States kill themselves (*Vital Statistics of the United States,* 1973, 1975). It has been estimated that each year anywhere from two to eight times that number, 50,000 to 200,000 persons, attempt suicide (Farberow & Shneidman, 1961; Parkin & Stengel, 1965; Shneidman, 1979; Stengel 1968). Dublin (1963) suggested that 1% of the population in the United States (2 million people) have at one time or another made suicide attempts. If the estimates are correct that anywhere from 10% to 20% of

---

I would like to express my deep gratitude to the members of our parasuicide research team: Paul Camper, Kelly Egan, Carol Ginsberg, André Ivanoff, Cinda Madonna, Sharon Medak, Stephen McCutcheon, and Elizabeth Trebow. Without their wit, hard work, and patience, this chapter would not have been written. Stephen McCutcheon's thoughtful comments on an earlier draft were invaluable.

those persons who have attempted suicide will eventually die by suicide (Dorpat & Ripley, 1967; Kreitman, 1977), then we can estimate that there are anywhere from 200,000 to 400,000 potential suicide victims in the United States alone. The rates for both suicide attempts and suicides are increasing almost everywhere in the world, including gradually increasing rates in the United States (Brown, 1979).

In contrast, suicide rates have decreased dramatically in England over the last several years. However, an equally dramatic increase in the number of suicide attempts suggests that the decreasing suicide rate may be a function of improved medical care for suicide attempters. A recent British study of persons who came to emergency rooms as a result of deliberate self-poisoning noted that such drug overdoses have increased so markedly over the past 20 years that among young women it is now the most common cause of emergency admissions to medical wards; it was speculated that if present trends continue, by 1984 adults who have poisoned themselves will fill all the emergency beds in British hospitals, (Jones, 1977). There have also been marked increases in adolescent suicides and attempted suicides in the last several years (Duncan, 1977; Hollinger, 1978; *Vital Statistics of the United States*, 1973, 1975).

Suicidal behavior often has been associated with depression, and the assumption has been made that if one knows how to treat depression, there is little else to know about treating suicidal patients. However, the association between depression and suicide is not as clear as was once thought. Whereas depressed persons often admit to having suicidal ideation, most do not actively engage in suicidal behavior beyond thinking about it. Nor do all persons experience depression prior to suicide attempts. It is probable that the inclusion of suicidal behavior among the criteria for diagnosis of depression has artificially raised the numbers of suicidal patients diagnosed as being depressed. For example, suicidal ideation, wishing to be dead, and suicide attempts are defined as part of the depressive syndrome in the APA *Diagnostic and Statistical Manual III* (American Psychiatric Association, in press) and in research diagnostic criteria (Spitzer et al., 1978); questions about suicidal ideation are included in depression inventories (e.g., Beck, Ward, Mendelson, Mock, & Erbaugh, 1961). These inclusions may not be justified; they may only further obscure what clear relationships there may be between depression and suicide. Certainly the statement by Silverman that "depression prior to suicide is probably universal" (1968, p. 887) is not justified by the data.

Depression does appear to be a factor in some suicidal behaviors. The rate of suicide is higher among patients diagnosed as being depressed than among patients with any other diagnoses (Miles, 1977). In addition, follow-up studies have shown that one-sixth of the mortality among depressives is the result of suicide, as compared with only 1% for the general population (Guze & Robins, 1970). Robin, Brooke, and Freeman-Browne (1968) found that 8% of male inpatients and 5% of female inpatients diagnosed as having affective disorders committed suicide within 6 to 11 years. Retrospective studies of diagnoses for psychiatric patients who later have committed suicide, as well as studies involving post hoc diagnoses made on the basis of interviews with significant others in the lives of psychiatric patients who have committed suicide, have revealed that a diagnosis of depression was indicated in 30% to 80% of the suicide cases (Barraclough et al., 1974; Dorpat & Ripley, 1960; Pokorny, 1964; Robin et al., 1959; Silver et al., 1971). These latter data should be interpreted cautiously; 20% to 70% of these patients were not diagnosed as being depressed. In reference to this point, Pokorny (1968) suggested that the belief that only depressed persons commit suicide is one of the major myths about suicidal behavior.

The purpose of this chapter is to present a social-behavioral model of suicidal behavior together with recommendations for assessment and treatment of suicidal patients. Methodological problems in conducting research on suicide will be discussed first in order to provide a background for evaluating the research data that are presented. Nonbehavioral models of suicide will be presented briefly; however, it is not the intent of this chapter to describe in detail the major nonbehavioral models in the current suicide literature nor their associated treatment recommendations. The interested reader is referred to the work of Douglas (1967), Resnik (1968), Hankoff and Einsidler (1979), and Farberow (1974) for reviews of relevant theories and treatment modalities.

Methodological Problems in Studying Suicidal Behavior

Research in the area of suicidal behavior has been notoriously difficult. Methodological problems exist at almost every level. Difficulties are encountered in the classification of suicidal behaviors, in the generalizability of data collected on patients who have engaged in one category of suicidal behavior to patients engaging in other categories, and in the applicability of findings collected after patients have already engaged in suicidal behavior to the understanding of patients before they engage in suicidal behavior. In addition, the relative infrequency of suicidal behavior, coupled with the ethical imperative to prevent suicidal acts if possible, precludes experimental analyses of factors inducing suicide.

Douglas (1967), in an excellent analysis of the definitions of suicide, suggested that there are several fundamentally independent but related dimensions in most definitions of suicide. Included in these dimensions are the ideas that suicide involves "the *initiation* of an act that leads to the death of the initiator," "*the motivation to be dead (or to die)* which leads to the initiation of an act that leads to the death of the initiator," and "the *knowledge* of an actor that [the actions initiated will] tend to produce the objective state of death" (Douglas, 1967, p. 351). Common to these dimensions is the notion that these persons know that their actions will lead to death and that engagement in the fatal actions is intended. Thus motivation, or intention, is central to the definition of suicide. Unfortunately, assessment of motivational states, as well as patients' thoughts prior to the act, is extremely difficult and necessarily inferential. The problems of inferring motivation and thoughts for the study population are, of course, compounded when some of the patients are dead. In addition, as Douglas pointed out, even though there is agreement that the intention to die must in some way be inferable if a death is to be labeled suicide, there is much disagreement among researchers, clinicians, coroners, and national and local legislators on how "suicide," "intention," and other related terms should be defined and what exactly constitutes adequate grounds for inferring intention and thus categorizing the behavior as suicide.

"Attempted suicide" is the term most often used to describe the behavior of persons who have engaged in deliberate but nonfatal self-injurious acts, but this could well be a misnomer; it implies that these persons were trying to end their lives and failed to complete the act. The term "suicide gesture" has been used by many to distinguish those persons who engage in suicidal behavior but do not intend to die from those persons who are trying to end up dead (i.e., commit suicide), the so-called real suicide attempters (Dorpat & Ripley, 1960; Motto, 1965; Nelson et al., 1977; Paykel et al., 1975; Schmidt et al., 1954). This distinction is pejorative, and it does not solve the problem of how to make an accurate assessment of suicidal intent. The term "parasuicide" has been suggested by Kreitman and associates (1969) as a substitute for all categories of suicide attempts; it does not require reliance on knowledge of one's conscious intent to die at the time of the act. Instead, parasuicide implies a behavioral analogue of suicide, but without imputing to the actor the intent to die; it has been defined as a "nonfatal act in which an individual deliberately causes self-injury or ingests a substance in excess of any prescribed or generally recognized therapeutic dosage" (Kreitman, 1977, p. 3). The label "parasuicide" will be used throughout this chapter. In the literature, the term "suicidal" generally refers to persons who engage in any suicide-related behavior, including suicide, parasuicide, suicide talk or threats, and/or suicidal ideation. An effort will be made in this chapter to specify, when possible, which class of behavior is meant. The more generic term will be used when all categories of suicidal behavior are meant to be included.

Much of the research on suicide has been done from the perspective that suicidal behavior represents a monotonic continuum; live attempters, threateners, and even ideators have been studied in attempts to make generalizations about dead completers. However, there are serious questions about the extent to which data collected for one category of suicidal persons can validly be generalized to other categories of suicidal persons. Although there is overlap between attempters and completers, as revealed by statistics showing that the best predictor of suicide is the finding that a person is a former parasuicide (Diekstra, 1973), suicide attempters do not greatly resemble suicide completers in terms of demographic and psychological variables (Murphy, 1977; Stengel, 1964). This distinction is important in that it suggests that assessment and treatment issues may be different for the two populations. In addition, it is doubtful that data collected on parasuicides after the act give a valid representation of the data that would have been collected if these persons had been evaluated before the act. The feedback effects of the parasuicide act itself, the physical damage resulting from the act, the differential treatment of parasuicide patients in hospital units, and the sometimes markedly different treatment of parasuicides by significant others can cause substantial changes in recall of prior events as well as in psychological functioning in the present.

Theoretical Approaches to Suicidal Behavior

Theoretical approaches to suicidal behavior can be classified into five general types: (1) sociological theories, (2) biological theories, (3) psychodynamic theories, (4) cognitive theories, and (5) learning theories.

Sociological Theories

Sociological theories view suicide as a function of a person's role and status in the social system. The classic sociological theory is that proposed by Emile Durkheim in 1897; it has influenced almost all later sociological theories. Durkheim's theory suggested that two characteristics of society, social integration and social regulation, together or singly determine social conditions, which in turn influence the suicide rate. More recent sociological theories introducing concepts such as the stability and durability of social relationships, social restraints, and social meaning as being important in suicidal behavior have been presented by Henry and Short (1954), Gibbs and Martin (1964), and Douglas (1967). The primary problem with these theories for the clinician is that although they are useful for predicting changes in the suicide rate for a total population or subgroup, they are not useful in individual cases, either for predicting suicide risk or for generating effective treatment procedures. Attempts to integrate personal variables with social factors have generated a comparatively new set of theories that can be classified as ecological. Thus, Braucht (1979) has suggested that "there is something special not only about the people who are cases of suicide or merely about the areas in which there are high rates of suicidal behavior, but about the interactions between individuals and their environments" (p. 658). This theoretical approach is similar to the interactional approach now popular in the psychology of personality (Endler & Magnusson, 1976).

Biological Theories

Biological theories of suicide suggest either that suicidal tendencies may be inherited (Kallman & Anastasio, 1947) or that chemical changes taking place in the body may precipitate suicidal behavior (Bunney & Fawcett, 1965; Bunney et al., 1969; Carroll & Mendels, 1976; Hornykiewicz, 1974; Levy & Hansen, 1969; Platman et al., 1971; Struve, 1979). The finding that among 24 twin pairs in which one twin committed suicide all surviving twins remained discordant as to suicide at follow-up, some as much as 49 years later (Kallman et al., 1949), tends to counter the genetic theory of suicide. Data on chemical correlates of suicidal behavior are equivocal, neither supporting nor refuting the theory.

Psychodynamic Theories

Psychodynamic theories, the most prominent theories in the clinical literature on suicidal behavior, view suicidal behavior as a product of internal unconscious motives. The classic motive imputed to suicidal persons by psychoanalytically oriented theorists has been that of hostility, or aggressive impulses, toward an introjected and ambivalently viewed love object (i.e., aggression turned inward). Menninger (1938) suggested that every suicide represents (1) the wish to kill, (2) the wish to be killed, and (3) the wish to die. Fantasies of identification with a lost object, rebirth and starting all over, reunion with one's mother, escape, elimination of a disliked part of oneself, autoscopy, and revenge have been posited as important motives in suicide (Furst & Ostow, 1979). Dynamic theories, including dynamic theories of suicide, assume that if an impulse is acted out against oneself, as in parasuicide and suicide, then the impulse will not be acted out against others at the same time; that is, the tendencies are located at opposite poles. As will be discussed at some length later, parasuicidal persons often are characterized by aggressive behavior toward both themselves and other people. Such data present a dilemma for psychodynamic theory in that, as aptly noted by Tapper (1975), "it is unlikely that aggression can be turned outward and then flip-flop inward at the same moment" (p. 18). Findings on the role of aggression in suicide have been contradictory. West (1965) found that one-third of the homicides in England and

Wales were murder-suicides, with the suicide occurring immediately after the murder. Other research indicating that persons who commit suicide behave less aggressively than persons who do not is consistent with psychodynamic theory. However, analyses of suicide notes have suggested that hostile motives may be infrequent in suicide (Farberow & Shneidman, 1957). Taken together, these data suggest that psychodynamic approaches do not provide an adequate account of suicide and parasuicide.

Cognitive Theories

Theories of suicidal behavior that view such behavior as an attempt to communicate or solve a problem, as well as theories that consider it to be the result of hopelessness and disordered thinking, can be classified as primarily cognitive in orientation. The classic approach to suicidal behavior, and especially parasuicide, as a method of communication was proposed by Farberow and Shneidman (1961), who coined the phrase "the cry for help" in reference to suicidal behavior: "The title, *The Cry for Help*, is meant to convey our feelings (from our work with suicidally disturbed persons) about the messages of suffering and anguish and the pleas for response that are expressed by and contained within suicidal behaviors" (p. xi). A similar approach was advocated by Kreitman and associates (1970), who suggest that many parasuicidal persons come from a population in which parasuicide is recognized as communicating a specific kind of information; thus persons who wish to convey such messages about their difficulties can perform an act (parasuicide) that carries a preformed meaning. Douglas (1967) discussed the social meaning of suicidal actions and suggested that they communicate to others that something is fundamentally wrong with the situation of the actor.

The theory that suicidal behavior is caused by persons' beliefs that their problems are insoluble has been advocated by Beck (1963); Zubin (1974) suggested that a sudden shift in one's locus of control might be a precipitating factor. A number of theorists have either directly or indirectly suggested that suicidal behavior is an instance of an attempt at problem solving (Applebaum, 1963; Grollman, 1971; Levenson & Neuringer, 1971; Neuringer, 1961; Stengel & Cook, 1958). From this vantage, both suicide and parasuicide are seen as attempts to solve the problems in one's life, usually those problems involving intense internal or environmental distress; in additon, one is attempting to get rid of problems (by death or "manipulation") rather than accommodate to them (Applebaum, 1963; Basescu, 1965; Kovacs et al., 1975b; Olin, 1976; Sifneos, 1966; Stengel, 1960, 1964). Maris (1971) has suggested that parasuicide, at least in some persons, can be usefully conceptualized as an attempt to cope with a difficult life situation. A problem-solving perspective of suicide is intimately related to the notion that hopelessness is a precipitant: Only those who see no solution to their problems while living attempt to solve their problems by dying. One might assume that the suicide act is successful in solving the precipitating problems; at a minimum, the person is no longer faced with the distressing event.

Learning Theories

The first formal attempt to conceptualize the development of suicidal behavior in learning terms was that of Frederick and Resnik (1971). Their approach is a blend of psychodynamic and behavioral theories and draws heavily on the work of Miller and Dollard (1941; Dollard & Miller, 1950). Frederick and Resnik presented the following formula: suicide potential = strength of past habits × drive strength. They concluded that suicidal behavior itself is a function of personality, motivating conditions, reinforcement, environment or setting, and strength of past responses in similar situations. Although a formulation of suicide in Hullian learning terms is not compatible with current behavioral thinking, the approach of Frederick and Resnik did lead to treatment strategies that currently are recommended by behavior therapists: desensitization and assertion training (Bartman, 1976; Liberman & Serber, Note 1).

Diekstra (1973) developed a social learning theory positing that suicidal behavior is a method of coping with a crisis and that, as such, it depends on the presence of suicidal behaviors in a person's repertoire, acquired through socialization. If suicidal responses are in a person's repertoire, then the probability of a suicidal response in a given situation is dependent on the person's expectations, the expectations of others in the person's environment, the availability of the means to engage in suicidal behavior, and the presence or absence of offers to help. Data presented by Diekstra and the data of many others to be reviewed later indicated that the factors suggesting that suicidal responses are in a person's repertoire (past suicidal behavior, past suicide threats, suicidal behavior among significant others) are the most powerful predictors of future suicidal responses. Little research has been done on the expectations about suicidal behavior of either suicidal persons or their significant others. Diekstra stated that suicidal behavior has a broad instrumental value, and it is interesting to note that the possible goals of suicide he suggested in the context of a social learning theory of suicide are remarkably similar to the fantasies associated with suicide reported by Furst and Ostow (1979) in the context of psychodynamic theory. The suicide outcome expectancies suggested by Diekstra included reunion with a deceased partner, revenue, hurting someone else, rest, and peace.

The observation that parasuicide often is followed by what appear to be rewarding consequences has led to a formulation of suicidal responses as operant behaviors (Bostock & Williams, 1974). The concept of suicidal behavior as an operant is quite similar to the belief held by many nonbehaviorists that parasuicide and suicide are, at least sometimes, functions of an intent to manipulate one's environment. However, the use of the designation manipulator not only is pejorative but also leads to the use of trait descriptions of the actor independent of the suicidal act; such labeling is not likely to engender a caring attitude among others who interact with the suicidal person. Thus, description of suicidal behavior as an operant seems quite preferable to description of the suicidal person as a manipulator.

A Social-Behavioral Model of Suicidal Behavior

The model of suicidal behavior presented here combines elements of each of the previously mentioned theories and is an extension of the social-behavioral model of personality presented by Staats (1963, 1975). An important aspect of this model is the notion that it can be profitable to conceptualize human functioning as occurring in one response system or a combination of three separate but interrelated response systems: the overt motor response system, the cognitive response system, and the physiological/affective response system. The lines between the systems are not always clear, and many molar responses are best viewed as cross-system response patterns. Thus, emotions include simultaneous physiological arousal together with specified cognitive contents. Since there is always a physiological aspect of any emotion, affect is defined as part of the physiological system. Social skills can include overt motor skills (such as the capacity to produce an appropriately assertive verbal response), cognitive skills (such as the capacity to discriminate when an assertive response is called for), and physiological/affective response skills (such as the capacity to manage one's own arousal in social situations) (Linehan, 1979). This tripartite model of behavior is similar to that suggested by Lang (1971) and recently reiterated by Wolpe (1978). Although the contention that cognitive processes should be considered as instances of behavior is controversial (Ledwidge, 1978), the model has been useful as an organizing principle for conceptualizing issues in behavioral assessment (Cone, 1977) and therapy (Linehan, 1979).

An important aspect of this approach to behavioral analysis is its emphasis on the interdependence of the three systems. Changes in one system will likely effect changes within the other two systems, thereby bringing about changes in the total organism. Whether or not such changes are maintained, and whether or not system responses are synchronous or desynchronous, is dependent on a number of complex factors (Hodgson & Rachman, 1974; Rachman & Hodgson, 1974). In a similar manner, from this theoretical vantage, people are viewed as being dynamically related to their environments. Thus, not only do situational stimuli affect people, people also influence their own situational surroundings; people create their own environments, both cognitively by acting on the stimuli impinging on the senses and objectively by influencing events (Bowers, 1973). The observed responses that people make are products of interactions both within these people (via the three response systems) and between these people and the environments in which they exist. The importance of this theoretical approach to suicidal behavior is threefold: (1) It highlights those areas of functioning important for an adequate understanding of suicide and parasuicide. (2) It points to the potential impact of the environment on the person and the potential impact of the person on environmental contingencies. (3) It suggests that interventions for the reduction of parasuicide and suicide will be most effective if focused on the individual person as an integrated and dynamic system of behavioral patterns.

In presenting this social-behavioral analysis of suicidal behavior, I have attempted to organize the empirical data relevant to assessment and treatment. There are thousands of research articles, case histories, theoretical discussions, and book chapters dealing with the characteristics of suicidal persons and their social settings; many are not relevant here. Great numbers of reports have been written by therapists experienced in treating suicidal patients; their descriptions of suicidal patients are considered here only if, at a minimum, they have presented frequency data on the characteristics of interest. As far as possible, data are excluded if the interpretations of their meanings are ambiguous (e.g., Rorschach data). Some of the findings presented here were based on multivariate data analysis techniques, but many were not.

An overview of the research on factors associated with suicide and parasuicide suggests that the developmental, situational, and behavioral pathways leading to suicide or parasuicide are multiple and complex. It is unlikely that there is a single behavioral or situational characteristic common to all parasuicides or suicides. For example, studies using cluster and component analysis procedures have found several typologies of parasuicidal and suicidal behaviors (Bagley et al., 1976; Colson, 1973; Henderson et al., 1977; Kiev, 1976). Nor is it likely that the locus of causality for suicidal behavior will be found in an analysis of the situation or of the person alone. The few studies using multivariate analysis have demonstrated that it is the combination of particular situational characteristics together with specific personal factors that best predicts future suicidal behavior.

Environmental Factors

Parasuicidogenic and suicidogenic environments appear to be characterized by four factors: negative changes, lack of social support, models for suicidal behavior, and predictable consequences for suicidal behavior. See the work of Clum and associates (1979) for a similar view.

Negative changes The notion that suicidal behavior is a result of negative and stressful environmental events has consistently been a part of attempts to explain suicidal behavior (Hankoff, 1979; Paykel, 1979). Recent research has suggested that both parasuicide and suicide are likely to be preceded by various patterns of negative life events (Breed, 1966; Cochrane & Robertson, 1975; Hankoff, 1979; Paykel et al., 1975). Data presented by Birtchnell (1970) and Levi and associates (1966) suggest that both parasuicidal and suicidal patients have experienced more recent losses of significant persons in their lives, as compared with other psychiatric patients. Humphrey (1977) suggested that losses, in general (e.g., persons, jobs), distinguish suicidal patients from nonsuicidal patients. Paykel (1979) found that parasuicides, when compared with depressives, reported a higher incidence of recent major events that were upsetting and uncontrollable. Braucht (1979) suggested that it may be possible to differentiate suicidal populations in terms of the specific types of environmental stresses to which they are exposed; however, it is not possible at this point to determine whether or not suicidal and parasuicidal persons can be differentiated in terms of the specific types of negative events occurring in their environments.

Taken together, these data suggest that both parasuicide and suicide can be conceptualized as responses to life events that are negative, stressful, and often uncontrollable. Thus, suicidal behavior is perhaps best viewed as an attempt on the part of a person in intolerable pain to solve a current personal problem. The effectiveness or ineffectiveness of such a solution depends on the outcomes associated with suicidal behavior, as compared with the possible outcomes if other behaviors are carried out. Whether or not an outcome of death by suicide can be considered an effective solution to a problem is dependent on one's values, ethics, and life priorities.

Lack of Social Support Evidence for lack of social support systems in the environments of suicidal persons comes from several sources. Suicides appear to hold minority status in their own cultural settings: Suicide rates for immigrants are higher than for natives of the new country as well as those who remained in the old country (Coombs & Miller, 1975); suicide rates for blacks and whites are inversely related to their proportions in a given population (Davis, 1979); those who have committed suicide are unrepresentative of the general population in their neighborhoods (Braucht, 1979). Both parasuicidal and suicidal persons are more often unemployed or retired than nonsuicidal persons (Bagley et al., 1976; Dublin, 1963; Humphrey, 1977; Kreitman, 1977), and thus they may lack the support and aid, in a number of life areas, provided by a work setting. The exception here, at least with respect to suicide, may be professional employment for young women, a status predictive of suicide among callers to a crisis center (Lettieri, 1974b). These women may experience fairly low life support and higher stresses because of their occupations.

Several investigators have found that absence of a spouse (because of death, divorce, or separation) predicts future suicidal behavior (Barraclough et al., 1974; Barraclough & Pallis, 1975; Farberow & MacKinnon, 1974; Greer et al., 1966; Kreitman, 1977; Lettieri, 1974b; Shneidman & Farberow, 1961). However, it has been found that among young men calling a crisis center, marriage may be conducive to suicide (Lettieri, 1974b). It must be kept in mind that in most of these studies control groups were not employed, and married suicidal and parasuicidal persons usually outnumbered nonmarrieds in absolute frequency. The meaning of this latter statistic is somewhat unclear, because report forms do not ordinarily make it easy to indicate a married-but-separated status. Suicide following parasuicide has been found to be more likely among the divorced, separated, and widowed (Kreitman, 1977; Tuckman & Youngman, 1963b, 1968b); marital separation and divorce have been found to characterize multiple parasuicides (Bagley & Greer, 1971; Kessel & McCulloch, 1966), although others have suggested that marital status is not a significant factor (Kreitman, 1977; Worden & Sterling-Smith, 1973).

Some 21% to 34% of persons who commit suicide live alone prior to death (Bagley et al., 1976; Shneidman et al., 1970); living alone is characteristic of persons who commit suicide following parasuicidal behavior (Paerregaard, 1975; Tuckman & Youngman, 1963b, 1968a), and families with few members may be predictive of both suicide (Humphrey, 1977; Lettieri, 1974b) and multiple parasuicide (Kreitman, 1977). However, other findings that 42% of persons who commit suicide live with spouses (Shneidman et al., 1970), that perhaps as few as 17% of parasuicidal persons live alone (Greer et al., 1966), and that overcrowded living arrangements may be most characteristic of multiple parasuicides (Chowdhury et al., 1973) suggest that both types of behavior may take place in an interpersonal context.

As with negative life events, it is not possible, given the current state of research, to distinguish suicidal persons from parasuicidal persons in terms of any qualitative differences in their respective support systems. However, it seems likely that parasuicidal persons generally may experience more hostile social environments than suicidal persons. As will be noted later, parasuicidal persons frequently interact with their environments in a hostile manner, a behavior pattern likely to generate reciprocal hostility. Rosenbaum and Richman (1970) interviewed relatives of parasuicides and found that they were hostile toward the parasuicides; in fact, they were more hostile toward the parasuicides than the parasuicides were toward them. However, if a parasuicidogenic environment is more hostile than the environment of the suicide, it may be that the parasuicide's environment also has greater potential for giving support than does the suicide's environment; that is, agents capable of giving support to the parasuicide may exist, but they may withhold support, whereas such agents may be absent from the suicide's environment. An overlap between the two environmental settings was suggested by Farberow and associates (1970), who found that medical patients who later committed suicide had experienced hospital ward staffs who had been more indifferent, less supportive, and, at times, more hostile than had the ward staffs for patients who did not subsequently commit suicide.

An absence of social support systems may be important in all types of suicidal behavior for several reasons. With a hostile or inattentive social network, or the absence of a social network, recognition of a person's crisis state will be unlikely, especially if there is unclear communication of the person's needs. Emotional support while weathering the crisis, active assistance in reducing the stress, and suggestions of possible alternatives that might be effective in solving the person's problems will not be forthcoming. In such situations people are dependent on their own behavioral capabilities for resolving problems and dealing with stressful situations. As will be noted later, the probability that these people will have the requisite capabilities is exceedingly low.

Models for Suicidal Behavior and Consequences As has been noted by many researchers, most people who have low social support and simultaneously experience negative life events do not engage in suicidal behavior. First, such a response must be part of the person's behavioral repertoire. Second, the person must expect the outcome of suicidal behavior to be more positive than the outcomes of other possible responses. Exposure to suicidal models may be important in terms of acquisition of the suicidal response and development of outcome expectations. Kreitman and associates (1970) found that parasuicidal persons, more often than nonparasuicidal persons, were linked socially with significant other persons who had previously been parasuicidal. Pokorny (1968) reviewed several family case histories in which 5 to 23 suicides had occurred in single families over three to five generations. Other studies have suggested that the suicide rate may be higher for family members of persons who commit suicide (Moss & Hamilton,

1957). Barraclough and associates (1977) found a statistical association between the number of reports of suicide inquests in a local newspaper and the subsequent suicide rate among men under 45 years of age.

As noted earlier, many suicides have previously engaged in parasuicidal behavior. The fact that most parasuicidal responses appear to be followed by large changes in the environment in directions desired by the parasuicide (Rubenstein et al., 1958) suggests that enactment of parasuicide as well as observation of it may be effective in producing expectations for positive change as a result of parasuicide. Other researchers have discovered that parasuicide not followed by therapy or other psychological interventions, especially when the person has not refused treatment, predicts another parasuicide (Bagley & Greer, 1971), more lethal second parasuicides for persons not in therapy prior to the initial act (Worden & Sterling-Smith, 1973), and eventual suicide (Motto, 1965). These findings, together with the association of hopelessness with suicide, suggest that when all other avenues of positive outcomes, including parasuicide, are exhausted, death via suicide may appear to provide the most positive outcome.

Demographic Factors

Sex The overwhelming preponderance of evidence suggests that parasuicide is more often engaged in by women (Bancroft & Marsack, 1977; Bogard, 1970; Greer et al., 1966; Hankoff, 1979; Paerregaard, 1975; Shneidman et al., 1970), whereas suicide is more often completed by men (Barraclough & Pallis, 1975; Farberow, 1974; Kreitman, 1977; Litman, 1974; *Vital Statistics of the United States*, 1973, 1975). Possible exceptions to these differential rates were suggested by Kreitman (1977), who found equal male and female parasuicide rates for older single persons and for persons repeating parasuicides. Linehan (1973) has suggested that the differential suicide and parasuicide rates by sex may be, at least partially, functions of differential sex-role expectations for males and females. The theory is based on the premise that, all other things being equal, a person will try parasuicide as a problem solution before trying suicide. Thus, if, for one reason or another, parasuicide is socially sanctioned or antithetical to sex-role expectations, a person entering a suicidal crisis will be more likely to skip the parasuicide phase and either commit suicide or leave the suicidal field altogether, turning to other nonsuicidal options. A variety of data sources lend tentative support to this contention. Among young men who call suicide crisis centers, rigid adherence to a male sex role predicts suicide; similarly, among young women, professional status, suggesting movement toward the male sex role, also predicts suicide (Lettieri, 1974b; Litman, 1974). Suicide has been evaluated as being more masculine than parasuicide by adult men and women (Linehan, 1973). Finally, the fact that women outnumber men in total suicidal behavior, whereas men more often than women use alcohol excessively and engage in criminal behavior (Mensh, 1965, Millon, 1969), suggests that men indeed may be leaving the suicidal field more often than women. It should be noted that the common idea that men are more likely to succeed at suicide because they choose more lethal methods does not explain the differential rates; even when the method is the same, men commit suicide more than women (Lester, 1969).

Age With few exceptions, parasuicide rates have been found to decrease with age (Bogard, 1970; Kreitman, 1977; Shneidman et al., 1970); 75% to 78% of instances are estimated to involve persons between ages 18 and 45 years (Greer & Lee, 1967); Paerregaard, 1975; Tuckman & Youngman, 1968b). Suicide rates, on the other hand, increase with age for men and increase to middle age or the early sixties for women (Barraclough et al., 1974; Bogard, 1970; Farberow, 1974; Kreitman, 1977; *Vital Statistics of the United States*, 1973, 1975). The major exception is for nonwhite populations (at least in the United States): Suicide rates for blacks decrease with age, with a peak age between 20 and 34 years (Davis, 1979; Farberow, 1974). As with parasuicide, suicide rates among adolescents are increasing rapidly (Davis, 1979). As noted by Charatan (1979), psychological, physiological, social, ethical, cultural, economic, and situational factors all can play roles in suicide among the elderly. An accumulation of losses over time and the threat of future losses, together with reduced resources, both environmental and behavioral, for coping with stress and reducing pain, are likely mediating factors. The high parasuicide rate among the young may be a function of a tendency to parasuicide before committing suicide; young people may be more likely to believe that they can produce some changes in their adverse environments. Finally, the association between hostility and antisocial behaviors and parasuicide, to be discussed later, suggests that parasuicide among the young may be simply another instance of the greater overall hostility and sociopathic behaviors among younger persons as compared with older persons (Millon, 1969; Weissman, 1974).

Race Studies of parasuicides admitted to hospital emergency rooms have suggested that nonwhites (especially women) are overrepresented in the parasuicide population relative to their presence in the general population (Parkin, 1974; Pederson et al., 1973; Piler, 1938; Tuckman & Youngman, 1968b). Other studies have found the rates to be similar to the proportions of nonwhites living in the neighborhoods around the emergency rooms (Bogard, 1970; Hankoff, 1979; Steele, 1977). Still others have suggested that overrepresentation of nonwhites may be due to a greater tendency for nonwhite parasuicides to be treated in hospital emergency rooms. In contrast, whites (in the United States) tend to be overrepresented in the suicide population (Davis, 1979; Farberow, 1974; *Vital Statistics of the United States*, 1973, 1975). The exception here is the younger (age 25-29 years) male population, where black suicide rates are higher than those for whites (Davis, 1979; Lettieri, 1974b).

The mechanisms by which race affects parasuicide and suicide rates are not immediately obvious. However, it seems clear that the important question here is not why whites commit suicide at higher rates than blacks but rather why blacks commit suicide less. For example, the higher suicide rates for minority persons mentioned earlier suggest that United States black suicide rates should be high. It seems possible that to answer this question we will need to study more closely the characteristics of persons who cope with and survive adverse environmental conditions. The roles of future expectations, beliefs about life's meaning, and group solidarity and support found to be important in survival of persons in concentration camps (Despres, 1976; Frankl, 1959) are likely important here.

Behavioral Factors

Cognitive System The cognitive characteristics of suicidal persons can be considered from either of two perspectives: (1) the person's cognitive style; (2) the person's cognitive content. Cognitive style refers to a person's manner of processing, organizing, and using information. Stylistic characteristics commonly linked to suicidal behavior include rigidity versus flexibility, impulsiveness versus reflectiveness, and field independence versus dependence. Several studies have found that parasuicides appear to be more rigid in their thinking (Levenson, 1972; Neuringer, 1964b; Patsiokas et al., 1979; Vinoda, 1966), less capable of abstract problem solving (Levenson & Neuringer, 1971), frequently impulsive (Farberow et al., 1970; Fox & Weissman, 1975; Kessel & McCulloch, 1966), and possibly more field-dependent (Levenson, 1972) than psychiatric control populations. However, the data on the latter two characteristics are contradictory (Patsiokas et al., 1979).

Each of these studies involved patients hospitalized after parasuicide acts, and the time lapses between the acts and the testing are not clear. Thus, it is possible that the stylistic responses noted were specific to high-stress states, a not unlikely occurrence for parasuicides. Cognitive rigidity, impulsiveness, field dependence, and overall poor problem-solving capabilities may be functionally related to parasuicide by limiting the range of problem solutions open to these people. When faced with seemingly catastrophic life problems and environmental stresses, those who eventually become parasuicides may be unable to generate alternative solutions to effect outcomes preferable to suicidal outcomes. A rigid style also suggests that in the face of changing environmental contingencies these people will be unable to change their expectancies and thus may experience even more negative changes than would be the case if they could monitor contingencies more effectively and change overt behavior accordingly.

Levenson and Neuringer (1971) stated that "problem solving incapacity is of lethal consequence" (p. 435). However, whether or not the findings on the cognitive styles of parasuicides are applicable to a suicide population is yet to be determined. Levenson and Neuringer, using intelligence test protocols cited by Patsiokas and associates (1979), found male suicide committers more field-dependent than nonsuicidal controls. The belief that committers are more rigid is, to some extent, probably a function of a belief that there is always a better solution than suicide and that if suicidal persons were just more flexible they not only would have figured this out but also would have chosen it, a conclusion based on both a value judgment and circular reasoning.

Models of suicidal behavior positing an important role for cognitive content as a precursor have focused on hopelessness, outcome expectancies of suicidal behavior, locus of control, and self-concept. One of the most influential theorists has been Beck (1963; Bedrosian & Beck, 1979; Beck et al., 1974), who suggested that the effect of depression on suicide is mediated by the hopelessness concomitant with the depression. Research by Farberow and MacKinnon (1974), Farberow and McEvoy (1966) and Barraclough and associates (1974) has suggested that hopelessness is frequent among people who commit suicide. However, the data of Barraclough and associates suggest that this may be true only in certain diagnostic categories. Studies have been published demonstrating (1) that the correlation between hopelessness and suicidal intent (measured by analyzing the parasuicide act and/or interviewing the patient) is higher than that between depression and suicidal intent and (2) that the latter correlation is reduced when the effect of hopelessness is partialed out (Beck, Kovacs, & Weissman, 1975; Kovacs et al., 1975a; Minkoff et al., 1973; Wetzel, 1976). As might be expected, inspection of these results, as well as data presented by Porkorny and associates (1975), suggests that this relationship is far stronger when current intent (as opposed to intent measured retrospectively at the time of parasuicide) is related to current hopelessness. Although this research was done on parasuicides, the suicidal intent measures employed have been shown to be positively related to suicide as compared with parasuicide (Beck, Morris, & Beck, 1974), and thus the result can tentatively be generalized to the suicide population. In fact, it should be noted that this research does not make a case for a relationship between hopelessness and parasuicide.

The relationship of hopelessness to parasuicide is not clear. The suicidal intent measure positively related to hopelessness is negatively related to parasuicide as compared with suicide (Beck, Morris, & Beck, 1974). Weissman and associates (1973) found controls to be equal to parasuicides in terms of hopelessness, whereas other investigators found parasuicides to be more hopeless (Paykel & Dienelt, 1971; Wetzel, 1976). It could be that the construct of hopelessness is ambiguous. Whereas the belief that there are not solutions to a person's problems, except for dying, would be taken as an indicator of hopelessness, a person's belief that life might be improved (but, only if the person resorts to parasuicide) might be taken as an indication of hope. Thus, although both groups might be expecting negative future events unless they engage in the respective acts, suicides would be viewed as hopeless and parasuicides would be viewed as hopeful. Thus, hopelessness as a construct is probably too global for differentiating the two groups. However, it is probable that future expectations of some type are functionally related to parasuicidal activity. Findings regarding rigidity suggest that parasuicides may not expect positive outcomes except by parasuicide, if only because they cannot think of alternatives. Wenz (1977) found that parasuicides rated themselves as more powerless than control subjects, although the groups failed to differ on externality generally. It should be noted that although one's cognitive style may make it less likely that one will recognize realistic positive outcome expectancies, the environmental data reviewed previously suggest that the negative expectancies may be influenced by an actual deficit of positive possibilities.

That the cognitive content for suicidal persons includes negative self-concepts, and feelings of being "one down" has been an axiomatic assumption of suicidologists (Neuringer, 1974b). Data with respect to parasuicide suggest that this assumption is well founded. In one of the few true predictive studies using psychological variables, Kaplan and Pokorny (1976) showed that among high-school students who said they had not had past suicidal thoughts and had not previously committed parasuicidal acts, those who scored high on a measure of self-derogation had higher incidences of suicidal thoughts and parasuicidal acts than did those who scored low when compared at a 1-year follow-up. Additionally, those students admitting to past suicidal thoughts and/or parasuicidal acts scored higher on self-derogation than did students with no previous history. Neuringer (1974b) found that parasuicides not only rated themselves lower on evaluative and potency scales than psychosomatic and general population controls but also had a greater tendency to rate themselves as being worse than other people. Negative self-concepts may function in a generalized way much as does low self-efficacy in any specific area (Bandura, 1977). Thus a person with a negative self-concept may feel unable to carry out behaviors that are more adaptive and more "capable" than parasuicide and that might be necessary to produce positive changes either within the person or in the situation. The resulting inaction may contribute to an absence of positive changes, setting up still other conditions conducive to parasuicide. The relationship between self-concepts and suicide is unclear.

The increasing rates of suicide with increasing age and the accompanying uncontrollable life stresses, as well as the association between suicide and loss, suggest that the functional relationship between hopelessness and suicidal behavior discussed earlier may be less often mediated by low self-concepts for suicidal persons than for parasuicidal persons.

In summary, parasuicidal persons appear to be rigid and possibly field-dependent and impulsive in their cognitive styles. They are likely poor problem solvers, a characteristic that may be functionally related to parasuicidal behavior as a method of coping with problems in living. Although suicidologists have presumed that these same characteristics apply to persons who commit suicide, the data simply do not exist to verify such an assumption. The notion that the act of suicide itself proves that these persons have poor problem-solving skills involves both circular reasoning and a value judgment. With respect to cognitive content, both parasuicides and suicides are likely to report hopelessness, although the construct itself is perhaps too global to be meaningful. Negative self-concepts are characteristic of persons who commit parasuicidal acts. However, data on self-concepts and suicide do not exist.

Physiological/Affective System   "In general, it is probably accurate to say that suicide always involves an individual's tortured and tunneled logic in a state of inner-felt, intolerable emotion" (Shneidman, 1979, p. 144). This statement points out the important role of the physiological/affective system in suicidal behavior. Empirical studies on the affective characteristics of suicidal persons have focused, for the most part, on interpersonal emotional responses, including hostility, friendliness and comfort with people, and feelings of depression, apathy, and dysphoria. Other studies have examined the roles of physical illness and somatic complaints in suicidal behavior.

With very few exceptions, these studies indicate that, at least after the fact, parasuicides appear to be more angry, hostile, and irritable, in general, and more dissatisfied with treatment than nonsuicidal psychiatric patients and general population control groups (Crook et al., 1975; Lester, 1968; Nelson et al., 1977; Richman & Charles, 1976; Vinoda, 1966). These findings hold up when one compares parasuicidal depressives with nonparasuicidal depressives when the variables of sex and age are controlled (Weissman et al., 1973). Some support for the view that the hostility is not a function of the parasuicidal behavior itself or of the subsequent survival of an attempt at suicide is suggested by data collected by Paykel and Dienelt (1971). During a 10-month follow-up of depressed inpatients, they found that prior psychiatrists' ratings, self-ratings, and mood ratings of high hostility levels were more characteristic of those who subsequently became parasuicidal than of those who did not. In contrast, persons who later commit suicide often are characterized as less angry (Dean et al., 1967; Litman, 1974) and more often apathetic and/or indifferent to treatment (Dean et al., 1967; Farberow & MacKinnon, 1974; Farberow & McEvoy, 1966; Farberow et al., 1970; Virkkunen, 1976).

Although the notion that parasuicide is motivated by a wish for revenge certainly fits the data, it is equally possible that angry people might resort to parasuicide because they can think of nothing better to do to lessen or escape from frustrating circumstances. Two studies (Colson, 1973; Henderson et al., 1977) employing cluster analysis on reported parasuicidal motives found a cluster characterized by low desire for revenge and low desire to hurt (not extrapunitive, not operant) as well as a cluster in which persons desired to get their own way and to get even (were operant and extrapunitive). Kovacs and associates (1975b) interviewed parasuicides and reported that 56% were motivated by a desire to give up and escape from life, 13% were gambling with death in order to effect environmental changes, and the remaining 31% had a combination of motives. It is interesting that a third cluster reported by Henderson and associates was characterized by both extrapunitive and nonoperant motives (i.e., a combination of the motives of the first two clusters).

The possibility that parasuicides experience an interpersonal approach-avoidance conflict is suggested by findings that they report wanting affiliation and affection from others more than do psychiatric control groups and general population controls (Cantor, 1976; Nelson et al., 1977). However, they also reported feeling more uncomfortable when approaching people (Cantor, 1976), they rated themselves as less friendly, in general, than nonparasuicides (Kreitman, 1977; Paykel & Dienelt, 1971), and they tended to resent those people to whom they reported they could turn for help in difficult situations (Lester, 1969). Farberow and associates described a dependent-dissatisfied pattern of behavior characteristic of one type of suicidal group (Farberow et al., 1961, 1970), suggesting that an approach-avoidance conflict might also be relevant for suicide.

As noted previously, a large percentage of suicidal patients are diagnosed, either prior to the act or retrospectively, as being depressed. The same is true for parasuicides; Weissman (1974) reviewed diagnostic studies of parasuicides from 1960 to 1971 and suggested that a diagnosis of depression accounts for 35% to 79% of all cases. It is not clear which behavioral patterns associated with the diagnosis are characteristic of suicide and parasuicide, nor is it clear whether or not the two suicidal classes differ. Litman (1974), for example, found that somatic depression and absence of affective depression predicted suicide among callers to a suicide crisis center. Several investigators have found insomnia to be associated with suicide (Bagley et al., 1976; Barraclough et al., 1974;

Farberow et al., 1970). Kreitman (1977) found that the diagnosis of depression among parasuicides predicts subsequent suicide; Pokorny (1966) suggested that less severe depression may be related to later suicide. Both Bagley and Greer (1971) and Kreitman (1977) found depression to be unrelated to repeated parasuicidal behavior. Worden and Sterling-Smith (1973) found depression to be more characteristic of nonrepeaters than of repeaters. A number of studies have found poor physical health to be associated with suicide. Investigators have reported that 25% to 70% of persons who commit suicide were in poor health immediately prior to the act (Andress & Corey, 1977; Bagley et al., 1976; Dorpat & Ripley, 1960). A group of persons characterized as focusing on their medical problems has been found in most attempts to develop a typology of suicide (e.g., Bagley et al., 1976; Farberow & McEvoy, 1966). As would be expected, the role of poor health as a precipitant of suicide increases with age (Dorpat & Ripley, 1960). The association between poor health and parasuicide is less marked, and control groups have been lacking in the relevant studies.

The emotional pictures that emerge appear to be different for the suicide and parasuicide. Although both may be depressed and interpersonally ambivalent, the parasuicide often is angry and hostile, whereas the suicide is more likely apathetic and indifferent. It may well be that the developmental stages suggested by Kubler-Ross (1969) as characteristic of the process of dying are also applicable to the process of suicide. The stages of denial, bargaining, anger, depression and acceptance that are important in dying seem somewhat similar to the patterns of demandingness, hostility, and depression that are characteristic of parasuicides, as well as the subsequent lessening of depression, indifference to treatment, and acceptance of suicide as a viable option that are characteristic of those who do commit suicide. Suicide appears to be clearly associated with other somatic problems, and both types of suicidal persons experience marked environmental stress and emotional pain.

It is also possible that the ability to tolerate pain (i.e., to accommodate to it) may be lower for suicidal persons than for other groups. Studies of parasuicides (Cantor, 1976) and of suicides (Farberow et al., 1970) have found that both groups may have a low tolerance for frustration. A more reactive physiological response system and/or inadequate coping skills for pain may be important here. In addition, a low pain tolerance combined with a tendency to react impulsively suggests that the suicidal person may be less capable of producing the sustained effort often needed to remedy adverse and frustrating environmental conditions.

Overt Motor System The overt behavioral characteristics of suicidal persons can be discussed in terms of two broad categories: interpersonal patterns and life styles. Both suicides and parasuicides exhibit low degrees of interpersonal interaction and social involvement (Breed, 1966; Crook et al., 1975; Farberow & MacKinnon, 1974; Farberow & McEvoy, 1966; Farberow et al., 1970; Nelson et al., 1977). Observations and self-reports of interpersonal patterns have suggested that both groups may be lacking important social skills. Neither group seems likely to ask for help, support, or attention (Cantor, 1976; Virkkunen, 1976) when in stressful situations; parasuicides may tend to believe that there is no one they can ask (Lester, 1969). Studies have consistently found that parasuicidal persons are rated by others as demanding, that their interpersonal relationships are most frequently characterized by friction and conflict, and that the parasuicide act itself often follows acute conflict, arguments, and relationship disruptions (Birtchnell & Alarcon, 1971; Greer et al., 1966; Pakyel et al., 1975; Weissman et al., 1973). Violence in key relationships and a diagnosis of sociopathy or antisocial personality are associated with multiple parasuicidal acts (Buglass & McCulloch, 1970; Kessel & McCulloch, 1966; Kreitman, 1977). In contrast to parasuicides, suicidal persons may be lower in hostile interpersonal behavior and possibly more passive and dependent in their actions than nonsuicidal psychiatric patients (Dean et al., 1967; Farberow et al., 1970; Kiev, 1974). However, the data are unclear here, because Farberow and associates (1970) found suicidal persons to be more demanding than nonsuicidal persons.

In summary, suicidal persons appear to interact with people less than nonsuicidals; they may be less successful at maintaining interpersonal relationships, and they are likely to be deficient in assertion capabilities, at least in difficult situations. Additionally, the interpersonal relationships of parasuicides appear to be characterized by marked conflict and antisocial patterns. The possible functional relationships of these interpersonal behaviors to suicidal behavior are obvious. The absence of mutually satisfying relationships may constitute (1) a source of emotional pain, (2) a state of affairs conducive to decreasing one's faith in the capacities of others to alleviate one's distress, and (3) a factor making it less likely that the social support needed by the suicidal person will be forthcoming. Without assertion skills, these people may be unable to raise an effective cry for help. The interpersonal friction experienced and generated by parasuicidal persons only further exacerbates an already untenable situation.

In addition to the problems posed by the ineffective interpersonal behavior of suicidal persons, the overwhelming preponderance of data suggests that across a broad array of situations, parasuicides and suicides engage in maladaptive life-styles. As noted previously, 20% to 65% of suicides and parasuicides have previously engaged in parasuicidal behavior. Both types of behavior are associated with high rates of alcoholism and drug addiction (Frankel et al., 1976; Kreitman, 1977;

Miles, 1977). Criminal behavior has been associated with multiple parasuicidal acts (Kreitman, 1977), suicide among young men (Lettieri, 1974b), and parasuicide followed by suicide (Ettlinger, 1964; Paerregaard, 1975). Finally, as mentioned earlier, unemployment and job loss are characteristics of suicidal persons. With so few effective coping styles, it is no wonder that such persons ultimately turn to suicidal behavior. These stylistic qualities make it unlikely that existing problems will be solved, and they also enhance the probability of further crisis.

System Relationships As has perhaps been clear throughout this summary of characteristics of suicidal environments and persons, parasuicide and suicide are products of dynamic interactions within the person, within the environment, and between the person and the environmental circumstances. Certainly, not all of the characteristics outlined here are necessary to a suicidal outcome; however, they do appear to constitute sufficient conditions for such activity. For a given individual, whether suicide or parasuicide occurs may depend on a unique confluence of events across each of the subsystems of environment and personal behavior. Changes in any one subsystem may be sufficient to upset the balance across the total system and prevent, at least momentarily, suicidal behavior. However, more permanent changes toward a nonsuicidal balance may require simultaneous interventions across a combination of subsystems. A simplified version of the theory outlined here is presented schematically in Figure 9.1.

Both the environment and the person's own behaviors are presented as subsystems in Figure 9.1. Demographic factors (with the possible exception of sex) are invariant and thus do not constitute a separate subsystem; however, they do influence environmental and behavioral functioning. For example, age, or the passage of time, is related to the probability of negative life changes (e.g., losses); sex is directly related to one's physiological responses; race may be functionally related to one's social support network. Within the environmental subsystem, it is usually that various events are linked together such that changes in one aspect of the environment will influence other aspects. For example, hospitalization as a consequence of parasuicide might lead to the loss of one's job (a negative life event), which might then decrease one's social support system by eliminating a work involvement after discharge. Having a spouse or parent commit suicide is usually both a negative life change and a loss of social support.

Similarly, within the behavioral subsystem, a person's own responses can serve as stimuli for further responding (Staats, 1975). The fundamental difference between the model of suicidal behavior presented here and other models or theories is that this social-behavioral model does not, in the abstract, posit that one behavioral system (e.g., the

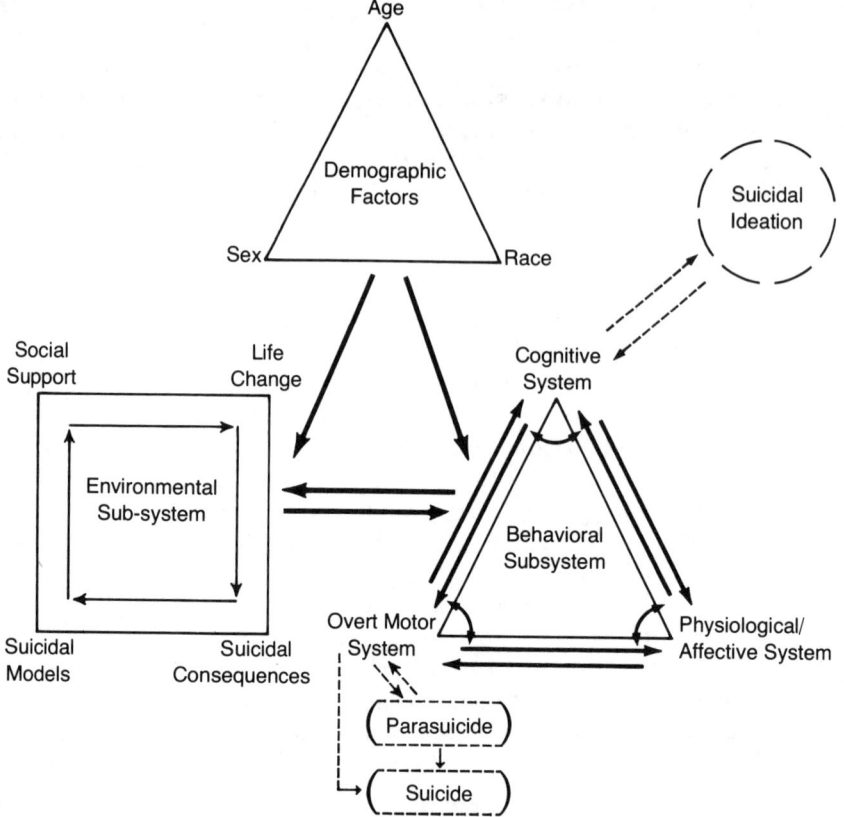

Figure 9.1 Social-behavioral model of suicidal behavior.

cognitive) is universally more important or more central than any other system. Instead, the perspective of the person as an integrated system presented here would suggest that an emphasis on one behavioral content area as causative in suicidal behavior represents an artificial break in the interactive relationship among behavioral responses. This same emphasis on within-person dynamics also distinguishes this social behavioral approach from a radical behavioral theory of suicide. However, the bidirectional arrows between the environmental and behavioral subsystems in Figure 9.1 indicate the theoretical importance of situational events in explaining suicidal behavior, both directly and indirectly. Overall, the level and content for each behavioral, demographic, and environmental variable, as well as the strength of any one variable or combination of variables as determinants of suicidal behavior, are factors that must be assessed in each individual case.

Assessment of Suicidal Patients

The assessment task in treating a suicidal patient is threefold: (1) The current risk and long-term risk for suicide and parasuicide must be estimated; (2) a social-behavioral analysis of the suicidal responses must be carried out; (3) a social-behavioral analysis of the problem or problems that precipitate suicidal behavior must be carried out. Knowledge of long-term suicide/parasuicide risks is useful for determining treatment priorities and for alerting the therapist to a need for specific suicide-prevention procedures. Estimation of short-term risk is important for day-to-day decisions and sometimes hour-to-hour decisions on how to handle crisis situations when they arise. Social-behavioral analyses of suicidal responses and precipitating problems are essential for treatment planning and assessment of the progress and effectiveness of therapy.

Risk Assessment for Suicide and Parasuicide

Assignment to Risk Populations The ideal would be to describe a method of assessment such that the likelihood of future parasuicide and/or suicide for a given patient could be predicted with some precision. However, ethical problems in determining if one's predictions are accurate, together with more general problems related to predicting infrequent events, make this task all but impossible (Beck, Resnik, & Lettieri, 1974; Lester, 1970; Neuringer, 1974a). The best that can be done is to describe the characteristics of populations in which rates of suicidal behavior are higher than in the population as a whole. Such a description can then be used to determine whether or not a given patient is part of a population at risk for eventual parasuicide or suicide.

Those factors associated with populations at risk for suicide, parasuicide, and either type of behavior following an initial parasuicide were discussed in the previous section. A summary of characteristics identifying suicidal populations is presented in Table 9.1. It is not at all clear how many, or what combination, of these characteristics a patient must have in order to be at high risk. Suicide prediction scales already developed suggest that the more suicidogenic or parasuicidogenic characteristics a person has, the more likely it is that suicidal behavior will occur (Farberow & MacKinnon, 1974; Lettieri, 1974a, 1974b). For example, Tuckman and Youngman (1963b) estimated suicide rates (per 100,000) following parasuicide as 3,751 for persons over 45 years, 3,708 for males, and 2,181 for whites. However, for white older males, the rate was 6,827 (as compared with a rate of 1,951 for previous parasuicides in general). Murphy (1974), on the other hand, has made a convincing argument for restricting the use of the high-risk designation

TABLE 9.1 Characteristics of Populations at Increased Risk for Suicidal Behavior

	Parasuicide	Suicide	Parasuicide following Parasuicide	Suicide following Parasuicide
I. Environmental characteristics				
A. Life changes	Losses	Losses	—	—
	Major upsetting events	—[a]	—	—
	Uncontrolled events	—	—	—
B. Social support				
1. Work	Absent	Absent (young women: professional setting)	Absent	Absent
2. Marital rates	Unmarried > married	Unmarried > married	Results mixed	Divorced/separated/widowed
3. Marital frequency	Married > unmarried	Married > unmarried	—	—
4. Family	Hostile	Less available	Less available	Less available
5. Ecology	—	Minority status	—	—
C. Models	Socially linked to other parasuicides	Family suicide rate higher		
D. Consequences	Desired changes	Death; survivor trauma	No treatment (for those not AMA) after index parasuicide	No follow-up by mental health community after index parasuicide
II. Demographic characteristics				
A. Sex	Female > male	Male > female	Female = male	Male > female
B. Age	Decreases with age	Increases with age (blacks: decreases with age)	Decreases with age	Increases with age

	Nonwhite over-represented	White > nonwhite (young males: blacks > white)	White = nonwhite	White > nonwhite
C. Race				
III. Behavioral characteristics				
A. Cognitive				
1. Style	Rigid	—	—	—
	Possibly impulsive	—	—	—
	Possibly field-dependent	—	—	—
	Poor problem solvers	—	—	—
2. Content	Possibly hopeless	hopeless	—	—
	Powerless	—	—	—
	Congruent—external attributions	—	—	—
	Negative self-concept	—	—	—
B. Physiological/ affective				
1. Affective	Angry, hostile	Apathetic	—	—
	Depressed	Depressed	Results on depression mixed	Results on depression mixed
	Dissatisfied with treatment	Indifferent to treatment	—	—
	High preference for affiliation and affection	Possibly dependent dissatisfied	—	—
	Uncomfortable with people			
2. Somatic	Possibly poor health	Poor health (increases with age)	—	Poor health
	—	Insomnia	—	—
	Low frustration tolerance	Low pain tolerance	—	—

TABLE 9.1 Characteristics of Populations at Increased Risk for Suicidal Behavior

	Parasuicide	Suicide	Parasuicide following Parasuicide	Suicide following Parasuicide
C. Overt motor				
1. Interpersonal	Low social involvement	Low social involvement	Low social involvement	Low social involvement
	Less likely to ask for help	Less likely to ask for support or attention	—	—
	High friction and conflict	Data mixed on friction and conflict	Violence; sociopathy	High friction and conflict
2. Styles	20%–55% previous parasuicide	20%–65% previous parasuicide	Multiple parasuicides	Multiple parasuicides
	Alcohol and drug abuse	Alcohol and drug abuse	Alcohol and drug abuse	Alcohol and drug abuse
	—	Criminal behavior (young men)	Criminal behavior	—
	Unemployed	Unemployed/retired	Unemployed	Unemployed/retired

[a] A dash indicates that there is no research relevant to that topic or that the research that does exist is too ambiguous to be useful.

to only those persons having all or most of the "suicide" characteristics. Using the Tuckman and Youngman (1968a) demographic correlates of high suicide risk, he identified a high-risk group of 5 million persons from the general population. However, as Murphy then noted, if all persons possessing those exact characteristics were prevented from committing suicide, only 21 (16%) of a sample of 134 consecutive suicides in one of his studies would have been prevented. Thus it must be stressed that persons who lack one or even many of the characteristics associated with suicide or parasuicide are not thereby immune to suicidal risk. If Table 9.1 is used for making treatment decisions, this should be done with some caution.

Table 9.1 is set up to discriminate, when possible, a parasuicidal population from a suicidal population. The chance of accidental death from a parasuicide attempt is such that it would be unwise to discount a person's suicide risk simply because that person falls in the parasuicidal population instead of the suicidal population. Additionally, the overlap between the two populations makes it improbable that one can distinguish, at least at the contiguous ends of the curves, between parasuicidal and suicidal populations. Finally, the increased suicide risk among former parasuicides suggests that identification as being at high risk for parasuicide, in itself, places one at high risk for suicide. Thus, although discrimination between the two suicidal groups may have important implications for treatment planning, one must be wary of attaching too much importance to any one factor or group of factors as critical in making such a distinction.

Attempts have been made to discriminate groups at minimal suicide risk from groups at low risk and to discriminate both from groups at moderate risk through high risk (e.g., Litman, 1974). However, the data across studies are not yet consistent enough (nor have adequate statistical models been applied) to allow useful precision in most clinical settings. Instead, data derived from using Table 9.1 should be used to cue continuous intensive clinical assessment of the likelihood of suicidal behavior with a particular patient. Most of the information called for will be obtained in routine assessment procedures. Unfortunately, the one area of information often not explored routinely in behavioral assessments is that of suicidal behavior in the patient's past and current life. The important roles of past parasuicide attempts, current suicidal ideation, and suicidal models among the patient's significant others suggest that such information is imperative for responsible assessment in the clinical setting. Previous parasuicide, for example, is the single best predictor of future suicide and parsuicide. Findings that nondepressed persons do commit suicide and parasuicide suggest that a policy of assessing suicidal risk only among depressives is clinically untenable.

Examination of the factors related to suicidal risk suggests that persons may move in and out of the risk populations depending on environmental and behavioral variations. Thus one's risk population status is not static. In clinical settings, therefore, Table 9.1 might be most useful as a sort of mental outline for tracking variations in risk. As will be noted later, one strategy in therapy with patients at high risk for suicide/parasuicide is to intervene in ways designed to move them into a lower-risk population.

Assessment of Current Risk   Ignorance of a patient's current intentions to engage in suicidal behavior forecloses the possibility of active intervention aimed specifically at reducing the threat of suicidal behavior. Assignment to a high-risk population, although useful, is not particularly helpful when trying to predict whether a patient is going to commit parasuicide or suicide in the near future (e.g., the next several hours, days, or weeks). Numerous important treatment decisions (e.g., whether or not to hospitalize, to actively "rescue," to see the patient more frequently, to limit the amount of time spent on the telephone call, to focus treatment time on the suicidal behaviors or on other conditions that may prove functionally related) are intimately tied to the clinician's assessment of the possibility that suicidal behavior is imminent. To a certain extent, as will be discussed extensively later, therapy with an acutely suicidal patient is much like walking a tightrope: One must constantly balance the need for an active, caring response, which can be essential in keeping the patient alive, with the equally important need to refrain from reinforcing suicidal responses and thus perhaps increasing the possibility that the patient will engage in parasuicide or suicide at a later time. How to weight the balance at any specific time is dependent on the current risk, given either course of action. Although frequently it is easier simply to assume high and imminent suicide danger, no matter what the actual level of risk, such a decision presupposes that active suicide-prevention techniques (e.g., hospitalization, calling significant others, intense expression of concern), when unnecessary, are benign in their effects, a premise that is, at best, doubtful with suicidal patients.

Once a patient fits the criteria for high risk described earlier, assessment of factors related to current circumstances, suicidal intent, and suicide-related response patterns must be carried out to judge the likelihood of suicidal behavior in the immediate or near future. Active reassessment of such risk is called for under a number of circumstances. The most obvious is that in which a patient communicates an intent to commit suicide. Such a communication may occur in a crisis situation, in which case the clinician is faced with determining the immediate risk, possibly at an inconvenient time and over the telephone. In other instances the intent to commit suicide may be communicated during a scheduled treatment session, with the threatened suicidal behavior to take place either very soon (e.g., that night) or only if some future event occurs, such as an anticipated rejection or failure of the therapy.

It must be stated at the outset that the data required for accurate prediction of imminent risk of suicidal behavior do not exist. There have been no studies of persons who have been in a crisis state or who otherwise have been believed to be at high and imminent risk who have then committed suicide or parasuicide and have been compared with a similar group who have not engaged in either suicidal act. Naturally, such research would involve significant ethical problems. If one believes that certain factors make suicidal behavior imminent, then active intervention usually is mandated. The predicted suicide or parasuicide is thereby artificially, so to speak, constrained by the investigator. Thus, although cases that failed to come to the attention of intervention agents and cases in which intervention did not succeed may give some idea of the rate of false negatives for various predictors, success in the prevention of suicidal behavior makes it impossible to gain an accurate estimate of the rate of false positives for those same predictors.

Items that may be useful for assessing current risk for suicide and parasuicide are listed in Table 9.2 under one of three categories: (1) direct indices of imminent risk for suicide or parasuicide; (2) indirect indices of imminent risk for suicide or parasuicide; (3) circumstantial factors related to suicidal behavior in the next several hours or days. An item is included here if it discriminates persons who commit suicide or parasuicide from those who do not, if it discriminates persons who commit suicide from those who commit parasuicide, or if it seems to occur in conjunction with suicidal behavior in a high percentage of cases. The items are not ordered according to any hierarchical design, although, logically, certain indices will occur before others. For example, suicidal ideation generally precedes suicide threats. The presence of any of the factors listed should lead directly to an exploration for other indices. Because this type of information is most frequently needed when a patient is in a state of crisis, the clinician may have to use an array of interpersonal skills to induce the patient to divulge the necessary information. Unless the patient is new to therapy, most of the background information needed to put the current information in perspective should be available. For example, a crisis situation is not the time for the therapist to be asking for the first time about the details of any previous suicidal behavior.

Direct indices of imminent suicide and/or parasuicide include suicide threats, suicide planning and/or preparation, suicidal ideation, and recent parasuicide. Contrary to popular myth, persons who commit suicide and parasuicide frequently communicate their intent ahead of time; 50% to 80% threaten suicide or talk about death beforehand (Bagley et al., 1976; Dorpat & Boswell, 1963; Kreitman, 1977. The

Table 9.2 Factors Associated with Imminent Risk for Suicide or Parasuicide

I. Direct indices of imminent risk for suicide or parasuicide
  1. Suicide threats
  2. Suicide planning and/or preparation
  3. Parasuicide in the last year
  4. Suicidal ideation
II. Indirect indices of imminent risk for suicide or parasuicide
  5. Patient falls in suicide or parasuicide risk population
  6. Recent disruption or loss of interpersonal relationship; negative environmental changes in past month
  7. Indifference to or dissatisfaction with therapy; elopements and early pass returns by hospitalized patients
  8. Current hopelessness or anger or both
  9. Recent medical care
  10. Indirect references to own death; arrangements for death
III. Circumstances associated with suicide and/or parasuicide in the next several hours/days
  11. Alcohol consumption
  12. Suicide note written or in progress
  13. Methods available or easily obtained
  14. Isolation
  15. Precautions against discovery or intervention; deception or concealment about timing, place, etc.

suicide rate for suicide threateners is 40 times that for a comparable nonsuicidal population (Pokorny, 1966). The rate at which these people called suicide crisis centers during the previous year is 1400 per 100,000 per year, a rate 100 times that for the general population (Litman, 1974). Of course, it should be noted here that parasuicides rarely signal their intention to commit parasuicidal acts; instead, they generally communicate an intent to commit suicide. Although, after the fact, parasuicides may report intending to bring about outcomes other than death (i.e., suicide was not actually intended), it is unlikely that before the fact these persons clearly discriminated the difference between suicide and parasuicide. Even if such a discrimination is made, the future parasuicide probably will not reveal this true intent; the effect simply is not the same as the effect produced by a threat to commit suicide.

Once a patient threatens suicide, an immediate concern should be what, if any, planning and/or preparations the patient has made. Questions about planning are contained in both the Suicide Intent Scale (SIS) and the Scale for Suicide Ideation developed by Beck and associates (Beck, Schuyler, & Herman, 1979; Beck, Kovacs, & Weissman,

1979). Some construct validity has been demonstrated for both instruments (Beck, Morris, & Beck, 1974; Beck, Schuyler, & Herman, 1979; Minkoff et al., 1973), and the SIS is capable of discriminating, at least retrospectively, between a suicidal group and a parasuicidal group (Beck & Lester, 1976). Dorpat and Ripley (1960) suggested that 50% to 80% of suicides are planned ahead of time.

The suicide risk among those who previously have committed parasuicide has been estimated at 80 to 200 times that for the general population (Motto, 1965; Tuckman & Youngman, 1963a), and parasuicide is the best predictor of a subsequent parasuicide (Dorpat & Ripley, 1967; Kreitman, 1977). The risk of suicidal behavior of either type is greater during the first year after a parasuicide (Bancroft & Marsack, 1977; Dorpat & Ripley, 1967). The relationship between the circumstances of the initial parasuicide and further suicidal behavior is unclear and likely is complex. A number of researchers have found the lethality, or potential fatality, of the initial parasuicide to be positively related to the occurrence of subsequent suicide (Lettieri, 1974b; Motto, 1965; Schmidt et al., 1954; Worden & Sterling-Smith, 1973); others have found lethality to be nonsignificant in predicting future suicide (Greer & Lee, 1967; Kessel & McCulloch, 1966; Pokorny, 1966). Worden and Sterling-Smith (1973) found low lethality of the initial attempt to be predictive of multiple parasuicidal acts, whereas Kessel and McCulloch (1966) obtained nonsignificant results. Thus, although one is perhaps safe in assuming that a high risk for parasuicide is associated with a higher risk for suicide, it is less clear when a previous low-lethal parasuicide (due to nonlethal methods or a high rescue potential or both) should be considered a warning signal for future suicide rather than another parasuicide. If suicidal behavior is viewed as problem-solving behavior, then it seems logical to predict that a person with a history of using parasuicide successfully is likely to continue to use parasuicide in difficult situations. On the other hand, if, for any reason, parasuicide stops working and if, at the same time, the person does not believe that there are other means of ameliorating the difficult situation, then suicide should be likely. It would appear to be critical that the therapist carefully assess the consequences to the patient of any previous suicidal behavior.

Current suicidal ideation, even in the absence of suicide threats, is also indicative of higher risk for suicidal behavior (Paykel & Dienelt, 1971). Pokorny (1966) estimated that the risk for suicide among ideators is 35 times that for a comparable nonsuicidal population. Often the relevant assessment issue is whether or not one ought to ask the patient about suicidal ideation if the patient has not brought up the topic. Many authors (e.g., Pokorny, 1968) have noted the persistent myth that one can increase the risk of suicide by suggesting the topic for discussion. The assumption is that somehow patients might suicide if only the therapist gives them the idea to do it. Clinical experience suggests that patients who are thinking about suicide usually are relieved if the therapist asks about it. Certainly there are no data to verify that anyone ever died because someone asked about suicidal thoughts. However, it is possible that someone might die if the question is not asked.

Several events might cue the clinician to probe for suicidal ideation. Simple recognition that the patient is part of a high-risk population, no matter the reasons, is cause to ask if suicide is being considered. Specific events frequently found to precede suicide and/or parasuicide should also prompt such questioning. As noted previously, frequently disruptions in interpersonal relationships, as well as other negative environmental events, have occurred in the month preceding suicidal behaviors; dissatisfaction with or indifference to therapy is characteristic of patients who commit suicide and parasuicide; current hopelessness and anger-hostility often accompany suicide and parasuicide, respectively. Farberow suggested that hospitalized patients who later commit suicide are more likely than nonsuicides to have histories of hospital elopements and early returns from passes (Farberow & MacKinnon, 1974; Farberow & McEvoy, 1966). Up to 65% of suicides see physicians in the 3 months prior to death, and as many as 48% see physicians in the week immediately prior to death (Bagley et al., 1976; Barraclough et al., 1974). Seeing a physician, in itself, is perhaps not important in predicting suicide. However, in conjunction with other indicators, it might be a useful clue. Finally, data presented by Dorpat and Ripley (1960) indicate that substantial numbers of suicide committers have communicated their intention beforehand in an indirect way by making references to their own deaths (e.g., "You would be better off without me.").

Circumstances surrounding the actual act of suicide or parasuicide are summarized in Table 9.2. A large proportion of persons who engage in either type of behavior consume alcohol immediately prior to the act (Frankel et al., 1976; Kreitman, 1977). However, the amount of alcohol ingested appears to be unrelated to the potential lethality of the method used (Frankel et al., 1976); thus, explanations for the role of alcohol in suicidal behavior based on its effect on risk taking or inhibition and self-control appear to have little support. Other explanations offered by Frankel and associates include a possible role for alcohol in deteriorating social relationships; it is also possible that alcohol consumption and suicidal behavior have a common cause.

Logically one might assume that the probability of imminent suicidal behavior would be related to the availability of appropriate methods and that an increased risk of suicide, as opposed to parasuicide, would be related to whether or not lethal methods were available. Some tentative support for this notion has been provided by Linden and Hale (1972), who found a positive correlation between rate of suicide and method availability when the latter was operationally defined as the rate of accidental death by a given method. A number of studies have reported that suicide completers use more lethal and less reversible methods than do parasuicides (Dorpat & Boswell, 1963; Freeman et al., 1974). It is beyond the scope of this chapter to review the probable lethality and medical reversibility of the various methods commonly employed in suicidal activities. However, the nonmedical practitioner working with suicidal patients should obtain a summary of such information or, at a minimum, should have a medical consultant. The *Physicians' Desk Reference,* as well as local poison control centers, can be useful for determining the lethality of ingestants; Freeman and associates (1974) have summarized the reversibility for most other common methods of suicide.

Knowledge of several additional factors in the patient's circumstances may be useful in predicting the imminent risk of suicide versus the risk of parasuicide. Written suicide notes are more characteristic of suicides than parasuicides (Shneidman & Farberow, 1961; Yessler et al., 1960). The degree of isolation and the precautions against discovery or intervention are both included in the SIS (Beck, Morris, & Beck, 1974), which has been used to discriminate between the circumstances surrounding parasuicide and those surrounding suicide. Freeman and associates (1974) presented data indicating that suicide, to a greater extent than parasuicide, is likely to take place in isolation. However, they also found that in a sample of 34 suicides, 10 (29%) took place either in the presence of another person or with another person in the immediate vicinity but not visible. The comparable percentage for parasuicide was 65.4%. These data make it clear that the presence of other people does not, in itself, eliminate the risk of suicide.

Social-Behavioral Analyses of Suicidal and Other Problem Behaviors

Patients rarely come to therapy complaining of suicidal behaviors. Instead, the presenting problems of suicidal patients usually are any number of other behavioral patterns or environmental events or combinations thereof. What is generally true is that the problem is sufficiently painful, at least from the patient's point of view, to precipitate suicidal behavior if it is not resolved. The first task of the clinician, therefore, is to conduct a comprehensive social-behavioral analysis of both the presenting problems and the current suicidal behaviors. An assessment outline for use with suicidal patients is shown in Table 9.3. With the exception of those items explicitly dealing with suicidal behaviors and risk, the outline is not specific to suicidal patients. Furthermore, the method for carrying out such analysis in the clinical setting is no different for suicidal patients than for any other patients

Table 9.3 Social-Behavioral Analysis of Suicidal Behavior[a]

A. Suicidal behaviors (ideation, threats, planning/preparation, parasuicide)
  1. Identification and description
  2. Dimensions of suicidal behavior (duration, pervasiveness, frequency, severity)
  3. History of suicidal behavior (patient and family)
  4. Apparent situational determinants (preceding/consequent events)
  5. Apparent behavioral determinants (preceding/consequent patient behaviors)
B. Problems precipitating suicidal behavior; presenting problems
  1. Nature of problems: identification and description
  2. Dimensions of problems, (duration, pervasiveness, frequency, severity)
  3. Historical setting for problems
  4. Current situational determinants (preceding/consequent events)
  5. Current behavioral determinants (preceding/consequent patient behaviors)
C. Patient/environment characteristics relevant to suicide risk
  1. Environmental characteristics that increase the risk of suicide and parasuicide (life events, social support, models, consequences of suicidal and nonsuicidal behaviors)
  2. Patient characteristics that increase the risk of suicide and parasuicide (demographic variables; cognitive, physiological/affective, and overt motor behavioral patterns)
  3. Environmental and patient characteristics that reduce the risk of suicidal behaviors
D. Patient/environment characteristics relevant to treatment
  1. Client assets (physical, aptitudes, abilities, interests, etc.)
  2. Patient deficiencies (physical, aptitude, abilities, interests, etc.)
  3. Environmental assets
  4. Environmental deficiencies
E. Objectives
  1. Targets for modification (list in priority order)
  2. Outcome criteria and how progress will be measured (by target)
F. Interventions
  1. Immediate steps needed to reduce current suicide or parasuicide risk
  2. Intervention strategies (list by target)

[a] Adapted from Pomeranz and Goldfried (1970).

and thus is not discussed in detail here. The reader interested in further discussion of such a format as a guide to behavioral assessment in general is referred to the work of Linehan (1977).

A functional analysis of current suicidal responses per se (ideation, verbalizations, planning, parasuicide) is important insofar as the suicidal behavior interacts with nonsuicidal presenting problems and also as a guide to planning interventions aimed directly at reducing the duration, pervasiveness, frequency, and severity of the suicidal behaviors and determining the probability of future suicide. In addition, information regarding the current dimensions of suicidal responses is essential for determining therapeutic efficacy. A comprehensive assessment should also include examination of those factors that have been found to be associated with suicidal behavior in other patients. The specific events, both environmental and behavioral, that might be important as precipitants, mediators, or determinants of suicidal responses are listed in Table 9.1. The roles of any of these events in a particular patient's behavioral patterns provide an important focus of the social-behavioral analysis.

Treatment Strategies

There have been innumerable articles on psychotherapy with suicidal patients (e.g., Jeger, 1979; Kiev, 1975; Kopell, 1977; Kovacs et al., 1975b; Lesse, 1975; Mintz, 1968; Moss, 1966; Moss & Hamilton, 1957; Olin, 1976; Ringel, 1976; Seale & McNichol, 1965; Shein & Stone, 1969), and many theoretical articles on suicide include treatment recommendations (e.g., Frederick & Resnik, 1971). In contrast, there are few empirical data on the effectiveness of the recommended treatments in reducing suicidal behavior. The paucity of clinical research on treatment of suicide may be due to several factors. The ethical problems involved in using no-treatment, delayed-treatment, and even minimal-treatment control groups have seriously hampered efforts to validate treatment programs empirically. The infrequency of parasuicide and the irreversibility of suicide prohibit, except in rare cases, investigation via single-patient research designs. The high dropout rate for parasuicides in traditional therapies (Bogard, 1970; Paykel et al., 1974) suggests that patients' refusals to participate in research programs may hinder the implementation of any outcome study. Finally, the relative lack of behavioral models of suicidal behavior may account for the absence of behavioral research in this area.

The treatment strategies presented here are based on clinical experience with suicidal and parasuicidal patients as well as on the empirical data describing behavioral and environmental variables likely to interact with suicidal responses. In the absence of data to the contrary, it is assumed that behavioral treatment procedures that work with nonsuicidal patients will also be effective with suicidal patients. Therefore, the recommendations discussed here are proposed for use in addition to whatever one would ordinarily do in clinical practice. The treatment strategies described are presented as treatment recommendations; it cannot be stressed too strongly that, as yet, there are no empirical data to verify their effectiveness in suicide and parasuicide prevention. Thus, constant assessment of suicidal risk, even during intensive treatment interventions, should be continued. The ideographic data collected can then be used to guide modifications and supplements to the interventions suggested here. The recommendations can be broken down into four general categories: (1) pretreatment recommendations; (2) long-term treatment recommendations; (3) suicide-specific treatment recommendations; (4) suicide-crisis management recommendations. Before discussing therapeutic strategies, a few comments are needed on the ethical and legal issues surrounding the treatment of acutely suicidal patients and whether or not reluctant patients should be recruited into therapy.

Ethical and Legal Issues of Suicide Prevention

Treatment situations in which therapist and patient collaborate together in developing and implementing interventions designed to reduce the likelihood of suicide do not pose serious problems concerning the value of such efforts. However, preventive techniques, which often are intrusive, sometimes are actively avoided, and frequently are unwanted, can raise important ethical and legal issues. Most often these issues have been formulated as questions of whether or not a person has the right to commit suicide and, if so, whether or not the act can ever be rationally motivated. Vigorous and well-reasoned arguments have been made upholding both sides of such questions (Brandt, 1975; Cassidy & Russo, 1979; Diggory, 1968; Moskop & Engelhardt, 1979; Siegel, 1979; Szasz, 1979). Although the right to commit suicide is an important consideration for anyone contemplating suicide, its relevance to how a therapist ought to respond to a patient's suicidal behavior is unclear. The important questions, instead, would seem to be two: Does a person, and in this case a therapist, have a right to intervene against another person's explicit wishes in that person's attempt to commit suicide? If such a right exists, what limits should there be on such intervention?

When intervention is defined broadly to include indirect social influence techniques, such as praise or verbal persuasion at one end of the continuum all the way to involuntary hospitalization and inpatient "suicide precautions" at the other end, it seems clear that one has the right to intervene, but the limits of that right are debatable. At what point the therapist limits the intervention is dependent both on the state of the patient who is threatening suicide and on ethical and legal considerations. Attention to the patient's current state of functioning as an important variable in determining the limits of intervention suggests a belief that suicide is in some situations a rational act, in some not. This premise is not shared by all; suicide is most often viewed as a product, or symptom, of mental illness (e.g., Shein & Stone,

1969) or, at least, of deficient problem-solving capabilities (e.g., Applebaum, 1963). There are circumstances, of course, in which even the strongest advocate of the right to suicide would agree that the act is most likely a product of irrational thought processes and thus should be prevented. A person clearly under the influence of potent mind-altering chemicals or a person with equally serious chemical imbalances due to organic disease, to give an extreme example, would be forcibly stopped from committing suicide by most observers. However, the usual suicide case does not present such an extreme, and thus the limits of responsible intervention are considerably less clear. Arguments for and against considering suicide to be rational have been summarized by Brandt (1975).

Independent of the rationality of the act, the question of unilateral intervention still remains. Szasz (1979) presented a strong set of arguments against forcible intervention techniques and concluded as follows:

> In short, I submit that preventing people from killing themselves is like preventing people from leaving their homeland: Whether those who so curtail other people's liberties act with complete sincerity or with utter cynicism hardly matters. What matters is what happens—the abridgment of individual liberty, justified, in the case of suicide prevention, by psychiatric rhetoric; and, in the case of emigration prevention, by political rhetoric (p. 72).

Szasz based his arguments on philosophical grounds. The reasons for active suicide prevention (including, at times, involuntary hospitalization) are in practice, if not in theory, often based on legal considerations. Often the issue is whether or not one can be sued, or even charged with a crime, if one does not intervene. Case law is almost totally inconsistent on this issue. Most legal problems arise when a person is hospitalized and is thereby considered at imminent risk for suicide; comparatively few outpatient cases have been litigated, and even fewer successfully so (Perr, 1979).

No matter what an individual therapist's stand on the permissible limits of suicide prevention, it is critical that those limits be determined before a patient becomes acutely suicidal. A middle-of-the-night crisis, with a patient telephoning and threatening to take a fatal dose of barbiturates, is not the time to think these issues out. All things considered, a decision during an acute crisis to employ involuntary prevention techniques, such as calling an emergency rescue squad and/or committing the patient to a hospital, is far easier on the clinician in terms of both effort expended and risk taken. If stricter intervention limits are accepted (e.g., if only those techniques that do not infringe on the patient's civil liberties are permitted), then the clinician opposing suicide must be far more active when a patient is acutely suicidal. If the patient refuses hospitalization, the therapist must remain more readily available, and home visits may be necessary. Significant others must also be coordinated to provide additional emotional support and physical presence. The risk of immediate suicide is clearly less if a patient is hospitalized under intensive suicide precautions, such as constant observation. For the short term, anyone can be prevented from committing suicide. Whether such interventions decrease or possibly increase the long-term risk of suicide is not clear. What is possible is that most clinicians believe that they can reduce their own responsibility and the consequent risk of malpractice suit or professional censure if they forcibly intervene to save patients' lives.

The contention here is that therapists' rights to protect themselves from both psychological harm and legal jeopardy and to act in accordance with their values are at least as valid as patients' rights to commit suicide without forcible intervention. However, a suicidal patient has a right to know ahead of time both how the therapist intends to respond to various suicidal crises and what the therapist's true reasons are for such actions. After discussion of these points, the patient then has the right to terminate treatment or be referred to another therapist. For example, I once had a young woman patient who threatened suicide and then took sublethal drug overdoses on the average of once a month. The overdoses were not serious enough to require extensive medical attention ordinarily no more than stomach lavage and thus had not come to the attention of her parents, an outcome important to the patient. However, after several parasuicide incidents, I told the patient that if she took an overdose again or did anything to make me think a drug overdose was imminent, I would immediately inform her parents, who lived nearby. I explained to her that I was unwilling to remain solely responsible for responding to her drug overdoses, and we discussed the possible legal implications for me of not responding more actively should she actually carry out her threat to commit suicide. She had been told previously that I would not, under any foreseeable circumstances, initiate involuntary commitment proceedings. I could not, of course, guarantee that her parents would not institute commitment proceedings, although she and I agreed that hospitalization would be more harmful than helpful for her. She was offered referral to other therapists if she did not wish to continue with me under these circumstances. She continued with her therapy and refrained from further parasuicides.

Therapy Recruitment

Very few research studies have examined whether or not therapeutic intervention of any sort is effective in reducing the incidence of parasuicide and suicide. Only four studies have been located in which patients were randomly assigned to experimental and control groups;

an additional four studies retrospectively compared treated and control parasuicidal patients for subsequent parasuicide. These studies are summarized in Table 9.4. Among the experimental studies, three of four (Chowdhury et al., 1973; Gibbons et al., 1978; Motto, 1976) showed no significant differences at follow-up on suicidal behavior. However, Motto's data suggest that attempts to maintain contact, if only by letter, may be successful over the long run in reducing subsequent suicide among suicidal persons who refuse treatment. Bartman (1976) found significant effects at a 6-week follow-up, but his sample was extremely small, and thus generalizations are hard to make. Furthermore, his patients did not differ at posttreatment examination on most outcome measures, including paper-and-pencil measures of assertion; thus, in the absence of 6-week follow-up parasuicide data on similar nontreated patients, it is difficult to determine if the assertion training helped the experimental group or if the discussion treatment harmed the controls.

Those studies that examined treatment versus no treatment, retrospectively, present a more hopeful picture. In three of the four studies, patients receiving (or obtaining) professional intervention appeared to have been less parasuicidal at follow-up. However, neither study that examined subsequent suicide rates (Ettlinger, 1975; Greer & Bagley, 1971) found any differences between groups. Examination of all eight studies suggests that when professional contact of any kind is compared with no contact of any kind (Greer & Bagley, 1971; Kennedy, 1972; Motto, 1976; Termansen & Bywater, 1975), the contact group may subsequently have lower rates of suicidal behavior. Thus there is tentative support for the idea that continued professional contact, no matter how limited, may be effective in reducing suicidal behavior. Therefore, attempts to recruit suicidal persons into therapy appear to be warranted.

A number of investigators have found that most attempts to get parasuicides to follow up on outpatient psychotherapy referrals are less than successful. For example, Oast and Zitrin (1974) attempted to contact 265 parasuicides immediately after discharge from a psychiatric hospital. They sent letters (including registered letters), contacted relatives and collateral agencies, and, as a final procedure, made home visits. Only 139 patients (52%) were successfully traced. Seventy (50%) of these patients refused referral for continued care. Thus, only 26% of the entire sample were successfully referred. Bogard (1970) reported that only 4 of 44 parasuicides (9%) referred for outpatient care actually began treatment; 13 of 27 persons (48%) showed up for treatment in a study reported by Paykel and associates (1974). When a person refuses treatment or does not show up, the sending of intermittent nondemanding letters expressing continued interest, leaving open the door for the person to reestablish contact, is the treatment of choice. Motto's data suggest that this simple procedure may have important risk-reducing effects.

TABLE 9.4 Experimental and Quasi-experimental Treatment Outcome Studies with Suicidal Persons

Authors	Sample	Intervention	Follow-up	Results
Experimental design				
Bartman (1976)	Consecutive parasuicides admitted to inpatient psychiatric unit	1. Assertion training + milieu ($n = 7$) 2. Discussion control + milieu ($n = 7$)	6 weeks	1 < 2: parasuicide (3 vs. 0)
Chowdhury et al. (1973)	Multiple parasuicides admitted to poison center (high risk excluded)	1. Outpatient clinic; domiciliary visits; 24-hr emergency service ($n = 71$) 2. Conventional care ($n = 84$)	6 months	1 = 2: parasuicide (24% vs. 23%)
Gibbons et al. (1978)	Parasuicides admitted to emergency room (high risks and those already in treatment excluded)	1. Time-limited task-centered casework in patient's home ($n = 200$) 2. Routine services, referral	1 year	1 = 2: parasuicide (13.5% vs. 14.5%)
Motto (1976)	High-suicide-risk psychiatric inpatients refusing further treatment	1. Intermittent, nondemanding letters 2. No follow-up	4 years	1 = 2: suicide (trend toward significance) (5.2% vs. 8.3%)

Quasi-experimental designs

Study	Sample	Treatment	Follow-up	Results
Greer & Bagley (1971)	Parasuicides admitted to emergency room	1. Prolonged contact; two session ($n = 88$) 2. Brief contact; one or two sessions ($n = 76$) 3. No treatment ($n = 47$)	1–2 years	$(1 = 2) < 3$: parasuicide (20% vs. 26% vs. 39%); $1 = 2 = 3$: suicide (1% vs. 1% vs. 4%)
Ettlinger (1975)	Parasuicides admitted needing intensive medical treatment	1. Intensive treatment, relative contact, planned follow-up ($n = 222$) 2. Less therapy time than in 1 ($n = 233$)	5 years	$1 = 2$: parasuicide (32% vs. 29%); $1 = 2$: suicide (17% vs. 17%)
Kennedy (1972)	Parasuicides under care of general practitioners	1. Admitted to psychiatric treatment center ($n = 142$) 2. Referred to psychiatrist ($n = 32$) 3. Not referred ($n = 30$)	1 year	$1 < (2 = 3)$: parasuicide (12% vs. 38% vs. 37%)
Termansen & Bywater (1975)	Parasuicides admitted to emergency room	1. Short-term intensive follow-up by mental health worker ($n = 45$) 2. Same as 1, but by volunteer ($n = 32$) 3. No follow-up ($n = 32$)	3 months	$1 < (2 + 3)$: parasuicide (1% vs. 2% vs. 7%)

Pretreatment Recommendations

Once a patient accepts therapeutic intervention, preparation for behavioral change may be necessary if therapy is to be used effectively by certain patient populations. Some patients may be in such a state of crisis and high physiological arousal that they are unable to focus on any structured attempts to assess their problems and plan and implement appropriate interventions. Other suicidal patients may be so apathetic, depressed, and/or hopeless about possibilities for change that they are unwilling or unable to exert even minimal efforts to bring about therapeutic change. The high dropout rate for parasuicides, as well as the low socioeconomic status of many chronic parasuicides (Kreitman, 1977), suggests that with this population, in particular, a concerted effort to socialize patients for therapy may be needed if treatment is to be effective. The issues encountered here are often referred to as counter-control issues by behavior therapists (Davison, 1973) and "resistance" by more traditional therapists.

Role Induction Role induction, or an explanation of the events and behaviors patients can expect to encounter during treatment, is a significant factor in creating and maintaining a beneficial therapeutic relationship (Goldstein, 1975). Heitler (1976), in an extensive review of the literature on therapy preparatory techniques, concluded that therapy is more acceptable and more accessible to patients of low socioeconomic status when adequate preparation and explanation have occurred. Patients who are in behavior therapy for the first time may feel uncomfortable if their expectations are not met; as a result, the therapeutic relationship may suffer, resulting in greater likelihood of dropout from therapy (Baekeland & Lundwall, 1975). Effective role-induction interviews have been developed (Hoehn-Saric et al., 1964; Orne & Wender, 1968), and with appropriate modifications they might be effective with suicidal populations.

Reattribution Training An expectation that one can control outcomes as a result of one's behavior is considered an important prerequisite for maximizing the effect of a given behavioral treatment (Kanfer, 1980). The hopelessness characteristic of many suicidal patients suggests that they may have abandoned any belief that they can control the outcomes needed for life to be improved in important ways. Recent attributional reconceptualizations of learned helplessness may be especially relevant for parasuicidal patients. Miller and Norman (1979) pointed out that although depression is a common response to the learned helplessness manipulation, hostility has been an unexpected and unexplained finding with some patients. Anecdotal evidence suggests that those who respond with depression tend to make internal attributions, whereas those who respond with hostility and anger may make external attributions (Miller & Seligman, 1976; Seligman, 1975). Such external attributions may be characteristic of parasuicides, a group frequently characterized as hostile. Therefore, reattribution training procedures may be necessary to teach patients the skills necessary to make more accurate attributions about the causes of their own behavior and the behavior of others. The premise here is that therapy will be most effective if patients come to believe that they can positively influence outcomes while also learning to more accurately discriminate when they are and are not influential in negative outcomes. Explicit procedures toward this end are placed under pretreatment strategies rather than under long-term treatment strategies because of their critical importance in getting patients to agree to any focused attempts to bring about changes in their other behavior patterns.

Several methods can be effective in attribution retraining. Semantic procedures include the following: (1) didactic and bibliographic presentations, such as providing patients with information on learning theory and behavioral analysis principles, first in the abstract and then gradually using more relevant examples; (2) verbal persuasion procedures, such as confrontation and the foot-in-the-door technique of cognitive restructuring developed by Goldfried and associates (1974); (3) imaginal rehearsal of veridical response-outcome relationships. However, active experience with veridical response-outcome relationships appears to be more powerful than discussion in changing unrealistic attributions (Ross et al., 1975; Wortman & Dinzer, 1978). Having patients actively perform social-behavioral analyses of their own behaviors and the behaviors of others during initial therapy sessions, as well as self-monitoring between sessions, may be useful here. Mahoney (1977) suggested several methods of increasing self-monitoring compliance.

Relationship Enhancement Clinical experience clearly suggests that these attributional changes are unlikely to occur outside of a supportive therapeutic relationship. Indeed, the relatively high dropout rate for parasuicides and the high level of social isolation of suicidal patients in general (characteristic of therapy dropouts, according to Baekeland & Lundwall, 1975) emphasize the need for developing a positive therapeutic relationship during the initial stages of treatment. Thus, special emphasis on relationship-enhancement techniques, such as those suggested by Brammer (1979) and Goldstein (1975), seems essential for creating an atmosphere of trust and genuine caring. Moreover, such an atmosphere will provide a foundation for attitude change (Johnson & Matross, 1975) and will foster a willingness to proceed with behavior therapy.

Long-term Treatment Recommendations

Recommendations for long-term treatment planning with a specific suicidal patient are impossible in the abstract. Treatment targets and effective procedures are dependent on the functional analysis of the suicidal behavior accomplished during the social-behavioral assessment. However, if suicidal behavior is generally viewed as problem-solving behavior (i.e., behavior functionally related to ameliorating painful internal or external stress), then a therapy model designed to teach nonsuicidal behavioral skills for solving such problems might be useful. The premise here is that, with few exceptions, suicidal behavior represents an ineffective solution to one's problems in living. (Ineffectiveness is defined an an excess of negative effects in relation to the number of positive effects.) Presumably, if a patient acquires other behavioral skills for bringing about desired outcomes, then suicidal behavior will be avoided.

The concept of skills, as used here, is broad, and it includes behavioral capabilities within each of the three behavioral systems. An examination of the behavioral characteristics associated with suicide and parasuicide (Table 9.1) suggests that any one or more of several treatment strategies might be appropriate. For example, treatment targets and associated therapy strategies might include the following: (1) changes in cognitive styles via problem-solving therapies (e.g., Jacobson, 1979; Platt & Spivack, 1974); (2) changes in cognitive contents via cognitive restructuring therapies (e.g., Goldfried et al., 1974) or other cognitive intervention strategies; (3) acquisition of emotional control skills via desensitization, stress management training programs, meditation, or relaxation training; (4) reduction of physical pain via structured biofeedback and pain-control therapies (e.g., Turk, 1978); (5) acquisition of more constructive interpersonal behavioral patterns, including reduction of demanding and nonassertive response frequencies and an increase in interpersonal comfort, via social skills treatment packages (e.g., Linehan et al., 1979); (6) reduction in addictive and other excessive maladaptive behaviors via treatment packages designed to teach self-control skills (e.g., Marlatt & Gordon, 1978). As predicted by the social-behavioral personality model presented at the beginning of this chapter, even when treatment is aimed at a specific behavioral target or system, changes across the other two systems can be expected (Zeiss et al., 1979). With suicidal populations, simultaneous interventions in each of the behavioral systems, and possibly direct interventions in patients' environmental settings, probably are necessary to effect permanent changes. Whether or not these changes will extend to suicidal response patterns is dependent on the functional relationship between those suicidal responses and the targeted behavior.

Suicide-specific Treatment Recommendations

The recommendations presented earlier for long-term treatment planning are essentially the same as might be recommended for any number of nonsuicidal problems. The treatment recommendations discussed in this section are more specifically related to therapy with suicidal patients. For the most part, these ideas come under the heading "clinical wisdom" and are based on clinical experience, both mine and that of others, as well as on a theoretical application of the social-behavioral model of suicidal behavior to the clinical setting. Twenty-one recommendations are presented in the following paragraphs. Certainly the list is not comprehensive, and the efficacy of any one of the recommendations is dependent on its application within the context of an overall therapeutic intervention strategy. The list can be divided into three categories: (1) general procedures, (2) precrisis planning procedures, and (3) therapeutic maintenance for suicidal and nonsuicidal behaviors. Some of the recommendations are obvious.

General Procedures 1. *Talk about suicide openly and matter-of-factly.* Occasionally, patients are fearful about the therapist's potential reaction to suicidal ideation and/or planning, and thus they do not bring the topic up for discussion. A matter-of-fact tone on the therapist's part may make discussion easier. Additionally, such a posture reduces the possibility that the therapist's response to suicidal communications will reinforce suicidal responding.

2. *Avoid pejorative explanations of suicidal behavior or motives.* Suicidal patients often are extremely sensitive to pejorative explanations of their suicidal behaviors. Attempts to suggest that such behaviors may have been motivated by a desire to get attention or to manipulate others are likely to be met by firm insistence that the behaviors were motivated by terrible pain and a desire to die. Labeling "suicide attempts" as gestures, or even as parasuicide, can be equally aversive. Because nonsuicidal deliberate self-injury may be socially sanctioned to a greater extent than suicide attempts ("She was only trying to get attention."), it seems possible that patients might learn suicidal intent as an explanation for their own contemplated or overt behavior. Pejorative labeling on the part of the therapist may increase this tendency.

3. *Present a problem-solving theory of suicidal behavior, and maintain the stance that suicide is a maladaptive and/or ineffective solution.* Labeling suicidogenic circumstances as problems to be solved and teaching patients to use suicidal ideation as a cue to problem solving might facilitate alternative nonsuicidal problem solving. Occasionally, however, even the therapist may not immediately see how a problem situation can otherwise be resolved. At such times it seems helpful to point out that not being able to solve the problem immediately does not

mean that it cannot be solved eventually. At other times it may be clear to both patient and therapist that there is no hope of reducing the patient's emotional and/or physical pain. Whether or not, in such an instance, it is ever therapeutic to help a patient commit suicide is a decision that must be based on careful reflection of one's own values. Many suicidologists emphasize the role of the therapist in supporting life (e.g., Lesse, 1975; Mintz, 1968). Most of the time there is some chance that problems can be solved effectively with nonsuicidal responses. The therapist's task, in these instances, is to consistently remind patients of the relative ineffectiveness of suicidal behavior.

4. *Involve significant others, including other therapists.* Many suicide therapists recommend involvement of significant others in therapy (Kiev, 1975; Kopell, 1977; Lesse, 1975; Mintz, 1968; Moss & Hamilton, 1957; Shein & Stone, 1969; Wekstein, 1979). Accurate perception of the likely responses of significant others to suicidal behavior depends on communication with these other people. Additionally, the likelihood that social interactions play at least a contributory role in subsequent suicidal behavior suggests that involvement of the significant others in therapy might be useful. In some situations even other therapists may be rewarding suicidal behaviors; it is not uncommon for chronic parasuicidal patients to be involved with a number of mental health professionals and community agencies.

5. *Schedule sessions frequently enough, and maintain session discipline such that at least some therapy time is devoted to long-term treatment goals.* Most therapists have experienced, at least once, a crisis-of-the-week patient, with whom it seems almost impossible to move from crisis intervention to focusing on the behavioral changes necessary to prevent future maladaptive crisis responses. Application of crisis intervention procedures, as discussed in the next session, is useful here. However, the scheduling of extra sessions, as well as maintaining better control over the use of session time, might also be necessary.

6. *Stay aware of the multitude of variables impinging on patients, and avoid omnipotent taking or accepting of responsibility for patients' suicidal behaviors.* Beliefs about personal responsibility for one's own behavior or the behavior of others involve primarily ethical considerations; however, such beliefs may have important practical implications. Once it begins to appear that the therapist is the only variable or the most potent variable influencing a patient's suicidal behavior, then extraordinary methods of behavioral control may become justified, and the focus of intervention likely will slip from concentration on remedying problems functionally related to the suicidal behavior to a more exclusive concentration on preventing the suicidal behaviors in the short run. As was noted earlier, such short-run considerations may be inimical to the long-term interests of patients. Additionally, communication to the patient that the therapist has assumed final responsibility

for the patient's behavior may lead to counter-control problems in which the patient believes that freedom of choice has been lost. In my own experience I have found it useful to communicate to patients that I will be responsible for providing the best therapy possible, given my capabilities, and that I will expect the patients to take responsibility for their own behavior, including any suicidal behavior.

7. *Maintain professional consultation with a colleague.* Maintaining perspective of one's own sense of responsibility for patient's suicidal behaviors can be much easier if progress is intermittently discussed with a professional colleague. Such discussion is especially critical following a successful suicide attempt.

8. *Maintain contact with persons who reject therapy.* As noted in the section dealing with recruitment of patients, simply sending intermittent follow-up letters to persons who reject therapy or drop out of therapy may be a successful suicide-prevention technique. Certainly the effort needed here appears to be minimal, given the possible therapeutic outcome.

Precrisis Planning Procedures 9. *Anticipate and plan for crisis situations.* Ideally, suicidal patients will be taught to generate more adaptive solutions to problem situations. However, until such skills are developed, it is critical that therapist and patient together discuss events that might trigger suicidal behavior and develop a plan for how the patient should respond in such a situation. For example, the patient might be instructed to follow one of these procedures: to call the therapist; to make a self-statement that the suicide can always be carried out at a later time (and thus does not have to be done immediately, before talking with the therapist); to invite friends over; to go to a movie; to use any other response that both patient and therapist think might avert suicidal behavior. The point here is to plan these responses ahead of time, because during the crisis the patient may be unable to conceive alternative behaviors.

10. *Continually assess the risk of suicide and parasuicide.* This point was discussed previously, but it cannot be overemphasized.

11. *Be accessible.* Clinical experience suggests that the patient's access to the therapist during times of crisis can be critical in preventing suicidal behaviors (Basescu, 1965; Chowdhury et al., 1973; Mintz, 1968). Certainly it makes no sense to instruct a patient to call the therapist before committing suicide if the therapist is not going to be accessible. Although from the point of view of the therapist's personal life it is preferable that patients handle their problems without the aid of the therapist, this is simply not possible for many suicidal patients.

12. *Use emergency/crisis/suicide services in the area.* The use of local crisis services is especially recommended when patients are in acute suicidal crisis. Often, therapeutic interventions can be coordinated,

ensuring consistent responses to patients. A crisis service can also be used to provide immediate attention to a patient's suicidal behaviors without at the same time possibly rewarding such activities with the therapist's attention.

13. Give the patient a crisis card: telephone numbers of therapist, policy emergency, hospital, significant others. Patients often do not think too clearly during crises because of their high physiological arousal. Such a card will provide a directive cue as to what to do in such situations.

14. Keep telephone numbers and addresses of patients and their significant others with you. Having such information available can be extremely useful if a patient calls threatening suicide, especially if the patient then hangs up the telephone or becomes unconscious.

15. Make a short-term antisuicide contract, and keep it up to date. Several suicidologists have suggested making a contract with the patient stating that the patient will not commit suicide for a certain period of time (Gibbons et al., 1978; Wekstein, 1979). However, it is important that the contract not cover an unrealistically long period of time; such a long agreement would have little meaning for an acutely suicidal patient. When the short-term contract is made, it is critical that it be kept up to date by the therapist. Forgetting to update the contract can lead to the belief that the therapist does not care whether or not the patient commits suicide or that the therapist does not attach much importance to the contract.

16. Contact the patient's physician regarding the risks of overprescribing medications. A number of suicide therapists have recommended an interdisciplinary approach to treatment (Bogard, 1970; Chowdhury et al., 1973; Gibbons et al., 1978; Holland, 1970; Moss & Hamilton, 1957). Barraclough and associates (1974) and Jacobson and associates (1976) presented data suggesting that 75% to 80% of the physicians treating patients who later commit suicide prescribe psychotropic drugs; Jacobson and associates reported that the prescribed drugs were the causes of death in 54% of their cases.

Therapeutic Maintenance Procedures *17. Do not force the patient to resort to suicidal talk or ideation in order to get your attention.* If a patient wants the therapist's attention and cannot get it any other way, the patient may resort to suicidal behavior. Patients should be explicitly instructed that they don't have to be suicidal before calling the therapist; care should be taken that extra sessions are not scheduled *only* when patients threaten suicide. Some patients feel guilty about asking for the therapist's time or are otherwise unable to directly ask for the therapist's time unless they are suicidal; however, asking for extra attention is acceptable to most patients if it is needed to save their lives. Thus, with some patients, the therapist must make a considerable effort to ensure that suicidal ideation is not prompted by inability to call the therapist. An approach such as that recommended here requires that the therapist develop ways of dealing directly with patients who request or demand more time than is easily available or who call at inappropriate times.

18. Express your caring openly; provide noncontingent warmth and attention. As noted previously, strong interpersonal relationships between patients and therapist probably are critical for keeping many suicidal patients in therapy. In addition, such relationships can be powerful aids in keeping patients alive when they are faced with overwhelming crisis situations. Noncontingent warmth, attention, and expressions of caring are important in developing positive relationships with anyone, including suicidal patients. Such expressions should obviate the need for the patient to engage in suicidal behavior to get the therapist's attention. Finally, such open expressions of caring might be conducive to helping suicidal patients change their self-attitudes to become less negative and less self-derogatory. However, insincere expressions of caring are likely to be found out in the long run. Thus it might be preferable to refer a disliked patient to another therapist.

19. Clarify and reinforce nonsuicidal responses to problems. In some instances patients may not be aware that they have the capacity to solve problems in nonsuicidal ways. Rewarding a patient's adaptive activities may be useful in increasing the probability of such responses, thereby reducing the likelihood of suicidal responses.

20. Identify the possible therapeutic responses to patient's suicidal behaviors. Once a patient has a realistic expectation of what the therapist's response to suicidal behavior is likely to be, the attractiveness of such behavior may be reduced. It seems to be important that the patient know at least two things: (1) that the therapist will be sad or disappointed if the patient dies and (2) that the therapist will continue on with life if the patient dies. The therapist's reactions to parasuicide probably will depend on the circumstances surrounding the act, as well as on other assessment information about the patient. However, accurate expectations about the therapist's reactions may influence the patient to decide against parasuicidal acts. At least, it seems to be preferable for the patient to be told the therapist's probable responses ahead of time. With respect to suicidal ideation, the patient who expects negative consequences to follow communication of suicidal intent is unlikely to divulge such thoughts to the therapist. Therefore, it might be beneficial to state at the outset how one plans to deal with such verbalized thoughts. It is perhaps obvious at this point that promises should not be made if one does not intend to keep them. Thus, if the therapist's policy is to inform the family or civil authorities when a patient resorts to parasuicide or threatens to, confidentiality should not be promised.

21. Ensure that the patient has realistic expectations about the re-

sponses of others to future suicidal behavior. Realistic expectations about the responses of others to suicidal behavior may help to reduce the possibility of suicidal behavior in much the same way as do accurate expectations about the therapist's responses. It is especially important to help patients confront the fact that after suicide they will not be around to experience any expected positive responses from other people. Although parasuicide may, in fact, produce the consequences the patient desires, accurate understanding ahead of time of the probable negative side effects may be helpful in preventing parasuicide. A careful line must be maintained here such that one does not present a negative picture of parasuicide consequences without also presenting some hope for obtaining positive outcomes by other means; removing parasuicide as an option, when patients can find no other solutions to their problems, might increase the possibility of suicide.

Suicide-Crisis Management Recommendations

As Mintz (1968) pointed out, "all forms of psychotherapy are ineffective with a dead patient" (p. 285). Suicidal behavior often is a response to a crisis situation in a patient's life, and the therapist's ability to manage such crises, especially if the patient is threatening imminent suicide, often is critical to whether or not the patient commits parasuicide or suicide. In these cases, standard crisis intervention techniques should be employed. It is beyond the scope of this chapter to discuss such procedures in detail. However, Butcher and Maudal (1976) have provided an excellent discussion of crisis intervention, and the procedures they recommend are listed in Table 9.5.

Recommendations specific to handling a suicide crisis are also listed in Table 9.5. Once again, assessment of risk is critical. After such an assessment is carried out, the therapist will be in a position to determine if immediate and more active steps are needed to prevent death or injury. If a suicide attempt is in progress (e.g., if the patient has taken a drug overdose), then it may be necessary to call the police or an emergency rescue squad, or a home visit by the therapist may be appropriate. The latter is especially appropriate when the degree of risk is low or when there is concern that more active measures might reinforce parasuicide. Techniques that may be of use in preventing suicide or parasuicide include persuading the patient to remove lethal items, emphatically instructing the patient not to commit suicide, persisting with statements that the threatened suicide is not a good solution and that a better solution can be found, and generating hopeful statements and alternative solutions.

In some situations the best thing the therapist can do is to randomly generate solutions, so to speak, and hope that one affects the patient. Focusing on the problem situation, rather than on the planned suicidal

Table 9.5 Suicide-Crisis Management Recommendations

General crisis management procedures (Butcher & Maudal, 1976)
1. Offer emotional support
2. Provide opportunity for catharsis
3. Communicate hope and optimism
4. Be interested and actively involved
5. Listen selectively; respond to workable material, and ignore irrelevant or unmanageable aspects of the case
6. Provide needed factual information
7. Formulate the problem situation
8. Be emphatic and to the point
9. Predict future consequences of various plans of action
10. Give advice and make direct suggestions
11. Set limits; establish rules
12. Clarify and reinforce adaptive responses
13. Confront the patient's ideas and behavior directly
14. Terminate sessions abruptly if patients are not at the point of working on their problems
15. Make concrete demands or requirements of patients before the next contact
16. Work out an explicit time-limited contract
17. Enlist the aid of others

Suicide-crisis management procedures
18. Assess circumstances associated with imminent risk
19. Make a home visit or call the police or emergency rescue squad when appropriate
20. Remove, or convince the patient to remove, lethal items
21. Emphatically instruct the patient not to commit suicide or parasuicide
22. Persists with statements that suicide is not a good solution, that a better one can be found
23. Generate hopeful statements and alternative solutions
24. Keep the focus on the problem situation, not on the planned suicidal behavior
25. Stay in contact with the patient until the immediate crisis is resolved
26. Anticipate a recurrence of the crisis response
27. Plan or structure the patient's time during the crisis period until your next contact
28. Suggest temporary hospitalization until the crisis eases

behavior, is useful here, because undue emphasis on the latter will divert attention from finding alternative solutions. Until the patient convincingly agrees not to commit suicide, it is a good idea for the therapist to stay in close contact or, if this is not possible, to arrange for another person to be with the patient. Once the immediate crisis is reduced and the patient is no longer threatening suicide, it is important that a recurrence of the crisis response be anticipated and planned for. Structuring the patient's time for the period before the next contact with the therapist might be useful in reducing the likelihood of such a response. Finally, if the immediate crisis cannot be resolved, or if either the patient or the therapist expects a recurrence of the crisis state before other interventions can be made, temporary hospitalization might be useful.

Therapist Qualifications

Not every therapist is suited to working with suicidal patients. Unfortunately, however, every therapist must be prepared for the eventuality of a patient threatening suicide. Certainly, a suicidal crisis is not the time for the unprepared or unwilling therapist to refer the patient to someone else. Effective therapeutic management of suicidal patients requires certain appropriate personal characteristics, as well as a range of relevant information and treatment skills.

At a minimum, the therapist working with suicidal patients must have good interpersonal relationship skills and must be willing to invest the time, caring, and energy that suicidal patients often require. The ability to maintain a positive regard for life and a sense of hope in the face of the patient's hopelessness and desire to die, the ability to tolerate aggressive, rejecting, and often hostile patient behavior and not react in a reciprocal manner, and the ability to be honest with the patient about one's own limits, both for giving attention and for bearing the risk that the patient may commit suicide, are perhaps critical for working with a suicidal population. Practically, adequate preparation for working with suicidal patients requires that the therapist know the mechanisms for admitting patients to psychiatric hospital units during emergencies and for obtaining emergency rescue services; the therapist must find out about the crisis services available and acquire a fair knowledge of the ethical and legal implications of various treatment decisions. The therapist must also be acquainted with the range of therapeutic interventions likely to be needed for suicidal patients and must be trained in the assessment procedures needed to determine their timely application. Finally, the therapist must be willing to ask for professional consultation when in doubt, especially when therapy does not appear to be effective in reducing suicide risk.

NOTE

1. Liberman, R., & Serber, M. *Behavior therapy with suicidal patients.* NIMH grant proposal submitted 1972.

REFERENCES

American Psychiatric Association. *Diagnostic and statistical manual of mental disorders* (3rd ed.). Washington, D.C.: American Psychiatric Association, 1980.

Andress, V., & Corey, D. Suicide motives: Comparison of assignment of motives by coroners and psychologists. *Psychological Reports*, 1977, *40*, 11-14.

Applebaum, S.A. The problem-solving aspect of suicide. *Journal of Projective Technology*, 1963, *27*, 259.

Baekeland, F., & Lundwall, L. Dropping out of treatment: A critical review. *Psychological Bulletin*, 1975, *82*, 738-783.

Bagley, C., & Greer, S. Clinical and social predictors of repeated attempted suicide: A multi-variate analysis. *British Journal of Psychiatry*, 1971, *119*, 515-521.

Bagley, C. Jacobson, S., & Rehin, A. Completed suicide: A taxonomic analysis of clinical and social data. *Psychological Medicine*, 1976, *6*, 429-438.

Bancroft, J., & Marsack, P. The repetitiveness of self-poisoning and self-injury. *British Journal of Psychiatry*, 1977, *131*, 394-399.

Bandura, A. Self-efficacy: Toward a unified theory of behavioral change. *Psychological Review*, 1977, *84*, 191-215.

Barraclough, B., Bunch, J., Nelson, B., & Sainsbury, P. A hundred cases of suicide: Clinical aspects. *British Journal of Psychiatry*, 1974, *125*, 355-373.

Barraclough, B.M., & Pallis, D.J. Depression followed by suicide: A comparison of depressed suicide attempters with living depressives. *Psychological Medicine*, 1975, *5*, 55-61.

Barraclough, B., Shepard, D., & Jennings, C. Do newspaper reports of coroners' inquests incite people to commit suicide? *British Journal of Psychiatry*, 1977, *131*, 528-532.

Bartman, E.R. *Assertive training with hospitalized suicide attempters.* Doctoral dissertation, Catholic University of America, 1976.

Basescu, S. The threat of suicide in psychotherapy. *American Journal of Psychotherapy*, 1965, *19*, 99.

Beck, A.T. Thinking and depression: Idiosyncratic content and cognitive distortions. *Archives of General Psychiatry*, 1963, *9*, 324-333.

Beck, A.T., Kovacs, N., & Wiessman, A. Hopelessness and suicidal behavior. *Journal of the American Medical Association*, 1975, *234*, 1146-1149.

Beck, A.T., Kovacs, M., & Weissman, A. Assessment of suicidal intention: The scale for suicide ideation. *Journal of Consulting and Clinical Psychology*, 1979, *47*, 343-352.

Beck, A.T., & Lester, D. Components of suicidal intent in completed and attempted suicides. *The Journal of Psychology*, 1976, *92*, 35-38.

Beck, A.T., Resnik, H.L.P., & Lettieri, D.J. (Eds.). *The prediction of suicide.* Bowie, Md.: Charles Press, 1974.

Beck, A.T., Schuyler, D., & Herman, I. Development of suicidal intent scales. In A.T. Beck, H.L.P. Resnik, and D.J. Lettieri (Eds.), *The prediction of suicide*, Bowie, Md.: Charles Press, 1974.

Beck, A.T., Ward, C.H., Mendelson, M., Mock, J., & Erbaugh, J. An inventory for measuring depression. *Archives of General Psychiatry*, 1961, *4*, 561-571.

Beck, A.T., Weissman, A., Lester, D., and Trexler L. Measurement of pessimism, the Beck hopelessness scale. *Journal of Consulting and Clinical Psychology*, 1974, *42*, 861-865.

Beck, R.W., Morris, J.B., & Beck, A.T. Cross-validation of the suicidal intent scale. *Psychological Reports*, 1974, *34*, 445-446.

Bedrosian, R.C. and Beck, A.T. Cognitive aspects of suicidal behavior. *Suicide and life threatening behavior*, 1979, *9*, 87-96.

Birtchnell, J. The relationship between attempted suicide, depression and parent death. *British Journal of Psychiatry*, 1970, *116*, 307-313.

Birtchnell, J., & Alarcon, J. Depression and attempted suicide: A study of 91 cases seen in a casualty department. *British Journal of Psychiatry*, 1971, *118*, 289-296.

Bogard, H.M. Follow-up study of suicidal patients seen on emergency room consultation. *American Journal of Psychiatry*, 1970, *126*, 1017-1020.

Bostock, T., & Williams, C.L. Attempted suicide as an operant behavior. *Archives of General Psychiatry*, 1974, *31*, 482-486.

Bowers, R.S. Situationism in psychology: An analysis and a critique. *Psychological Review*, 1973, *80*, 307-336.

Brammer, L. *The helping relationship: Process and skills.* Englewood Cliffs, N.J.: Prentice-Hall, 1979.

Brandt, R.B. The mortality and rationality of suicide. In S. Perlin (Ed.), *A handbook for the study of suicide*, New York: Oxford University Press, 1975.

Braucht, G.N. Interactional analysis of suicidal behavior. *Journal of Consulting and Clinical Psychology*, 1979, *47*, 653-669.

Breed, W. Suicide, migration, and race: A study of cases in New Orleans. *Journal of Social Issues*, 1966, *22*, 30-45.

Brown, J.H. Suicide in Britain. *Archives of General Psychiatry*, 1979, *36*, 1119-1124.

Buglass, D., & McCulloch, J.W. Further suicidal behavior: The development and validation of predictive scales. *British Journal of Psychiatry*, 1970, *116*, 483-491.

Bunney, W.E., Jr., & Fawcett, J.A. A possibility of a biochemical test for suicide potential. *Archives of General Psychiatry*, 1965, *13*, 232-239.

Bunney, W.E., Jr., Fawcett, J.A., Davis, J.M., & Gifford, S. Further evaluation of urinary 17-hydroxycorticosteroids in patients. *Archives of General Psychiatry*, 1969, *21*, 138-150.

Butcher, J.N., & Maudal, G.R. Crisis intervention. In I.B. Weiner (Ed.), *Clinical methods of psychology*, New York: Wiley, 1976.

Cantor, P.C. Personality characteristics found among youthful female suicide attempters. *Journal of Abnormal Psychology*, 1976, *85*, 324-329.

Carroll, B.J., & Mendels, J. Neuroendocrine regulation in affective disorders. In E.J. Sschar (Ed.), *Hormones, behaviors and psychopathology*, New York: Raven, 1976.

Cassidy, J.P., & Russo, P.M. Religion: A catholic view. In L.D. Hankoff and B. Einsidler (Eds.), *Suicide: Theory and clinical aspects*, 73-82. Littleton, Mass.: P.S.G. Publishing, 1979.

Charatan, F.B. The aged. In L.D. Hankoff and B. Einsidler (Eds.), *Suicide: Theory and clinical aspects*, Littleton, Mass.: P.S.G. Publishing, 1979.

Chowdhury, N., Hicks, R.C., & Kreitman, N. Evaluation of an after-care service for parasuicide (attempted suicide) patients. *Social Psychiatry*, 1973, *8*, 67-81.

Clum, G.A., Patsiokas, A.T., & Luscomb, R.L. Empirically based compre-

hensive treatment program for parasuicide. *Journal of Consulting and Clinical Psychology,* 1979, *47,* 937-945.
Cochrane, R., & Robertson, A. Stress in the lives of parasuicides. *Social Psychiatry,* 1975, *10,* 161-171.
Colson, C. An objective analytic approach to the classification of suicide motivation. *Acta Psychiatrica Scandinavica,* 1973, *49,* 105-113.
Cone, J.D. The relevance of reliability and validity for behavioral assessment. *Behavior Therapy,* 1977, *8,* 411-426.
Coombs, D., & Miller, H. The Scandinavian suicide phenomenon: Fact or artifact? Another look. *Psychological Reports,* 1975, *37,* 1075-1078.
Crook T., Raskin, A., & Davis, D. Factors associated with attempted suicide among hospitalized depressed patients. *Psychological Medicine,* 1975, *5,* 381-388.
Davis, R. Black suicide in the seventies: Current trends. *Suicide and Life-Threatening Behaviors,* 1979, *9,* 131-140.
Davison, G.C. Counter-control in behavior modification. In L.A. Hamerlynck, L. Handy, & E. Mash (Eds.), *Critical issues in behavior modification,* Champaign, Ill., Research Press, 1973.
Dean, R.A., Miskimins, W., Cook, R., Wilson, L.T., & Maley, R.E. Prediction of suicide in a psychiatric hospital. *Journal of Clinical Psychology,* 1967, *23,* 296-301.
Despres, T. *The survivor.* New York: Oxford University Press, 1976.
Diekstra, R. *A social learning theory approach to the prediction of suicidal behavior.* Presented at the Seventh International Congress on Suicide Prevention, Amsterdam, 1973.
Diggory, J.C. Suicide and value. In H.L. Resnick (Ed.), *Suicidal behaviors,* Boston: Little, Brown, 1968.
Dollard, J., & Miller, N.E. *Personality and psychotherapy: An analysis in terms of learning, thinking, and culture.* New York: McGraw-Hill, 1950.
Dorpat, T.L., & Boswell, J.W. An evaluation of suicidal intent in suicide attempts. *Comprehensive Psychiatry,* 1963, *4,* 117-125.
Dorpat, T.L., & Ripley, H. A study of suicide in the Seattle area. *Comparative Psychiatry,* 1960, *1,* 349-359.
Dorpat, T.L., & Ripley, H.S. The relationship between attempted suicide and committed suicide. *Comprehensive Psychiatry,* 1967, *2,* 74-79.
Douglas, J.D. *The social meaning of suicide.* Princeton, N.J.: Princeton University Press, 1967.
Dublin, L. *Suicide: A sociological and statistical study.* New York: Ronald Press, 1963.
Duncan, J.W. The immediate management of suicide attempts in children and adolescents: Psychological aspects. *Journal of Family Practice,* 1977, *4,* 77-80.
Endler, N.S., & Magnusson, D. *Interactional psychology and personality.* New York: Wiley, 1976.
Ettlinger, R.W. Suicides in a group of patients who had previously attempted suicide. *Acta Psychiatrica Scandinavica,* 1964, *40,* 363-379.
Ettlinger, R.W. Evaluation of suicide prevention after attempted suicide. *Acta Psychiatrica Scandinavica* [Suppl. 260], 1975.
Farberow, N.L. *Suicide.* Morristown, N.J.: General Learning Press, 1974.

Farberow, N.L., & MacKinnon, D. Prediction of suicide in neuropsychiatric hospital patients. In C. Neuringer (Ed.), *Psychological assessment of suicidal risk,* Springfield, Ill.: Thomas, 1974.

Farberow, N.L., & McEvoy, J.L. Suicide among patients with diagnoses of anxiety reaction or depressive reaction in general medical and surgical hospitals. *Journal of Abnormal Psychology,* 1966, *71,* 287-299.

Farberow, N., McKelligott, J., Cohn, S., & Darbonne, A. Suicide among cardiovascular patients. In E.S. Shneidman, N.L. Farberow, & R.E. Litman (Eds.), *The psychology of suicide,* New York: Science House, 1970.

Farberow, N.L., & Shneidman, E.S. Suicide and age. In E.S. Shneidman & N.L. Farberow (Eds.), *Clues to suicide,* New York: McGraw-Hill, 1957.

Farberow, N.L., & Shneidman, E.S. (Eds.). *The cry for help.* New York: McGraw-Hill, 1961.

Farberow, N.L., Shniedman, E.S., & Leonard, C.V. Suicide among schizophrenic mental hospital patients. In N.L. Farberow & E.S. Shniedman (Eds.), *The cry for help.* New York: McGraw-Hill, 1961.

Fox, K., & Weissman, M. Suicide attempts and drugs: Contradiction between method and intent. *Social Psychiatry,* 1975, *10,* 31-38.

Frankel, B.G., Ferrence, R.G., Johnson, F.G., & Whitehead, P.C. Drinking and self-injury: Toward untangling the dynamics. *British Journal of Addiction,* 1976, *71,* 299-306.

Frankl, V.E. *From death-camp to existentialism.* Boston: Beacon, 1959.

Frederick, C., & Resnik, H.L.P. How suicidal behaviors are learned. *American Journal of Psychotherapy,* 1971, *25,* 37-55.

Freeman, D., Wilson, K., Thigpen, J., & McGee, R. Assessing intention to die in self-injury behavior. In C. Neuringer (Ed.), *Psychological assessment of suicidal risk,* Springfield, Ill.: Thomas, 1974.

Furst, S.S., & Ostow, M. The psychodynamics of suicide. In L.G. Hankoff & B. Einsidler (Eds.), *Suicide: Theory and clinical aspects,* Littleton, Mass.: P.S.G. Publishing, 1979.

Gibbons, J.S., Butler, J., Urwin, P., & Gibbons, J.L. Evaluation of a social work service for self-poisoning patients. *British Journal of Psychiatry,* 1978, *133,* 111-118.

Gibbs, J.P., & Martin, W.L. *Status integration and suicide: A sociological study.* Eugene: University of Oregon Press, 1964.

Goldfried, M.R., Decenteceo, E.T., & Weinberg, L. Systematic rational restructuring as a self-control technique. *Behavior Therapy,* 1974, *5,* 247-254.

Goldstein, A. Relationship enhancement methods. In F. Kahfer & A. Goldstein (Eds.), *Helping people change,* New York: Pergamon, 1975.

Greer, S., & Bagley, C. Effect of psychiatric intervention in attempted suicide: A controlled study. *British Medical Journal,* 1971, *1,* 310-312.

Greer, S., Gunn, J.C., & Koller, K.M. Aetiological factors in attempted suicide. *British Medical Journal,* 1966, *2,* 1352-1355.

Greer, S., & Lee, H.A. Subsequent progress of potentially lethal attempted suicides. *Acta Psychiatrica Scandinavica,* 1967, *40,* 361-371.

Grollman, E.A. *Suicide prevention, intervention, postvention.* Boston: Beacon Press, 1971.

Guze, S.B., & Robins, E. Suicide and primary affective disorders. *British Journal of Psychiatry,* 1970, *117,* 437-483.

Hankoff, L.D. Situational categories. In L.D. Hankoff & B. Einsidler (Eds.), *Suicide: Theory and clinical aspects*, Littleton, Mass.: P.S.G. Publishing, 1979.

Hankoff, L.D., & Einsidler, B. (Eds.). *Suicide: Theory and clinical aspects.* Littleton, Mass.: P.S.G. Publishing, 1979.

Heitler, J. Preparatory techniques in initiating expressive psychotherapy with lower class, unsophisticated patients. *Psychological Bulletin*, 1976, *83*, 339-352.

Henderson, A.S., Hartigan, J., Davidson, J., Lance, G.N., Duncan-Jones, P., Koller, K.M., Ritchie, K., McAuley, H., Williams, C.L., & Slaghuis, W.A. Typology of parasuicide. *British Journal of Psychiatry*, 1977, *131*, 631-641.

Henry, A.F., & Short, J.F. *Suicide and homocide.* London: Free Press, Glencoe, Collier-Macmillan, 1954.

Hodgson, R., & Rachman, S.I. Synchrony and dyssynchrony in fear and avoidance. *Behavior Research and Therapy*, 1974, *12*, 311-318.

Hoehn-Saric, R., Frank, J., Imber, S., Nash, E., Stone, A., & Battle, C. Systematic preparation of patients for psychotherapy: Effects on therapy and outcome. *Journal of Psychiatric Research*, 1964, *2*, 267-281.

Holland, J. *Basic issues in suicide prevention: Medical and psychiatric aspects.* Presented at the Summer Institute in Suicidology, Washington, D.C., 1970.

Hollinger, P. Adolescent suicide: Recent trends. *American Journal of Psychiatry*, 1978, *13*, 754-756.

Hornykiewicz, O. Some remarks concerning the possible role of the brain monoamines (dopamine, noradrenaline, serotinin) in mental disorders. *Journal of Psychiatric Research*, 1974, *11*, 249-253.

Humphrey, J.A. Social loss: A comparison of suicide victims, homocide offenders and non-violent individuals. *Diseases of the Nervous System*, 1977, *38*, 157-160.

Jacobson, N.S. Increasing positive behavior in severely distressed marital relationships: The effects of problem-solving training. *Behavior Therapy*, 1979, *10*, 311-326.

Jacobson, S.A., Bagley, C., & Rehin, A. Clinical and social variables which differentiate suicide, open and accident verdicts. *Psychological Medicine*, 1976, *6*, 417-421.

Jeger, A.M. Behavior theories and their application. In L.D. Hankoff & B. Einsidler (Eds.), *Suicide: Theory and clinical aspects.* Littleton, Mass.: P.S.G. Publishing, 1979.

Jones, D.I.R. Self-poisoning with drugs: The past twenty years in Sheffield. *British Medical Journal*, 1977, *1*, 28-29.

Kallman, F.J., & Anastasio, M.M. Twin studies on the psychopathology of suicide. *Journal of Nervous and Mental Disease*, 1947, *105*, 40-55.

Kallman, F.J., Deporte, J., Deporte, E., & Feingold, L. Suicide in twins and only children. *American Journal of Human Genetics*, 1949, *1*, 113-126.

Kanfer, F. Self-management methods. In F. Kanfer & A. Goldstein (Eds.), *Helping people change* (2nd ed.), 334-389. New York: Pergamon, 1980.

Kaplan, H.B., & Pokorny, A.D. Self-attitudes and suicidal behavior. *Suicide and Life-Threatening Behavior,* 1976, *6,* 23-35.

Kennedy, L. Efficacy of a regional poisoning treatment center in preventing further suicidal behavior. *British Medical Journal,* 1972, *4,* 255-257.

Kessel, N., & McCulloch, W. Repeated acts of self-poisoning and self-injury. *Proceedings of the Royal Society of Medicine,* 1966, *59,* 89-92.

Kiev, A. Prognostic factors in attempted suicide. *American Journal of Psychiatry,* 1974, *131,* 987-990.

Kiev, A. Psychotherapeutic strategies in the management of depressed and suicidal patients. *American Journal of Psychotherapy,* 1975, *29,* 345-354.

Kiev, A. Cluster analysis profiles of suicide attempts. *American Journal of Psychiatry,* 1976, *133,* 150-153.

Kopell, B.S. Treating the suicidal patient. *Geriatrics,* 1977, *32,* 65-67.

Kovacs, M., Beck, A.T., & Weissman, A. Hopelessness: An indicator of suicidal risk. *Suicide,* 1975, *5,* 98-103. (a)

Kovacs, M., Beck, A.T., & Weissman, A. The use of suicidal motives in the psychotherapy of attempted suicides. *American Journal of Psychotherapy,* 1975, *29,* 363-368. (b)

Kreitman, N. *Parasuicide.* London: Wiley, 1977.

Kreitman, N., Phillip, A.E., Greer, S., & Bagley, C. Parasuicide. *British Journal of Psychiatry,* 1969, *115,* 746-747.

Kreitman, N., Smith, P., & Tan, E. Attempted suicide as a language: An empirical study. *British Journal of Psychiatry,* 1970, *116,* 465-473.

Kubler-Ross, E. *On death and dying.* New York: Macmillan, 1969.

Lang, P.J. The application of psychophysiological methods to the study of psychotherapy and behavior change. In A.E. Bergin & S.L. Garfield (Eds.), *Handbook of psychotherapy and behavior change,* pp. 90-109. New York: Wiley, 1971.

Ledwidge, B. Cognitive behavior modification: A step in the wrong direction? *Psychological Bulletin,* 1978, *85,* 353-375.

Lesse, S. The range of therapies in the treatment of severely depressed suicidal patients. *American Journal of Psychotherapy,* 1975, *29,* 308-326.

Lester, D. Suicide as an aggressive act: A replication with a control for neuroticism. *Journal of General Psychology,* 1968, *79,* 83-86.

Lester, D. Suicidal behavior in men and women. *Mental Hygiene,* 1969, *53,* 340-345.

Lester, D. Attempts to predict suicidal risk using psychological tests. *Psychological Bulletin,* 1970, *74,* 1.

Lester, D. Effects of suicide prevention centers on suicide rates in the United States. *Health Services Reports,* 1974, *89,* 37-39.

Lettieri, D.J. Research issues in developing prediction scales. In C. Neuringer (Ed.), *Psychological assessment of suicidal risk,* Springfield, Ill.: Thomas, 1974. (a)

Lettieri, D.J. Suicidal death prediction scales. In A.T. Beck, H.C.P. Resnik, & D.J. Lettieri (Eds.), *The prediction of suicide,* Bowie, Md.: Charles Press, 1974. (b)

Levenson, M. *Cognitive and perceptual factors in suicidal individuals.* Unpublished doctoral dissertation, University of Kansas, 1972.

Levenson, M., & Neuringer, C. Problem-solving behavior in suicidal adolescents. *Journal of Consulting and Clinical Psychology,* 1971, *37,* 433-436.

Levi, D., Fales, C., Stein, M., & Sharp, V. Separation and attempted suicide. *Archives of General Psychiatry,* 1966, *15,* 158-164.

Levy, B., & Hansen, E. Failure of the urinary test for suicide potential: Analysis of urinary 17-OHCS steroid findings prior to suicide in two patients. *Archives of General Psychiatry,* 1969, *20,* 415-418.

Linden, L.L., & Hale, B.E. Choice of suicidal methods: Availability of lethality. In R. Litman (Ed.), *Proceedings of the 6th International conference for suicide prevention,* Ann Arbor: Edwards Brothers, 1972.

Linehan, M.M. Suicide and attempted suicide: A study of perceived sex differences. *Perceptual and Motor Skills,* 1973, *37,* 31-34.

Linehan, M.M. Behavioral interviews. In J.D. Cone & R.P. Hawkins (Eds.), *Behavioral assessment: New directions in clinical psychology,* New York: Brunner/Mazel, 1977.

Linehan, M.M. Structured cognitive-behavioral treatment of assertion problems. In P.C. Kendall & S.P. Hollon (Eds.), *Cognitive-behavioral interventions: Theory, research, and procedures,* New York: Academic, 1979.

Linehan, M.M., Goldfried, M.R., & Goldfried, A.P. Assertion therapy: Skill training or cognitive restructuring? *Behavior Therapy,* 1979, *10,* 372-388.

Litman, R.E. Models for predicting suicide risk. In C. Neuringer (Ed.), *Psychological assessment of suicidal risk,* Springfield, Ill.: Thomas, 1974.

Mahoney, M.J. Some applied issues in self-monitoring. In J.D. Cone & R.P. Hawkins (Eds.), *Behavioral assessment: New directions in clinical psychology,* New York: Brunner/Mazel, 1977.

Maris, R.W. Deviance as therapy: The paradox of the self-destructive female. *Journal of Health and Social Behavior,* 1971, *12,* 113-124.

Marlatt, G.A., & Gordon, J.R. *Determinants of relapse: Implications for the maintenance of behavior change.* Alcoholism and Drug Abuse Institute Technical Report No. 78-07, University of Washington, 1978.

Menninger, K. *Man against himself.* New York: Harcourt, Brace, 1938.

Mensh, I.N. Psychopathic condition, addictions, and sexual deviation. In B.J. Wolman (Ed.), *Handbook of clinical psychology,* New York: McGraw-Hill, 1965.

Miles, P.C. Condition predisposing to suicide: A review. *Journal of Nervous and Mental Disease,* 1977, *164,* 231-256.

Miller, I.W., & Norman, W.H. Learned helplessness in humans: A review and attribution theory model. *Psychological Bulletin,* 1979, *86,* 93-118.

Miller, N.E., & Dollard, J. *Social learning and imitation.* New Haven: Yale University Press, 1941.

Miller, W., & Seligman, M. Learned helplessness, depression and reinforcement. *Behavior Research and Therapy,* 1976, *14,* 7-17.

Millon, T. *Modern psychopathology.* Philadelphia: Saunders, 1969.

Minkoff, K., Bergman, E., Beck, A.T., & Beck, R. Hopelessness, depression, and attempted suicide. *American Journal of Psychiatry,* 1973, *130,* 455-459.

Mintz, R.S. Psychotherapy of the suicidal patient. In H.L.P. Resnik (Ed.), *Suicidal behaviors: Diagnoses and management,* Boston: Little, Brown, 1968.

Moskop, J., & Englehardt, H.T. The ethics of suicide: A secular view. In L.D. Hankoff & B. Einsidler (Eds.), *Suicide: Theory and clinical aspects*, Littleton, Mass.: P.S.G. Publishing, 1979.

Moss, L.M. Psychotherapy of the suicidal patient. *New York State Journal of Medicine*, December 1, 1966, 3020-3025.

Moss, L.M., & Hamilton, D.M. Psychotherapy of the suicidal patient. In E.S. Shneidman & N.L. Farberow (Eds.), *Clues to suicide*, New York: McGraw-Hill, 1957.

Motto, J. Suicide attempts. *Archives of General Psychiatry*, 1965, *13*, 516-520.

Motto, J.A. Suicide prevention for high-risk persons who refuse treatment. *Suicide and Life-Threatening Behavior*, 1976, *6*, 223-230.

Murphy, G.E. The clinical identification of suicidal risk. In A.T. Beck, L.P. Resnik, & D.J. Lettieri (Eds.), *The prediction of suicide*, Bowie, Md.: Charles Press, 1974.

Murphy, G.E. Suicide and attempted suicide. *Hospital Practice*, 1977, 73-81.

Nelson, V.L., Nielsen, E.C., & Checketts, K.T. Interpersonal attitudes of suicidal individuals. *Psychological Reports*, 1977, *40*, 983-989.

Neuringer, C. Dichotomous evaluations in suicidal individuals. *Journal of Consulting Psychology*, 1961, *25*, 445-449.

Neuringer, C. Reactions to interpersonal crises in suicidal individuals. *Journal of General Psychology*, 1964, *71*, 47-55. (a)

Neuringer, C. Rigid thinking in suicidal individuals. *Journal of Consulting and Clinical Psychology*, 1964, *28*, 54-58. (b)

Neuringer, C. *Psychological assessment of suicide risk*. Springfield, Ill.: Thomas, 1974. (a)

Neuringer, C. Self- and other -appraisals by suicidal, psychosomatic and normal hospitalized patients. *Journal of Consulting and Clinical Psychology*, 1974, *42*, 306. (b)

Oast, S.P., and Zitrin, A. A public health approach to suicide prevention. *American Journal of Public Health*, 1974, *65*, 144-147.

Olin, H.S. Psychotherapy of the chronically suicidal patient. *American Journal of Psychotherapy*, 1976, *30*, 570-575.

Orne, M.I. and Wender, P.H. Anticipatory socialization for psychotherapy: Method and rationale. *American Journal of Psychiatry*, 1968, *124*, 207-1212.

Paerregaard, G. Suicide among attempted suicides: A 10-year follow-up. *Suicide*, 1975, *5*, 140-144.

Parkin, M. Suicide and culture in Fairbanks: A comparison of three cultural groups in a small city of interior Alaska. *Psychiatry*, 1974, *37*, 60-67.

Parkin, D., & Stengel, E. Incidence of suicidal attempts in an urban community. *British Medical Journal*, 1965, *2*, 133-138.

Patsiokas, A., Clum, G., & Luscomb, R. Cognitive characteristics of suicide attempters. *Journal of Consulting and Clinical Psychology*, 1979, *47*, 478-484.

Paykel, E.S. Life stress. In L.D. Hankoff & B. Einsidler (Eds.), *Suicide: Theory and clinical aspects*, Littleton, Mass.: P.S.G. Publishing, 1979.

Paykel, E.S., & Dienelt, M.N. Suicide attempts following acute depression. *Journal of Nervous and Mental Disease*, 1971, *153*, 234-243.

Paykel, E.S., Hallowell, C., Dressier, D.M., Shapiro, D.L., & Weissman, M.M. Treatment of suicide attempters. *Archives of General Psychiatry*, 1974, *31*, 487-491.

Paykel, E.S., Prusoff, B.A., & Meyers, J.K. Suicide attempts and recent life events, *Archives of General Psychiatry*, 1975, *32*, 327-333.

Pederson, A., Awad, G., & Kindler, A. Epidemiological differences between white and non-white suicide attempters. *American Journal of Psychiatry*, 1973, *130*, 1071-1076.

Perr, I.N. Legal aspects of suicide. In L.D. Hankoff & B. Einsidler (Eds.), *Suicide: Theory and clinical aspects*, Littleton, Mass.: P.S.G. Publishing, 1979.

Piler, P. Eighteen hundred and seventeen cases of suicidal attempts: A preliminary statistical survey. *American Journal of Psychiatry*, 1938, *95*, 97-115.

Platman, S.R., Plutchik, R., & Weinstein, B. Psychiatric, psychological, behavioral and self-report measures in relation to a suicide attempt. *Journal of Psychiatric Research*, 1971, *8*, 127-137.

Platt, J.J., & Spivack, B. Means of solving real-life problems: Psychiatric patients vs. controls and cross-cultural comparisons of normal females. *Journal of Community Psychology*, 1974, *2*, 45-48.

Pokorny, A.D. Suicide rates in various psychiatric disorders. *Journal of Nervous and Mental Disorders*, 1964, *139*, 499.

Pokorny, A.D. A follow-up study of 618 suicidal patients. *American Journal of Psychiatry*, 1966, *112*, 1109-1116.

Pokorny, A.D. Myths about suicide. In H.L.P. Resnik (Ed.), *Suicide behaviors*, Boston: Little, Brown, 1968.

Pokorny, A.D., Kaplan, H.B., & Tsai, S.Y. Hopelessness and attempted suicide: A reconsideration. *American Journal of Psychiatry*, 1975, *9*, 954-956.

Pomeranz, D.M. & Goldfried, M.R. An intake report outline for modification. *Psychological Report*, 1970, *26*, 447-450.

Rachman, S., & Hodgson, R.I. Synchrony and dyssynchrony in fear and avoidance. *Behavior Research and Therapy*, 1974, *12*, 311-318.

Resnik, H.L.P. *Suicide behaviors*. Boston: Little, Brown, 1968.

Richman, J., & Charles, E. Patient dissatisfaction and attempted suicide. *Community Mental Health Journal*, 1976, *12*, 301-305.

Ringel, E. The parasuicide syndrome. *Suicide and Life-Threatening Behavior*, 1976, *6*, 131-149.

Robin, A.A., Brooke, E.M., & Freeman-Browne, D.L. Some aspects of suicide in psychiatric patients in Southead. *British Journal of Psychiatry*, 1968, *114*, 739-747.

Robin, E.M.D., Murphy, G.E., Wilkinson, R.H., Gasner, S., & Kayes, J. Some clinical considerations in the prevention of suicide based on a study of 134 successful suicides. *American Journal of Public Health*, 1959, *49*, 888-889.

Rosenbaum, M., & Richman, J. Suicide: The role of hostility and death wishes from the family and significant others. *American Journal of Psychiatry*, 1970, *126*, 1652-1655.

Ross, L., Lepper, M., & Hubbard, M. Perseverance in self-perception and social perception: Biased attributional processes in the debriefing paradigm. *Journal of Personality and Social Psychology*, 1975, *32*, 880-887.

Rubenstein, R., Moses, R., & Lidz, T. On attempted suicide. *American Medical Association Archives of Neurology and Psychiatry*, 1958, *79*, 103-112.

Schmidt, E.H., O'Neal, P., & Robins, E. Evaluation of suicide attempts as a guide to therapy. *Journal of the Amercian Medical Association*, 1954, *155*, 549-557.

Seale, A.L., & McNichol, R.W. Treatment of the suicidal patient: Community psychiatry approach. *Southern Medical Journal*, 1965, *58*, 1159-1162.

Seligman, M. *Helplessness: On depression, development, and death.* San Francisco: Freeman, 1975.

Shein, H.M., & Stone, A.A. Psychotherapy designed to detect and treat suicidal potential. *American Journal of Psychiatry*, 1969, *125*, 1247-1251.

Shneidman, E.S. An overview: Personality, motivation and behavior theories. In L.D. Hankoff & B. Einsidler (Eds.), *Suicide: Theory and clinical aspects*, Littleton, Mass.: P.S.G. Publishing, 1979.

Shneidman, E.S., & Farberow, N.L. Statistical comparisons between attempted and committed suicides. In N.C. Farberow & E.S. Shneidman (Eds.), *The cry for help*, New York: McGraw-Hill, 1961.

Shneidman, E.S., Farberow, N.L., & Litman, R.E. (Eds.). *The psychology of suicide.* New York: Science House, 1970.

Siegel, S. Religion: A Jewish view. In L.D. Hankoff & B. Einsidler (Eds.), *Suicide: Theory and clinical aspects*, Littleton, Mass.: P.S.G. Publishing, 1979.

Sifneos, P. Manipulative suicide. *Psychiatric Quarterly*, 1966, *40*, 525-537.

Silver, M., Bohnert, M., Beck, A., & Marcus, D. Relation of depression to attempted suicide and seriousness of intent. *Archives of General Psychiatry*, 1971, *25*, 573-576.

Silverman, C. The epidemiology of depression—A review. *American Journal of Psychiatry*, 1968, *124*, 883-891.

Spitzer, R., Endicott, J., & Robins, E. Research diagnostic criteria. *Archives of General Psychiatry*, 1978, *35*, 773-786.

Staats, A.W. *Social behaviorism.* New York: Dorsey, 1975.

Staats, W., & Staats, C.K. *Complex human behavior.* New York: Holt, Rinehart, 1963.

Steele, R.E. Clinical comparison of black and white suicidal attempters. *Journal of Consulting and Clinical Psychology*, 1977, *45*, 982-986.

Stengel, E. The complexity of motivations to suicidal attempts. *Journal of Mental Science*, 1960, *106*, 1388.

Stengel, E. *Suicide and attempted suicide.* Baltimore: Penguin, 1964.

Stengel, E. Attempted suicides. In H.L.P. Resnick (Ed.), *Suicidal behaviors: Diagnoses and management*, Boston: Little, Brown, 1968.

Stengel, E., & Cook, N. *Attempted suicide.* London: Oxford University Press, 1958.

Struve, F.A. Clinical electro-encephalography. In L.D. Hankoff & B. Einsidler (Eds.), *Suicide: Theory and clinical aspects*, Littleton, Mass.: P.S.G. Publishing, 1979.

Szasz, T.S. A critique of professional ethics. In L.D. Hankoff & B. Einsidler (Eds.), *Suicide: Theory and clinical aspects*, Littleton, Mass.: P.S.G. Publishing, 1979.

Tapper, B., *A behavioral assessment of the reinforcement contingencies associated with the occurrence of suicidal behaviors.* Unpublished doctoral dissertation, University of Southern California, 1975.
Termansen, P.E., & Bywater, C. S.A.F.E.R.: A follow-up service for attempted suicide in Vancouver. *Canadian Psychiatry Association Journal,* 1975, *20,* 29-34.
Tuckman, J., & Youngman, W. Suicide risks among persons attempting suicide. *Public Health Reports,* 1963, *78,* 585-587. (a)
Tuckman, J., & Youngman, W. Identifying suicide risk groups among attempted suicides. *Public Health Reports,* 1963, *78,* 763-766. (b)
Tuckman, J., & Youngman, W. A scale for assessing suicide risk of attempted suicides. *Journal of Clinical Psychology,* 1968, *24,* 17-19. (a)
Tuckman, J., & Youngman, W. Assessment of suicide risk in attempted suicides. In H.L.P. Resnick (Ed.), *Suicide behaviors.* Boston: Little, Brown, 1968. (b)
Turk, D. Cognitive behavioral techniques in the management of pain. In J. Foreyt & D. Rathjen (Eds.), *Cognitive behavior therapy: Research and application,* New York: Plenum, 1978.
Vinoda, K.S. Personality characteristics of attempted suicides. *British Journal of Psychiatry,* 1966, *112,* 1143-1150.
Virkkunen, M. Attitude to psychiatric treatment before suicide in schizophrenia and paranoid psychoses. *British Journal of Psychiatry,* 1976, *128,* 47-49.
Vital Statistics of the United States (Vol. II, Part A, 1973). U.S. Department of Health, Education, and Welfare, National Center for Health Statistics, Hyattsville, 1977.
Vital Statistics of the United States (Vol. II, Part B, 1975). U.S. Department of Health, Education, and Welfare, National Center for Health Statistics, Hyattsville, 1977.
Weissman, M.M. The epidemiology of suicide attempts 1960 to 1974. *Archives of General Psychiatry,* 1974, *30,* 737-746.
Weissman, M., Fox, K., & Kleiman, G.L. Hostility and depression associated with suicide attempts. *American Journal of Psychiatry,* 1973, *130,* 450-454.
Wekstein, L. *Handbook of suicidology.* New York: Brunner/Mazel, 1979.
Wenz, R.V. Subjective powerlessness, sex, and suicide potential. *Psychological Reports,* 1977, *40,* 927-928.
West, D.J. *Murder Followed by Suicide.* Cambridge, Mass.: Harvard University Press, 1966.
Wetzel, R.D. Sematic differential ratings of concepts and suicide intent. *Journal of Clinical Psychology,* 1976, *32,* 11-12.
Wolpe, J. Cognition and causation in human behavior and its therapy. *American Psychologist,* 1978, *33,* 437-446.
Worden, J.W., & Sterling-Smith, R.S. Lethality patterns in multiple suicide attempts. *Life-Threatening Behavior,* 1973, *3,* 95-104.
Wortman, C., & Dinzer, L. Is an attributional analysis of the learned helplessness phenomenon viable? A critique of the Abramson-Seligman-Teasdale reformulation. *Journal of Abnormal Psychology,* 1978, *87,* 75-90.

Zeiss, A.M., Lewinsohn, P.M., & Muñroz, R.F. Nonspecific improvement effects in depression using interpersonal skills training, pleasant activity schedules, or cognitive training. *Journal of Consulting and Clinical Psychology*, 1979, *47*, 427–439.

Zubin, J. Observations on nosological issues in the classification of suicide behavior. In A.T. Beck, H.L.P. Resnik, & S.J. Lettieri (Eds.), *The prediction of suicide*, Bowie, Md.: Charles Press, 1974.

Somatic Treatment for Depression
James Kocsis

The purpose of this chapter is to discuss the factors that enter into the decision to prescribe somatic treatments for depression. The therapeutic armamentarium available for depressive syndromes is broad, and it includes supportive and psychodynamic psychotherapies, behavioral and cognitive therapies, medications, and electroconvulsive therapy (ECT). ECT, which was introduced by Cerletti and Bini in 1938, has gradually become accepted as being particularly effective in selected cases of severe depression. The modern antidepressant chemotherapies, the monoamine oxidase inhibitors (MAOIs) and the tricyclic compounds, were discovered in 1952 (Selikoff et al., 1952) and 1957 (Kuhn, 1958), respectively. The latter have become predominant among all antidepressant treatments currently in use. In recent years lithium ion has been found to have antidepressant activity in selected cases (Mendels, 1976), and antipsychotic drugs of the phenothiazine type also have been described as having a role in the management of certain types of depression (Nelson & Bowers, 1978). The current evidence pertinent to the selection of depressed patients for whom the various somatic therapies are likely to be useful will be discussed. No attempt will be made to outline basic pharmacology or such aspects of clinical use of these treatments as dosage, blood concentrations, or side effects. Several recent psychopharmacology texts have adequately summarized these areas (Baldessarini, 1977; Lipton et al., 1979; Shader, 1975).

The major complicating factors in the selection of appropriate treatment modalities for depression are the likely heterogeneity of depressive syndromes in terms of etiology and pathogenesis and the lack of valid predictors of differential effectiveness for the various antidepressant treatments. Although there is preliminary evidence from several laboratories that disturbances in particular biological parameters occur in some depressive subtypes and that these disturbances can be used to predict responses to certain antidepressant medications, these tests are not widely available, and they are difficult to perform in a nonresearch setting without strict control of diet and other factors that might affect their results (Maas, 1975). From a practical standpoint, physicians and therapists treating depression currently are restricted to consideration of clinical parameters when making treatment selections. The use of clinical predictors for the selection of somatic treatments for depression will be the major focus of this review.

It is important to recognize that evaluations of efficacy of antidepressant treatments, as well as evaluation of the clinical response to treatment in a given depressed patient, are complicated by the spontaneously relapsing and remitting nature of depressive disorders. From the standpoint of research design, this necessitates the use of random assignment and control groups for determining the efficacy of antidepressant treatments. Furthermore, because milder forms of depression of the kind usually seen in outpatient settings are highly placebo-responsive, it may be difficult to demonstrate differences between active treatments and placebo treatments. Because of these considerations, it is imperative to use double-blind treatment trials of active and placebo treatments, with reliable formal ratings of treatment responses, before the efficacy of any given therapy can be accepted. Recent studies have also suggested the importance of monitoring the concentrations of drugs in the blood to ensure the adequacy of medication treatments. The theoretical basis for this practice was noted by Jenner and Lee (1976), who observed that apparent drug responders are heterogeneous in that some are pharmacologic responders, whereas others remit spontaneously while on drugs. Likewise, apparent drug nonresponders are heterogeneous in that some are inadequately treated or are noncompliant. An evaluation of the pharmacologic response to medication in an individual patient is enhanced by the use of blood-level monitoring to determine the adequacy of the medication trial. Another technique that may be used for this purpose is blind substitution of placebo for active drug and observation for relapse. Researchers interested in the effects of psychotherapy on depression have also taken cognizance of the issue of assuring the homogeneity and adequacy of the treatment delivered in order to properly evaluate the antidepressant efficacy of that treatment (Waskow & Parloff, 1975).

Many studies have shown correlations between the antidepressant effectiveness of various treatments and such clinical parameters as severity, symptom profile, and natural history. However, methodologic flaws (such as lack of placebo control groups and failure to report interrater reliability, rates of treatment compliance, and characteristics of dropouts) have diluted the value of the reported correlations for predictive purposes (Bielski & Friedel, 1976). Furthermore, it is difficult to draw conclusions when studies are conducted in multiple locations using variable diagnostic criteria and different treatment settings (inpatient, outpatient, etc.) unless such correlations are replicated.

Recognition of the importance of the ability to predict differential effectiveness for antidepressant therapies, as well as interest in biochemical and hormonal aberrations in some depressives, has led to a number of attempts to reclassify these disorders. Classifications of both dimensional and categorical types have been made (Paykel, 1979). The assumptions underlying dimensional classifications, which are based on the application of linear multiple regression to psychiatric rating variables, have been subject to criticism (Klein et al., 1969), and most studies of treatment outcome for depression have employed categorical classifications. Most attention has been devoted to the endogenous–characterologic dichotomy and its variants. These categories will be described here because of evidence indicating that they indeed have usefulness for treatment selection.

Endogenous Depression

Endogenous depressions, which have also been called endogenomorphic, psychotic, vital, or vegetative depressions, tend to occur in later life in persons who have had "good" premorbid personalities. The mood is almost always dysphoric, but it may be described as low, worn out, or anxious, rather than depressed. This syndrome may appear in relationship to a disappointment or loss, but often it appears to arise de novo. There may be a history of prior depressive episodes that have remitted with or without treatment, and there may be a family history of depression. The most distinctive characteristic of the endogenous depressions is the accompanying physical or "vegetative" symptoms that give this syndrome a particularly biological aspect. These include the following: psychomotor agitation or retardation; insomnia, particularly early morning awakening; diurnal variations of mood, with the worst time being the morning; anorexia with weight loss; decreased libido, sometimes with impotence in men and amenorrhea in women; constipation. This syndrome shares with other forms of depression such common associated features as guilt, self-depreciation, loss of usual interests, decreased ability to function, social withdrawal, and suicidal tendencies. Overvalued ideas, distortions or frank delusions of guilt, poverty, and bodily decay are common in the more severe forms, and they have implications for treatment selection, as will be discussed later.

Endogenous depression with vegetative signs has been hypothesized by psychobiologic researchers to reflect dysfunction of limbic-hypothalamic brain centers involved in the regulation of mood and appetitive functions (Goodwin, 1977). This theory has received support from two sources: preliminary findings by several laboratories of depression-associated deficits in turnover of amine neurotransmitters (norepinephrine, serotonin) known to be importantly represented in these brain areas; the known central-monoamine-facilitating effects of the antidepressant medications.

Several variants of the endogenous depressive syndrome have been described, and these have implications for treatment selection.

The Unipolar-Bipolar Distinction

Unipolar depression consists in recurrent relapsing and remitting depressive episodes, usually endogenous in nature, without episodes of hypomania or mania. Bipolar depression is a relatively rare condition in which episodes of depression alternate, usually on an irregular basis, with periods of euphoric overactivity and poor judgment leading to self-detrimental behavior, so-called hypomanic or manic phases.

The Primary-Secondary Distinction

This distinction, first proposed by Robins and Guze (1972), divides depressions into those arising in the absence of preexisting medical or psychiatric disorders, which are termed primary, and those that arise during the course of a serious medical illness or preexisting psychiatric disorder such as alcoholism or schizophrenia, which are termed secondary. Because most research on the natural history, prognosis, and treatment of depression has been confined to the primary form, less is known about the course and pharmacologic responsiveness of secondary depression.

Depressive Equivalents or Masked Depression

It is particularly important for clinicians to recognize that patients who present with predominant hypochondriasis or exaggerated responses to real physical illnesses may have a hidden or masked form of endogenous depression. Common clues that should lead to consideration of this diagnosis include physical signs and symptoms that elude explanation, multiple symptoms involving many organ systems, and symptoms that resist treatment by ordinary methods. Inquiries about the presence of dysphoria, guilt, self-depreciation, and suicidal ideation, as well as vegetative signs of depression, will aid the therapist in arriving at the correct diagnosis.

Characterologic Depression

Characterologic depressive syndromes, which have also been termed reactive, neurotic, or personal depressions, may be acute or chronic, and they tend to occur in patients with long-standing neurotic problems or personality disorders. Typically the complaints of depression are bitter, often with angry, demanding, or manipulative overtones. However, these patients often fail to appear especially depressed, and they may lack vegetative signs of depression. Anxiety often is prominent and is associated with initial insomnia and diarrhea; appetite may be transiently diminished, and oversleeping and overeating are common. The depressed mood often is markedly labile, responding dramatically to environmental or interpersonal events. Attention-seeking suicidal gestures (often wrist scratching or mild drug overdose) are common. Completed suicide, whether intentional or accidental, at times with bizarre manipulative qualities, may occur. Rosenthal and Guderman (1967) emphasized the self-pitying aspect of some of these states and described the characteristic irritability, reactivity, and fluctuating symptoms.

Although nonendogenous depressive disorders are extremely common, their nosologic status remains uncertain, and they are subjects of much confusion in theory, research, and clinical practice. Klerman and associates (1979) have observed that one source of the confusion stems from the multiple meanings that have accrued to the term *neurotic depression,* which has been used to label depressive syndromes having one or a combination of the following features: nonincapacitating; nonpsychotic; nonendogenous; reactivity; occurrence in persons with long-standing maladaptive personality patterns; occurrence as a result of unconscious conflict.

Thus, whereas the unipolar and bipolar endogenous depressive conditions have been fairly well delineated and validated by studies of family history, course, and treatment response (Winokur et al., 1968), nonendogenous depressions seemingly represent a more diffuse group of disorders.

Mild and Combined Syndromes

An evaluation of a depressed patient should take into account the occurrence of sadness as a normal mood in reaction to negative life events, the occurrence of normal grief, which may share many features of endogenous depression, including vegetative signs, and the likelihood of mixed syndromes.

Endogenous depressions also occur episodically in some patients who are characterologically depressed or who suffer from other primary medical or psychiatric illnesses such as cancer, schizophrenia, or alcoholism. Accurate differential diagnosis and optimum treatment selection await the development of improved nosology based on better knowledge of etiology and pathogenesis and the development of validating biological markers.

Prediction of Responses to Tricyclic Antidepressant

Six tricyclic antidepressants are currently marketed in the United States: imipramine (Tofranil, etc.), amitriptyline (Elavil, etc.), desmethylimipramine (Norapramine, Pertofrane), Nortriptyline (Aventyl, Pamelor), protriptyline (Vivactil), and doxepin (Sinequan, Adapin). Although differing somewhat in side effects and potency, they have approximately equal effectiveness as antidepressants. The improvement rates reported in mixed depressive samples usually have been 60% to 80%. Because of high placebo response rates, some studies have failed to demonstrate efficacy for these drugs.

There is consistent evidence that the presence of the so-called endogenous symptom pattern predicts a favorable response to the tricyclic drugs (Bielski & Friedel, 1976). However, the clinical features and tricyclic drug responsiveness of endogenous depressive syndromes vary, and this has led to investigations of the predictive value of individual symptoms. Klein (1974) suggested that the presence of anhedonia constitutes the sine qua non of "endogemorphic" depression and is predictive of imipramine response, but this idea has not been systematically tested by others. Glassman and associates (1975) reported that depressed inpatients with delusions showed more unfavorable responses to imipramine than did nondelusional patients, and they recommended ECT as the treatment of first choice for the former. Of note in this regard is that Nelson and Bowers (1978) recently reported successful treatment of 12 of 13 delusionally depressed patients with a combination of tricyclic and antipsychotic drugs. A final point is that to date there have been few studies of the predictive value of individual vegetative signs for tricyclic antidepressant response.

Clinical practice and anecdotal reports have suggested that some nonendogenous depressions respond to tricyclics. Undoubtedly there is overlap between endogenous and nonendogenous syndromes in terms of clinical presentation. Mild vegetative disturbances such as initial insomnia and mild anorexia with the loss of a few pounds are common and difficult to evaluate. Klerman and associates (1979) have observed that clinicians' recommendations regarding the value of drug treatment for neurotic depressions tend to follow their conceptions of the nature of the disorder, but they have asserted that "clinical experience and recent research trials increasingly support the value of tricyclics for neurotic depressions." It seems likely that some neurotic depressions are mild forms of true manic-depressive conditions, whereas others are not, and that there is a place for medication in the management of some of these states, although the correct diagnosis may be difficult to make.

Among the demographic and natural history variables examined in various studies of the prediction of tricyclic responses, only one, a history of multiple prior episodes of depression, has been consistently found to have predictive value, and it predicts a negative response to tricyclics (Bielski & Friedel, 1976).

In summary, the modal responder to the tricyclic antidepressants would seem to be the endogenous depressive with vegetative signs and a good premorbid personality who is anhedonic and nondelusional and has experienced few previous episodes or none.

Although tricyclic antidepressants have commonly been used clinically for patients with so-called secondary depression (i.e., those with preexisting psychiatric diagnoses such as schizophrenia or alcoholism and those with life-threatening physical illness), there have been few studies of the efficacy of tricyclics for this population.

Although there is considerable anecdotal support for a pharmacologic value (as opposed to placebo value) of the tricyclics for some patients with so-called neurotic or characterologic depressions, research must be carried out to define the characteristics of subgroupings in these groups for whom these drugs are likely to have value.

Comparisons of Behavioral and Cognitive Therapies with Chemotherapy

A number of behavioral and cognitive approaches to the treatment of depression have now been developed (Rush & Beck, 1978). Controlled studies have demonstrated efficacy for these techniques in the treatment of nonbipolar, nonpsychotic depressed outpatients free of serious suicide attempts and suicidal ideation (Fuchs & Rehm, 1977; Morris, 1975; Rehm et al., 1979; Schmickley, 1976).

Rush and associates (1977) compared cognitive therapy with tricyclic treatment in 41 depressed outpatients treated for a mean of 11 weeks. They reported a lower dropout rate and better symptom reductions in the cognitive therapy group.

Several studies have been conducted to compare psychotherapeutic modalities to chemotherapy for depressed outpatients and to examine the effects of combining these treatments. Group therapy (Covi et al., 1974), marital therapy (Friedman, 1975), and interpersonal therapy (Weissman et al., 1979) have been found to be less effective than tricyclics alone or equally as effective as tricyclics alone, but they have generally been found to improve outcomes (particularly long-term outcomes) when used in combination with drugs. A new collaborative study being conducted by the National Institute of Mental Health will examine the effects of cognitive therapy alone and in combination with tricyclics, as compared with drug only, for the treatment of outpatient depressives. Given the consistent findings of the particular usefulness of tricyclic antidepressants for endogenous depression, it is important for studies of other treatments to report the incidences of vegetative signs among their subject samples so that clinicians can judge the relative utility of various treatments by depressive subtype.

Prediction of Antidepressant Responses to MAOIs

Several methodologically sound clinical trials comparing the MAOI phenelzine (Nardil) to placebo have now been conducted. Phenelzine has been found to be effective for the treatment of nonendogenous (Nies et al., 1975) or "neurotic" outpatients (Johnstone & Marsh, 1975) and ineffective for the treatment of (presumably mostly endogenously) depressed inpatients (Medical Research Council, 1965). Robinson and associates (1978) have pointed out the importance of proper patient selection and adequate doses (> 60 mg/day) for effective use of phenelzine.

A retrospective study by West and Dally (1959) found that patients who responded favorably to another MAOI, iproniazid, had hysterical features and an absence of endogenous symptoms. A third MAOI, tranylcypromine, has also been used in the treatment of depression. Bartholomew (1962) found it to be superior to placebo in reactive depressions, whereas two studies with inpatients found little or no advantage over placebo (Gottfries, 1963; Khanna et al., 1963).

Because of the possibility of serious toxic effects from these compounds, they should be prescribed only by psychiatrists knowledgeable about these drugs and about the prevention and management of their side effects and toxicity. An inconvenient aspect of their use is the necessity that patients maintain a restricted diet to avoid their potential for inducing severe hypertension.

Because those patient populations for whom MAOIs have been reported to be effective are known to be highly responsive to a wide variety of therapeutic interventions, including placebo, the importance of placebo control groups in the evaluation of MAOI efficacy and comparisons of drug, nondrug, and combined treatments should be emphasized. No studies have been found that have sought to examine possible synergistic effects between MAOIs and verbal or behavioral therapies.

Lithium as an Antidepressant

The clinical use of lithium as an antidepressant generally should be restricted to bipolar patients who are actively depressed and to other depressed patients who fail to respond to usual antidepressant treatments. Using the method of within-patient crossover to placebo, three studies have demonstrated more frequent antidepressant responses among bipolar than unipolar depressed patients (Baron et al., 1975; Goodwin et al., 1972; Noyes et al., 1974). Mendels (1976) has suggested that a family history of bipolar illness or of lithium-responsive depression may enhance the clinical indication for a trial of lithium as an antidepressant. Lithium and antidepressant drugs may act synergistically in the treatment of depression, particularly in bipolar patients.

Use of ECT

ECT is indicated for severe psychotic depressions with vegetative symptoms, regardless of subtype (bipolar, unipolar, involutional melancholia). Reported success rates vary from 60% to 90% and they are equal to or higher than rates for tricyclics and higher than rates for MAOIs for these conditions (Fink, 1978).

ECT is the treatment of choice for depressions complicated by imminent suicidal risk, physical debilitation, or medical contraindications to antidepressant drug use. Although it is a controversial matter, it is believed by some psychopharmacologists that delusional depressions should be treated with ECT (Glassman et al., 1975). On the other hand, there has been a report of comparable rates of responses from the use of a combination of antidepressant and antipsychotic drugs (Nelson & Bowers, 1978).

Although ECT possesses the advantage over drugs of having a high rate of initial favorable responses, the treatment often is less acceptable to patients and families, and there is substantial risk of early relapse. For these reasons, some clinicians, including the author, prefer to begin the treatment of endogenous depressions with medication, unless there are emergency complications. Drug responders have the advantage of little risk from early relapse if the medication is maintained for several months after the resolution of the acute episode. Drug nonresponders may still receive ECT and have a high rate of favorable response.

Studies comparing ECT to placebo for the treatment of nonendogenous (reactive or characterologic) depressions have failed to demonstrate efficacy of ECT for these conditions (Carney & Sheffield, 1974).

Summary and Guidelines for Antidepressant Treatment Selection

The most clear-cut indications for somatic treatments for depression occur in those depressive states that are bipolar or are accompanied by delusions or imminent risk of suicide. These states generally should not be treated solely by nonsomatic treatments.

Endogenous depressions that are not delusional, not bipolar, and not accompanied by grave suicidal risk generally should be treated with tricyclic medications alone or in combination with nonsomatic therapies. A problem is the evaluation of the severity of vegetative signs. The presence of marked weight loss over several weeks and early morning awakening with diurnal variations in mood and decreases in libido and sexual activity generally should constitute grounds for referral for tricyclic medication. Some patients with mild insomnia and anorexia without persistent severe weight loss might be treated initially with psychotherapy or cognitive-behavioral approaches, with consideration of addition of medication if these prove ineffective after several weeks.

Treatment selection for nonendogenous neurotic and characterologic depressions is even less certain. The author's strategy generally is to try a nonsomatic treatment first and take the attitude (both for oneself and for the patient)that sequential adequate trials of various somatic and nonsomatic treatments will be attempted until something helps. A serious mistake to be avoided with these conditions is the attitude that any treatment given is the "right" one. These guidelines for treatment selection are summarized in Figure 10.1.

A final note applies to maintenance treatment with somatic therapies. Successful treatment of a first episode of depression with medication or ECT will generally be followed by 3 to 6 months of antidepressant maintenance. A similar schedule applies to patients who have very

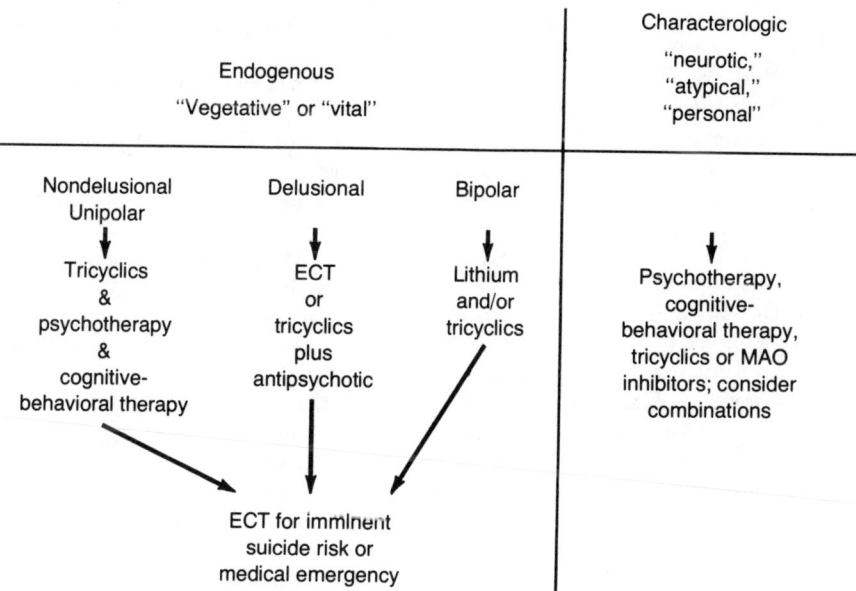

Figure 10.1. Depressive Subtypes and Choice of Treatment

infrequent episodes. Other patients with histories of frequent depressive occurrences may require prolonged or even lifelong medication maintenance. When patients on medication are being concurrently treated by psychotherapists or behavior therapists, it is useful for the latter to communicate with the psychopharmacologist and to be informed about the recommendations for maintenance treatment.

REFERENCES

Baldessarini, R.J. *Chemotherapy in psychiatry.* Cambridge: Harvard University Press, 1977.

Baron, M., Gershon, E.S., Rudy, V., Jonas, W., & Buchsbaum, M. Lithium carbonate response in depression. *Archives of General Psychiatry,* 1975, *32,* 1107.

Bartholomew, A.A. Evaluation of tranylcypromine in treatment of depression. *Medical Journal of Australia,* 1962, *49,* 655.

Bielski, R.J., & Friedel, R.O. Prediction of tricyclic antidepressant response. *Archives of General Psychiatry,* 1976, *33,* 1479–1489.

Carney, M.W.P., & Sheffield, B.F. The effects of pulse ECT in neurotic and endogenous depression. *British Journal of Psychiatry,* 1974, *125,* 91–94.

Cerletti, U., & Bini, L. L'electroshock. *Archives General di Neurology, Psychiatry e Psychoanalyasis,* 1938, *19,* 266.

Covi, L., Lipman, R.S., Derogatis, L.R., Smith, J.E., & Pattison, J.H. Drugs and group psychotherapy in neurotic depression. *American Journal of Psychiatry,* 1974, *131,* 191-198.

Fink, M. Efficacy and safety of induced seizures (EST) in man. *Comprehensive Psychiatry,* 1978, *19,* 1-8.

Friedman, A.S. Interaction of drug therapy with marital therapy in depressed patients. *Archives of General Psychiatry,* 1975, *32,* 619-637.

Fuchs, C.Z., Rehm, P.L. A self-control behavior therapy program for depression. *Journal of Consulting and Clinical Psychology,* 1977, *45,* 206-215.

Glassman, A.H., Kantor, S.J., & Shostak, M. Depression, delusions and drug response. *American Journal of Psychiatry,* 1975, *132,* 716-719.

Goodwin, F.K. Biologic basis of drug action in the affective disorders. In M.E. Jarvik (Ed.), *Psychopharmacology in the practice of medicine,* New York: Appleton-Century-Crofts, 1977.

Goodwin, F.K., Murphy, D.L., Dunner, D.L., & Bunney, E., Jr. Lithium response in unipolar versus bipolar depression. *American Journal of Psychiatry,* 1972, *129,* 44-47.

Gottfries, C.G. Clinical trial with the monoamine oxidase inhibitor tranylcypromine on a psychiatric clientele. *Acta Psychiatrica Scandinavica,* 1963, *39,* 463.

Jenner, F.A., & Lee, C.P. Intracellular lithium and clinical response. *Lancet,* 1976, *1,* 641.

Johnstone, E.C., & Marsh, W. Acetylator status and response to phenelzine in depressed patients. *Lancet,* 1975, *1,* 567-570.

Khanna, J.L., Pratt, S., Burdizk, E.G., & Chaddha, R.L. A study of certain effects of tranylcypromine, a new antidepressant. *Journal of New Drugs,* 1963, *3,* 227.

Klein, D.R. Endogenomorphic depression: A conceptual and terminologic revision. *Archives of General Psychiatry,* 1974, *31,* 447-454.

Klein, D.F., Honigfeld, G., & Feldman, S. Prediction of drug effects by a successive screening, decision tree diagnostic technique. In P.R.A. May & J.R. Wittenbern (Eds.), *Psychotropic drug response: Advances in prediction,* Springfield, Ill.: Thomas, 1969.

Klerman, G.L., Endicott, J., Spitzer, R., & Hirschfeld, M.A. Neurotic depression: A systematic analysis of multiple criteria and meanings. *American Journal of Psychiatry,* 1979, *136,* 57-61.

Kuhn, R. The treatment of depressive states with imipramine hydrochloride. *American Journal of Psychiatry,* 1958, *115,* 459-464.

Lipton, M.A., Dimascio, A., & Killian, D.F. *Psychopharmacology: A generation of progress.* New York: Raven, 1979.

Maas, J.W. Clinical biochemistry and the choice of the appropriate medication for the psychiatric patient. In J. Mendels (Ed.), *The psychology of depression.* New York: Spectrum, 1975.

Medical Research Council. Clinical trial of the treatment of depressive illness. *British Medical Journal,* 1965, *1,* 881-886.

Mendels, J. Lithium in the treatment of depression. *American Journal of Psychiatry,* 1976, *133,* 373-378.

Morris, N.E. *A group self-instruction method for the treatment of depressed outpatients.* Doctoral dissertation, University of Toronto, 1975.

Nelson, J.C., & Bowers, M.B. Delusional unipolar depression. *Archives of General Psychiatry*, 1978, *35*, 1321-1328.

Nies, A., Robinson, D.S., Lamorn, K.R., Ravaris, C.L., & Ives, J.O. The efficacy of the MAO inhibitor phenelzine. Dose effects and prediction of response. In *Neuropsychopharmacology*, Amsterdam: Excerpta Medica, 1975.

Noyes, R., Jr., Dempsey, G.N., Blume, A., & Cavanaugh, G.L. Lithium treatment of depression. *Comprehensive Psychiatry*, 1974, *15*, 187.

Paykel, E.S. Predictors of treatment response. In S.E. Paykel & A. Cappen (Eds.), *Psychopharmacology of affective disorders*, New York: Oxford University Press, 1979.

Rehm, L.P., Fuchs, C.Z., Roth, D.M., Kornblith, S.J., & Romano, J.M. A comparison of self-control and assertion training treatments of depression. *Behavior Therapy*, 1979, *10*, 429-442.

Robins, E., & Guze, S.B. Classification of depression. In T.A. Williams, M.M. Katz, & J.A. Shields (Eds.), *Recent advances in the psychobiology of depressive illness*, Washington, D.C.: DHEW publication 70-9053, 1972.

Robinson, D.S., Nies, A., & Ravaris, C.L. Clinical pharmacology of phenelzine. *Archives of General Psychiatry*, 1978, *35*, 629-635.

Rosenthal, S., & Guderman, J.E. The self-pitying constellation in depression. *British Journal of Psychiatry*, 1967, *113*, 485-489.

Rush, A.J., & Beck, A.T. Adults with affective disorders. In M. Hersen & A.S. Bellack (Eds.), *Behavior therapy in the psychiatric setting*, Baltimore: Williams & Wilkins, 1978.

Rush, A.J., Beck, A.T., Kovacs, M., & Hollon, S. Comparative efficacy of cognitive therapy and pharmacotherapy in the treatment of depressed outpatients. *Cognitive Therapy and Research*, 1977, *1*, 17-37.

Schmickley, V.G. *The effects of cognitive-behavior modification upon depressed outpatients*. Doctoral dissertation, Michigan State University, 1976.

Selikoff, I.J., Robitzek, E.H., & Ornstein, G.G. Toxicity of hydrazine derivatives of isonicotinic acid in the chemotherapy of human tuberculosis. *Quarterly Bulletin of the Sea View Hospital*, 1952, *13*, 17.

Shader, R.I. *Manual of psychiatric therapeutics*. Boston: Little, Brown, 1975.

Waskow, I.E., & Parloff, M.B. *Psychotherapy change measures*. Washington, D.C.: DHEW publication (ADM) 74-120, 1975.

Weissman, M.M., Prusoff, B.A., Dimascio, A., Neu, C., Goklaney, M., & Klerman, G. The efficacy of drugs and psychotherapy in the treatment of acute depressive episodes. *American Journal of Psychiatry*, 1979, *136*, 555-558.

West, E.D., & Dally, P.J. Effects of iproniazid in depressive syndrome. *British Medical Journal*, 1959, *1*, 1491.

Winokur, G., Clayton, P., & Reich, T. *Manic depressive illness*. St. Louis: Mosby, 1968.

Special Population Groups

PART IV

Active Treatment of Childhood Depression

Theodore A. Petti

Clinically significant depressed or dysphoric mood among children is being recognized with increasing frequency by clinicians, and treatment strategies are being devised for its amelioration. Most clinicians agree that there are large numbers of depressed children who need treatment. Within any given clinic population the proportion of depressed children is surprisingly high. Among those seen for outpatient care, the estimates vary upward to 12% to 20%, and even as high as 63%, for children presenting to educational diagnostic clinics with problems of deviant behavior and poor school performance (Weinberg et al., 1973). Murray (1970) found that over 60% of a sample of schoolchildren referred for evaluation had four or more groups of symptoms that he considered to be diagnostic of depression. He noted that the combination of depression and aggression, as well as school nonattendance, seems to occur quite frequently in childhood.

There are, of course, lower estimates of the general incidence of childhood depression. Rutter and associates (1970), in a study on the Isle of Wight, demonstrated that only 2 of 1000 young boys demonstrated "pure" depression. Kashani and Simonds (1979) recently reported that 1.6% of children whose parents participated in a family health plan or who were delivered at a university hospital showed clear-cut depression. However, they reported that about 12% of the children demonstrated clinically significant sadness and/or depression. The proportion of depressed children in residential settings approaches 50% or more (Petti et al., 1980).

Given the prevalence of depressive symptoms among children, the development of treatment strategies to alleviate such symptoms is an important issue. Psychopharmacological agents have been found efficacious for both depressed adults (Davis, 1976) and children (Petti et al., 1980; Petti & Wells, 1980; Puig-Antich et al., 1978). However, there has been public concern over the use of psychotropic drugs with children. The trend to refrain from drug use has stemmed in part from the development of behavior-oriented learning techniques that have been touted as adjuncts or alternatives, in some instances, to drug therapies.

A major problem, prior to instituting treatment, is to make the diagnosis of depression. A review of the literature concerning this vexing problem has been presented elsewhere (Petti, 1978). Diagnostic criteria range from the soft "depressive equivalents" described by Toolan (1962), which are seen as manifestations of depression leading to an inference of its existence, to the very strict criteria of Puig-Antich and associates (1978) and Kashani and Simonds (1979). Hollon (1970) considered depression to be a major causative factor in poor school performance and listed depressive features as feelings of inadequacy, worthlessness, rejection by others, helplessness, hopelessness, and guilt. Glaser (1967) described "masked depressions" as existing when there are expressed feelings of hopelessness, inadequacy, helplessness, worthlessness, and rejection by others that do not correspond to the patient's immediate environment or the examiner's observation of the actual situation. More detailed descriptions of depressive diagnosis and symptoms may be found elsewhere (McConville & Boag, 1976; Petti, 1978; Puig-Antich et al., 1978; Schulterbrandt & Raskin, 1977).

Clinicians should remain alert to the possibility of depression as a symptom complex that demands attention when a child presents with a history that includes prolonged periods of sadness, unhappiness, or loneliness, recent periods of moodiness and irritability, and negative or oppositional behavior. These patients should also experience a decrease in self-esteem, as manifest by excessive guilt, demeaning self-statements, feelings of worthlessness or hopelessness, and suicidal ideation or suicide attempts. These are the core symptoms around which other categories of depression-related behaviors can cluster. These other behaviors include aggressive or assaultive activity that is out of character for the individual child, disturbances in sleep and school performance decreased desire for socialization, somatic complaints, and changes in energy level or in appetite. When a child meets such criteria, as defined in the Bellevue Index of Depression (Petti, 1978), the Weinberg criteria (Weinberg et al., 1973), the unmodified Research Diagnostic Criteria (RDC) (Puig-Antich et al., 1978), or the DSM-III criteria (Kashani & Simonds, 1979), a program should be implemented to deal with the depressive disorder.

Wide-ranging therapeutic approaches have been used in the treatment of depressed children, and, in general, each reflects the hypothesized cause of the disorder as viewed by the therapist. A number of case reports (Bene, 1975; Furman, 1974; Sacks, 1977), have presented a psychoanalytically oriented approach. Cytryn and McKnew (1979) advocated the use of short-term hospitalization for effective treatment. Behavioral and active treatments of depressed children will be described later in this chapter.

A number of uncontrolled studies have demonstrated that tricyclic antidepressants such as imipramine (Tofranil) and amitriptyline are effective in treating depressed children (Ossofsky, 1974; Puig-Antich et al., 1978; Weinberg et al., 1973). A review of this literature is available (Petti, 1980). Several workers have described multimodal approaches (McConville & Boag, 1976; Petti et al., 1980; Petti & Wells, 1980). We believe this is the most efficacious and most efficient program for treating depressed children, and it will be described in more detail later.

Behavioral Approaches in Childhood Psychotherapy

Many reviews of the history of behavioral or active therapies with children have been presented (Gelfand & Hartman, 1968; Graziano, 1971; Yates, 1970). Some of the earliest uses of learning theory in the treatment of deviant behavior have been listed by Yates (1970). A number of recent publications have dealt exclusively with behavioral or active treatment of children (Graziano, 1971, 1975; Lahey & Kazdin, 1977; Marholin, 1978; Phillips & Ray, 1980; Pizzat, 1973).

The principles of learning theory have gradually been accepted as applicable to clinical disorders of childhood. The number of reports dealing with behavioral treatment of childhood psychologic disorders has maintained an exponential growth pattern. The history of this development is enlightening and reflects the primary concerns of clinicians in each decade. These active treatments are in stark contrast to the more psychoanalytic approach that has been the predominant form of therapy. Greenwald (1967) noted the difference, characterizing active psychotherapy as "being concerned with those techniques that focus directly on the removal of symptoms," whereas insight-oriented therapies are variations of psychoanalysis focusing on the dynamic forces that motivate behavior.

Rationale for Active Treatment of Depressed Children

There have been various cognitive and behavioral models postulated to account for depression that tend to augment the physiological view of the problem. These theories have been succinctly outline by Akiskal and McKinney (1975). Despite the considerable amount of work that has been done with adults, attention to this aspect of depression in children has been glaringly absent. In the cognitive model of depression, the symptoms manifested are depressed levels of motivation, mood, and behavior, resulting mainly from the person's distorted negative ways of thinking (Kovacs & Beck, 1977). Such persons see themselves as deficient, helpless, and hopeless, and their view of life is influenced by the triad of negative conceptions of themselves, their experiences, and their future (Beck, 1967). In a recent publication, Kovacs and Beck (1977) restated the possibility of a circular feedback model of depression in which affect feeds into cognition and vice versa, and they addressed a major shortcoming, attempting to explain how such persistently negative views are created. However, it is rare for even the most depressed children to manifest the triad in as completely negative a manner as is found in adults, largely because of developmental factors. It is easy to postulate a course in which the symptoms observed in children (e.g., depressed affect, lowered energy levels, poorly directed negative behavior) and their lack of skills to derive positive reinforcement from the environment could lead to the negative triad so dramatically described by Beck (1967). In addition, it should be noted that these inappropriate behaviors can be exacerbated as children grow into adults.

The theory of learned helplessness (Seligman, 1973) depicts another view of how the negative cognition of depression is derived and also provides a model that accounts for much of the prior experience reported with hospitalized depressed emotionally disturbed children. This theory of depression is based on experimental work with animals. The relationship to clinical depression rests on similarities between the nonadaptive passive behavior in animals and the inability of patients to initiate new behaviors that would free them from aversive situations. In many respects, the treatment for learned helplessness in dogs closely resembles the cognitive approach of Beck. That is, the animal is forced to learn to respond in a way that will provide reinforcement for appropriate action. This model can help explain the phenomenon of depression in children. For example, depressed hospitalized children exposed to repeated episodes of inescapable aversive situations may be left with impairment in their future adaptive behaviors in similar environments. In addition, the failure to respond often generalizes to other situations. Thus these children are exposed to consecutive trials in which they cannot obtain reinforcement, and they develop low self-esteem, hopelessness, helplessness, and depression.

A model that most nearly approaches what can best be measured in terms of treatment is the one proposed by Lewinsohn and associates (1970). As in the Beck (1967) and Seligman (1973) models, pathological habits that have become established through continued practice are the primary areas for remediation. In this model, depression results from two causes: decreases in the types of activities that normally would provide pleasant experiences, either through avoidance of such activities or because of a decrease in the number of situations that could provide the required positive reinforcement; increases in behaviors such as complaining, whining, and delay in responding or failure to respond to environmental cues.

Lewinsohn and associates (1970) noted that treatment should concentrate more on the low rate of response-contingent positive reinforcement than on the total amount of positive reinforcement that is available in the environment. An increase in positive experiences also seems to be suggested by Beck and Seligman. The social environment is seen as reinforcing the depressive behavior by sympathy giving, which, over time, increases the self-pity of depressed persons and leads to a decrease in the elicitation of even this unhealthy intercourse. As a result, depressed persons become even more isolated. Moreover, depressed persons have great difficulty in programming their lives, and as compared with normals they have great deficits in social skills (i.e., the instrumental behaviors that will elicit positive reinforcement from others, not behaviors that will be punished or ignored by others). Lewinsohn and Atwood (1969) reported that the issues are complicated by the observation that depressed persons actually know what to do, and when questioned they say that they do it, but in practice they do not act appropriately. Lewinsohn's techniques are described in a series of reports based on a teaching model for a course entitled "Coping with Depression."

In all the models described here, lack of reinforcement for social interactions and frequent withdrawal from social interactions are recognized. These difficulties may account for Lewinsohn's emphasis on a combination of active therapies, including social skills training, cognitive transformation (thinking more positively), systematic muscular relaxation, and scheduled involvement in pleasant events as major components in treating depression.

Another reason for active treatment of childhood depression involves the inadequate or ineffective parenting of caretakers who themselves are depressed. Such children are then faced with double obstacles. First, they do not have proper role models to emulate in regard to getting pleasure from life, which normally would be derived from being effective in interpersonal interactions. Second, there is no one to model the learning of general approaches to problem solving. Philips (1979), a psychoanalyst, reported on five cases of depression in children whose parents were themselves depressed. In each of these cases the depressed parent was the mother. Philips noted that the predominant response to the mother's depression was passive or active aggression and that the child's response to the mother's depression was aggression directed outward or inner passivity and withdrawal, ultimately culminating in depression. Philips noted that the underlying themes in therapy for these children were related to the children's efforts to compensate for the experienced repetitive bereavement by the few (though deviant) channels available to the children for such expressions.

McLean (1976) described parental depression as incompatible with effective parenting, and he concluded that children of depressed parents have a great deal of difficulty in developing a strong sense of self-esteem because their parents are less capable of effective parenting. These children repeatedly observe ineffective interpersonal coping strategies because of the defective parenting with which they are in contact. Teaching such children more appropriate ways of dealing with their environments through effective modeling by therapists, teaching them how to gain access to positive reinforcement, and helping them develop more effective interpersonal skills for problem solving and conflict resolution are critical to helping them develop a sense of self-esteem and gain a greater sense of control over their environments.

A number of techniques for active therapy for depressed children have been employed. Many have been used to treat the symptoms related to the depression, but there have been recent reports in which the depression itself has been the targeted behavior. The techniques range from social-skills/assertion training to biofeedback, antidepressant medication, token economy systems, contingency management systems, and cost-response models.

Active Therapy for Symptoms Related to Depression

Various active therapies have been used in the treatment of behaviors and symptoms frequently related to depression in children. Behavioral approaches have been directed toward enuresis, school phobia or refusal, hyperactivity, aggression, social withdrawal and isolation, and gastrointestinal disorders. All of these symptom complexes have been associated to some extent with depression.

Enuresis was one of the first symptoms related to depression in children that was treated with a behavioral approach, the bell-and-pad method (Mowrer & Mowrer, 1938). Lovibond and Coote (1970) provided a more detailed description of this widely used procedure. It has been reported to be more effective for childhood enuresis than psychotherapy (DeLeon & Mandell, 1966) or limited drug therapy. More complete reviews are available (Doleys, 1977; Siegel & Richards, 1978).

Bladder control training for retention has also been extensively researched and has been shown to have some promise as an effective treatment for childhood enuresis and to be deserving of further investigation (Doleys, 1977). Targeting the oppositional behavior of a 5-year-old boy, Nordquist (1971) used an ABAB design to effectively eliminate his enuresis, and this success was maintained during the 16-month follow-up period. The various other approaches used in the treatment of childhood enuresis (Doleys, 1977) include punishment, operant conditioning, and a combination of the bell-and-pad method and bladder control training. Azrin and associates (1974) reported that the latter is more effective than the bell-and-pad method alone; however, an attempt at replication of the study failed to demonstrate the same dramatic results (Doleys, 1977).

School phobia or refusal to attend school often accompanies the clinical syndrome of depression in children, and numerous case studies are available describing behavioral techniques used with school refusal (Gelfand, 1978; Richards & Siegel, 1978; Schaefer & Millman, 1977). Defining school attendance as the target behavior, Ayllon and associates (1970) treated an 8-year-old black girl with a positive reinforcement program. The child responded with voluntary, noncoerced, pleasureable attendance at school and an improvement in grades from a C average to A's and B's.

Systematic desensitization has also been used successfully with school-phobic children: The child is trained to relax and then assists in developing a hierarchy of stimuli that elicit the targeted behavior or symptom, finally progressing through the hierarchy until the most noxious stimuli can be imagined without invoking the targeted symptom or behavior. Richards and Siegel (1978) noted that many case studies support its use, but few controlled studies are available to demonstrate any superiority over other therapies.

Hyperactive, agitated behavior has also been noted to be a "depressive equivalent" or symptom in the depressive syndrome of children. In fact, side effects of stimulant medication control of hyperactive/distractible behavior noted in up to 20% of these children have been dysphoria and excessive crying. Such children generally have not been screened for depression. Ayllon and Rosenbaum (1977) described a variety of behavioral approaches used in the treatment of disruption of hyperactivity in school settings. They described the role of the teacher in controlling misbehavior through the use of teacher attention and contingent reinforcement by means of verbal praise and ignoring or expressing disapproval of inappropriate behaviors. They also described the role of peers in controlling misbehavior by removing peer attention to misconduct through the use of group contingency. Token systems have also been demonstrated to be highly effective in minimizing misbehavior in classroom settings. Feedback (implemented by informing children of their behavior ratings), a reinforcement schedule (implemented by differentially reinforcing low rates of misbehavior in the classroom), and the use of free time as a reinforcer were all found to show positive results. A form of self-regulation in which children evaluate their own behaviors and provide their own reinforcement has also been found to be highly effective.

Other successful methods of dealing with disruption and hyperactivity in school settings include a delayed time-out procedure, home-based reinforcement in which appropriate behavior in school is reinforced in the home, rearranging the classroom structure so that more time is spent with systematically presented academic instruction, instruction in appropriate behavior and modeling of that behavior, setting time limits for completion of academic tasks, and reinforcement for academic achievement and for nondisruption (Ayllon & Rosenbaum, 1977).

Backman and Firestone (1979) reviewed the literature on psychopharmacological and behavioral approaches to the treatment of hyperactive children. They concluded that the available data suggest superior efficacy for methylphenidate over behavioral approaches for the treatment of hyperactivity, particularly regarding short-term improvement in classroom behavior and attentional process. Academic performance seemed to improve more with behavioral treatments conducted in special research classrooms. They suggested that a combination of various techniques would provide a more efficacious regimen than any one technique or medication alone. This is borne out by the result of Gittelman-Klein and associates (1976) and Williamson and associates (1981).

In the latter study, an extremely hyperactive and distractible 9-year-old boy from a chaotic home situation, who met modified RDC criteria for depression (Petti, 1978), was treated in the following sequential manner, following an initial baseline period (A); dextroamphetamine (B); return to baseline (A); reintroduction of dextroamphetamine (B); dextroamphetamine plus instruction (BC); dextroamphetamine, instruction, and modeling and guided practice (BCD); finally, dextroamphetamine, instruction, modeling and guided practice, and goal setting, feedback, and reinforcement (BCDE). Feedback and goal setting were provided by a Large Scale Integrated Activity monitor. The results showed marked improvement in a variety of measures. Classroom on-task behavior, for example, with an interrater reliability of 92% (range 80%–100%), when from means of 73% on A to 96% on B, back down to below the initial baseline level on A, up to 85% on B, and stabilized at an average of 94% for the final three phases. There were marked reductions in mechanical and gross motor behaviors in a variety of settings, and time-sampled appropriate behaviors with peers were optimal during the final phases. The child's depression also improved considerably, and qualitatively his interactions with peers became more positive.

Douglas and associates (1976) have demonstrated how modeling, self-verbalization, and self-reinforcement techniques can be used to train more adaptive behaviors in hyperactive children. These children were taught more deliberate and more effective strategies for coping with social situations, academic problems, and cognitive tasks. There were significant differences on pretest, posttest, and follow-up comparisons between the 18 boys who received the cognitive training program and the 11 boys in the control group who had been matched for age, IQ, and measures of hyperactivity and impulsiveness. There was also some generalization of this training to dealing with responses to frustrating situations: "it could appear that the training we gave in considering consequences of events and of one's own actions had a generalized effect on the ability of children to cope less aggressively and more effectively with frustration at least when it is portrayed in story form" (Douglas et al., 1976, p. 403).

Biofeedback has been used effectively in the treatment of hyperactivity. Lubar and Shouse (1977) have presented a review of this literature. However, there is a paucity of clinical data related to the use of biofeedback with children (Conners, 1979). Lubar and Shouse have demonstrated that hyperactivity can be controlled with biofeedback using sensorimotor rhythm (SMR), and they have suggested that the combination of stimulant medication and SMR conditioning leads to more desirable changes in hyperkinetic behaviors than does use of the drug alone and that such positive changes are maintained following withdrawal of medication. The greatest improvement was a decrease in undesirable behaviors, mainly those of a motor nature.

Somatic complaints, including those involving the digestive tract, frequently accompany depression in both adults and children (Brumbach et al., 1977). Behavioral approaches have been highly effective in treating a number of symptoms and behaviors related to the gastrointestinal system, including vomiting and rumination, anorexia and food refusal, obesity, encopresis, and constipation. The techniques used include punishment, manipulation of social contingencies, operant techniques, token economy systems, systematic desensitization, multiple behavioral approaches, biofeedback, and hypnosis with reinforcement (Conners, 1979; Graziano, 1975; Schaefer & Millman, 1977; Siegel & Richards, 1978).

Aggressive, impulsive behavior (Burks & Harrison, 1962) and oppositional behavior (Symonds, 1970) have been linked to childhood depression. Many children act angry or misbehave as a way of handling feelings of inadequacy, sadness, or insecurity. Wide-ranging interventions have been used in treating such behaviors. Patterson and associates at the Oregon Research Institute have developed a series of assessment procedures and interventions directed to the treatment of hyperaggressive children (Patterson, 1974). These interventions are conducted in the home by training the parents in the use of social learning, particularly contingency contracting, and they include withdrawal of privileges, loss of points on a token system, the use of time-out procedures, and the use of positive reinforcement for appropriate behaviors. The emphasis is on modifying the coercive family system and teaching parents the fundamental concepts of child management and appropriate norms of child behavior. Socially aggressive behavior often can exclude or prevent children from receiving positive reinforcement from their environments. Modeling procedures have resulted in short-term decreases in aggression (Kirkland & Thelen, 1977). Maloney and associates (1978) described a number of behavioral strategies to treat antisocial behavior, such as contingent praise and attention, behavioral contracting, and token economy. They suggested that it is necessary to add skills teaching methods to token economies to provide alternative prosocial behaviors.

A series of studies by Camp and associates at the University of Colorado have delineated some of the difficulties with verbal mediation of conflict for young aggressive boys. Much of this difficulty relates to the sense of helplessness and inability to cope that such children experience. In a well-designed study (Camp et al., 1977), 12 aggressive second-grade boys participated in a training program that involved modeling and verbalization of cognitive activity in order to foster the use of verbal mediation skills around both cognitive and interpersonal problems. This "think aloud" program for developing self-control in these 6- to 8-year-old boys was highly successful in fostering prosocial behaviors and significantly improving their patterns of performance on cognitive tests. Major emphasis was placed on assisting these children in developing answers to the following four basic questions: What is my problem? What is my plan? Am I using my plan? How did I do? The program lasted for 6 weeks, and its one shortcoming was that the treated aggressive boys did have some difficulty in channeling their voluminous verbal output. Overall, this type of program offers great hope for teaching such children the skills necessary to function more effectively in interpersonal situations.

Bornstein and associates (1980) reviewed the rationale for providing aggressive children with social skills training. It was hypothesized that aggressive behavior as a response to frustration would be reduced if these children were instructed in the appropriate expression of feelings, social and adaptive interaction, and assertion of rights and needs. The subjects were two boys, ages 8 and 12 years, and two girls, ages 9 and 12 years, who were inpatients at a children's psychiatric unit. Direct ward observations and past history indicated that each child manifested high levels of aggression with peers and inability to express dissatisfaction or to be assertive in a nonhostile manner. All four children were noted to be deficient in appropriate interpersonal behaviors on the unit and in a creative dramatics therapy group when asked to role-play social interactions. These scenes paralleled those used for the primary dependent measures of behavioral assessment, the Behavioral Assertiveness Test for Children (BAT-C) (Bornstein et al., 1977).

Training consisted of three sessions for each of the targeted behaviors: eye contact as a ratio of speech duration; decreasing one's hostile tone of voice; requesting new behaviors. Overall assertiveness was monitored but not specifically trained. One subject was rated on another variable: smiling in response to positive prompts. The results indicated substantial improvements for each child for each targeted behavior, and the changes occurred only after sequential training for each behavior. Overall assertiveness improved moderately. Generalization of improvement was inconsistently noted and quite variable at follow-up assessment. The authors noted that the variability of results highlights the necessity for careful, individualized assessment and treatment planning for social skills training with children.

Slaby and Crowley (1977) reported decreases in verbal and physical aggression in a group of children whose teacher used contingent attention to reinforce verbally cooperative interactions. The rate of cooperative behaviors increased, but it decreased when the teacher began attending to verbal aggression. The aggressive behaviors also increased in this second phase.

A number of other studies have demonstrated how the effect of training in more positive social interaction can lead to improvement in socially desirable behavior and can allow these children effective alternative behaviors to replace their negative repertoire. Combs and Slaby (1977) provided a well-reasoned and comprehensive review that conveys the rationale for social skills training with aggressive, unpopular children. Drawing on work from a number of investigations, they noted that the aggressive behavior manifested by children considered unpopular usually is unprovoked, immature, disruptive, and undirected, as compared with the aggression manifested by children who are well accepted by their peers; moreover, aggression as a response to physical provocation is generally seen by peers as acceptable. They also cited data indicating that popular children differ from unpopular classmates on two of six designated tasks ("making friends" and "referential-communication"), in addition to giving and receiving more positive reinforcement, and they noted that these may be crucial issues in helping these children learn socially adequate behaviors to replace their unsocialized, aggressive, or immature behaviors.

Elder and associates (1979) reported the successful training of four adolescent patients who demonstrated verbally and physically aggressive behaviors on the adolescent unit of a state psychiatric hospital. Training these youths consisted in teaching them the appropriate skills of interrupting, requesting new behaviors, and responding to negative communications of peers, such as teasing and threats. Using a multiple baseline across the three behavior designs, with the therapist providing instructions, modeling, and feedback, these workers were able to demonstrate increased social appropriateness to both training and generalization in role-playing scenes, as well as in extratreatment settings, including decreases in fines from the token economy system and decreased time in seclusion. At follow-up, three of the subjects were maintaining residence in the community more than 6 months after hospital discharge. These workers asserted that their subjects learned both to punish and to acquire rewards from their peers in socially acceptable ways, and they believe that social skills training offers aggressive adolescents a better chance for survival than would punishment or reinforcement of incompatible behaviors.

Depressed children who do not attempt to deny or hide their dysphoric feelings frequently become withdrawn or isolated. Numerous behavioral interventions have been used to treat these target symptoms. Coaching as a training method to allow isolated third-grade and fourth-grade children to become more popular has been described by Oden and associates (Combs & Slaby, 1977). The procedure consisted in (1) individually teaching the isolated children how to play with other children, (2) practicing these techniques, (3) playing selected social games with peers, and (4) being given feedback on their play. The individual teaching centered on the actual participation in play, the concepts involved in sharing and taking turns, and ways to communicate verbally with peers and provide assistance to peers in a supportive manner. These children were compared with a group who played the same games with peer partners, but without the coaching, and with a group who played without peer partners. Significant pretreatment-to-posttreatment effects in sociometric ratings by peers were attained only by the coached group. These children maintained these gains on 1-year follow-up ratings conducted by a different group of peers.

Gelfand (1978) described behavior therapy in the treatment of social withdrawal and negative emotional states in children, listing a number of investigators and noting the treatment method, treatment length, outcome, and duration of the period for which follow-up data were collected. Gelfand (1978) also noted that shyness and social withdrawal were responsive to behavioral approaches, and her review of the literature of "socialization experiences," which involve placing socially isolated children in collaborative interactions with other children, offering advice to their parents, or involving the children in nondirective play therapy, demonstrated that such techniques have limited effectiveness. Gelfand referred to earlier work by Anderson, Paige, and Jack showing that social assertiveness can be increased by providing nursery-school children with methods for coping and praising them for good performances.

O'Connor (1969) has demonstrated that modeling is an effective treatment for decreasing the social withdrawal of certain nursery-school children. A modeling film, as compared with a film of dolphins swimming, was highly effective in increasing social interactions among children who had been designated as being socially withdrawn and who had low peer interaction rates as determined by classroom observations. At follow-up, children who had viewed the modeling film were indistinguishable from socially normal classmates on observations conducted shortly after the film. The other group of withdrawn children, who viewed the control film, were distinguishable from their normal classmates because of their low interactions. The raters were blind to the condition. In a later study, O'Connor (1972) found that the effects of modeling were still evident at 3-week follow-up observations, during which time the interaction rates remained at normal levels. A similar group of children were treated by graduate students who praised them for social approaches to peers, and their results were less durable. The children treated by the shaping procedure had returned to their own low initial baseline rates of interaction. Gelfand (1978) also discussed sources of treatment failure and noted that most of the work in treating shyness and social withdrawl in children has been with the pre-school-age group.

Weinrott and associates (1979) reviewed a number of reports describing techniques targeted at changing the response patterns of withdrawn children, and they noted that most either were single-case treatment studies or lacked adequate controls and that treatment generally focused on single behaviors rather than on the multiple deficits of such children. In a more strictly controlled protocol, these workers demonstrated significant positive changes from baseline values in social withdrawal and appropriate interactions with peers, as well as on the withdrawal scale of the Walker Problem Behavior Identification Checklist for children whose teachers were trained in the use of symbolic modeling, adult social reinforcement, and individual and group contingencies. These changes persisted through the 5-week follow-up, at which time the treated children were indistinguishable from normal peers on a variety of measures and were more sociable than the untreated controls. Perhaps even more telling are the anecdotal reports of teachers to the effect that the trained children were experiencing increased peer contact in the lunchroom and on the playground and that they were inviting and being invited by friends to one another's homes. They were also described as happier, more alert, and eager to assume tasks of greater responsibility. This study combined many of the approaches that have been used previously for treatment of withdrawn children, and it has significant relevance for treating depressed children.

An earlier pioneering study by Walker and Hops (1973) demonstrated how the use of group and individual reinforcement contingencies was effective in the modification of social withdrawal. They found that training a withdrawn subject in social interaction skills using the symbolic modeling procedure of O'Connor (1969) and then implementing a reinforcement contingency for using those skills was highly effective. So was the converse, in which after identical training of the withdrawn child, the peer group would be rewarded for initiation of appropriate interactions by that child. A combination of individual and group contingencies for initiation of social interactions by the withdrawn child following social skills training proved to be the most powerful form of change agent for such children.

A case report by Rhodes and associates (1979) detailed an important consideration in the social skills training of withdrawn or unassertive children. Using a procedure very similar to that of Bornstein and associates (1977), they trained a 15-year-old boy in three component behaviors of assertiveness (requests for new behaviors, ratio of eye contact to duration of speech, and loudness of speech) and found that he made significant gains in the first two behaviors and in overall assertiveness, but not in the third, and that the training effects generalized to his interactions with peers in his natural environment. However, his teachers noticed that some of his more aggressive peers, usually the "bullies," became physically aggressive toward the boy as a response to his assertiveness. They suggested that a "discrimination" component be built into this training protocol.

Many depressed children are socially ineffective. Allen and associates (1975) reviewed the relevant literature regarding the seriousness of social ineffectiveness among children. They then presented a successful behavior therapy group treatment program for such children that emphasized group interaction followed by development of poise and flexibility in a group setting and, finally, social play behavior outside the group. Throughout the three phases, tokens were given as tangible reinforcers for the appropriate, specified behaviors. The children were chosen for the study by means of a sociogram completed by the children in class and by identification of specific behaviors by their teachers. Children who were more socially isolated than socially inept were excluded. The 23 socially inept children who were given the behavioral group training showed significantly more social gains in the sociometric outcome evaluation than the 10 control children in the no-treatment comparison group. The social gains drawn from the reinforcement program persisted through the 12-month follow-up. The controls showed only minimal improvement.

Bornstein and associates (1977) described a training program consisting of instructions, feedback, behavioral rehearsal, and modeling in a multiple baseline analysis for training social skills in four unassertive children. The targeted behaviors selected for modification were ratio of eye contact to speech duration, loudness of speech, requests for new behaviors, and duration of speech. An overall assertiveness rating was also assessed for each child. The results indicated considerable improvement in the overall component behaviors, as well as overall assertiveness, for all four subjects. Eye contact, loudness of speech, speech duration, and requests for new behaviors were all enhanced, and the multiple baseline analysis demonstrated that the targeted behaviors were independent of one another and that the change from the baseline level was directly related to training for that specific behavior. Moreover, the authors reported generalization of the gains in social skills to untreated scenes and changes in both treated and untreated scenes that persisted through the 1-month follow-up period after treatment. The four children were assessed as unassertive, and they came from a group of 12 children who were described as excessively cooperative, passive, shy, unassertive, and conforming and had been referred by their teachers. The four subjects in this study met the criteria of deficiencies in at least three verbal and nonverbal target behaviors during the baseline assessment.

Rekers (1978), in a series of case reports, has noted the direct functional relationship between sex type behavior and reinforcement contingencies. One case was that of Carl, an 8-year-old boy who had had a variety of unsuccessful therapies to alleviate his transsexual problems and difficulties in social relationships. These behaviors were causing him to be socially isolated and a subject of ridicule; he was chronically unhappy. Behavioral treatment was aimed at decreasing his social isolation, emotional depression, and anxiety associated with the sexual deviance. Treatment was conducted across stimulus environments and across behaviors with a multiple baseline intrasubject design. Treatment settings included the home, clinic, and school. A differential social reinforcement contingency was used to shape masculine and feminine speech content. This contingency resulted in a sharp decrease in feminine speech and an increase in masculine content. There was also suppression of the feminine voice inflection, even though this behavior was not specifically treated. The mother employed a token economy reinforcement procedure in the home, targeted to increase masculine play with his brother and to decrease feminine play gestures and speech content with his sister. The teacher in school used response cost for his feminine gesture mannerisms and disobedient "brat" behaviors. The latter immediately decreased, but the feminine gestures and speech had a more gradual decline and were stimulus-specific to the setting. This necessitated reintroducing the contingencies into his new classroom the following year.

Individuals in the school and the home setting, as well as psychologists who interviewed and tested Carl, indicated that his feminine behaviors had been markedly reduced, and there was no evidence for cross-gender identification following treatment. His social and emotional adjustment was also improved markedly. His treatment was extended an additional 15 months because Carl was not able to play games or sports generally expected of boys. A specific set of shaping procedures to overcome problems of throwing and kicking was combined with a modeling program between Carl and a psychology student regarding appropriate masculine behaviors, and Carl was taken on trips to the park and beach. A follow-up 1 year beyond this additional treatment showed continuous stability of all the therapeutic gains and normalization of sexual development. Rekers (1978) did caution against using behavior therapy for a gender-disturbed child unless one is able to obtain reliable observational data on the child's sex type behavior and unless the therapist can monitor progress when the training is carried out by paraprofessionals, such as teachers and parents.

Active Therapy for Depressed Children

There have been few accounts of behavioral approaches applied to children designated as being depressed. The reasons for this, perhaps, are that the operational definition of what constitutes the components of childhood depression is elusive and that treatment of the symptom complex encounters numerous obstacles. For example, most depressed children have a sense of hopelessness, helplessness, and low self-esteem. Although these feelings are intermittent rather than constant, they are accompanied in many instances by oppositional, self-defeating, and negative behaviors or by apathy, anhedonia, and a superficial lack of motivation for change. Specific types of active therapy have included social skills training, self-monitoring, conflict resolution/assertion training, and a multimodality approach that emphasizes all these methods.

Calpin and Cinciripini (1978) described a multiple baseline analysis of social skills training for two depressed children, a 10-year-old girl and an 11-year-old boy. Both were hospitalized for severe and incapacitating behavior; both had marked difficulty with peer relationships. A systematic assessment of social skills by the Behavioral Assertiveness Test for Children (BAT-C) (Bornstein et al., 1977) demonstrated gross deficiencies in both children. Target behaviors were selected on the basis of the assessment. For the girl, these consisted of the ratio of eye contact to speech duration, the frequency of noncompliance to unreasonable requests by peers, and mean overall social skills. Target behaviors for the boy included the ratio of eye contact to speech duration, the frequency of praise statements in scenes in which such behavior would be appropriate, expressing affect, requesting new behaviors in response to unreasonable requests by peers, and mean overall social skills. The girl had a trial of antidepressant medication (imipramine) after an initial baseline was established, and she demonstrated no change in the ratio of eye contact to speech duration or in the number of noncompliance behaviors to unreasonable requests, but she did show a minimal increase in mean overall social skills, and subjectively she appeared less depressed. Both children demonstrated significant improvement following a program of instruction in appropriate interactions, modeling of these behaviors, and videotape feedback of their own responses.

The videotaped scenes were evaluated, and interrater reliability was obtained on 50% of randomly chosen sessions. They ranged from 100% for the girl's noncompliance behaviors to 85% on overall social skills and 92% for ratio of eye contact to speech duration. The reliability varied for the boy from 100% on affect expression to 71% on overall social skills. Examples of improvement include the girl's going from near-zero rates on both baseline and imipramine treatment for eye contact and noncompliance to a mean of .88 for the final five sessions for the ratio of eye contact to speech duration and the optimal 4 for 4 noncompliances during all the assessment scenes. Similar results were obtained for the generalization scenes. The boy evidenced like changes in assessed behaviors, achieving maximum levels in ratio of eye contact to speech duration, number of praise statements, requests for new behaviors, and mean overall social skills. He made some improvement on being able to make affect statements, but at 1-month and 3-month follow-ups he had dropped back to the near-zero baseline levels. His suicidal ideation had cleared, but he continued to evidence some degree of mood swings and oppositional behavior outside the training environment on the unit.

These authors made two salient points: (1) the girl was prevented from completing her social skills training and hospital treatment because her mother had difficulty in dealing with the seemingly positive changes in her daughter's behavior as perceived by the ward staff; (2) the need to program the acceptability of affect statements, such as those targeted for the boy, in the natural environment. Both suggestions relate to the often cited need to program the adults and peers in the child's natural environment to reinforce the newly acquired skills of the child.

Calpin and Kornblith (1977) reported the effects of social skills training on the interpersonal behaviors of four hospitalized children with marked aggressive behavior who met modified RDC criteria for depression. They all had chronic histories of poor peer relationships and were found to be deficient in interpersonal skills, as assessed by the BAT-C (Bornstein et al., 1977) as modified by Calpin and Cinciripini (1978). The four boys were of low average or borderline intelligence. The targeted behaviors were requested for new behaviors, affect statements, and overall social skills. Reliability was assessed as in the study of Calpin and Cinciripini (1978). The training package consisted of instructions concerning appropriate responses, modeling, behavioral rehearsal, and videotape feedback.

The training was conducted with a multiple baseline design across subjects. The mean interrater reliabilities for requests for new behaviors and affect expression were 85% and 91%, respectively, and 81% for overall social skills, with a range from 75% to 90%. Improvements on all three targeted behaviors were noted for all four boys. Follow-ups at 1 month and 3 months found three of the boys retaining many of their new skills, but one boy returned to baseline levels of functioning.

Matson and associates (1980) reported the treatment of four depressed children, two boys (9 and 11 years) and two girls (both 11 years of age). The children met modified RDC criteria (Petti, 1978) and had failed to respond to an intensive behavior-oriented milieu. Various approaches were tested in this study: the effectiveness of modeling and observational learning in the acquisition of social skills; the effects of social skills training on depressed, emotionally disturbed children; the benefits derived from using "booster session" training in maintaining gains with social skills training; assessing the generalization of targeted social skills from the modeling or observational learning training and the more conventional training.

The skills assessed and then trained were the following: appropriate verbal responses in particular situations, such as giving compliments, giving help or assistance, and making appropriate requests; demonstrating appropriate affect; making appropriate eye contact; demonstrating appropriate psychomotor behavior for a given situation. Scenes involving behaviors that posed problems for these children were developed for assessment. The children were also assessed by direct-care staff on the unit, who filled out questionnaires to rate six behaviors, including giving compliments, giving help, making appropriate requests, and demonstrating affect. Overall social ability and responses to negative interactions were also assessed in this questionnaire. The raters were blind to the experimental conditions. As in the previously reported studies, the training involved instruction, information feedback, modeling, role playing, and social reinforcement. A multiple baseline design across behaviors and subjects was used in the study. Verbal behavior, psychomotor behavior, affect, and eye contact were the target behaviors that were trained sequentially. The two most skilled subjects were trained first, while the two least skilled were observers. Following the attainment of criteria by the first and then the second skills-trained subjects, the other two subjects received sequential treatment. One of the most skilled and one of the least skilled children were given the booster sessions, which were identical with the social skills training sessions and were held 2.5 weeks following conclusion of the social skills training phase. Follow-up was conducted for 10 weeks after the conclusion of training.

The results indicated that social skills training effects were immediate, but the process of observing a peer demonstrating appropriate social skills was not effective. The least skilled subjects also took longer and were less consistent in their acquisition of skills. Direct-care staff ratings of the four children indicated that three showed significant improvements on the trained components, as well as on overall behavior rating, but one child did not change significantly. One of the two children who did not receive the booster sessions scored at optimum levels on follow-up. This study demonstrated that social skills could be trained in groups and that treatment gains could generalize to untreated but similar social scenes and also to the natural environment. The child whose scores did not change significantly, as rated by the direct-care staff, did generalize his treatment gains to the ward situation. Modeling alone by the more skilled subjects was ineffective in training positive social skills for the unskilled children.

Using a format similar to the BASIC ID (Lazarus, 1973), we (Petti & Wells, 1980; Petti et al., 1980) have advocated the use of a multimodal approach in the treatment of childhood depression for children hospitalized in psychiatric facilities.

Ross, for instance, was a 12.5-year-old Caucasian boy who was referred because of increasingly disruptive and uncontrolled behavior both at home and in school. He had been suspended from school for allegedly setting a fire, slashing tires and breaking windows in the neighborhood, and making homicidal threats toward neighborhood children and his parents. He also made frequent suicide threats, but no attempts. On admission to the hospital, his affect was somewhat flat, but responsive within a limited range. There was marked self-deprecatory ideation, and he would not attempt any task with which he was not already familiar. He could not name a single friend, nor any shared activities with peers. The initial interview was marked by extreme oppositionalism, with frequent responses of "I don't know" and massive denial of all problems. There was no evidence of a formal thought disorder. He did admit to minor problems of being irritable and easily annoyed, having difficulty in falling asleep, having trouble waking up in the morning, losing his interest in school, not playing with groups of children as much as before, and not wanting to attend school. He reported moderate problems with daydreaming and poor concentration in school, having a drop in his school grades, not being as friendly and outgoing as previously, and having a decreased appetite. He reported several problems with chest pain.

Ross scored very high and was positive for depression on the Bellevue Index of Depression (Petti, 1978). The early period of hospitalization was marked by extreme oppositionalism, intrusiveness into the activities of staff and peers, intense crying spells, and destructive antisocial activities that varied from minor stealing, urinating in his room, and putting toys in the toilet to flooding the bathroom, setting up staff members against each other, and instigating peer against one another.

Following successful treatment with imipramine, 200 mg/day, which decreased his depressed affect, allowed him to verbalize feelings about his situation, and resulted in his desire to make some basic changes in his behavior, Ross was begun on a self-monitoring program in which he would label and identify the social consequences of behaviors that were particularly disruptive to peer relationships, such as tattling, interfering with staff redirection, escalating other children, and taking on the staff role. Significant behavior changes were noted with the institution of this program. His participation with peers increased, and he began expressing sadness about having to leave the unit. Tapering him off medication resulted in some regression to previous behaviors. He was restarted on imipramine, 75 mg/day, and marked improvement recurred. By the time of discharge, his destructive acting-out behavior was controlled, and he showed significant improvement in relationships with peers and staff members, although interpersonal relationships still were tinged with difficulties. He was able to be verbally more expressive of his affect and concerns and usually was able to talk with someone about his feelings, rather than act immediately on impulse, as had been his previous pattern. His attempts at intrusiveness and controlling were decreased, but not absent, at the time of discharge. His affect did brighten, and he was better able to tolerate uncertainty and frustration.

A formal follow-up 2 months after discharge indicated, by parent report, marked improvement in all areas of functioning, as measured before and after treatment on the Deviant Behavior Inventory of Novick and associates (1966). At the time of admission he had averaged a total score of 55 out of a possible 237 items on the true-false inventory. At follow-up, the average was 13.5. On admission, his average score for inappropriate affect and self-feeling/interpersonal behavior was 17.5, and on follow-up it was 3. His score for the category of discipline, competition, peer relations, and delinquencies was 22.5 on admission and 7 at follow-up. The parents noted marked improvement in all areas. Ross himself reported an absence of symptoms and enthusiasm for the future. An informal follow-up 8 months later indicated that he was functioning adequately, and an exacerbation of the oppositional, destructive, and depressive symptoms had not occurred. His full-scale IQ was 106. Inpatient evaluation and treatment were deemed necessary in this case because of the severity of his symptoms. However, the judicious use of medication and the self-monitoring program are interventions that lend themselves to outpatient treatment.

Keat (1976) described multimodal therapy for two children who presented with behaviors related to depression. The pragmatic approach used by Keat is an operationalization of the BASIC ID of Lazarus (1973). The first child, a 9-year-old adopted boy, presented with problems involving cheating, stealing, inhibited expressions of feelings, tension, poor reading skills, low self-image, severe sibling rivalry, and hyperactivity. Keat described the problems and treatment strategy. The second case involved Percy, who was almost 7 years old and was having difficulties with nighttime phobias, lack of friends, sibling rivalry, and limit testing. Nocturnal enuresis and depression were also considered to be problems. Various behavioral approaches were used, employed within the format of the BASIC ID. Keat described a systematic approach to analyzing the problem and developing treatment strategies for this wide range of disorders, including dealing with the father and his depression. Both of the cases discussed by Keat (1976) allow the reader to appreciate the thought processes that make up a comprehensive therapeutic approach and are directly applicable to the treatment of depressed children.

The following case history will be used as a vehicle to integrate what has been outlined thus far concerning active treatment of depressed children. It will typify an integrated and systematic progression of treatment modalities.

Case History

Van was a 6.5-year-old Caucasian boy who was referred for treatment because of his attempt to burn down the family home. He had been evaluated at a local mental health clinic 1 year earlier because of increasing problems with aggressiveness, tantrums, whining, and "hyperactivity." These difficulties were said to have been intensified by the divorce of his parents 3 months earlier. Following this evaluation, Van entered kindergarten, and his performance was marked by aggressive behavior toward peers, disruptiveness, distractibility, and inattentiveness. A psychiatric evaluation 3 months after he started school revealed Van to be anxious, impulsive, and distractible. Gross and fine motor developmental delays were also noted. Psychological testing depicted a child with average intelligence who lacked a "sense of himself as a responsible self-controlled and intact person." Special school placement in a class for socially and emotionally disturbed children, individual dynamically oriented psychotherapy for Van, and supportive counseling for his mother were recommended.

After more than 8 months of individual therapy for Van and counseling for his mother, referral for intensive short-term hospitalization was made based on increased frequency and intensity of oppositional and noncompliant behavior and aggressive behavior with peers and a younger brother, marked by kicking, biting, and distractibility. These behaviors had worsened during the summertime; they remained the same at home, but diminished somewhat at school.

His past history was notable in a number of respects. The parents were constantly involved in marital strife, and neither the birth of Van nor that of his older brother had been planned. The mother was particularly upset at Van's birth because he was so close in age to his brother and he was not a girl. The mother was sick throughout her pregnancy with gallbladder attacks that culminated in the removal of over 40 gallstones when Van was 2 months old. Except for the unavailability of the mother during his first 4 months, Van's delivery and neonatal period had been unremarkable. He did develop colic about the time of his mother's hospitalization, which lasted for several months, and he was described as very active and a head banger. Developmental milestones were reported as normal, except for persistent nocturnal enuresis, which continued into the hospitalization period. He was described as stubborn and headstrong by both parents; temper tantrums with screaming and destructive behavior began at the age of 2.5 to 3 years. The latter behavior included breaking windows and setting three dangerous fires. Van had been described as his father's favorite, whereas his older brother was the mother's favorite. The mother scored at the upper limits for mild depression, and the maternal grandmother, who often cared for him, scored in the moderately depressed range on the Zung Inventory of Depression (Zung, 1965).

On the Bellevue Index of Depression (BID) (Petti, 1978), Van reported the following areas of depressive symptoms: severe problems with loneliness and unhappiness, moodiness, irritability, easy crying, negativism, self-deprecatory ideation, beliefs of persecution (all items related to aggressive behavior and agitation and restless sleep); mild problems with falling asleep and early morning awakening; chronic problems with not being friendly and outgoing, bedwetting, and being tired a great deal. His mother corroborated each of these ratings and added that decreased socialization was more extensive than Van had reported.

Hospital Course *Physical and Mental Status Examination.* On admission, Van presented as an attractive, well-developed 6.5-year-old white male with alternating strabismus. The neurological examination revealed multiple nonfocal signs, such as difficulty with graphesthesia, stereognosis, gross motor tasks, two-point discrimination, and persistence measures. No unusual movements or mannerisms were noted, but he did demonstrate much impulsive, intrusive gross motor activity, and he was distractible and fidgity. Oppositional, negative, and silly behaviors were present at a moderate level. He appeared mildly depressed, but not suicidal, homicidal, delusional, or psychotic.

Baseline observations. During the first 3 weeks of hospitalization, Van exhibited much aggressive, oppositional, and negative behavior. He occasionally requested punishment and actively sought time-outs in a quiet room and in locked seclusion for assaultive or destructive behavior. In psychoeducational testing he required eight sessions to complete a basic battery, and he demonstrated fear and anxiety, particularly in paper/pencil tasks and tasks requiring independent functioning, because of his overwhelming need for reassurance and direct one-to-one supervision. His attention span and concentration level were adequate until he met a task that had the potential for frustration. His IQ (verbal 101, performance 100, full-scale 100) on the WISC-R was well within normal levels. No evidence for a specific learning disability was found. In the classroom, his behavior and performance were adequate. Disruptive behaviors consisted of "calling out, pouting and defying authority." He was noted to respond "to positive reinforcement and requires firm and consistent limits."

The mother and her mother were noted to be tired and exhausted when observed in a family art evaluation; the mother and grandmother appeared irritated by Van's reasonable requests for attention. The grandmother was critical and often threatened to punish, particularly the older brother, and she gave virtually no positive attention. Van was cooperative and pleasant during the session, but his brother, who had been described previously as better behaved, appeared extremely tense, uncomfortable, negative, oppositional, and whining in an attention-getting manner. The grandmother appeared to be a stronger figure in the family than her daughter. The father failed to keep appointments for the family evaluation and continued his previous pattern of sporadic involvement. The mother and grandmother were continuing their twice-weekly counseling sessions at the child guidance center. Interactions between Van's father and mother were noted to be clearly dysfunctional. Laboratory studies, including basic and special procedures, were within accepted limits. Speech, hearing, and language assessments were normal, except for slightly reduced hearing bilaterally. A social skills assessment indicated several deficits that will be described later.

With this multiproblem child from a multiproblem family, the following treatment plan was developed to deal comprehensively with this child's depression and deviant behavior. Targeted problems included the following: unsocialized aggression, depression, inadequate socialization skills, family dysfunction, and performance anxiety in the classroom or testing setting. We elected to target the social deficits and family dysfunction prior to considering the use for medication.

Supportive Psychotherapy, Dynamically Oriented The outpatient therapist who had been treating Van continued to see him weekly throughout the hospitalization. The goal of this modality was to assist Van in developing greater insight into his behavior, through the sharing of feelings. Except for the relationship aspect of this behavior, little was gained from this relatively nondirective approach. The relationship to the therapist remained very positive, and Van expressed pleasure in anticipation of its continuation beyond his discharge from the hospital.

Structured Milieu Therapy, Behaviorally Oriented A positively oriented milieu therapy that uses a time-out procedure for specified behaviors related to noncompliance and assaultive or aggressive behaviors and encourages development of internal controls by the child is routinely available at this unit. The goals for Van and other children admitted to the unit are to provide them with sufficient appropriate reinforcement to allow them to develop a greater sense of self-worth, to decrease their sense of lack of control and learned helplessness, to decrease their need to obtain negative attention by negative behaviors, and to increase their adaptive social interactions.

In Van's case, specific goals included decreasing the level of time-outs and locked seclusions by at least 50% and subjective assessment of his use of social skills appropriately in conflict situations. Other expectations included attainment of a more positive self-concept and consistent demonstration of "adaptive sharing of feelings, ability to make two positive self-statements (per day), accept redirection, and name one friend." A program was initiated to increase his frequency of adaptive peer interactions and to decrease the behaviors that caused peers to avoid him. Specific targets included lowering his voice level to an acceptable range and decreasing his touching and shoving behaviors.

Wearing his glasses regularly and complete cessation of his tendency to damage or destroy them was one goal related to well-child care that directly reflected on his self-esteem and self-concept. Without his glasses he had great difficulty in reading and hence would be unable to attain the satisfaction of high achievement—something that is highly reinforcing. He had broken many pairs of glasses in the past.

The rewards for achieving the goals in his program involved situations that would provide him with extensions of his behavioral programs toward increasing his self-esteem and adaptive interactions with peers. Examples of reinforcers chosen by Van included serving himself at breakfast, being able to spend his "light time" before bed on the unit with peers and staff, and going on short excursions with a peer he chose and a staff person. Material rewards such as an extra fruit drink for breakfast or for a snack, chocolate milk with a meal, or items from the reinforcement closet were also available.

Psychoeducational Therapy The primary goal of this intervention with depressed children is to get them "turned back on" to school. Most depressed children have used school as the forum to show their depression, and many have academic deficits as a result of this. Also, a large proportion of depressed children have either specific learning disabilities or major areas of academic dysfunction. We routinely address these issues by first assessing the level of school functioning, identifying areas of strength that we can use and problems that require work, and then developing and implementing specific interventions.

Van did not require such a major undertaking. What we wanted to do was maximize his academic success by praising his positive achievements and, just as important, provide him with teacher-pleasing behaviors that not only would make him manageable in the classroom but also would make him someone his teacher and his peers would consider a good student and great pal, respectively. We wanted to enhance school as a conflict-free sphere so that one area of positive social and achievement reinforcement would be available to provide him with some immunity to the potentially destructive future conflicts at home. In school, specific behavioral goals included achieving above the 90% level in raising his hand for the teacher's attention and remaining in his seat unless given permission to leave it.

Supportive Family Work and Parent Skills Training The mother and grandmother continued the supportive outpatient counseling they had been receiving at the child guidance center. They were noted to be more spontaneous in sharing concerns and feelings, and they were requesting help in being more assertive. The mother worked with our social worker on concrete issues such as marital conflict centering around the hospitalization and visitation. Because the children, particularly Van, were caught in the parental cross fire, we worked with the mother on handling the marital conflict in more constructive ways. Both mother and father began to participate in parent management training sessions. These sessions consisted of a series of didactic discussion, practice, and feedback components that addressed the following issues: how to observe behavior and label it; how to reinforce positive behavior; how to phrase requests in a constructive and positive manner; how to determine what to punish and how to do it in an appropriate manner, including the use of time-outs from reinforcement; how to set up behavioral programs involving contingency reinforcement. The entire thrust of this intervention related to providing the parents with a consistent approach to interacting with Van and giving them skills to ensure a home environment in which they could demonstrate sufficient control that Van and his brother would feel comfortable in growing up.

The mother continued these sessions through the hospitalization and employed them successfully with her older son (who had begun to act up as soon as Van was hospitalized) and with Van when he was home for visits. Van and his mother grew more responsive to each other through the course of the training. The father became more involved with the boys with increasing consistency, but he failed to continue with the training. Through the hospital course, the mother and father continued to meet jointly with our social worker to work on visitation rights after discharge, and both were seen to have made gains in working out conflicts in their postmarital relationship.

Social Skills Training Van had manifested numerous deficits in social skills and conflict-resolution behaviors. These included poor eye contact and moving away from anyone talking to him or with him, showing an inability to modulate his high-pitched whiny voice, swearing when addressed, withdrawing, isolating or increasing nondirected gross motor activity when anxious, and being unable to play adaptively with peers, to deal with anger-arousing situations, or to sustain any semblance of a positive interaction.

A formal social skills assessment using scenes (Matson et al., 1980) similar in style and format to those described elsewhere (Bornstein et al., 1980; Petti et al., 1980) involved the following definitions and findings:

1. Eye contact: looking at the role-model prompter while responding to the prompt: 8 out of 10.
2. Appropriate facial: demonstrating socially acceptable facial mannerisms for a particular response: 6 out of 10.
3. Appropriate motor: approaching and facing the prompter and not moving arms, legs, or torso while responding: 3 out of 10.
4. Words spoken: number of single words in the subject's response: 32.
5. Intonation: scored as 1 = flat unemotional tone and 5 = full and/or lively tone with emotional expressiveness: 27 out of 50.
6. Appropriate verbal content: verbal responses that match the scene being role-played: 8 out of 10.
7. Overall social skills: a global rating for each scene: 26 out of 50.

Thus, except for the surprisingly adequate performance on eye contact, the formal assessment substantiated our clinical impression, particularly in regard to deficits in appropriate facial and motor responses, paucity of the number of words in his responses (averaging 3.2 words per cue), inadequate vocal intonation of feeling, and overall deficits in social skills.

A program was instituted as part of a protocol for treating depressed children. Over a 4-week period he was coached at least four times per week in the manner described previously (Bornstein et al., 1980; Petti et al., 1980). He was encouraged to practice his skills on the unit and was praised for his attempts.

The results at the end of this period bore out the success of this program regarding social skills development. His eye contact and appropriate verbal content were perfect, 10 for 10. Appropriate facial expression responses went to 8, appropriate motor to 9, and intonation to 41. His total words went up to 78, or 7.8 per scene, and his overall social skills were rated at 40. On the unit he was noted to be less sassy and to display more insight into his behavior. His loudness and irritability at meals decreased. He rarely complimented others, but he did begin to request peers to allow him to join in with their play.

However, even with all these intensive interventions, he remained clinically depressed. His score on the BID increased from 57 to 68; on the School Age Depression Listed Inventory (SADLI), another interview format that rates behavior as well as self-report of depression, his score went from 52 to 64, thus indicating continued significant depression. He stated that he felt sad and unhappy as well as hopeless about not having many friends. On the unit, he reported multiple somatic complaints, being tired and having a decreased appetite. In his individual therapy, he played dead and said that he was glad to be dead because he was "ugly."

Psychopharmacologic Treatment: Tricyclic Antidepressants Because Van had been treated with what we believed was the entire range of our available therapeutic armamentarium, and because of our very positive experience with the responses of such children to tricyclic antidepressant therapy, Van was placed on imipramine therapy. The dosage was increased to 5 mg/kg/day over a 1-week period. The response was dramatic. He showed increased success on his behavior programs (90%), and he developed a "good supporting relationship" with a new roommate ("praising more easily and accepting it better"). His voice level became more appropriate. He began using his behavior program to gauge his own behavior. His BID was negative, with very few symptoms reported as problem areas. He still had difficulties with loud, silly, disruptive behavior during activities.

His medication was tapered over a period of 1 week (we now advocate that this be done over 2 weeks), and he had some minor increases in symptoms (Law et al., 1981) during a period of a few days. A few weeks later, at discharge, it was noted that his adaptive peer interactions and progress on his behavior program had increased with the medication and been maintained. He was able to use adaptive social skills. He related feeling better about himself, and he had fewer mood swings. His affect was reported as brighter, with much less irritability. It must be remarked that part of this might be attributed to his approaching discharge. However, he expressed realistic concerns about going home, his mother's ability to provide for his needs, and the potential for being torn in loyalty between his parents. We did not observe the result of greater openness and sharing that we anticipated as one of the benefits of imipramine treatment. His locked seclusions were completely eliminated as a problem, and his gross motor level dropped from 51% during time-sampled free-play observations to 13%

during the period prior to discharge. Hyperactivity was not considered a problem, even after the medication had been terminated. His peers were genuinely sorry that he was leaving them, and he expressed reciprocal feelings of missing them.

Why a Multimodal Approach? This case, presented in the lean manner it was, demonstrates the multiple roots that must be considered when diagnosing and treating depressed children. Many of the factors related to depression in adults (learned helplessness and perceived lack of control over their environments, a negative cognitive set, and inability to gain access to or receive positive reinforcers) were present in this child. One positive part of his life, school, could have been expected to cause problems for him soon, because his performance anxiety would have limited his ability to function and caused him to react in his characteristic maladaptive manner to his frustration (he had been hospitalized shortly after he had begun the first grade).

Treatment in each of the areas described was perceived as necessary to correct or attempt to help this child deal with his feelings of helpless, hopeless inadequacy. Each dealt with one part of the total picture necessary to give him a perception of internal control, the skills to face the external environment both socially and academically, and an acceptable and suitable environment, with parenting figures who would offer the external controls necessary for a secure feeling and awareness of the necessity for positive reinforcement.

This case also touches on many of the symptoms associated with depression in children and how past experience in their treatment can be applied to comprehensive treatment of significant depression in children. This child was cared for on a clinical research unit; hence the separation of two of the major active treatment modalities. Our experience has been that a total modality integrated approach is the most efficacious and most cost-effective. However, a systematic approach, a single-case approach, a multiple baseline approach (Hersen & Barlow, 1976), or a group treatment double-blind protocol may be necessary to determine which children can benefit best from less or more of these active therapeutic modalities.

An inpatient setting allows for maximum documentation of such a multimodal, multidisciplinary approach. However, aside from the highly structured milieu, all the other modalities employed for this child have ready application for outpatient or day-hospital treatment. It is difficult but not impossible to gain the cooperation of teachers and parents in monitoring and reinforcing adaptive behaviors and dealing with negative behaviors in an appropriate manner. The greater range of reinforcers available outside the hospital setting adds to the chances of success on an outpatient basis. The provision of a suitable psychoeducational component can be supplemented in the community through the employment of empathic, knowledgeable, and competent tutors. Creative solutions to decreasing negative family interactions without physical separation of the child from the home, while helping the parents approach parenting in a more efficacious manner, are quite feasible (Patterson, 1974). Social skills training for children has been conducted successfully on an outpatient basis (Bornstein et al., 1977), as have the number of other behaviorally oriented interventions described throughout this chapter. The use of tricyclic antidepressant therapy on an outpatient basis requires more graduated increases in dosage and a longer period of drug reduction than those reported for hospital work, but with careful monitoring (Petti, 1980) it can be accomplished.

In summary, depression in children that reaches clinically significant magnitude occurs frequently. This symptom complex has a multitude of causes, presents in a variety of ways, and demands comprehensive treatment. The active treatments described in this chapter provide such an approach.

REFERENCES

Akiskal, H.S., & McKinney, W.T. Overview of recent research in depression. *Archives of General Psychiatry*, 1975, *32*, 285-305.

Allen, R.P., Safer, D.J., Heaton, R., Ward, A., & Barrell, M. Behavior therapy for socially ineffective children. *Journal of the American Academy of Child Psychiatry*, 1975, *14*, 500-548.

Ayllon, T., & Rosenbaum, M.S. The behavioral treatment of disruption and hyperactivity in school settings. In B.B. Lahey, & A.E. Kazdin (Eds.), *Advances in Clinical Child Psychology*, New York: Plenum, 1977.

Ayllon, T., Smith, D., & Rogers, M. Behavioral management of school phobia. *Journal of Behavior Therapy and Experimental Psychiatry*, 1970, *1*, 125-138.

Azrin, N.H., Sneed, T.J., & Fox, R.M. Dry bed: Rapid elimination of childhood enuresis. *Behavior Research and Therapy*, 1974, *12*, 147-156.

Backman, J., & Firestone, P. A review of psychopharmacological and behavioral approaches to the treatment of hyperactive children. *American Journal of Orthopsychiatry*, 1979, *49*, 500-504.

Beck, A.T. *Depression: Clinical, experimental and theoretical aspects.* New York: Harper & Row, 1967.

Bene, A. Depressive phenomena in childhood: Their open and disguised manifestations in analytic treatment. In *Studies in child psychoanalysis: Pure and applied*, New Haven: Yale University Press, 1975.

Bornstein, M.R., Bellack, A.S., & Hersen, M. Social skills training for unassertive children: A multiple baseline analysis. *Journal of Applied Behavior Analysis*, 1977, *10*, 183-195.

Bornstein, M., Bellack, A.S., & Hersen, M. Social skills training for highly aggressive children in an inpatient psychiatric setting. *Behavior Modification*, 1980, *4*, 173-186.

Brumbach, R.A., Dietz-Schmidt, S.G., & Weinberg, W.A. Depression in children referred to an educational diagnostic center: Diagnosis and treatment and analysis of criteria and literature review. *Diseases of the Nervous System*, 1977, *38*, 529-535.

Burks, H.L., & Harrison, S.I. Aggressive behavior as a means of avoiding depression. *American Journal of Orthopsychiatry*, 1962, *32*, 416-422.

Calpin, J.P., & Cinciripini, P.M. A multiple baseline analysis of social skills training in children. Presented at Midwestern Association for Behavior Analysis, Chicago, May, 1978.

Calpin, J.P., & Kornblith, S.J., *Training of aggressive children in conflict resolution skills*. Presented at the annual convention of the Association for the Advancement of Behavior Therapy, Chicago, 1977.

Camp, B.W., Bloom, G.E., Hebert, F., & van Doorninck, W.M. "Think aloud": A program for developing self-control in young aggressive boys. *Journal of Abnormal Child Psychology*, 1977, *5*, 157-169.

Combs, M.S., & Slaby, O.A. Social skills training with children. In B.B. Lahey, & A.E. Kazdin (Eds.), *Advances in clinical child psychology*, New York: Plenum, 1977.

Conners, C.K. Application of biofeedback to treatment of children. *Journal of the American Academy of Child Psychiatry*, 1979, *18*, 143-151.

Cytryn, L., & McKnew, D.J., Jr. Affective disorders. In J. Nosphitz (Ed.), *Disturbances in development of the basic handbook of child psychiatry* (Vol. 2), pp. 321-340, 1979.

Davis, J.M. Overview: Maintenance therapy in psychiatry: II. Affective disorders. *American Journal of Psychiatry*, 1976, *133*, 1-13.

DeLeon, G., & Mandell, W.A. Comparison of conditioning and psychotherapy in the treatment of functional enuresis. *Journal of Clinical Psychology*, 1966, *22*, 326-330.

Doleys, D.M. Behavioral treatments for nocturnal enuresis in children: A review of the recent literature. *Psychological Bulletin*, 1977, *84*, 30-54.

Douglas, V.I., Parry, P., Marton, P., & Garson, C. Assessment of a cognitive training program for hyperactive children. *Journal of Abnormal Child Psychology*, 1976, *4*, 389-410.

Elder, J.P., Edelstein, B.A., & Narick, M.M. Adolescent psychiatric patients: Modifying aggressive behavior with social skills training. *Behavior Modification*, 1979, *3*, 161-178.

Furman, E. *A child's parent dies. Studies in childhood bereavement*. New Haven: Yale University Press, 1974.

Gelfand, D.M. Social withdrawal and negative emotional states: Behavior therapy. In B.B. Wolman, J. Egan, & A.O. Ross (Eds.), *Handbook of treatment of mental disorders in childhood and adolescence*, Englewood Cliffs, N.J.: Prentice-Hall, 1978.

Gelfand, D.M., & Hartman, D.P. Behavior therapy with children: A review and evaluation of research methodology. *Psychological Bulletin*, 1968, *79*, 204-215.

Gittelman-Klein, R., Klein, D.F., Abikoff, H., Katz, S., Gloisten, A.C., & Kates, W. Relative efficacy of methylphenidate and behavior modification in hyperkinetic children: An interim report. *Journal of Abnormal Child Psychology*, 1976, *4*, 361-379.

Glaser, K. Masked depression in children and adolescents. *American Journal of Psychotherapy*, 1967, *21*, 565–574.
Graziano, A.M. (Ed.). *Behavior therapy with children.* Chicago: Aldine, 1971.
Graziano, A.M. (Ed.). *Behavior therapy with children.* Chicago: Aldine, 1975.
Greenwald, H. (Ed.). *Active psychotherapy.* New York: Atherton, 1967.
Hersen, M., & Barlow, D.H. *Single case experimental designs.* New York: Pergamon Press, Inc., 1976.
Hollon, T.H. Poor school performance as a symptom of masked depression in children and adolescents. *American Journal of Psychotherapy*, 1970, *25*, 258–263.
Kashani, J., & Simonds, J.F. The incidence of depression in children. *American Journal of Psychiatry*, 1979, *136*, 1203–1205.
Kazdin, A.E. *History of behavior modification—Experimental foundations of contemporary research.* Baltimore: University Park Press, 1978.
Keat, D.B., II. Multimodal therapy with children: Two case histories. In A. Lazarus (Ed.), *Multimodal behavior therapy*, New York: Springer, 1976.
Kirkland, K.D., & Thelen, M.H. Uses of modeling in child treatment. In B.B. Lahey, & E. Kazdin (Eds.), *Advances in clinical child psychology*, New York: Plenum, 1977.
Kovacs, M., & Beck, A. An empirical-clinical approach toward a definition of childhood depression. In J.G. Schulterbrandt & A. Raskin (Eds.), *Depression in childhood: Diagnosis, treatment, and conceptual modesls,* New York: Raven, 1977.
Lahey, B.B., & Kazdin, A.E. *Advances in clinical child psychology*, New York: Plenum, 1977.
Law, W., Petti, T.A., & Kazdin, A.E. Withdrawal symptoms after graduated cessation of imipramine in children. *American Journal of Psychiatry*, 1981, *138*, 647–650.
Lazarus, A.A. Multimodal behavior therapy: Treating the "Basic ID." *Journal of Nervous and Mental Disease*, 1973, *156*, 404–411.
Lewinsohn, P.M., & Atwood, G.E. Depression: A clinical-research approach. *Psychotherapy: Theory, Research, and Practice*, 1969, *6*, 166–171.
Lewinsohn, P.M., Weinstein, M.S., & Alper, T. A behavioral approach to the group treatment of depressed persons: A methodological contribution. *Journal of Clinical Psychology*, 1970, *26*, 525–532.
Lovibond, S.H., & Coote, M.A. Enuresis. In C.G. Costello (Ed.), *Symptoms of psychopathology,* New York: Wiley, 1970.
Lubar, J.F., & Shouse, M.N. Use of biofeedback in the treatment of seizure disorders and hyperactivity. In B.B. Lahey & A.E. Kazdin (Eds.), *Advances in clinical child psychology,* New York: Plenum, 1977.
Maloney, D.M., Fixsen, D.L., & Maloney, K.B. Antisocial behavior: Behavior modification. In B.B. Wolman, J. Egan, & A.O. Ross (Eds.), *Handbook of treatment of mental disorders in childhood and adolescence,* Englewood Cliffs, N.J.: Prentice-Hall, 1978.
Marholin, D., II (Ed.). *Child behavior therapy.* New York: Gardner, 1978.
Matson, J.L., Esvelt-Dawson, K., Andrasik, F., Ollendick, T.H., Petti, T.A., & Hersen, M. Observation and generalization effects of social skills training with emotionally disturbed children. *Behavior Therapy*, 1980, *11*, 522–531.

McConville, B.J., & Boag, L.C. *Therapeutic approaches in childhood depression*. 1976.
McLean, P.D. Parent depression: Incompatible with effective parenting. In E.J. Mash, L.E. Handy, & L.A. Hamerlynck (Eds.), *Behavior modification approaches to parenting*, New York: Brunner/Mazel, 1976.
Mowrer, O.H., & Mowrer, W.M. Enuresis: A method for its study and treatment. *American Journal of Orthopsychiatry*, 1938, *8*, 436-459.
Murray, P.A. The clinical picture of depression in school children. *Journal of the Irish Medical Association*, 1970, *63*, 53-56.
Nordquist, V.M. The modification of a child's enuresis: Some response-response relationships. *Journal of Applied Behavior Analysis*, 1971, *4*, 241-247.
Novick, J., Rosenfeld, E., Bloch, D.A., & Dawson, D. Ascertaining deviant behavior in children. *Journal of Consulting Psychology*, 1966, *30*, 230-238.
O'Connor, R.D. Modification of social withdrawal through symbolic modeling. *Journal of Applied Behavior Analysis*, 1969, *2*, 15-22.
O'Connor, R.D. Relative efficacy of modeling, shaping, and the combined procedures for modification of social withdrawal. *Journal of Abnormal Psychology*, 1972, *79*, 327-334.
Ossofsky, H.J. Endogenous depression in infancy and childhood. *Comprehensive Psychiatry*, 1974, *15*, 19-25.
Patterson, G.R. Interventions for boys with conduct problems: Multiple settings, treatments, and criteria. *Journal of Consulting and Clinical Psychology*, 1974, *42*, 471-481.
Petti, T.A. Depression in hospitalized child psychiatry patients: Approaches to measuring depression. *Journal of the American Academy of Child Psychiatry*, 1978, *17*, 49-59.
Petti, T.A. Imipramine in the treatment of depressed children. In D.P. Cantwell & G. Carlson (Eds.), *Childhood depression*, New York: Spectrum, 1980.
Petti, T.A., Bornstein, M., Delamater, A., & Conners, C.K. Evaluation and multimodality treatment of a depressed pre-pubertal girl. *Journal of the American Academy of Child Psychiatry*, 1980, *19*, 690-702.
Petti, T.A., & Wells, K. Crisis treatment of a preadolescent who accidentally killed his twin. *American Journal of Psychotherapy*, 1980, *34*, 434-443.
Philips, I. Childhood depression: Interpersonal interactions and depressive phenomena. *American Journal of Psychiatry*, 1979, *136*, 511-515.
Phillips, J.S., & Ray, R.S. Behavioral approaches to childhood disorders: Review and critique. *Behavior Modification*, 1980, *4*, 3-34.
Pizzat, F.J. *Behavior modification in residential treatment for children: Model of a program*. New York: Behavioral Publications, 1973.
Puig-Antich, J., Blau, S., Marx, N., Greenhill, L.L., & Chambers, W. Prepubertal major depressive disorder. A pilot study. *Journal of the American Academy of Child Psychiatry*, 1978, *17*, 695-707.
Rekers, G.A. Sexual problems: Behavior modification. In B.B. Wolman, J. Egan, & A.O. Ross (Eds.), *Handbook of treatment of mental disorders in childhood and adolescence*, Englewood Cliffs, N.J.: Prentice-Hall, 1978.
Rhodes, W.A., Redd, W.H., & Berggren, L. Social skills training for an unassertive adolescent. *Journal of Clinical Child Psychology*, 1979, *8*, 18-21.
Richards, C.S., & Siegel, L.J. Behavioral treatment of anxiety states and

avoidance behaviors in children. In D. Marholin II (Ed.), *Child behavior therapy*, New York: Gardner, 1978.

Rutter, M., Tizard, J., & Whitmore, K. (Eds.). *Education, health, and behavior.* London: Longmans, 1970.

Sacks, J.M. The need for subtlety: A critical session with a suicidal child. *Psychotherapy, Theory, Research and Practice*, 1977, *14*, 434–437.

Schaefer, C.E., & Millman, H.L. *Therapies for children: A handbook of effective treatments for problem behaviors.* San Francisco: Jossey-Bass, 1977.

Schulterbrandt, J.G., & Raskin, A. *Depression in childhood; Diagnosis, treatment, and conceptual models.* New York: Raven, 1977.

Seligman, M.E.P. Fall into learned helplessness. *Psychology Today*, 1973, *7*, 43–49.

Siegel, L.J., & Richards, C.S. Behavioral intervention with somatic disorders in children. In D. Marholin II (Ed.), *Child behavior therapy*, New York. Gardner, 1978.

Slaby, R.G., & Crowley, C.G. Modification of cooperation and aggression through teacher attention to children's speech. *Journal of Experimental Child Psychology*, 1977, *23*, 442–458.

Symonds, M. Depression in adolescence. *Science and Psychoanalysis*, 1970, *17*, 66–74.

Toolan, J.M. Depression in children and adolescents. *American Journal of Orthopsychiatry*, 1962, *32*, 404–415.

Walker, H.M., & Hops, H. The use of group and individual reinforcement contingencies in the modification of social withdrawal. In L.A. Hamerlynck, L.C. Handy, & E.J. Mash (Eds.), *Behavior change; Methodology, concepts, and practice*, Research Press, 1973.

Weinberg, W.A., Rutman, J., Sullivan, L., Penick, E.C. & Dietz, S.G. Depression in children referred to an educational diagnostic center. *Journal of Pediatrics*, 1973, *83*, 1065–1072.

Weinrott, M.R., Corson, J.A., & Wilchesky, M. Teacher-mediated treatment of social withdrawal. *Behavior Therapy*, 1979, *10*, 281–294.

Williamson, D.A., Calpin, J.P., DiLorenzo, T.M., Garris, R.P., & Petti, T.A. Combining Dexedrine (dextro-amphetamine) and activity feedback for the treatment of hyperactivity. *Behavior Modification*, 1981, *5* (in press).

Yates, A.J. *Behavior therapy*. New York: Wiley, 1970.

Zung, W.W.K. A self-rating depression scale. *Archives of General Psychiatry*, 1965, *12*, 63–70.

Behavioral Treatment of Elderly Patients with Depression

Joseph P. Cautela

The theoretical model presented focuses on certain assumptions concerning the relationship between aging and depression. Depression as viewed here is not an entity that causes psychological and organic behavior; it is not an entity that is caused by either organic or environmental events. Depression, as used in this chapter, is a construct, an abstraction, a shorthand term to describe a well-known set of behaviors.

Three major behavioral models have been proposed to explain the causes of these common behaviors: Beck's cognitive theory (1967), Seligman's learned helplessness theory (1975), and Lewinsohn's theory of insufficient response-contingent positive reinforcement (1974).

Beck's theory essentially holds that negative cognitions (negative scanning) are the major factors causing depression. In Seligman's theory, depression is considered to be the result of feelings of helplessness; it occurs when persons perceive that their behaviors are controlled by unpredictable environmental contingencies. Lewinsohn's model assumes that depressive behavior is a result of insufficient positive reinforcement, specifically insufficient response-contingent positive reinforcement.

It is difficult to determine to what extent these negative cognitions, feelings of helplessness, and low reinforcement levels interact in a causal manner to produce depressive behavior. In this regard, Blaney (1977) presented an excellent discussion of these three theories of depression. Blaney concluded that the evidence does not exclude any of the three models, nor does it point to any one model as the only viable one.

My clinical observations of patients labeled by themselves or by a professional as depressed have revealed that invariably they are negative scanners who feel helpless and are experiencing low levels of reinforcement. Generally, my therapeutic strategies are aimed at decreasing these patients' negative scanning, giving them a feeling of control, and increasing the levels of reinforcement in their lives.

Although some of the antecedents and consequences of depressive behavior may differ in the elderly, the goals and therapeutic strategies are similar to those for younger adults.

It is important to distinguish between the process of aging, which is a phenomenon common to all persons, and the behaviors of elderly persons, which are shaped primarily by cultural forces. It is also important to avoid misleading etiological assumptions about both aging and depression. Aging does not explain behavior, nor is it caused by behavior. It is a mistake to assume that any behavior is due to senility or to old age. Although there is no doubt that aging has some influence on behavior, it is almost impossible to determine its influence on a particular behavior. Even if we could determine the extent of its influence, we usually have only other variables available for manipulation.

Aging is a multifactorial process (Butler & Engel, 1978). The danger of ascribing certain behaviors to aging is that the attribution will discourage therapeutic strategies that could modify the behaviors. An obvious example is to attribute poor memory among elderly persons to the aging process. This attribution might discourage the clinician from trying to increase a patient's attention span or teach memory strategies. It could also result in the clinician not encouraging a patient to participate in activities that require retention of information, such as college courses.

The primary focus of this chapter is to describe my approach in treating elderly (65 years and over) depressed patients. The patient population referred to is that encountered in my private practice. In a previous article (Cautela, 1969b) I described a classical conditioning approach to treating the elderly. Other authors, such as Hoyer (1973), have described the application of operant techniques in treating the elderly. It must be emphasized that the ages of persons considered elderly can cover a span of at least 30 years. Classification of the elderly in terms of a specific age is completely a cultural bias.

Recently I have focused more on combining a respondent approach and an operant approach when treating elderly patients (Cautela & Mansfield, 1977). In this chapter, special emphasis will be given to covert conditioning procedures (Cautela, 1973, 1976a, 1977b). In the use of covert conditioning, the patient is instructed to imagine the target behavior and then imagine consequences that affect the probability of the target behavior.

Covert conditioning procedures are analogous to operant procedures: covert sensitization (Cautela, 1966, 1969b) (punishment), covert reinforcement (Cautela, 1970b) (positive reinforcement), covert extinction (Cautela, 1971) (extinction), covert negative reinforcement (Cautela, 1970a) (negative reinforcement), covert modeling (Cautela, 1976a) (modeling is a concept used within the operant framework), and covert response cost (Cautela, 1976b) (response cost). These procedures will be discussed in more detail later when they are presented as treatment strategies for particular behaviors. The covert conditioning assumptions are the following:

1. Covert behaviors obey the same laws as overt behaviors (the homogeneity assumption).
2. The most heuristic model for covert and overt behaviors is a conditioning model, more specifically, operant conditioning.
3. All behavioral events, for convenience, are classified in three categories: covert behavior (thoughts, images, feelings), overt (observable) behavior, and physiological behavior (events occurring under the skin). All three categories of behaviors obey the same laws and interact with one another.
4. All behavioral events are organic events. This is an important assumption, especially in dealing with speculation and treatment of organic dysfunction.

Behavioral Analysis

During the first interview, the therapist attempts a preliminary behavioral analysis of the target behavior, establishes the role of therapist as a social reinforcer, makes all credentials known, and explains the rationale and possible treatment approach.

When proceeding with a behavioral analysis, the therapist must discover the ABCs of the target behavior. In determining B, the therapist defines the target behavior operationally and determines its frequency, intensity, and duration. After B has been specified, the antecedents of B and the consequences occurring after B are to be made explicit.

Behavioral analysis in treating depression among the elderly proceeds in the same manner as treatment of other problem behaviors. It is interesting to note that in my private practice, more than 70% of elderly patients referred for treatment are diagnosed as being depressed. It is also important to emphasize that many elderly patients respond to treatment as well as younger adults (Gilbert, 1969). The primary task is to gain an operational definition of what patients are referring to when they say that they are depressed. This is done by interviewing patients using behavior inventories (Cautela, 1970) and interviewing significant others.

While interviewing, it is important to shape competing behaviors to patients' verbal statements that make attributions for their "depression" or their "old age." Often it is helpful to restructure the attributions so that some other, more adaptive, attributions are also considered. Also, the "old age" or "depression" attributions are ignored, and competing attributions are suggested. It must be remembered that therapy is always taking place while one is interviewing patients, whether for behavioral analysis or for determination of treatment procedures. When a patient makes any verbal or nonverbal responses, the therapist is influencing these responses, whether the therapist means to or not. The therapist is always responding when the patient is behaving. There is no choice; the therapist must reinforce, extinguish, or punish the behavior of the patient. For example, if a patient professes to feel all washed up, the therapist can say nothing but give a little body language (extinction) or nod (positive reinforcement); or the therapist can say, "You don't really believe that, do you?" (punishment).

In addition to interviewing the patient, the therapist should administer behavioral inventories to the patient and interview significant others to aid in the behavioral analysis.

Inventories

All patients are routinely given the Behavioral Analysis History Questionnaire (BAHQ) (Cautela, 1977a, pp. 3-13), the Self-Rating Behavior Scale (SRBS) (Cautela, 1977a, pp. 15-19), The Reinforcement Survey Schedule (RSS) (Cautela, 1977a, pp. 45-52), and the Imagery Survey Schedule (ISS) (Cautela, 1977a, pp. 123-134); for elderly patients referred because of depressive symptoms, the Depressive Behavior Survey Schedule (DBSS) (Cautela, 1977a, pp. 197-199) is also administered.

The BAHQ is a self-administered questionnaire geared toward obtaining general information about the patient in a number of areas such as health, sexuality, and family.

The SRBS consists of a listing of problem behaviors (both covert and overt). Patients are asked to indicate which behaviors they think they have to learn in order to function more effectively or to be more comfortable. Each item is observed briefly, a decision is made whether or not to try to modify the problem behavior, and a preliminary behavioral analysis is performed to determine the nature and relevance of the behavior (Upper & Cautela, 1977).

The RSS is a list of 54 major items. Patients are asked to rate the reinforcement values of a variety of stimuli and experiences that can be used as reinforcers in overt and covert conditioning procedures. Patients use a 5-point rating scale to indicate the enjoyability or satisfaction provided by each stimulus. Patients are also asked to list the things they think about relatively frequently. A number of ways have been outlined in which the RSS can be used to aid in the implementation of treatment in institutional and individual therapy settings. Research studies have indicated that the reliability and validity of the RSS warrant its use as a clinical and research instrument (Cautela & Kastenbaum, 1967).

The ISS provides an assessment of a patient's ability to imagine. This scale assesses a variety of imagery abilities, such as physical imagery ability (physical feelings or sensations) and psychological imagery ability (mental feelings elicited by words). Specific words and more general categories are rated for pleasantness, vividness, and ease or rapidity in producing images.

The DBSS requires patients to rate the frequencies of their thoughts, feelings, and behaviors (e.g., somatic complaints, decreased activities) on a scale of 1 to 5.

My own experience has taught me that the RSS, which usually is given to young adults, is not as useful with the elderly population. Recently, Bob Kastenbaum and I (Note 2) have developed the Elderly Reinforcement Survey Schedule (ERSS) (Appendix K).

The ERSS consists of 161 items, with the patient expressing various degrees of liking or dislike for the items. The patient's possible response choices are similar to those in the RSS. The categories of items include food, shopping, music, scenery, reading, entertainment, spectator sports, hobbies, activities, odors, quiet and reflective times, participation in entertainment and activities, trips, animals and people, going places, and being recognized and socialization. Patients are also asked to list their three most favorite people in all the world and the three most wonderful experiences they can imagine. For some patients, two sessions may be needed to administer the ERSS, depending on the patient's level of receptivity and cooperation.

The ERSS is used in a manner similar to that for the RSS. I rely a great deal on this schedule to help develop rapport with patients. Also, the schedule is used to help determine what activities can be targeted for reinforcer sampling or for an increase in frequency. Reinforcer sampling is used when patients express either neutral feelings or great preference for a particular experience without having had direct contact with the experience. For example, a patient might express great liking for gardening, only to reveal later never really having had experience in gardening. I would then suggest some ways to become involved in gardening. If the patient shows some avoidance of implementing these suggestions, then I employ covert reinforcement to increase the probability of sampling the passive reinforcing experience. The patient is asked to imagine experiencing the activity sampled, such as planting seeds, and then is asked to imagine a known reinforcing experience, such as eating ice cream. After a number of trials of covert reinforcement in the office and as homework, the patient attempts reinforcer sampling with continual prodding from the therapist. Covert reinforcement is also used to increase the frequency of an activity previously experienced by the patient but currently being experienced at only a low frequency. A typical example is a patient who expresses a preference for watching baseball games but lately hasn't been in the mood to go. Assuming that there is no physical or financial reason for this avoidance, he can be asked to imagine the following: He is traveling to the ballpark, is finding a seat (covert reinforcement), is enjoying watching his favorite team score a few runs (covert reinforcement), and is leaving the game very satisfied (covert reinforcement).

The ERSS has special value in dealing with elderly depressed patients, because one of the main goals of treatment is to increase the reinforcement level. The reinforcement level can be defined in terms of the number and quality of reinforcing experiences that currently are occurring (e.g., on a particular day). Other survey schedules are employed if needed, such as the Thought-Stopping Survey Schedule (TSSS) (Cautela, 1977a, pp. 101-105), which consists of 51 items regarding which the patient is likely to be maladaptive. Here the patient is asked to indicate how often a particular thought occurs, using a 5-point scale ranging from "not at all" to "very much." Patients are also asked to list other thoughts that bother them or that occur more than 10 to 20 times per day (Cautela & Upper, 1975).

The Assertive Behavior Survey Schedule (ABSS) (Cautela, 1977a, pp. 111-114) consists of four sections in which patients rate their degrees of assertiveness, determine what might occur if they asserted themselves, estimate what the responses might be if they asserted themselves, and estimate how they might respond to other individuals if they believe that they are giving more than is being received.

The Social Performance Survey Schedule (SPSS) (Cautela, 1977a, pp. 137-145) was designed for use with patients experiencing social anxiety. This schedule is filled out by the patient concerning the patient's own social performance or the social performance of a significant other (Lowe & Cautela, 1978).

Interviewing Significant Others

There are three main objectives in interviewing significant others: (1) Obtain information that will be helpful in treating the patient. (2) Explain the treatment rationale to the patient's significant others. This helps increase the probability of effective cooperation. (3) Instruct the significant others in the consequences of desirable and undesirable behaviors. The optimal frequency for meeting with significant others depends on the nature and extent of their interaction with the patient, as well as on their degrees of cooperation. In treating a patient with severe depressive behavior, the significant others should be seen at least once a week until the crisis is averted and some progress is evident. The patient is then seen on a biweekly schedule until significant progress is made, then once a week until discharge. When interviewing significant others of an elderly patient, it is important to emphasize that they not treat the patient as a child or as if the patient were senile. It is important that the patient be treated as a mature adult.

Record Keeping

Depending on the degree of cooperation, it is desirable to have the patient record the ABCs of at least one target behavior after the first week. The choice of target behaviors depends on a number of factors, such as ease of recording, pervasiveness, and percentage of possible incapacities. Besides the usual advantages cited for recording behaviors (Kimaki, 1978; Nelson et al., 1978; Sieck & McFall, 1976), when depressed patients record behaviors such as suicidal thoughts, the behaviors are seen more objectively and partake less of an uncontrollable intrapsychic force. After the record keeping reveals a reliable sample of the target behaviors, the treatment strategy is planned with the aid of the patient. Record keeping and mutual planning of strategy give the patient a greater feeling of self-control and thereby reduce feelings of helplessness. This is especially true if the behavior is an organic dysfunction such as asthma or nausea.

Treatment

Although the focus of this chapter is a behavioral approach to depression in the elderly, there will be no descriptions of the use of electric shock or drugs in the treatment strategy. This is not to deny their effectiveness either alone or with behavior therapy. Most patients referred are already on some form of drug therapy. Whether drugs do or do not benefit these patients, it appears that drugs are not sufficient in these cases to effect the behavioral changes desired; otherwise these patients would not be referred.

As previously mentioned, the treatment strategy is aimed at achieving three primary goals:

1. Decrease the effects of (covert and physiological) aversive stimuli.
2. Increase the level of reinforcement.
3. Give a feeling of greater self-control.

The strategies employed for the three objectives naturally overlap. Some strategies are applicable in achieving all three objectives. Table 12.1 depicts the strategies employed for each of the objectives. This table by no means includes all the strategies that might be employed, but it is representative of the common strategies for all patients labeled depressive. Because the uses of most of these strategies have been reported elsewhere in many contexts, my description focuses on the use of covert conditioning, either in modifying behavior directly or in making more effective use of other strategies.

The Elderly and Depression

Elderly patients referred for treatment have primary diagnoses of depression more frequently than any other diagnosis. The elderly are more likely to experience depression, and as a corollary they are more prone to make suicide attempts (Linden & Breed, 1975). In a previous report I outlined the theoretical bases and treatment procedures for presuicidal behavior among the elderly (Cautela, Note 1). Since the presentation of that report, I have employed covert procedures to modify the probability of suicide attempts. It is assumed that in some

TABLE 12:1 Strategies Employed to Achieve Three Primary Goals in the Treatment of Depressive Behaviors

Strategies	Decrease Aversive Stimuli	Increase Level of Reinforcement	Increase Self-control
Relaxation	X		X
Thought stopping	X		X
Social skills training	X	X	X
Record keeping	X	X	X
Physical exercise	X	X	X
Teaching crime control tips			X
Teaching self-defense			X
Shared Living		X	
Foster care (day care)	X	X	
Group therapy		X	
Contingency contract	X	X	X
Reinforcer sampling		X	X
Vocational counseling		X	X
Nutritional counseling	X	X	
Covert conditioning processes			
Covert reinforcement	X	X	X
Covert sensitization			X
Covert extinction	X		X
Covert negative reinforcement	X	X	X
Covert response cost			X
Covert modeling	X	X	X

cases suicidal thoughts can be reinforcing, because they represent an attempt to escape from aversive stimulation. This assumption appears to have some merit, because one observes that often suicidal patients feel and act much calmer after they have decided on the means. In other cases patients report that suicidal thoughts are accompanied by anxiety. When it is apparent that a patient is getting reinforcement from anticipatory suicidal thoughts, thought stopping and covert sensitization are employed to change the suicidal thoughts. Covert reinforcement is also employed on the patient's tendencies not to commit suicide. When a patient reports that suicidal thoughts are accompanied by anxiety, thought stopping, which becomes reinforcing in itself, is accompanied by a decrease in anxiety, and covert reinforcement is used. Covert reinforcement is also employed for competing responses (not committing suicide and enjoying certain aspects of one's life), and it appears to be particularly effective.

Whereas depression in the elderly involves negative scanning, low levels of reinforcement, and feelings of helplessness, as is the case with a younger population, the variables influencing these factors vary with chronological age and cultural influence. Loss of reinforcers through loss of loved ones and friends is more apt to occur among the elderly. Retirement is likely to result in a decrease in reinforcement because of loss of work-involved relationships, lack of working status, and decreased income. Feelings of helplessness are more common because the elderly have little control over a number of factors: looking older, diminishing sensory acuity, decreased income, and debilitating diseases. Low levels of reinforcement and feelings of helplessness result in increased negative scanning, which in turn lowers reinforcement levels and increases feelings of helplessness. A crucial problem for the therapist in treating the elderly depressed is how to modify negative scanning, levels of reinforcement, and feelings of control in the face of the reality of these patients' situations.

Decreasing Negative Scanning

There are several strategies employed to decrease negative scanning. The first obvious strategy is to try to reduce the reasons or the sources for negative scanning. Elderly patients who engage in negative scanning when going out of the house and visiting relatives can be desensitized for their fear of public transportation. Covert reinforcement can be employed by having these patients imagine that they are enjoying various forms of public transportation, followed by imagining pleasant scenes.

Thought stopping is used a great deal on negative self-statements and negative scanning of past, present, and future events (Cautela & Wisocki, 1977). For this to be effective, training must be extensive in the office and through homework assignments. Record keeping will reveal to patients the gradual effectiveness of thought stopping. It is important to teach patients how to positively scan themselves and their environments. Patients fill out daily reinforcement records to note any possible reinforcement that has occurred each day. This forces patients to positively scan their environments, and they usually become aware that more reinforcing events occur than would have been predicted. Positive scanning can also be reinforced by having patients imagine positively scanning situations and then imagining pleasant scenes. An example would be imagining noticing beautiful scenery while driving, and then imagining an experience that is pleasant, such as hearing one's favorite song. The therapist can enhance positive scanning by pointing out to patients positive attributes, such as kindness or a sense of humor, and any skills, such as skill in playing bridge. As previously mentioned, repetitive negative scanning must be ignored after the therapist has attempted to restructure some of the negative statements. Not only must the therapist attempt to ignore the negative scanning statements; significant others are also taught to ignore such statements and to try to reinforce positive scanning. If significant others are not able to ignore self-derogatory statements and other kinds of negative scanning, then covert extinction is employed. In covert extinction, the patient is instructed to imagine the targeted behavior to be reduced (e.g., statements of despair) and to imagine that the reinforcement is withheld. The patient is asked to imagine this behavior occurring in the presence of others, who pay not the slightest bit of attention to the patient. It is important to inform the patient and the significant others that when the patient first begins to use extinction, there is a possibility that at first there will be an increase in negative scanning (extinction burst) (Reynolds, 1968, p. 28), and some negative behavior is likely to occur (extinction-produced aggression) (Azrin et al., 1966). The patient and the significant others must be instructed not to despair about the increased statements of negative scanning; they must be told that this situation is only temporary, and gradually the statements will decrease to nearly zero, if everyone is cooperative. They must also be instructed to try to ignore but understand the aggressive behavior.

Some depressed patients who are intense negative scanners claim that they cannot imagine any positive experiences. Covert positive reinforcement cannot be used with this group, because they are not able to imagine pleasant scenes. In some of these cases covert negative reinevent is occuring (e.g., being caught in a storm) and then imagines the response to be increased (e.g., calling a friend), which terminates the aversive experience.

Another source of negative scanning can be aversive stimulation due to pain or physical discomfort. If a patient is experiencing frequent or constant pain caused by some physical disability, such as arthritis or neuralgia, it is almost impossible to eliminate irritability, low levels of frustration tolerance, and negative scanning. Feelings of helplessness are also usually concomitants.

In treating depressive behaviors it is necessary to target pain behavior as soon as possible. Behavioral procedures are employed in addition to medical therapy. Behavioral treatment of pain involves viewing pain as the cause of behaviors that must be analyzed according to the ABC paradigm. The pain behavior is operationally defined, and the usual procedure for discovering the antecedents and consequences is used. A procedure that appears effective in modifying pain behavior is the self-control triad (Cautela, 1977c; Cautela & McCullough, 1978).

The self-control triad consists in teaching the patient to say "stop" to take a deep breath and relax while exhaling, and then to imagine a pleasant scene. After the patient is taught the use of this sequence well in the office and by homework, the triad technique can be employed every time pain is noticed or an increase in pain is experienced. The patient is told to keep repeating the triad procedure until there is a noticeable decrease in pain and discomfort.

Use of the triad usually results in some decrement in pain, probably because of distraction, reciprocal inhibition due to relaxing and imagining a pleasant scene. Covert reinforcing properties of the pleasant scenes reinforce the behavior of saying "stop" and breathing deeply when the patient is experiencing an aversive stimulation. The triad is also employed in a similar manner to modify pervasive anxiety. The triad can be used to modify phobic behavior in two ways. The patient is asked to imagine gradually approaching a phobic stimulus, and the triad technique is performed whenever anxiety is experienced anywhere along the approach to the stimulus. The patient is instructed to repeat this sequence over and over as many times as necessary until the whole approach sequence can be imagined without having to employ the triad. The patient is also instructed in the use of a self-control triad that is used when approaching the phobic stimulus in a real situation.

Elderly depressed patients are taught to employ the triad in a wide variety of situations, such as negative thinking, experiencing pain or discomfort, being rejected, and when feeling anxious in the presence of others.

Changing the Level of Reinforcement

As indicated earlier, one of the main objectives in treating depression among the elderly is to increase their levels of reinforcement. This level of reinforcement is defined in terms of the number and quality of reinforcements occurring during any selected time period. Here the term *reinforcement* is used in the narrow sense as a stimulus, which as a consequence, increases the probability of a response. Of course, this implies that the stimulus must impact as a reinforcer on the patient. There are numerous relevant assumptions and generalizations involving the level of reinforcement:

1. For optimal functioning, each patient must have a particular level of reinforcement. Optimal functioning requires the following: (a) Patients report or feel that they are happy. (b) Crises are handled as effectively as possible. (c) Functioning is effective in vocational and academic activities. (d) Distress and anxiety are minimal or non-existent. (e) Maladaptive behaviors do not occur.
2. The level of reinforcement is determined by the following factors: (a) the degree of positive or negative scanning of past events; (b) the numbers of reinforcing activities currently occurring in patients' lives. (c) The degree of anticipation of future reinforcing or aversive activities.
3. A low reinforcement level is concomitant with the following: (a) feeling "down," depressed, unhappy; (b) minimal activity; (c) increased susceptibility to developing maladaptive behaviors, such as phobias (e.g., fear of being bitten by a dog).
4. Treatment of a behavior disorder is more successful if the patient's general level of reinforcement (GLR) is high.
5. Lack of cooperation in the treatment program, especially if the behavior is highly maintained by reinforcement, will be more likely to occur if the GLR is low.
6. In any treatment procedure, regardless of the behavior to modified, the therapist should determine the GLR by the use of questionnaires (e.g., the Reinforcement Survey Schedule, the Fear Survey Schedule, and the Behavioral Analysis History Questionnaire), by asking what reinforcing activities the patient currently is pursuing (e.g., job, hobbies, interests, family, school, etc.), and by asking the patient what types of images are occuring regarding the past, present, and future.

In addition to theoretical assumptions, several empirical generalizations can be made concerning the level of reinforcement:

1. The lower the GLR, the greater the depressed mood (Lewinsohn & Libet, 1972).
2. The amount of positive reinforcement experienced is less in depressed patients (MacPhillamy & Lewinsohn, 1974).
3. Depressed patients are more sensitive to aversive contingencies.
4. Depressed patients usually have poorer social skills (Libet and Lewinsohn, 1973).

It is assumed that the by-products and concomitants of the level of reinforcement are similar for different age groups.

Increasing the levels of reinforcement among the elderly is more difficult than in younger populations. This is especially true of the elderly retired who have lost their spouses and have little or no social support from relatives, friends, and acquaintances. Also, aversive stimulation in the form of discomfort due to physical illness is more likely to occur among the elderly. Even though the elderly population presents a special problem to the therapist in terms of increasing the general level of reinforcement, the procedures used are similar for mature adults and young adults. As presented earlier, the techniques for eliminating aversive stimulation include covert conditioning to reduce fear, pain, and other kinds of discomfort. Positive scanning is shaped in the patient by the therapist's responses during the interview. The use of a daily reinforcement schedule is encouraged, and covert reinforcement is employed as a consequence to the imagining of positive scanning behavior.

In addition to the therapist's attempts to reinforce the patient as much as possible, significant others must be instructed how to reinforce the patient in any manner possible. The behaviors to be reinforced are positive scanning, maintaining a pleasing appearance, engaging in new activities, and use of any new ability demonstrated to even the slightest degree.

As previously indicated, depressed patients tend to have poor social skills, which means that they probably receive relatively little social reinforcement. One of the behaviors that tends to be aversive to others is constant complaining about health. The high frequency of complaining is not surprising, because the elderly are more likely to have a number of physical disabilities simply because people tend to have more things go wrong as they become older. In addition, complaining is sometimes reinforced by attention from others. It is important to point out to patients that complaining behavior of any kind tends to become boring and aversive to others, especially if it is continually repeated; patients must be told that this is probably the case even though listeners may appear to be sympathetic. In addition, the therapist should warn that expressions of sympathy and concern from others can actually result in an increase in overt and covert complaining behavior. After the rationale is presented to patients, they are instructed not to complain to anyone except a physician or the therapist, unless it is a symptom that requires immediate attention. Patients must be told that their families and significant others have been instructed to ignore repeated complaints; in this way, significant others will actually be more helpful. If patients find it difficult to stop unnecessary complaining, and their families find it difficult to ignore the complaining, then covert extinction should be used. These patients are instructed to imagine a number of situations in which they are complaining but nobody pays attention to their complaints. Patients are also instructed to use covert extinction concerning particular situations in which there is unnecessary complaining. In this way patients can rectify mistakes that have occurred during the day. Not only are patients asked to reduce or eliminate unnecessary complaining; they also are encouraged to reinforce others.

One common mistake of the elderly is to criticize relatives and friends for what they have not done, rather than reinforcing them for what they have done. A common example is scolding one's children for not telephoning or visiting often enough, rather than reinforcing them by thanking them for calling or visiting. Because a number of factors contribute to the poor self-images of elderly patients, compliments from others often are punished by disclaiming the attribute complimented. These patients must be encouraged to express their thanks when they are complimented. Elderly patients often say that they feel inadequate when conversing with younger adults. Being out of the work force and not being physically active can influence them to believe that they have nothing to say that is worthwhile. Patients who are not current in public affairs should be encouraged to read at least one news magazine each week and to read a newspaper in its entirety every day. This often will result in increased feelings of competence in communicating with others. Patients who fear that they have nothing to say can often benefit by being taught nondirective counseling procedures. After being taught the nondirective approach, these patients usually report that they feel more at ease in dealing with others in social situations.

One of the social skills usually lacking in elderly depressed patients is proper expression of assertive behavior (Corby, 1975). They often tend to be overly aggressive or not assertive enough. Assertive behavior is necessary for the elderly to maintain their feeling of control and personal worth. The elderly need to be assertive with their immediate families, especially with their children, because it is the children who tend to believe that age tends to make parents incompetent to plan or to make practical decisions. Elderly patients often are fearful about being assertive, because they might be rejected by those who supply their only social support. It must be pointed out that if children and other relatives are thanked for their concern and advice, and if the patient is assertive (speaks up when an injustice is done) when necessary, the patient will be more respected. Record keeping and behavioral rehearsals often help in increasing assertive behavior. If assertive behavior does not occur, because of fear of rejection, the patient must be desensitized by covert reinforcement.

A covert conditioning procedure that appears to be particularly effective in increasing assertive behavior is covert modeling (Cautela, 1976a). In covert modeling, the patient is asked to imagine watching someone else being comfortable while being assertive in a variety of situations. In these scenes, the model is usually successful and always appears more satisfied after being assertive. Covert modeling must be specifically tailored to the patient's experience (Kazdin, 1975, 1976a, 1976b).

A case history will illustrate the effects of lack of assertive behavior in an elderly patient. The patient reported that his son had bought him a season ticket to attend a particular summer theater each week. The son had arranged for the father to be dropped off at the theater and picked up when the show had ended. The father was afraid to tell his son that he disliked the theater, for fear that the son would feel rejected and would stop showing his father kindness in other ways.

The father was told to explain the situation to his son in the same manner that he had explained it to the therapist. The father expressed great concern and discomfort at the prospect of relating his feelings to his son. Covert reinforcement was employed so that the father would feel comfortable when explaining the dilemma to his son. After a week of practice sessions of covert reinforcement, the father was able to relate his feelings openly to his son. The son apologized and told his father that if he ever felt coerced again, he hoped his father would speak up immediately. The son further explained that if he felt assured that his father would speak up about his preferences, he would not be afraid to attempt to do other things for his father.

At the end of a day when a patient should have been assertive but was not, then sometime before retiring for the night the patient should practice a covert modeling scene in which the model makes the proper assertions in the same situations.

Another form of behavior that can lead to avoidance by others is criticism. It must be continually emphasized to patients that their criticisms should not be expressed unless they are constructive and can be sandwiched between two compliments. If a patient wants to express criticism about her grandchildren's behavior to the parents, she can express criticism in the following manner: "It is a delight to have the children visit me, but they tend to run around a lot and make too much noise. I know that they are excited to be here, and I appreciate that, but I wish you would try to get them to calm down a bit and slow down when going through the house."

During each session, the patient should describe the social interactions that have taken place since the last session. The successful interactions must be reinforced. The problems that occurred must be discussed and treatment strategies devised with mutual input.

Other ways in which the level of reinforcement can be increased include encouraging patients to engage in activities that will lead to reinforcement. Among such activities are those that lead to better health, increased feelings of competence, and more opportunities for social reinforcement. Elderly patients must be encouraged to engage in some form of exercise, because this will increase feelings of well-being (reinforcement), will increase agility and mobility, and will result in social reinforcement from others. It is wise to consult a physician to select exercise that is optimally reinforcing and at the same time has beneficial effects. Even elderly patients with apparent debilitating conditions should be urged to exercise within the limits allowed by their physicians.

Elderly patients should be asked to investigate the possibility of joining various self-help groups for senior citizens. The activities of the self-help groups can lead to greater feelings of self-worth and can decrease feelings of helplessness. Self-help groups can provide a nucleus for the friendships that often develop when persons are involved in similar pursuits.

Modifying Feelings of Helplessness

In targeting the feeling of helplessness, the behaviors to be accelerated are those that promote feelings of self-control. Self-control (Cautela, 1969a) can be defined as making a response to control the frequency of another response. If the targeted behavior is excessive drinking of alcohol, then self-control concerning alcoholic beverages occurs when a patient makes a response that decreases the probability of drinking alcohol at any particular time. If the targeted behavior is a reduction of anxiety in a social situation, then self-control behavior is being performed when the patient is able to make responses to reduce anxiety in these social situations.

The feeling of self-control results when patients believe that they are able to make responses that will alter the frequencies of undesirable behaviors. It is important to note that self-control is not a unitary trait. Patients may be able to exercise control over a number of classes of behavior, but there may be inability to control one or two classes of behavior, such as smoking or overeating. It is important to point out to patients that inability to control one or more classes of behavior does not mean that they are weak or incapable because of old age or depression. Patients must be told that achieving self-control or mastery of a particular behavior involves using procedures to break old habits and to develop new competing habits.

The elderly appear to be particularly prone to believe that their behavior is under the control of unpredictable external contingencies and biological factors involved in the aging process. The tendency for this belief among the elderly arises because there is some decreased mobility that accompanies chronological aging, because there is increased probability of disease processes, and because of cultural expectancies.

Young adults are quick to assume that the elderly have declined in reasoning power as well as in bodily functions. Young adults are also quick to dismiss some of the aspirations of the elderly as being unrealistic, as examples of faltering mental ability.

Procedures

There are a numerous procedures that can be used routinely with almost all elderly patients who are capable of cooperating. There are some pervasive self-control procedures that can, for the most part, be used to control almost any behavior. Many general anxiety feelings, phobic responses, and maladaptive behaviors are due to faulty thought processes. If patients can be taught thought stopping effectively, then they are assured a self-control procedure that can be employed in a wide variety of situations for the rest of their lives.

Among the elderly, thoughts of helplessness and hopelessness are quite common. As a part of behavioral analysis, patients are asked to describe the usual general negative scanning, but thoughts of being incompetent, helpless, and hopeless regarding the future are also focal points. This is done by having the patient put negative thoughts on cards, which are used by the therapist to practice thought stopping in the office. The therapist shuffles the cards while the patient's eyes are closed. The patient is told that the therapist is going to read a thought from one of the cards. Then, with eyes closed, the patient begins to think the particular thought. When the patient begins the thought, the right index finger is raised. As soon as the index finger is raised, the therapist shouts "Stop!" in a loud voice. After the therapist proceeds through the pack of cards two or three times in this manner, the patient is asked to take the deck of cards and read a thought aloud, with eyes closed, and yell "Stop!" covertly. The patient proceeds in this manner until the act of yelling "Stop!" immediately eliminates the thoughts. The patient is then asked to practice going through the cards twice a day at home and at least five times each practice session. The patient is also instructed to use thought stopping in real situations whenever these thoughts occur. The patient must be strongly urged to continue saying the word "Stop!" covertly until a particular thought stays away for at least a few minutes. The patient is also instructed to keep a frequency count for each of the thoughts on the cards. Patients frequently report that this combination of recording and thought stopping reduces the frequency of undesirable thoughts and, more important, gives them a feeling of control.

Another pervasive procedure that appears helpful in self-control is the use of deep breathing, with the word "relax" being said while exhaling (Cautela & Groden, 1977). This procedure appears to be maximally effective if the patient has been taught deep muscle relaxation. The patient can use the deep breathing relaxation exercise to reduce maladaptive avoidance behaviors. Patients can take deep breaths during job interviews and when they perceive that they are about to engage in maladaptive approach behaviors, such as taking a deep breath when one feels the need to smoke or to be aggressively critical.

During behavioral rehearsals, the patient becomes anxious, then takes a deep breath and relaxes. This deep breathing relaxation response serves at least three functions. First, it causes a temporary decrease in anxiety or temptation. Second, if it is practiced continually with a given situation, desensitization to that situation is likely to occur. Finally, the patient experiences coping behavior, which enhances feelings of self-control. Another procedure that encompasses thought stopping and relaxation is the self-control triad described previously.

The combination of thought stopping, deep breathing, relaxation, and imagining a pleasant scene appears to be more effective than any of the three procedures used alone. The reason that thought stopping and deep breathing relaxation are taught alone is that a number of patients find the self-control triad difficult to master at first. Because the elderly are more likely to have feelings of incompetence, it is advantageous to approach the self-control triad gradually by teaching the component parts individually.

Elderly patients who live in areas beset by high crime rates should be encouraged to learn self-defense tactics and anticrime tips. In some areas the police departments have special classes for the elderly. After patients have learned some self-defense tactics and anticrime tactics, they often report that they feel less at the mercy of the environment.

Covert Conditioning as a Self-control Procedure

One of the goals of treatment for any patient is to teach procedures that can be used after therapy has been terminated, even though treatment has been successful. Before patients leave treatment, the rationale of covert conditioning should be explained to them, and they should be taught how to use covert conditioning as a self-control procedure.

Patients should be instructed to scan their behaviors as they occurred in different situations throughout the day. If they find that they have made inappropriate responses during the day, then at some time before going to sleep at night they are to imagine that they are making the desirable correct responses, using one or more covert conditioning procedures. For example, if a patient determines that she should have been more assertive to her roommate, then she can imagine that the situation is occurring again, but this time she makes the appropriate assertive response, feels comfortable, and then imagines a pleasant scene (covert reinforcement).

If patients deliberately did not take their medicine during the day, they are to imagine observing someone else not taking prescribed medicine and then immediately becoming ill (covert modeling). Also, they can imagine that when significant others discover that they are not taking prescribed medication, the others ignore the matter completely (covert extinction). Again, in dealing with the same responses, patients can imagine that they are about to throw medications down the drain, but decide not to, feel very good about this, and then imagine pleasant scenes (covert reinforcement). Covert sensitization can also be used by having patients imagine that medication has been omitted for some time and that this has been followed by serious illness. Another covert conditioning procedure that can be used to decrease maladaptive behaviors is covert response cost. The patient is instructed to imagine the response to be induced (refusing medication) and then imagine that a reinforcer is removed (finding one's wallet is missing). On an a priori basis, one would expect that patients such as the elderly, who experience many losses, would find that this procedure would only reinforce their feelings of loss or abandonment. Empirically, it appears that they not only feel less alone and less helpless but also recognize that they have a procedure that they can use to control their behaviors.

Patients can use one or more covert conditioning procedures on almost any inappropriate response that occurs during the day. They should repeat each procedure until the desired effect is achieved. In the example just cited, the patient continues to repeat the procedure until it is possible to imagine being very comfortable in that situation. The use of covert conditioning in this manner on a day-to-day basis can gradually result in elimination of inappropriate behavior or can prevent behavior from occurring at such a high rate that it becomes inappropriate.

Patients can be told that they have procedures that can be used to modify any response if they apply them diligently and appropriately. If they empirically demonstrate this for themselves, they develop strong feelings of coping ability and competence. Patients should practice daily use of covert conditioning as a means of self-control before therapy is terminated. Also, they should be told that if they ever need reeducation concerning any procedures at any time in their lives, they should feel free to contact the therapist for an appointment.

Special Considerations in Treating the Elderly

In dealing with an elderly population, one sometimes must alter procedures slightly to enhance treatment effects and avoid aversive results. When teaching relaxation, one must be careful to modify the teaching in a progressive manner so as to allow for possible complications, such as those imposed by arthritis, arterial sclerosis, and poor muscle tone. Sometimes the teaching of deep muscle relaxation can be more effective if one proceeds slowly and omits certain muscle groups. Also, covert relaxation training, which is somewhat similar to hypnosis, can be employed with the elderly. This emphasizes suggestions of relaxation and the production of various forms of imagery.

When using thought stopping, one might modify the procedure so that the word "Stop!" is not shouted unexpectedly after the patient is told to think of a particular thought. When using thought stopping with the elderly, it may be of advantage to spend more time teaching them to achieve good auditory imagery on the word "Stop!" so that it can be applied as effectively as possible. This caution appears necessary to avoid a startle response that might lead to a heart attack, as well as quick bodily movements that could result in a pinched nerve, a muscle strain, or some other type of injury.

The therapist can be a more effective social reinforcer to elderly patients if they are treated as acquaintances or friends. Before and after therapeutic sessions the therapist can chat with patients about current events and about their various recreational activities.

When employing covert conditioning with the elderly, it has been found necessary to make the scenes shorter and to describe them in more detail. Also, it appears to be more efficient to use fewer trials during the session and to use rest periods more frequently between blocks of trials.

At the beginning of treatment, patients should be encouraged not to hesitate to call to make immediate appointments with the therapist if they think they need support or advice. After patients have been taught the self-control procedures, the frequency of telephone calls to the therapist should decrease to almost zero, and patients will proudly report their progress in solving problems themselves using these procedures.

It is quite obvious that when dealing with the elderly it often is necessary to be knowledgeable about outside agencies that can benefit patients in any way. In this regard, patients often are referred to a social worker or guidance counselor who is familiar with local institutions and agencies especially for the elderly.

REFERENCE NOTES

1. Cautela, J.R. *The modification of behaviors that influence the probability of suicide in elders.* Presented at a symposium of the Eastern Psychological Association, 1976.
2. Cautela, J.R., & Kastenbaum, R. *Elderly Reinforcement Schedule (ERSS).* Unpublished manuscript, 1979.

REFERENCES

Azrin, N.H., Hutchinson, R.R., & Hake, D.F. Extinction-induced aggression. *Journal of Experimental Analysis of Behavior,* 1966, *9,* 191–204.

Beck, A.T. *Depression: Clinical, experimental, and theoretical aspects.* New York: Hoeber, 1967.

Blaney, P.H. Contemporary theories of depression: Critique and comparison. *Journal of Abnormal Psychology,* 1977, *86,* 203–223.

Butler, R.N., & Engel, B.T. Psychosomatic medicine and aging research. *Psychosomatic Medicine*, 1978, *40*, 365-367.

Cautela, J.R. Treatment of compulsive behavior by covert sensitization. *Psychological Records*, 1966, *16*, 33-41.

Cautela, J.R. Covert sensitization. *Psychological Reports*, 1967, *74*, 459-468.

Cautela, J.R. Behavior therapy and self-control: Techniques and implication. In C.M. Franks (Ed.), *Behavior therapy: Appraisal and status*, New York: McGraw-Hill, 1969. (a)

Cautela, J.R. A classical conditioning apprach to the development and modification of behavior in the aged. *Gerontologist*, 1969, *9*, 109-113. (b)

Cautela, J.R. Covert negative reinforcement. *Behavior Therapy and Experimental Psychiatry*, 1970, *1*, 272-278. (a)

Cautela, J.R. Covert reinforcement. *Behavior Therapy*, 1970, *1*, 35-50. (b)

Cautela, J.R. Covert extinction. *Behavior Therapy*, 1971, *2*, 192-200.

Cautela, J.R. Covert processes. *Journal of Nervous and Mental Diseases*, 1973, *157*, 27-36.

Cautela, J.R. Present status of covert modeling. *Journal of Behavior Therapy and Experimental Psychiatry*, 1976, *6*, 323-326. (a)

Cautela, J.R. Covert response cost. *Psychotherapy: Theory, Research, and Practice*, 1976, *13*, 397-404. (b)

Cautela, J.R. *Behavior analysis forms for clinical intervention*. Champaign, Ill.: Research Press, 1977. (a)

Cautela, J.R. Covert conditioning: Assumptions and procedures. *Journal of Mental Imagery*, 1977, *1*, 53-64. (b)

Cautela, J.R. The use of covert conditioning in modifying pain behavior. *Journal of Behavior Therapy and Experimental Psychiatry*, 1977, *8*, 45-52. (c)

Cautela, J.R., & Groden, J. *Relaxation: A comprehensive manual*. Champaign, Ill.: Research Press, 1977.

Cautela, J.R., & Kastenbaum, R. A reinforcement survey schedule for use in therapy, training, and research. *Psychological Reports*, 1967, *20*, 1115-1130.

Cautela, J.R., & Mansfield, L. A behavioral approach to geriatrics. In W.D. Gentry (Ed.), *Geropsychology: A model of training and clinical service*, Cambridge, Mass.: Ballinger, 1977.

Cautela, J.R., & McCullough, L. Covert conditioning: A learning theory perspective on imagery. In J. Singer (Ed.), *The power of human imagination*, 1978.

Cautela, J.R., & Upper, D. The process of individual behavior therapy. In M. Hersen & R.M. Eilser (Eds.), *Progress in behavior modification*, New York: Academic, 1975.

Cautela, J.R., & Wisocki, P.A. The thought-stopping procedure: Description, application, and learning theory interpretations. *Psychological Record*, 1977, *2*, 255-264.

Corby, V. Assertion training with aged populations. *Counseling Psychology*, 1975, 69-74.

Gilbert, J.G. Geriatric counseling. In E.J. Weizedl (Ed.), *Contemporary pastoral counseling*, Milwaukee: Bruce Publishing, 1969.

Hoyer, W.J. Application of operant techniques to the modification of elderly behavior. *Gerontologist*, 1973, *13*, 18-22.

Kazdin, A.E. Covert modeling, imagery assessment, and assertive behavior. *Journal of Consulting and Clinical Psychology*, 1975, *43*, 716-724.

Kazdin, A.E. Assessment of imagery during covert modeling treatment of assertive behavior. *Journal of Behavior Therapy and Experimental Psychiatry*, 1976, *7*, 213-219. (a)

Kazdin, A.E. Effects of covert modeling, multiple models, and model reinforcement on assertive behavior. *Behavior Therapy*, 1976, *7*, 211-222. (b)

Kimaki, J. Self-recording: Its effects on individuals high and low in motivation. *Behavior Therapy*, 1978, *9*, 65-72.

Lewinsohn, P.M. A behavioral approach to depression. In R.J. Friedman & M.M. Katz (Eds.), *The psychology of depression: Contemporary theory and research*, Washington: Winston-Wiley, 1974.

Lewinsohn, P.M., & Libet, J. Pleasant events, activity schedules, and depression. *Journal of Abnormal Psychology*, 1972, *79*, 291-295.

Libet, J.M., & Lewinsohn, P.M. Concept of social skill with reference to the behavior of depressed persons. *Journal of Consulting Psychology*, 1973, *40*, 304-312.

Linden, L.L., & Breed, W. The demographic epidemiology of suicide. In E.S. Shneidman (Ed.), *Suicidology: Contemporary developments*, New York: Grune & Stratton, 1975.

Lowe, M.R., & Cautela, J.R. A self-report measure of social skill. *Behavior Therapy*, 1978, *9*, 535-544.

MacPhillamy, D.J., & Lewinsohn, P.M. Depression as a function of levels of desired and obtained pleasure. *Journal of Abnormal Psychology*, 1974, *83*, 651-657.

Nelson, R.O., Lipinski, D.P., & Boykin, R.A. The effects of self-recorders training and obtrusiveness of the self-recording device on the accuracy and reactivity of self-monitoring. *Behavior Therapy*, 1978, *9*, 200-208.

Reynolds, G.S. *A primer of operant conditioning*. Glenview, Ill.: Scott, Foresman, 1968.

Seligman, M.E. *Helplessness: On depression, development and death*. San Francisco: Freeman, 1975.

Sieck, W.A., & McFall, R.M. Some determinants of self-monitoring effects. *Journal of Consulting and Clinical Psychology*, 1976, *44*, 958-965.

Upper, D., & Cautela, J.R. Behavior analysis, assessment and diagnosis. Section I. Behavioral vs. "traditional" approaches to assessment. In D. Upper (Ed.), *Presepctives in behavior therapy*, Kalamazoo: Behaviordelia, 1977.

Appendixes

APPENDIX A Activity Schedule

Part A

Name: _____ Date: _____

Please check within the parentheses to indicate the activities of this day. Only activities that were at least a little pleasant should be checked.

Activity	Frequency check	Activity	Frequency check
1. Laughing	( )	28. Learning to do something new	( )
2. Being relaxed	( )	29. Complimenting or praising someone	( )
3. Talking about other people	( )	30. Amusing people	( )
4. Thinking about something good in the future	( )	31. Being with someone I love	( )
5. Having people show interest in what I say	( )	32. Watching people	( )
		33. Making a new friend	( )
6. Being with friends	( )	34. Being complimented or told I have done well	( )
7. Eating good meals	( )	35. Expressing my love to someone	( )
8. Breathing clean air	( )	36. Having sexual relations with a partner of the opposite sex	( )
9. Seeing beautiful scenery	( )	37. Having spare time	( )
10. Thinking about people I like	( )	38. Helping someone	( )
11. Having a frank and open conversation	( )	39. Having friends come to visit	( )
12. Wearing clean clothes	( )	40. Listening to the sounds of nature	( )
13. Having coffee, tea, a coke, etc., with friends	( )	41. Watching wild animals	( )
14. Wearing informal clothes	( )	42. Driving skillfully	( )
15. Being noticed as sexually attractive	( )	43. Talking about sports	( )
16. Having peace and quiet	( )	44. Meeting someone new of the same sex	( )
17. Smiling at people	( )	45. Planning trips or vacations	( )
18. Sleeping soundly at night	( )	46. Having lunch with friends or associates	( )
19. Feeling the presence of the Lord in my life	( )	47. Being with animals	( )
20. Kissing	( )	48. Going to a party	( )
21. Doing a job well	( )	49. Sitting in the sun	( )
22. Having a lively talk	( )	50. Being praised by people I admire	( )
23. Seeing good things happen to family or friends	( )	51. Doing a project in my own way	( )
24. Being popular at a gathering	( )	52. Being told I am needed	( )
25. Saying something clearly	( )	53. Watching attractive women or men	( )
26. Reading stories, novels, poems, or plays	( )	54. Being told I am loved	( )
27. Planning or organizing something	( )	55. Seeing old friends	( )

APPENDIX A (Continued)

Activity	Frequency check	Activity	Frequency check
56. Staying up late	( )	69. Having an original idea	( )
57. Beachcombing	( )	70. Social drinking	( )
58. Snowballing or dune-buggy riding	( )	71. Getting massages or back-rubs	( )
59. Petting, necking	( )	72. Meeting someone of the opposite sex	( )
60. Listening to music	( )	73. Being in the country	( )
61. Visiting friends	( )	74. Seeing or smelling a flower or plant	( )
62. Being invited out	( )		
63. Going to a restaurant	( )	75. Being asked for my help or advice	( )
64. Talking about philosophy or religion	( )	76. Doing housework or laundry, cleaning things	( )
65. Singing to myself	( )		
66. Thinking about myself or my problems	( )	77. Sleeping late	( )
		78. Playing in sand, a stream, the grass, etc.	( )
67. Solving a problem, puzzle, crossword puzzle, etc.	( )	79. Being with happy people	( )
68. Completing a difficult task	( )	80. Looking at the stars or moon	( )

Part B

Name: _____ Date: _____

Please check within the parentheses to indicate the events of this day. Only events and interactions that were at least somewhat unpleasant should be checked.

Activity	Frequency check	Activity	Frequency check
1. Being dissatisfied with my spouse (living partner, mate)	( )	8. Having someone criticize or evaluate me (grades, rating, etc.)	( )
2. Working on something when I am tired	( )	9. Having too much to do	( )
3. Arguments with spouse (living partner, mate)	( )	10. Realizing that I can't do what I thought I could	( )
4. Being disabled (unable to work, go to school, etc.)	( )	11. Taking an exam (test, license examination, etc.)	( )
5. Having a minor illness or injury (toothache, allergy attack, cold, flu, hangover, acne breakout, etc.)	( )	12. Job hunting (applying, interviewing, etc.)	( )
		13. Leaving a task uncompleted, procrastinating	( )
6. Having my spouse (living partner, mate) dissatisfied with me	( )	14. Working at something I don't care about	( )
7. Working on something I don't enjoy	( )	15. Being rushed	( )
		16. Being near unpleasant people	

APPENDIX A (Continued)

Activity	Frequency check	Activity	Frequency check
(drunk, bigoted, inconsiderate, etc.)	( )	do something I disapprove (giving up religious training, dropping out of school, drinking, taking drugs, etc.)	( )
17. Having someone disagree with me	( )		
18. Being insulted	( )	39. Learning that someone is angry with me or wants to hurt me	( )
19. Having a project or assignment overdue	( )	40. Being misled, bluffed, or tricked	( )
20. Having something break or run poorly (car, appliances, etc.)	( )	41. Being nagged	( )
21. Living in a dirty or messy place	( )	42. Being bothered with red tape, administrative hassles, paperwork, etc.	( )
22. Bad weather	( )	43. Being away from someone I love	( )
23. Not having enough money for extras	( )	44. Listening to people complain	( )
24. Failing at something (a test, a class, etc.)	( )	45. Having a relative or friend living in unsatisfactory surroundings	( )
25. Seeing animals misbehave (making a mess, chasing cars, etc.)	( )	46. Knowing a close friend or relative is working under adverse conditions	( )
26. Being without privacy	( )	47. Learning of local, national, or international news (corruption, government decisions, crime, etc.)	( )
27. Eating food I don't enjoy	( )		
28. Working under pressure	( )		
29. Performing poorly in athletics	( )		
30. Talking with an unpleasant person (stubborn, unreasonable, aggressive, conceited, etc.)	( )	48. Being alone	( )
		49. Disciplining a child	( )
31. Realizing that I and someone I love are growing apart	( )	50. Saying something unclearly	( )
		51. Lying to someone	( )
32. Doing something I don't want to do in order to please someone else	( )	52. Breathing foul air	( )
		53. Being asked something I could not or did not want to answer	( )
33. Doing a job poorly (cooking something that tastes bad, etc.)	( )	54. Being in very hot weather	( )
34. Learning a friend or relative has just become ill, injured, or hospitalized, or is in need of an operation	( )	55. Being awakened when I am trying to sleep	( )
		56. Doing something embarrassing in the presence of others	( )
35. Being told what to do	( )	57. Being clumsy (dropping, spilling, knocking something over, etc.)	( )
36. Driving under adverse conditions (heavy traffic, poor weather, night, etc.)	( )	58. Receiving contradictory information from different sources	( )
37. Having a major unexpected expense (hospital bill, home repairs, etc.)	( )	59. Having family members or friends do something that makes me ashamed of them	( )
38. Having family members or friends		60. Being excluded or left out	( )
		61. Losing or misplacing something	

APPENDIX A (Continued)

Activity	Frequency check	Activity	Frequency check
(wallet, keys, golf ball, fish on a line, etc.)	( )	72. Being with sad people	( )
62. Learning that someone would stop at nothing to get ahead	( )	73. Having people ignore what I have said	( )
63. Being in a dirty or dusty place	( )	74. Being physically uncomfortable (dizzy, constipated, headache, itchy, cold, undergoing a rectal exam, having the hiccups, etc.)	( )
64. Not having sufficient time by myself, with my spouse (living partner, mate)	( )	75. Having people I care about fail at things (job, school, etc.) that are important to them	( )
65. Making a mistake (in sports, my job, etc.)	( )	76. Being with people who don't share my interests	( )
66. Running out of money	( )	77. Having someone owe me money or something else that belongs to me	( )
67. Having a relative or friend with a mental health problem	( )	78. Having someone I know drink, smoke, or take drugs	( )
68. Losing a friend	( )	79. Being misunderstood or misquoted	( )
69. Doing housework or laundry, cleaning things	( )	80. Being forced to do something	( )
70. Listening to someone who doesn't stop talking, can't keep to the point, or talks only about one subject	( )		
71. Living with a relative or roommate who is in poor physical or mental health	( )		

APPENDIX B Daily Mood Rating Form

Please rate your mood for this day (i.e., how good or bad you felt) using the 9-point scale shown below. If you felt really great (the best you have ever felt or can imagine yourself feeling), mark 1. If you felt really bad (the worst you have ever felt or can imagine yourself feeling), mark 9. If it was a so-so (or mixed) day, mark 5.

If you felt worse than so-so, mark a number between 6 and 9. If you felt better than so-so, mark a low number, between 2 and 4. Remember, a low number signifies that you felt good, and a high number means that you felt bad today.

very happy _____ very depressed
            1 2 3 4 5 6 7 8 9

Enter the date of your mood rating in the second column and your mood score in the third column.

Monitoring Mood			Monitoring Mood			Monitoring Mood		
Day	Date	Score	Day	Date	Score	Day	Date	Score
1			21			41		
2			22			42		
3			23			43		
4			24			44		
5			25			45		
6			26			46		
7			27			47		
8			28			48		
9			29			49		
10			30			50		
11			31			51		
12			32			52		
13			33			53		
14			34			54		
15			35			55		
16			36			56		
17			37			57		
18			38			58		
19			39			59		
20			40			60		

APPENDIX C Daily Monitoring Form for Relaxation Technique

Relaxation rating: 0 = most relaxed you have ever been
10 = most tense you have ever been

Dates: _____ to _____

	Monday	Tuesday	Wednesday	Thursday	Friday	Saturday	Sunday	Average Score (add your scores and divide by 7)
Average score for the day								
Least relaxed time								
Score								
When								
Where								
Situation								
Most relaxed time								
Score								
When								
Where								
Situation								
Occurrence of tension symptoms								
H = headache								
SA = stomachache								
SP = sleep problem								
Relaxation practice								
When								
For how long								
Score before								
Score after								

APPENDIX D Samples of Daily Monitoring of Relaxation

Malcolm		Barbara	
Average score	7	**Average score**	6
Least relaxed		**Least relaxed**	
Score	8	Score	7
When	Late morning	When	8–9 A.M.
Where	Office	Where	Home
Situation	Turning down Joe's request for salary increase	Situation	Trying to settle kid's argument
Most Relaxed		**Most Relaxed**	
Score	4	Score	3
When	5–6 P.M.	When	Early evening
Where	Home	Where	Park
Situation	Having drink and reading newspaper	Situation	Taking dog for walk
Occurrence of tension		**Occurrence of tension**	
symptoms	(SP)	symptoms	(H) In morning when kids were bickering
			(H) In late afternoon cooking dinner

Symbols for tension-related symptoms:
(SP) = sleep problem
(SA) = stomachache
(H) = headache

APPENDIX E Daily Monitoring of Relaxation in Problem Situations

Relaxation rating: 0 = most relaxed you have ever been
10 = most tense you have ever been   Dates: _____

Problem situations	Monday	Tuesday	Wednesday	Thursday	Friday	Saturday	Sunday
1. Initiating a conversation with a stranger							
2. Talking with a co-worker							
3. Joining the rest of the group at a coffee break							
4. Introducing myself to someone							
5. Inviting an acquaintance to join me for some social activity							
6. Accepting a social invitation							
7. Going to a service or social club meeting							
8. Inviting a neighbor over for coffee							
9. Appointment with my supervisor for a salary increase and/or promotion							
10. Professional meeting in which I have to give a talk before a group							

APPENDIX F Self-monitoring Log

Day: _____   Date: _____

Positive Activity   **Positive-Activity List Number**

1. _____
2. _____
3. _____
4. _____
5. _____
6. _____
7. _____
8. _____
9. _____
10. _____
11. _____
12. _____
13. _____
14. _____
15. _____
16. _____
17. _____
18. _____
19. _____
20. _____

Day's mood rating: 0   1   2   3   4   5   6   7   8   9   10
                        unhappiest   happiest
                        ever   ever

APPENDIX G Mood and Activity Exercise

The purpose of this exercise is to look closely at the relationship between activity and mood. The assumption is that mood is influenced by activity level generally and by specific types of activities.

1. Mood and activity graph: Using your self-monitoring logs for the last week, graph the number of positive activities for each day using the scale at the right. Now graph your week's mood using the scale at the left. Are the lines roughly parallel? Do the peaks and valleys correspond?

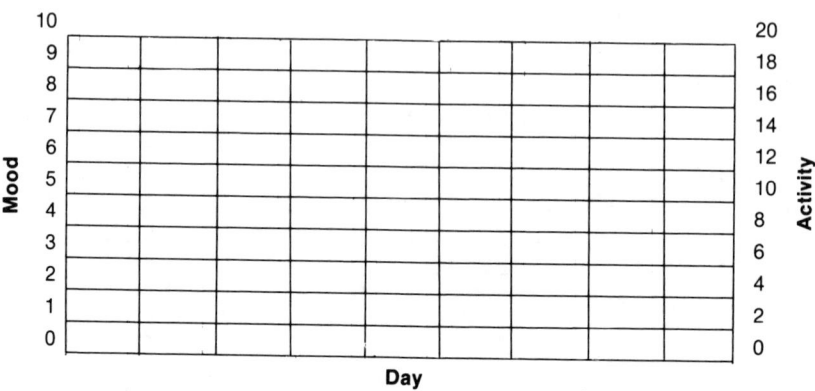

2. Pick out the 2 or 3 days on which your mood was the highest. Determine the average number of positive activities for those days. Next, do the same for the 2 or 3 days on which your mood was the lowest. Is the average number of activities higher on the better mood days?
3. Look at your self-monitoring logs for the 2 or 3 days on which your mood was the highest. What particular activities happened on those days? Compare these logs to the logs for your 2 or 3 worst mood days. What happened on the high mood days that did not happen on the low mood days?
4. Can you see a connection between your activity and your mood? People usually find a connection between mood and either general activity level or some specific type of activity. One week's records may not show this relationship clearly, but the program is based on the idea that mood can be changed by changing one's activities.
5. Repeat this exercise using the next week's records.

APPENDIX H Immediate Effects versus Delayed Effects

1. Choose four different activities that you recorded during the past week on your self-monitoring logs. Write them in the spaces at the left on the worksheet.
2. For each activity, fill in the effects in the four quadrants to the right. Effects can be payoffs or consequences of an activity (i.e., the reason you do it, the meaning it has for you). Effects can be either positive or negative. Most activities have both positive and negative effects (rewards and punishments, benefits and costs). Effects also can be immediate or delayed. Most activities have an effect at the moment but also may have a long-range cost or benefit. See the following examples.
3. Examples:

	Effects	
Activity	**Immediate**	**Delayed**
1. Ate an ice cream cone	Good taste, nice break, rested	Get more done if take breaks
	Expense	Gain weight
2. Called friend to come over for coffee	Enjoy talk	Better friendship
	Nervous about call	Less work done

4. Which were easier to think of: immediate effects or long-term effects? Positive or negative effects? Which are you more likely to be aware of at the time you are doing something? Did you think of effects that had not occurred to you before? Are there instances in which you might do things differently if you concentrate more on the delayed effects than on the immediate effects or vice versa?
5. During the coming week, use the extra column on your self-monitoring log to fill in a positive delayed effect of at least one positive activity per day.

Worksheet

Activity	Effects
	Immediate — Delayed

Columns (repeating): Negative Positive Negative Positive Negative Positive Negative Positive Negative Positive

1. _____
   _____
   _____

2. _____
   _____
   _____

3. _____
   _____
   _____

4. _____
   _____
   _____

5. _____
   _____
   _____

APPENDIX I Self-evaluation Worksheet

Goal (broad or long-range):
I want to increase _____
_____
_____

Subgoals:
1. _____
2. _____
3. _____
4. _____
5. _____

Assignment:
1. Establish goals and subgoals. The general idea is to break down the overall goal into small individual steps. To begin with, you may have to make a whole list of possible steps and then select from this list the best and most orderly steps. Subgoals should be defined such that they are (1) positive, (2) attainable, (3) within your capacity, and (4) operational.
2. Revise worksheets or make up additional worksheets for the preceding or different subgoals (two at most, for now).
3. Continue monitoring, as in previous weeks, all positive activities.
4. If an activity falls within your goal category, make a check mark in the extra column of your self-monitoring log.
5. Try to increase goal-related activities.

APPENDIX J Attribution of Responsibility

The purpose of this exercise is to look closely at assumptions people make in assigning credit, blame, or responsibility for events. The assumption is that people who tend to be depressed often make faulty assumptions about their responsibility for events.

1. List two fairly important events from your positive-activity logs for the last 2 weeks.
   Event a: _____
   Event b: _____
2. In what ways were other people, chance, or luck responsible for these events?
   Event a: _____
   Event b: _____
3. In what ways were you (your efforts, skills, abilities, etc.) responsible for these events?
   Event a: _____
   Event b: _____
4. What percentage of the responsibility for these events was attributable to you?
   Event a: _____ %
   Event b: _____ %

In most cases you will probably find that you have considerable responsibility for positive events in your life. Although positive events sometimes occur purely by chance (winning a lottery), positive events usually are things you have worked for or contributed to. It is nearly always within your power to influence these events or increase their effects. If you did not conclude that you had more than 50% responsibility for these events, go back to items 2 and 3 and reexamine them. Perhaps you can think of other ways in which you were responsible for the events.

5. Look at the reasons you wrote down in item 3. To what extent are these reasons examples of something generally true about yourself? That is, do they represent a stable pattern or characteristic of you that you show in many situations, or do they represent an unusual or limited aspect of your behavior?

Event a: General-stable 100-0% 75-25% 50-50% 25-75% 0-100% Unusual-specific

Event b: General-stable 100-0% 75-25% 50-50% 25-75% 0-100% Unusual-specific

In most cases you will probably find that the ways in which you were responsible for your positive activities were examples of general and stable characteristics that are true of you in many situations. If you did not conclude that general characteristics were involved, go back and reexamine your response to item 3. Perhaps you can think of general traits that were involved.

6. List two unpleasant or unhappy events that occurred during the last 2 weeks.
   Event c: _____
   Event d: _____
7. In what ways were other people, chance, or bad luck responsible for these events?
   Event c: _____
   Event d: _____
8. In what ways were you (your efforts, skills, and abilities or lack of effort, skill, and ability) responsible for these events?
   Event c: _____
   Event d: _____

9. What percentage of the responsibility for these events was attributable to you?
Event c: _____%
Event d: _____%

In most cases you will probably find that you are not solely responsible for the unpleasant events in your life. In most cases, unpleasant events are attributable to others or to chance. There is one exception to this rule. Being passive, and thus being bored or excessively dependent on others, can be an unpleasant event for which you may be responsible. That is, you could have chosen to act more assertively. If you did not conclude that your unpleasant events (other than passivity) were attributable to external causes or to luck, go back over items 7 and 8 and reexamine them. Perhaps you can think of other ways in which chance or other people were responsible for these events. It is important to be able to recognize accurately that certain unpleasant events are not under your control, whereas others may be. Only by separating these can you control and direct yourself and your mood.

10. Assignment for the coming week: Continue record keeping on your self-monitoring logs for the next week. Continue, especially, recording activities that you have defined as subgoals on your self-evaluation worksheets. For this week, use the extra column on your self-monitoring logs to record the percentage to which you were responsible for each of your positive activities.

APPENDIX K Elderly Reinforcement Survey Schedule

Name _____

Age _____ **Date** _____

We would like to ask you to rate how much you enjoy or like certain experiences. Your cooperation is appreciated.

We would like to use this information to find out what makes life worthwhile and enjoyable for individuals.

Indicate how much you would enjoy the experiences in the following list by checking one of the following:

  not at all ( )
  a little ( )
  a fair amount ( )
  much ( )
  very much ( )

If you have any trouble answering how you feel about any experience presented, perhaps it might be helpful for you to try to imagine that the experience is actually happening to you. Remember, this is not a test in any way. There are no right or wrong answers. Just answer how you would feel at this time in your life.

I Food

1. I like eating pastry: not at all ( ), a little ( ), a fair amount ( ), much ( ), very much ( ).
2. I like to eat cake: not at all ( ), a little ( ), a fair amount ( ), **much** ( ), very much ( ).
3. I like eating cookies: not at all ( ), a little ( ), a fair amount ( ), much ( ), very much ( ).
4. I like to eat donuts: not at all ( ), a little ( ), a fair amount ( ), much ( ), very much ( ).
5. I like eating ice cream: not at all ( ), a little ( ), a fair amount ( ), much ( ), very much ( ).
6. I like eating candy: not at all ( ), a little ( ), a fair amount ( ), much ( ), very much ( ).
7. I like drinking water: not at all ( ), a little ( ), a fair amount ( ), much ( ), very much ( ).
8. I like drinking milk: not at all ( ), a little ( ), a fair amount ( ), much ( ), very much ( ).
9. I like drinking soft drinks: not at all ( ), a little ( ), a fair amount ( ), much ( ), very much ( ).
10. I like drinking tea: not at all ( ), a little ( ), a fair amount ( ), much ( ), very much ( ).
11. I like drinking coffee: not at all ( ), a little ( ), a fair amount ( ), much ( ), very much ( ).
12. I like drinking hard liquor: not at all ( ), a little ( ), a fair amount ( ), much ( ), very much ( ).

13. I like drinking wine: not at all ( ), a little ( ), a fair amount ( ), much ( ), very much ( ).
14. I like drinking beer: not at all ( ), a little ( ), a fair amount ( ), much ( ), very much ( ).
15. I like to chew gum: not at all ( ), a little ( ), a fair amount ( ), much ( ), very much ( ).
16. I like malts: not at all ( ), a little ( ), a fair amount ( ), much ( ), very much ( ).
17. I like to eat popcorn: not at all ( ), a little ( ), a fair amount ( ), much ( ), very much ( ).
18. I like to eat candy: not at all ( ), a little ( ), a fair amount ( ), much ( ), very much ( ).
19. I like smoking cigars or a pipe: not at all ( ), a little ( ), a fair amount ( ), much ( ), very much ( ).
20. I like smoking cigarettes: not at all ( ), a little ( ), a fair amount ( ), much ( ), very much ( ).

II Shopping
21. I enjoy grocery shopping: not at all ( ), a little ( ), a fair amount ( ), much ( ), very much ( ).
22. I like shopping for clothes: not at all ( ), a little ( ), a fair amount ( ), much ( ), very much ( ).
23. I like visiting a marketplace: not at all ( ), a little ( ), a fair amount ( ), much ( ), very much ( ).
24. I like going shopping: not at all ( ), a little ( ), a fair amount ( ), much ( ), very much ( ).
25. I like getting a good bargain at a store: not at all ( ), a little ( ), a fair amount ( ), much ( ), very much ( ).

III Music
26. I like music in general: not at all ( ), a little ( ), a fair amount ( ), much ( ), very much ( ).
27. I like playing or using a musical instrument: not at all ( ), a little ( ), a fair amount ( ), much ( ), very much ( ).
28. I like folk music: not at all ( ), a little ( ), a fair amount ( ), much ( ), very much ( ).
29. I like swing music: not at all ( ), a little ( ), a fair amount ( ), much ( ), very much ( ).
30. I like classical music: not at all ( ), a little ( ), a fair amount ( ), much ( ), very much ( ).
31. I like Dixieland music: not at all ( ), a little ( ), a fair amount ( ), much ( ), very much ( ).
32. I like blues music: not at all ( ), a little ( ), a fair amount ( ), much ( ), very much ( ).

APPENDIX K (*Continued*)

33. I like rock music: not at all ( ), a little ( ), a fair amount ( ), much ( ), very much ( ).
34. I like to sing with other people: not at all ( ), a little ( ), a fair amount ( ), much ( ), very much ( ).
35. I like to sing alone: not at all ( ), a little ( ), a fair amount ( ), much ( ), very much ( ).

IV Scenery
36. I like looking at the ocean: not at all ( ), a little ( ), a fair amount ( ), much ( ), very much ( ).
37. I like seeing a beautiful farm with rolling hills and animals: not at all ( ), a little ( ), a fair amount ( ), much ( ), very much ( ).
38. I like looking at a lake: not at all ( ), a little ( ), a fair amount ( ), much ( ), very much ( ).
39. I like looking at the mountains: not at all ( ), a little ( ), a fair amount ( ), much ( ), very much ( ).
40. I like looking at beautiful sunsets: not at all ( ), a little ( ), a fair amount ( ), much ( ), very much ( ).
41. I like looking at a babbling brook: not at all ( ), a little ( ), a fair amount ( ), much ( ), very much ( ).
42. I like sitting in the sun: not at all ( ), a little ( ), a fair amount ( ), much ( ), very much ( ).
43. I enjoy watching and listening to birds: not at all ( ), a little ( ), a fair amount ( ), much ( ), very much ( ).

V Reading
44. I like reading: not at all ( ), a little ( ), a fair amount ( ), much ( ), very much ( ).
45. I like reading adventure stories: not at all ( ), a little ( ), a fair amount ( ), much ( ), very much ( ).
46. I like reading about romance: not at all ( ), a little ( ), a fair amount ( ), much ( ), very much ( ).
47. I like reading biographies: not at all ( ), a little ( ), a fair amount ( ), much ( ), very much ( ).
48. I like reading science fiction: not at all ( ), a little ( ), a fair amount ( ), much ( ), very much ( ).
49. I like reading detective stories: not at all ( ), a little ( ), a fair amount ( ), much ( ), very much ( ).
50. I like reading the newspaper: not at all ( ), a little ( ), a fair amount ( ), much ( ), very much ( ).
51. I like reading humor: not at all ( ), a little ( ), a fair amount ( ), much ( ), very much ( ).

VI Entertainment

52. I enjoy watching plays: not at all ( ), a little ( ), a fair amount ( ), much ( ), very much ( ).
53. I like watching television: not at all ( ), a little ( ), a fair amount ( ), much ( ), very much ( ).
54. I like watching movies: not at all ( ), a little ( ), a fair amount ( ), much ( ), very much ( ).
55. I like listening to the radio: not at all ( ), a little ( ), a fair amount ( ), much ( ), very much ( ).

VII Spectator Sports

56. I like watching pool: not at all ( ), a little ( ), a fair amount ( ), much ( ), very much ( ).
57. I enjoy watching hockey: not at all ( ), a little ( ), a fair amount ( ), much ( ), very much ( ).
58. I like watching golf: not at all ( ), a little ( ), a fair amount ( ), much ( ), very much ( ).
59. I like watching tennis: not at all ( ), a little ( ), a fair amount ( ), much ( ), very much ( ).
60. I like watching boxing: not at all ( ), a little ( ), a fair amount ( ), much ( ), very much ( ).
61. I like watching baseball: not at all ( ), a little ( ), a fair amount ( ), much ( ), very much ( ).
62. I like watching horse racing: not at all ( ), a little ( ), a fair amount ( ), much ( ), very much ( ).
63. I like watching track: not at all ( ), a little ( ), a fair amount ( ), much ( ), very much ( ).
64. I like watching ice skating: not at all ( ), a little ( ), a fair amount ( ), much ( ), very much ( ).
65. I like watching soccer: not at all ( ), a little ( ), a fair amount ( ), much ( ), very much ( ).
66. I like watching football: not at all ( ), a little ( ), a fair amount ( ), much ( ), very much ( ).
67. I like watching basketball: not at all ( ), a little ( ), a fair amount ( ), much ( ), very much ( ).

VIII Hobbies

68. I like collecting stamps: not at all ( ), a little ( ), a fair amount ( ), much ( ), very much ( ).
69. I like cooking: not at all ( ), a little ( ), a fair amount ( ), much ( ), very much ( ).
70. I like collecting coins: not at all ( ), a little ( ), a fair amount ( ), much ( ), very much ( ).
71. I like painting: not at all ( ), a little ( ), a fair amount ( ), much ( ), very much ( ).

APPENDIX K (Continued)

72. I like making things with my hands: not at all ( ), a little ( ), a fair amount ( ), much ( ), very much ( ).
73. I like being praised about my hobbies: not at all ( ), a little ( ), a fair amount ( ), much ( ), very much ( ).
74. I like needlepoint: not at all ( ), a little ( ), a fair amount ( ), much ( ), very much ( ).
75. I like knitting: not at all ( ), a little ( ), a fair amount ( ), much ( ), very much ( ).
76. I like showing photographs of my family and friends to other people: not at all ( ), a little ( ), a fair amount ( ), much ( ), very much ( ).
77. I like figuring out how something works: not at all ( ), a little ( ), a fair amount ( ), much ( ), very much ( ).
78. I like solving problems: not at all ( ), a little ( ), a fair amount ( ), much ( ), very much ( ).
79. I like playing cards: not at all ( ), a little ( ), a fair amount ( ), much ( ), very much ( ).
80. I like playing cribbage: not at all ( ), a little ( ), a fair amount ( ), much ( ), very much ( ).
81. I like playing whist: not at all ( ), a little ( ), a fair amount ( ), much ( ), very much ( ).
82. I like playing bridge: not at all ( ), a little ( ), a fair amount ( ), much ( ), very much ( ).
83. I like playing gin rummy: not at all ( ), a little ( ), a fair amount ( ), much ( ), very much ( ).
84. I like playing poker: not at all ( ), a little ( ), a fair amount ( ), much ( ), very much ( ).
85. I like playing Michigan rummy: not at all ( ), a little ( ), a fair amount ( ), much ( ), very much ( ).
86. I like playing bingo: not at all ( ), a little ( ), a fair amount ( ), much ( ), very much ( ).
87. I like playing chess: not at all ( ), a little ( ), a fair amount ( ), much ( ), very much ( ).
88. I like playing checkers: not at all ( ), a little ( ), a fair amount ( ), much ( ), very much ( ).

IX Activities
89. I like exercising: not at all ( ), a little ( ), a fair amount ( ), much ( ), very much ( ).
90. I like going for a walk: not at all ( ), a little ( ), a fair amount ( ), much ( ), very much ( ).
91. I like playing ping-pong: not at all ( ), a little ( ), a fair amount ( ), much ( ), very much ( ).
92. I like playing golf: not at all ( ), a little ( ), a fair amount ( ), much ( ), very much ( ).

93. I like dancing: not at all ( ), a little ( ), a fair amount ( ), much ( ), very much ( ).
94. I like swimming: not at all ( ), a little ( ), a fair amount ( ), much ( ), very much ( ).
95. I like bowling: not at all ( ), a little ( ), a fair amount ( ), much ( ), very much ( ).
96. I like playing horseshoes: not at all ( ), a little ( ), a fair amount ( ), much ( ), very much ( ).
97. I like playing croquet: not at all ( ), a little ( ), a fair amount ( ), much ( ), very much ( ).
98. I like gardening: not at all ( ), a little ( ), a fair amount ( ), much ( ), very much ( ).

X Odor
99. I like smelling flowers: not at all ( ), a little ( ), a fair amount ( ), much ( ), very much ( ).
100. I like smelling perfume: not at all ( ), a little ( ), a fair amount ( ), much ( ), very much ( ).
101. I like smelling food: not at all ( ), a little ( ), a fair amount ( ), much ( ), very much ( ).
102. I like smelling salt water: not at all ( ), a little ( ), a fair amount ( ), much ( ), very much ( ).
103. I like smelling freshly mowed grass: not at all ( ), a little ( ), a fair amount ( ), much ( ), very much ( ).
104. I like smelling fresh laundry: not at all ( ), a little ( ), a fair amount ( ), much ( ), very much ( ).

XI Quiet and Reflective Times
105. I like planning the day: not at all ( ), a little ( ), a fair amount ( ), much ( ), very much ( ).
106. I like taking naps: not at all ( ), a little ( ), a fair amount ( ), much ( ), very much ( ).
107. I like peace and quiet: not at all ( ), a little ( ), a fair amount ( ), much ( ), very much ( ).
108. I like feeling calm and relaxed when I go to sleep: not at all ( ), a little ( ), a fair amount ( ), much ( ), very much ( ).
109. I like feeling the future is going to be enjoyable: not at all ( ), a little ( ), a fair amount ( ), much ( ), very much ( ).
110. I like thinking about past experiences: not at all ( ), a little ( ), a fair amount ( ), much ( ), very much ( ).
111. I like following politics: not at all ( ), a little ( ), a fair amount ( ), much ( ), very much ( ).
112. I like helping with housekeeping: not at all ( ), a little ( ), a fair amount ( ), much ( ), very much ( ).
113. I like sewing: not at all ( ), a little ( ), a fair amount ( ), much ( ), very much ( ).

APPENDIX K (Continued)

XII Participation in Entertainment and Activities
114. I like parties or socials: not at all ( ), a little ( ), a fair amount ( ), much ( ), very much ( ).
115. I like going to the theater: not at all ( ), a little ( ), a fair amount ( ), much ( ), very much ( ).
116. I like going to restaurants: not at all ( ), a little ( ), a fair amount ( ), much ( ), very much ( ).
117. I like going on picnics: not at all ( ), a little ( ), a fair amount ( ), much ( ), very much ( ).
118. I like going to the zoo: not at all ( ), a little ( ), a fair amount ( ), much ( ), very much ( ).
119. I like going to museums: not at all ( ), a little ( ), a fair amount ( ), much ( ), very much ( ).

XIII Trips
120. I like riding in a car: not at all ( ), a little ( ), a fair amount ( ), much ( ), very much ( ).
121. I like going on a trip by bus: not at all ( ), a little ( ), a fair amount ( ), much ( ), very much ( ).
122. I like going on a trip by car: not at all ( ), a little ( ), a fair amount ( ), much ( ), very much ( ).
123. I like going on a trip by plane: not at all ( ), a little ( ), a fair amount ( ), much ( ), very much ( ).
124. I like going on a trip by boat: not at all ( ), a little ( ), a fair amount ( ), much ( ), very much ( ).

XIV Animals and People
125. I like horses: not at all ( ), a little ( ), a fair amount ( ), much ( ), very much ( ).
126. I like cats: not at all ( ), a little ( ), a fair amount ( ), much ( ), very much ( ).
127. I like dogs: not at all ( ), a little ( ), a fair amount ( ), much ( ), very much ( ).
128. I like listening to children laughing: not at all ( ), a little ( ), a fair amount ( ), much ( ), very much ( ).
129. I like playing with children: not at all ( ), a little ( ), a fair amount ( ), much ( ), very much ( ).
130. I like being near a handsome man: not at all ( ), a little ( ), a fair amount ( ), much ( ), very much ( ).
131. I like being near a handsome woman: not at all ( ), a little ( ), a fair amount ( ), much ( ), very much ( ).
132. I like babies: not at all ( ), a little ( ), a fair amount ( ), much ( ), very much ( ).

133. I like teenagers: not at all ( ), a little ( ), a fair amount ( ), much ( ), very much ( ).
134. I like elderly people: not at all ( ), a little ( ), a fair amount ( ), much ( ), very much ( ).

XV Going Places

135. I like going to church or temple: not at all ( ), a little ( ), a fair amount ( ), much ( ), very much ( ).
136. I like having visitors who are not relatives: not at all ( ), a little ( ), a fair amount ( ), much ( ), very much ( ).
137. I like visiting friends: not at all ( ), a little ( ), a fair amount ( ), much ( ), very much ( ).
138. I like visiting relatives: not at all ( ), a little ( ), a fair amount ( ), much ( ), very much ( ).
139. I like having visitors who are relatives: not at all ( ), a little ( ), a fair amount ( ), much ( ), very much ( ).
140. I like visiting restaurants: not at all ( ), a little ( ), a fair amount ( ), much ( ), very much ( ).

XVI Being Recognized and Socialization

141. I like being asked to tell stories about the early years of my life: not at all ( ), a little ( ), a fair amount ( ), much ( ), very much ( ).
142. I like being asked directions: not at all ( ), a little ( ), a fair amount ( ), much ( ), very much ( ).
143. I like having someone smile and say hello to me: not at all ( ), a little ( ), a fair amount ( ), much ( ), very much ( ).
144. I like being kissed by someone I like: not at all ( ), a little ( ), a fair amount ( ), much ( ), very much ( ).
145. I like being asked for my advice: not at all ( ), a little ( ), a fair amount ( ), much ( ), very much ( ).
146. I like having someone ask me how I am: not at all ( ), a little ( ), a fair amount ( ), much ( ), very much ( ).
147. I like receiving flowers: not at all ( ), a little ( ), a fair amount ( ), much ( ), very much ( ).
148. I like having somebody tell me jokes: not at all ( ), a little ( ), a fair amount ( ), much ( ), very much ( ).
149. I like getting presents: not at all ( ), a little ( ), a fair amount ( ), much ( ), very much ( ).
150. I like having a nice-looking stranger talk to me: not at all ( ), a little ( ), a fair amount ( ), much ( ), very much ( ).
151. I like having people pay careful attention when I speak: not at all ( ), a little ( ), a fair amount ( ), much ( ), very much ( ).
152. I like it when someone compliments me on my knowledge of current events: not at all ( ), a little ( ), a fair amount ( ), much ( ), very much ( ).

APPENDIX K (Continued)

153. I like having people seek me out for company: not at all ( ), a little ( ), a fair amount ( ), much ( ), very much ( ).
154. I like having sex with someone who cares for me: not at all ( ), a little ( ), a fair amount ( ), much ( ), very much ( ).
155. I like feeling that I am important to a person: not at all ( ), a little ( ), a fair amount ( ), much ( ), very much ( ).
156. I like being appreciated for my abilities: not at all ( ), a little ( ), a fair amount ( ), much ( ), very much ( ).
157. I enjoy being with other people: not at all ( ), a little ( ), a fair amount ( ), much ( ), very much ( ).
158. I like meeting new people: not at all ( ), a little ( ), a fair amount ( ), much ( ), very much ( ).
159. I like talking to other people: not at all ( ), a little ( ), a fair amount ( ), much ( ), very much ( ).
160. I like helping others: not at all ( ), a little ( ), a fair amount ( ), much ( ), very much ( ).
161. I like feeling that my life has contributed to the happiness of others: not at all ( ), a little ( ), a fair amount ( ), much ( ), very much ( ).

My three most favorite people in all the world are:
1. _____
2. _____
3. _____

The three most wonderful experiences I can imagine are:
1. _____
2. _____
3. _____

Index

ABSS (Assertive Behavior Survey Schedule), 349
Active treatment of childhood depression, 311-339; see also Children, depressed
Activity, increasing patient's, 225
Activity and mood exercise, 376
Activity Schedule, 367-370
Activity scheduling, 121
AER (automatic emotional reaction), 211-215, 218
Affect, depressed, 170, 175
  and performance, 162, 163
Affective/physiological system and suicide, 247-249, 255
Age and suicide, 243
Aging, process of, versus behaviors of elderly persons, 345
Aggressive, impulsive, oppositional, and negative behavior in children, 319-322, 327-328, 329-339
Anger
  with depression, 216
  and suicide, 248, 249
Antidepressant(s)
  evaluations of efficacy of, 296-297
  imipramine as, 330
  lithium as, 303
  versus multimodal approach, 176-177
  summary and guidelines for selection of, 304-305
  tricyclic
    for children, 337-338
    prediction of responses to, 300-301
Antidepressant responses to MAOI's, prediction of, 302-303
Arbitrary inference, 71-72
Aristotelian thinking, 222-223
Assertive Behavior Survey Schedule (ABSS), 349
Assertiveness
  in elderly, 357, 358
  as target behavior, 221-225

Assertiveness training
  and attributional styles, 155
  in remediation therapy, 194
  versus self-control therapy, 97-99
Assessment
  of depression, 3-26
    observational methods in, 22-23
    recommendations for, 23-24
    tools for, 14-22; see also Scales, reports, and schedules
  of risk for suicide and parasuicide, 253-263
  of suicidal behavior, 263-265
Assumption(s)
  and automatic thoughts, 145
  modification of, 127-129
  predisposing to depression, 127
Attribution of responsibility, 89-90, 380-381
Attributional reformulation, 131-160; see also Reattribution techniques
  clinical efficacy of therapeutic strategies in, 157-158
  decreasing vulnerability to depression in, 148-157
    attributing outcomes to internal, stable and global factors, 150-156
    judging outcomes as uncontrollable, 148-150
    subscribing to unrealistic goals, 156-157
  implications of, 136-137
  reversing current depressive episodes in, 140-148
    expectation of no control, 140-142
    internal attributions for uncontrollability, 146-148
    unattainable goals, 144-146
    unrealistic goals, 142-144
Attributional styles
  belief-based versus evidence-based, 155-156

Attributional styles (*cont.*)
    depressive, 150–156
Automatic emotional reaction (AER)
    and habit reinforcement, 218
    as target behavior, 211–215
Automatic thoughts, 195
    and assumption, 145
    identifying, 115–116
Aversive events, behavioral treatment
    managing of, 53–55
Aversive experience, 36
Aversive marital interchanges, 190

BAHQ (Behavioral Analysis History
    Questionnaire), 347
BDI (Beck Depression Inventory),
    17–18
Beck Depression Inventory (BDI), 17–18
    in behavioral treatment, 43
    dysfunctional attitude scale and, 156
Behavior
    depressed, 170, 175
    and mood and thoughts, 203
Behavior productivity in remediation
    therapy, 192–193, 198–199
Behavior rehearsal, 224
Behavior therapy, *see also* Behavioral
    treatment of depression
    attributional reformulation and,
        149–150
    versus behavioral treatment by cognitive therapy, 113–114
    clinical, for depression, 205–226
    and cognitive therapy versus chemotherapy, 301–302
    for socially ineffective children,
        group treatment program,
        324–325
Behavioral Analysis History Questionnaire (BAHQ), 347
Behavioral approaches
    in childhood psychotherapy, 313
    to somatic complaints in depression,
        319
Behavioral assessment of depression,
    8–14
    defining problem in, 9
    establishing patient-therapist contract in, 13–14
    functional analysis in, 9–12
    goals of, 24–25
    identification of specific behavioral
        excesses and deficits in, 12
    identifying personal and environmental assets in, 13
    interviewer rating instruments for,
        20–22
        Feelings and Concerns Checklist,
            21–22
        Hamilton Rating Scale, 20–21
        Schedule for Affective Disorders
            and Schizophrenia, 21
    selecting monitoring procedure and
        determining baseline in, 12–13
    self-monitoring instruments for,
        14–20
        Beck Depression Inventory, 17–18
        Depression Adjective Checklist,
            18–19
        MMPI depression scale, 16–17
        Pleasant Events Schedule, 19–20
        Pretreatment Questionnaire, 20
        Self-Rating Depression Scale, 18
    specifying behavioral goals in, 13
    therapeutic strategies in, 11–12
Behavioral factors in suicide, 244–252,
    255
Behavioral focus in remediation of
    skills and deficits, 196
Behavioral problems functionally
    related to depression, 43
Behavioral techniques in cognitive
    therapy, 120–122
    activity scheduling, 121
    graded task assignment, 122
    mastery and pleasure techniques,
        121–122
    presenting behavioral tasks, 122
Behavioral treatment of depression,
    33–63, 113–115, 344–363; *see
    also* Behavior therapy
    in cognitive therapy, 113–115
    components of: theory, strategy, and
        tactics, 33–35
    for successful short-term therapy,
        62–63
    desensitization in 211–215, 216, 218,
        317

Index **395**

in elderly patients, 344-363
new directions in, 60-62
practical concerns in, 59-60
remediation, common complications of, 201-203
strategy of, *see* Behavioral treatment strategy
tactics in, 49-58
  daily monitoring, 53
  evaluating progress, 57
  general considerations, 57-58
  managing of aversive events, 53-55
  relaxation training, 52, 55-57
  time management, 55
therapeutic efficacy of, 60-62
treatment modules in, 53
treatment paradigm in, 59
Behavioral treatment strategy, 38-49
conceptualization of problems in, 39-40
contracting and self-reinforcement schedules in, 48-49
daily monitoring in, 46-48
differential diagnosis in, 40-43
  interview outline, 42
home observations in, 43-44
identification of targets for intervention, 43-49
  behavioral problems functionally related to depression, 43
  interview outline for, 42
  pinpointing key events in, 44-46
  termination of, and follow-up assignments for, 48
  time limit for, 48
Bias(es)
  to attribute outcomes to internal, stable, and global factors, 150-156
  and illusions, cognitive, in nondepressed people, 158-160
  to judge outcomes as uncontrollable, 148-150
  to subscribe to unrealistic goals, 155-156
Biofeedback in treatment of hyperactivity, 319
Biological manifestations of depression, 171, 175

Biological theories of suicide, 234
Bladder control training, 317

Causal inferences and schemas, 153-155
Causes, search for, as complicating treatment, 202
Characterologic depression, 299
  treatment for, 301, 304-305
Chemotherapy versus behavioral and cognitive therapies, 301-302; *see also* Antidepressant(s)
Children, depressed
  active therapy for, 326-339
    rationale for, 314-316
    in symptoms related to depression, 316-326
  aggressive/impulsive/oppositional/negative behavior in, 319-322, 329-339
  multimodal approach for, 338-339
  psychoeducational therapy for, 334
  psychopharmacologic treatment: tricyclic antidepressants for, 337-338
  social skills training for, 336-337
  structured milieu therapy, behaviorally oriented, for, 334
  supportive psychotherapy, dynamically oriented, for, 333-334
  behavioral psychotherapy for, 313
  social skills training for, 320-322, 327-328, 336-337
Clinical practice, uses of theories in guiding, 131-134
Cognition, depressed, 170-171, 175
Cognitive biases and illusions in nondepressed people, 158-160
Cognitive content and suicide, 244-247, 255
Cognitive model of depression, 112-113
Cognitive-oriented therapy and belief-based styles, 155
Cognitive self-control in remediation of skills and performance deficits, 195-196
Cognitive skills, developing, 52

Cognitive style in suicide, 244-245
Cognitive system and suicide, 244-247
Cognitive theory(ies)
　versus multimodal orientation, 172
　of suicide, 235-236
Cognitive therapy, 111-129
　behavioral and, versus chemotherapy, 301-302
　behavioral treatments in, 113-115
　core data of, 116
　deuterolearning in, 120
　effectiveness of treatment in, 129
　homework in, 120
　identifying automatic thoughts in, 115-116
　logical empiricism and therapeutic collaboration in, 118-119
　maintaining functioning in, 127-129
　modifying underlying assumptions in, 127-129
　other schools versus, 141
　special process-debriefing and, 154
　specific behavioral techniques in, 120-122
　　activity scheduling, 121
　　graded task assignment, 122
　　mastery and pleasure techniques, 121-122
　　presenting behavioral tasks, 122
　specific cognitive techniques in, 123-125
　　alternative therapy, 124
　　reattribution, 125
　　triple-column, 123-124
　structure of therapeutic sessions in, 119-120
　suicide and, 125-127
　therapist in, 117-118
　typical course of treatment in, 119
Cognitive triad, negative, 112, 139
　in children, 314
Collaborative empiricism, 147
Communication, suicidal behavior as attempt at, 235
Communication skills, remediation of, 190-192
Complaining and criticizing in elderly, 356-358
Contingency management, 50-51

Contract
　antisuicide, 278
　therapist-patient, 13-14
Contracting and self-reinforcement schedules, 48-49
Control, expectations of lack of, 140-142, 146-150; see also Attributional reformulation
Coping techniques, inadequate, 188-189
"Coping with Depression" course, 60-62, 315
Covert conditioning procedures, 346
　for assertive behavior, 357-358
　as self-control procedure, 361-362, 363
Covert modeling, 357-358
Covert reinforcement of elderly, 352, 358

"D modality" (drug) treatment, 176-177; see also Antidepressant(s)
DAC (Depression Adjective Checklist), 18-19
Daily monitoring, see Monitoring, daily
DAS (Dysfunctional Attitude Scale), 156
DBSS (Depressive Behavior Survey Schedule), 347, 348
Decision making and problem solving in remediation of skills and performance deficits, 194-195
Demographic factors in suicide, 242-244, 254-255
Depressed affect and performance, 162, 163
Depression
　assessment of, 3-26
　　behavioral, 8-14
　atypical, 7
　characterologic, 299
　　treatment for, 301, 304-305
　classification of, 4-7
　　prototypic, 7
　complex nature of, 68-70
　context of, 26
　definition, 3
　endogenous, 297-299
　　treatment for, 300, 301, 304-305
　four-stage serial process in, 180-181

major, 6
masked, 298–299
  childhood, 312
mild and combined syndromes in, 300
"neurotic," 299, 301
primary versus secondary, 298
as resembling fever, 131
self-control model of, 70–80
subtypes of, 40, 69
symptoms of, 4, 5, 69
  endogenous, and tricyclic drugs, 300, 301
  physical or "vegetative," 297–298
  program noncompliance due to, 201
  symptoms related to active therapy for, 316–326
unipolar versus bipolar, 298
vulnerability to, 148–157
Depression Adjective Checklist (DACL), 18–19
Depression spectrum, different symptoms in, 169–171
Depressive Behavior Survey Schedule (DBSS), 347, 348
Depressive equivalent, 298–299
  hyperactive or agitated behavior as, 317–319
Depressive neurosis (dysthymic disorder), 6–7
Depressive subtypes and choice of treatment, 305
Desensitization, in behavioral treatment, 211–215, 216
  muscle tension and, 212
  of reinforcing person, 218
  of school-phobic children, 317
Deuterolearning in cognitive therapy, 120
Diagnostic subtypes, individual differences and, 184, 185
Drugs and suicide, 278
DSM-III classification system, 6–7
Dysfunctional Attitude Scale (DAS), 156
Dysthymic disorder (depressive neurosis), 6–7

ECT (electroconvulsive therapy), 295, 300

indications for, 303–304
Elderly, 344–363
behavioral analysis of, 347–350
  interviewing significant others, 349–350
  inventories, 347–349
  record keeping, 350
behavioral treatment of, 350–363
  changing level of reinforcement in, 354–359
  covert conditioning as self-control procedure in, 361–362, 363
  covert reinforcement in, 352, 358
  decreasing negative scanning in, 352–354
  modifying feeling of helplessness in, 359
  procedures in, 360–361
  special considerations in, 362–363
  strategy of, 350–351
  thought stopping in, 352–353, 360, 363
depression and, 351–352
depressive reactions among, 222
exercise for, 358–359
Elderly Reinforcement Survey Schedule (ERSS), 348–349, 382–390
Electroconvulsive therapy (ECT), 295, 300, 303–304
Emotional pictures of suicide versus parasuicide, 249–250
Emotional reactions, automatic (AER), 211–215, 218
Empiricism, collaborative, 147
Endogenous depression, 297–299
  treatment for, 300, 301, 304–305
  tricyclic drugs in, 300, 301
Enuresis in children, 316–317
Environmental factors in suicide, 239–242, 254
Environmental interventions in behavioral treatment, 50–51
ERSS (Elderly Reinforcement Survey Schedule), 348–349, 382–390

Family dysfunction and depressed child, 332–333, 335–336

Feedback
  false, and attributional style, 153–154
  negative and positive
    estimation of, 72–74
    nondepressed people and, 159
Feelings and Concerns Checklist, 21–22
  in behavioral treatment, 41
Flooding method
  avoiding, 212
  obsession and, 216
Functional analysis of depressive disorders, 9–12

Goal orientation, loss of, 201
Goals
  centered in area of self-respect, 223–224
  decreasing importance of unattainable, 144–146
  graduated attainment of, 197
  inappropriate and unobtainable, 222–223
  long-term and short-term, 87, 222
  personal and social recognition of, 197
  personal disuse and lack of, 187–188
  self-evaluation worksheet in, 379
  self-monitoring, 88
  setting of
    as problem in depression, 143
    in self-control therapy, 87–88
  specifying behavioral, 13
  unrealistic
    bias to subscribe to, 156–157
    modifying, 142–144
    and performance criteria, 186–187
Goals of behavioral assessment of depression, 24–25
Goals of treatment
  identification of, 196
  long-term, and suicide, 276
Graded task assignment in cognitive therapy, 122
Group research format, advantages of, 80–81
Guilt with depression, 216

Habit depressions, blind, 220–221
Habits, unwanted, as target behavior, 217–221
Habitual mild chronic hyperventilation (HMCH), 209–210
Hamilton Rating Scale, 20–21
Hedonism, 93
Helplessness in elderly, modifying feelings of, 359
Helplessness theories of depression, 135; see also Attributional reformulation; Learned helplessness
HMCH (habitual mild chronic hyperventilation), 209–210
Home observations in diagnosis, 43–44
Hopelessness and suicide, 126, 245–247
Hostility and suicide, 247–248, 249, 250
Humor in attributional reformulation, 146
Hyperactive or agitated behavior as "depressive equivalent", 317–319
Hyperventilation, habitual mild chronic, 209–210
Hypotheses of patient as complicating therapy, 202

Imagery, depressed, 170, 175
Imagery Survey Schedule (ISS), 347, 348
Immediate and delayed effects of specific activities, 85–86
Immediate and long-range goals, 87
Immediate Effects versus Delayed Effects (log), 377–378
Immediate versus long-term outcome of behavior, 74–75
Individual differences and diagnostic subtypes, 184, 185
Internal, stable, and global factors, outcomes and, 150–156
Interpersonal interaction, depressed, 171, 175
Interpersonal relationships, changing, 51–52
Interviewer rating instruments, 20–22
ISS (Imagery Survey Schedule), 347, 348

Index **399**

Key events, pinpointing, 44-46

Learned helplessness, 131-160, 207; see also Attributional reformulation
 depressed children and, 314-315
 reconceptualizations of, 272
Learning, social, as approach to depression, 33-63
Learning theory
 and clinical disorders of childhood, 313
 of suicide, 236-237
Life-stress events, 188
Lithium as antidepressant, 303
Logical empiricism and therapeutic collaboration in cognitive therapy, 118-119
Loss and automatic emotional reaction, 211

Manipulation and suicide, 126, 220, 237
MAOIs (monoamine oxidase inhibitors), 295
 prediction of antidepressant responses to, 302-303
Married couples, communication patterns of, 190-192
 aversive, 190
Masked depressions, 298-299
 childhood, 213
Mastery
 and assertiveness, 221-224
 and obsessive thoughts, 215
Mastery ratings, 121
Memory, distortions of, 72-73
MMPI Depression Scale, 16-17
Model of depression, atheoretical, 180-184
Models, types of, 133
Models approach to therapy, information for, 134
Monitoring, daily, 46-48, 53
 forms for
  Daily Monitoring Form for Relaxation Technique, 372, 373

 Daily Monitoring of Relaxation in Problem Situations, 374
 Daily Mood Rating Form, 371
Monoamine oxidase inhibitors (MAOIs), 295, 302-303
Mood and activity exercise, 376
Mood Rating Form, Daily, 371
Mood versus thoughts and behavior, 203
Motor behaviors, overt
 assessment of, 23
 suicide and, 249-251, 256
Multimodal orientation, personality according to, 171-172
Multimodal therapy, 169-177
 for children, 338-339
 intervention plans in, 173, 175-176
Muscle tension and desensitization, 212

Negative changes in suicidogenic environment, 239
Negative "cognitive triad," 112, 139
 in children, 314
Negative cueing, 191
Negative events, self-monitoring of, 71-74
Negative scanning in elderly, 352-354
Neurosis, depressive (dysthymic disorder), 6-7
Nondepressed people, cognitive biases and illusions in, 158-160
Normalization, role of, in remediation of skills and performance deficits, 198

Obsessions as target behavior, 215-216
Operant conditioning, stimuli and responses in, 10
Oppositional behavior and childhood depression, 319-320
Overt motor behavior assessment, 22-23
Overt motor system and suicide, 249-251, 256
Overt verbal behavior, 22-23

Pain or physical discomfort and negative scanning in elderly, 353–354
Parent skills training, 335–336
Parental depression, 315–316
Parenting, inadequate or ineffective, 315–316
"Passivity," 225
Patient-therapist contract, 13–14
Performance and effect, depressed, 162, 163
Performance criteria and unrealistic goals, 186–187
Performance deficits, remediation of, 179–203
Perfectionism, 87, 222
Personal and social recognition of gains, 197
Personal and social skills in remediation therapy, 189–196
Personal stress, sources of, 185–189
  inadequate coping techniques, 188–189
  life-stress events, 188
  personal disuse and lack of goals, 187–188
  unrealistic goals and performance criteria, 186–187
PES (Pleasant-Events Schedule), 19–20, 44–46
Phobia(s)
  school, 317
  treating depressions as, 211, 218
Phobic behavior in elderly, 354
Phobic reaction to depressive symptoms, 213
Physiological/affective system and suicide, 247–249, 255
Placebo treatments, 296
Pleasant and unpleasant events, daily monitoring of, 54
Pleasant-Events Schedule (PES), 19–20
  in behavioral treatment, 44–46
Pleasure ratings in cognitive therapy, 121–122
Pollyannaism, 92–93
Positive-Activities List, 84
Positive Activity Self-Monitoring Log, 375

Positive reinforcement and childhood depression, 315
Pretreatment Questionnaire, McLean, 20
Pretreatment recommendations in suicide treatment, 272–273
Primary versus secondary depression, 298
Problem-solving and suicidal behavior, 235–236, 239, 275–276, 279
Problem-solving therapy in attributional reformulation, 149–150
Problems and treatment goals, identifying, 196
"Process debriefing," special, 154
Productivity, behavior, 192–193, 198–199
Psychodynamic theories of suicide, 234–235
Psychoeducational therapy for children, 334
Psychopharmacologic treatment for children, 337–338
Psychotherapy, supportive, for children, 326–339
Public setting versus private, and self-reward, 78
Punishment and depression, 36

Race and suicide, 243–244
Rational-Emotive Therapy (RET), 157
RDC (Research Diagnostic Criteria), 70
Reattribution techniques, *see also* Attributional reformulation
  in cognitive therapy, 125
  in suicide treatment, 272–273
Reinforcement
  in behavioral treatment, 35–38
  contracting and, 48–49
  of habits by others, 217–219
  and automatic emotional reaction, 218
  self-, 48–49, 77–78, 90–92
  social
    for depression, 37
    for withdrawn children, 323–324
    in treatment of elderly
      changing level of, 354–359

covert, 352
Reinforcement contingencies and sex type behavior in children, 325–326
Reinforcement Survey Schedule (RSS), 347, 348, 382–390
Relationship enhancement in suicide treatment, 273
Relaxation, daily monitoring of, 372–374
Relaxation training, 52, 55–57
  in treatment of elderly
    deep breathing, 360–361
    deep muscle, 362
Remediation of skills and performance deficits, 179–203; see also Social skills training
  assertive action in, 194
  behavior productivity in, 192–193
  behavioral focus in, 196
  cognitive self-control in, 195–196
  communication skills in, 190–192
  complications of behavioral treatment programs in, 201–203
    conflicting hypotheses, 202
    confusion of relationships among mood, thoughts, and behavior, 203
    loss of goal orientation, 201
    program noncompliance due to symptoms, 201
    search for causes, 202
    suicidal ideation, 201–202
  decision making and problem solving, in, 194–195
  graduated attainment of goals in, 197
  identification of problems and treatment goals in, 196
  nonspecific factors in treatment in, 199–200
  personal and social recognition of gains in, 197
  personal and social skills in, 189–196
  serial treatment targets in, 197
  social interaction in, 193–194
  tapering treatment in, 198
  therapeutic tasks in, 198–199
    descriptive integration of program, 199
    focus on behavioral productivity, 198–199
    normalization, 198
    promotion of active social network, 199
Reporting instruments, see Scales, reports and schedules
Research Diagnostic Criteria (RDC), 42
"Resistance," 272
Responsibility, attribution of, 89–90, 380–381
RET (Rational-Emotive Therapy), 157
Rewards and punishments and behavioral motivation, 90–91
Rigidity and suicide, 244–245
Role induction in suicide treatment, 272
RSS (Reinforcement Survey Schedule), 347, 348

SADS (Schedule for Affective Disorders and Schizophrenia), 21
Scales, reports, and schedules
  Assertive Behavior Survey Schedule, 349
  Beck Depression Inventory, 17–18
  Behavioral Analysis History Questionnaire, 347
  Depression Adjective Checklist, 18–19
  Depressive Behavior Survey Schedule, 347, 348
  Dysfunctional Attitude Scale, 156
  Elderly Reinforcement Survey Schedule, 348–349, 382–390
  Feelings and Concerns Checklist, 21–22
  Hamilton Rating Scale, 20–21
  Imagery Survey Schedule, 347, 348
  Immediate Effects versus Delayed Effects, 377–378
  MMPI Depression Scale, 16–17
  Pleasant-Events Schedule, 19–20
  Pretreatment Questionnaire, McLean, 20
  Reinforcement Survey Schedule, 347, 348
  Schedule for Affective Disorders and Schizophrenia, 21
  Self-Rating Behavior Scale, 347

Scales, reports, and schedules (*cont.*)
  Self-Rating Depression Scale, 18
  Social Performance Survey Schedule, 348
  Thought-Stopping Survey Schedule, 349
  Unpleasant-Events Schedule (UES), 44–46
Schedule for Affective Disorders and Schizophrenia (SADS), 21
  in behavioral treatment, 41
Schemas
  and attribution styles, 152–153
  and causal inferences, 153–155
School phobia or refusal, 317
SDS (Self-rating Depression Scale), 18
Selective abstraction, 71
Self-attribution in depression, 76–77
Self-control
  cognitive, in remediation of skills and performance deficits, 195–196
  in elderly, 359
Self-control model of depression, 70–80
  general features of, 78–80
  immediate outcome of, 74–75
  negative events in, 71–74
  self-attribution in, 76–77
  self-reinforcement in, 77–78
  stringent criteria in, 75–76
Self-control procedure, covert conditioning as, 361–362, 363
Self-control therapy for treatment of depression, 68–105
  outcome studies in, 94–103
    comparison with assertion training, 97–99
    disassembly, 100–103
    one-year follow-up, 99–100
    validation, 95–97
  program of, 80–94
    general issues in, 92–94
    self-evaluation in, 87–90
    self-monitoring in, 81–87
    self-reinforcement in, 90–92
Self-control triad, 354
  in elderly, 361
Self-esteem
  and attributional style, 150–152

and helplessness, 146–147
and obsessive thoughts, 215
Self-help groups for senior citizens, 359
Self-image, idealized, 223–224
Self-judgments, idiosyncratic depressive, 112–113
Self-monitoring, in self-control therapy, 71–75, 81–87
  of immediate outcome, 74–75
  of negative events, 71–74
Self-Monitoring Log, Positive Activity, 375
Self-Rating Behavior Scale (SRBS), 347
Self-Rating Depression Scale (SDS), 18
Self-reinforcement
  in depression, 77–78
  in self-control therapy, 90–92
Self-reinforcement schedules and contracting, 48–49
Self-report instruments, 14–20; *see also* Scales, reports, and schedules
  Beck Depression Inventory, 17–18
  Depression Adjective Checklist, 18–19
  MMPI depression scale, 16–17
  Pleasant-Events Schedule, 19–20
  Pretreatment Questionnaire, 20
  Self-rating Depression Scale, 18
Self-respect, goals centered in area of, 223–224
Self-reward, 78
Sensation, depressed, 170, 175
Sex and suicide, 242–243
Sex type behavior and reinforcement contingencies in children, 325–326
Sexual behaviors, variant, 211
Significant others
  of elderly
    complaints and, 356
    interviewing, 349–350
    reinforcing by, 356
  and suicide, 276, 278
Skills, remediation of, *see* Remediation of skills and performance deficits; Social skills training
Social activities, increasing, 52
Social and personal recognition of

gains, 197
Social-behavioral analyses of suicidal and other problem behaviors, 263–265
Social-behavioral model of suicidal behavior, 237–252
Social competence, perceptions of, 159
Social interaction in remediation of skills and performance deficits, 193–194
Social learning approach to depression, 33–63; *see also* Behavioral treatment of depression
basic conceptualization in, 35–38
Social network, promotion of active, 199
Social Performance Survey Schedule (SPSS), 349
Social skills
and personal skills, remediation of, 189–196
and suicide, 250–251
Social skills training, *see also* Remediation of skills and performance deficits
for children, 320–329, 336–337
with aggressive behavior, 320–322, 327–328
who are depressed, 326–329
who are withdrawn, 322–324
and evidence-based attributional styles, 155
tactics for, 51
Social support lack in suicidogenic environment, 239–241
Social withdrawal in children, 322–324
Socially ineffective children, 324–325
Sociological theories of suicide, 233–234
Somatic complaints, behavioral approaches to, 319
Somatic factors in suicide, 255
Somatic treatment, 295–305
SPSS (Social Performance Survey Schedule), 349
SRBS (Self-Rating Behavior Scale), 347
Stimuli and responses in operant conditioning, 10
Stress, sources of personal, 185–189
inadequate coping techniques, 188–189
life-stress events, 188
personal disuse and lack of goals, 187–188
unrealistic goals and performance criteria, 186–187
Stress management skills, 52
Suicidal behavior, 237–252
as attempt at communication, 235
and consequences, models for, 241–242
methodological problems in studying, 231–233
social-behavioral analyses of, 263–265
theoretical approaches to, 233–237
Suicidal ideation
and remediation therapy, 201–202
as risk factor, 261–262
Suicidal intent, hopelessness and, 126, 245–247
Suicidal patients, assessment of, 253–265
Suicidal persons, outcome studies with, 270–271
Suicide and parasuicide
analysis of, 229–282
behavioral factors in, 244–252, 255
biological theories of, 234
in characterologic depression, 299
circumstances surrounding, 260, 262–263
cognitive system and, 244–247, 255
cognitive theories of, 235–236
cognitive therapy and, 125–127
demographic factors in, 242–244, 254–255
emotional pictures of, 249–250
environmental factors in, 239–242, 254
learning theories of, 236–237
manipulation and, 126, 220, 237
motives for, 125–126
parasuicide as predictor of subsequent parasuicide, 261
physiological/affective system and, 247–249
psychodynamic theories of, 234–235
risk assessment for, 253–263
social support and, 254

Suicide and parasuicide (*cont.*)
  sociological theories of, 233–234
  system relationships and, 251–252
  therapist qualifications in, 282
  therapy recruitment in, 268–271
  threatening, 259–261
  treatment strategies for, 263–282
    crisis management of recommendations, 280–282
    general procedures, 275–277
    long-term, 274
    precrisis, 277–278
    pretreatment, 272–273
    reattribution training, 272–273
    relationship enhancement, 273
    role induction, 272
    therapeutic maintenance, 278–280
Suicide attempts in elderly, 351–352
Suicide notes, 263
Suicide prevention, ethical and legal issues of, 266–268
Supportive family work for children, 335–336
Supportive psychotherapy for children, 326–339
Symbolic modeling for withdrawn children, 323–324
System relationships and suicide, 251–252

Target behaviors, 207–225
  assertiveness, 221–225
  automatic emotional reactions, 211–215
  general tension, 208–210
  obsessions, 215–216
  school phobia, 317
  unwanted habits, 217–221
Targeting deficiency and treatment, 181–182
  serial treatment targets, 197
Tension as target behavior, 208–210
Termination and follow-up assessments in behavioral treatment, 48
Theories as guiding clinical practice, 131–134
Therapeutic collaboration and logical empiricism in cognitive therapy, 118–119
Therapeutic effect as independent of treatment modality, 181
Therapeutic strategies in behavior therapy, 11–12
Therapist
  accessibility of, and suicide, 277
  adversary role of, 118–119
  in cognitive therapy, 117–118
  qualifications of, for treatment of suicidal patients, 282
Therapist-patient contract, 13–14
  antisuicide, 278
Therapy, *see* Treatment of depression
Therapy recruitment in suicide, 268–271
Thought stopping in elderly, 352–353, 360, 363
Thought-Stopping Survey Schedule (TSSS), 349
Time limit for behavioral treatment, 48
Time management in behavioral treatment, 55
Topographical analysis of depressive behaviors, 9
Treating depressions as phobias, 211, 218
Treatment modality, therapeutic effect as independent of, 181
Treatment of depression
  active, for children, 316–339
  antidepressant, 296–305, 337–338
  attributional reformulation, 131–160
  behavioral, 33–63, 205–226
    in children, 313
    in elderly, 350–363
    in somatic complaints, 319
  cognitive, 111–129
  remediation of skills and performance deficits, 179–203
  Rational-Emotive Therapy, 157
  self-control, 68–105
  somatic, 295–305
  targeting, 181–182
Treatment planning, differential, 25–26
Treatment program, behavioral
  descriptive integration of, 199
  noncompliance with, due to symp-

toms, 201
Triple-column technique in cognitive therapy, 123–124
TSSS (Thought-Stopping Survey Schedule), 349

UES (Unpleasant-Events Schedule), 44–46

"Unfair things," 212–213
Unipolar versus bipolar depression, 298
Unpleasant-Events Schedule (UES), 44–46

Vulnerability to depression, attributional, 148–157